Strategy Instruction
for Students with Learning Disabilities

WHAT WORKS FOR SPECIAL-NEEDS LEARNERS

Karen R. Harris and Steve Graham, *Editors*

www.guilford.com/WWFSNL

This series addresses a significant need in the education of students who are at risk, those with disabilities, and all children and adolescents who struggle with learning or behavior. While researchers in special education, educational psychology, curriculum and instruction, and other fields have made great progress in understanding what works for struggling learners, the practical application of this research base remains quite limited. Books in the series present assessment, instructional, and classroom management methods that have strong empirical evidence. Written in a user-friendly format, each volume provides specific how-to instructions and examples of the use of proven procedures in schools. Coverage is sufficiently thorough and detailed to enable practitioners to implement the practices described; many titles include reproducible practical tools. Recent titles have Web pages where purchasers can download and print the reproducible materials.

RECENT VOLUMES

Managing Challenging Behaviors in School:
Research-Based Strategies That Work
*Kathleen Lynne Lane, Holly Mariah Menzies, Allison L. Bruhn,
and Mary Crnobori*

Explicit Instruction: Effective and Efficient Teaching
Anita L. Archer and Charles A. Hughes

Teacher's Guide to ADHD
Robert Reid and Joseph Johnson

Vocabulary Instruction for Struggling Students
Patricia F. Vadasy and J. Ron Nelson

Preparing Effective Special Education Teachers
Nancy Mamlin

RTI for Reading at the Secondary Level:
Recommended Literacy Practices and Remaining Questions
Deborah K. Reed, Jade Wexler, and Sharon Vaughn

Inclusive Instruction:
Evidence-Based Practices for Teaching Students with Disabilities
Mary T. Brownell, Sean J. Smith, Jean B. Crockett, and Cynthia C. Griffin

Universal Design for Learning in the Classroom: Practical Applications
Tracey E. Hall, Anne Meyer, and David H. Rose, Editors

Teacher's Guide to Effective Sentence Writing
Bruce Saddler

Strategy Instruction for Students with Learning Disabilities, Second Edition
Robert Reid, Torri Ortiz Lienemann, and Jessica L. Hagaman

Promoting Social Skills in the Inclusive Classroom
Kimber L. Wilkerson, Aaron B. T. Perzigian, and Jill K. Schurr

Strategy Instruction
for Students with
Learning Disabilities

SECOND EDITION

Robert Reid
Torri Ortiz Lienemann
Jessica L. Hagaman

THE GUILFORD PRESS
New York   London

© 2013 The Guilford Press
A Division of Guilford Publications, Inc.
370 Seventh Avenue, Suite 1200, New York, NY 10001
www.guilford.com

Printed in the United States of America

This book is printed on acid-free paper.

Last digit is print number: 9   8   7   6   5   4   3   2

The authors have checked with sources believed to be reliable in their efforts to provide
information that is complete and generally in accord with the standards of practice that are
accepted at the time of publication. However, in view of the possibility of human error or
changes in behavioral, mental health, or medical sciences, neither the authors, nor the editors
and publisher, nor any other party who has been involved in the preparation or publication
of this work warrants that the information contained herein is in every respect accurate or
complete, and they are not responsible for any errors or omissions or the results obtained from
the use of such information. Readers are encouraged to confirm the information contained in
this book with other sources.

Library of Congress Cataloging-in-Publication Data

Reid, Robert (Robert Charles), 1950–
    Strategy instruction for students with learning disabilities / Robert Reid, Torri Ortiz
Lienemann, Jessica L. Hagaman. — Second edition.
        pages cm — (What works for special-needs learners)
    Includes bibliographical references and index.
    ISBN 978-1-4625-1198-3 (pbk.) — ISBN 978-1-4625-1220-1 (hardcover)
    1. Learning disabled children—Education—United States.   I. Lienemann, Torri Ortiz.
II. Hagaman, Jessica L. (Jessica Laurel).   III. Title.
    LC4705.R46 2013
    371.9—dc23
                                                                    2013011134

Once again, to Karen R. Harris,
who taught us what we needed to know

About the Authors

Robert Reid, PhD, is Professor in the Department of Special Education and Communication Disorders at the University of Nebraska–Lincoln. His research focuses on children with attention-deficit/hyperactivity disorder (ADHD) and on strategy instruction. Dr. Reid has published more than 100 articles and book chapters and has presented at national and international conferences. Additionally, he codeveloped the ADHD-IV Rating Scale. He serves on the editorial boards of five journals and actively reviews for several others.

Torri Ortiz Lienemann, PhD, is District Learning Coordinator and Assistant Special Education Director at Norris School District 160, Firth, Nebraska. Her work focuses on providing teachers with the necessary tools, specifically data-driven instructional interventions, to meet the needs of all students. Currently, Dr. Lienemann is involved in researching vocabulary and reading comprehension in at-risk students; teaching undergraduate and graduate courses; grant writing; and creating new programs to assist students with special needs and their teachers. She has been a classroom resource teacher at the elementary, middle, and high school levels.

Jessica L. Hagaman, PhD, is Assistant Professor in the Department of Special Education and Communication Disorders at the University of Nebraska–Omaha. She specializes in the education of students with learning disabilities and at-risk students. Dr. Hagaman has classroom experience at the early childhood and elementary school levels. Her research interests include early intervention for at-risk students, strategy instruction, and academic interventions.

Preface

The first edition of this book was created to fill what we saw as a serious need for a practical, user-friendly source of information on how to teach learning strategies to students with learning disabilities and to other struggling students. We were aware of the extensive data on the effectiveness of strategy instruction; however, we were equally aware that strategy instruction was not commonly used in the schools and that often the topic was not well covered in teacher preparation programs. This lacuna was at least partly because, despite the plethora of literature on the underlying theory of strategy instruction and on individual strategies, there was little, if any, information on how to actually teach strategies successfully. The research is clear that certain fundamental instructional tasks are necessary to facilitate successful strategy instruction, but many teachers were unaware of these tasks. They simply did not have the knowledge base to teach a strategy to a student with learning disabilities or other learning problems.

Our goal was to produce a volume that would provide teachers with practical knowledge of how to teach strategies to students with learning difficulties using a practical, validated instructional model—the Self-Regulated Strategy Development (SRSD) model—so that they could teach strategies successfully in the classroom. We include information on the theories that underlie strategy instruction and examples from research, but we focus on how the theories inform and relate to the *actual process of instruction*. We are able to draw on real-world examples to illustrate the process of strategy instruction because each of the authors has extensive experience in this area. All of us have conducted research on strategy instruction, taught strategies to struggling learners, and, most importantly, taught teachers how to use strategy instruction.

We were heartened by the success of the first edition of this book and by the feedback we received from classroom teachers and preservice teachers. Our teachers could observe how their students exhibited the difficulties that underlie many learning problems (e.g., problems with self-regulation, lack of metacognitive knowledge, maladaptive attributions), could now understand why they occurred, and, more importantly, could now know how to deal with them. They also appreciated how SRSD could make them more effective teachers. However, we also realized that some areas needed more attention and that some new issues needed to be addressed. In this second edition, we have greatly expanded our treatment of working memory, which is a key concept in strategy instruction. We have also added information on response to intervention (RTI), which is now widely used. Two new chapters have been added: one shows examples of how the steps in SRSD can be combined into lesson plans; the other provides information on handwriting and spelling. Additionally, we have updated the new edition with new strategies in the content areas and added information on using SRSD with students with attention-deficit/hyperactivity disorder (ADHD).

Chapter 1 provides a rationale for why teachers should learn a strategies-based approach to teaching. In Chapter 2 we define a *strategy*, present background knowledge on critical concepts fundamental to strategy instruction, and explain common misconceptions about strategy instruction. In Chapter 3 we present the SRSD model, explaining each of the steps in the model, the rationale for each step, and the importance of each step. We stress that the SRSD model is an invaluable tool for teachers. In Chapter 4 we provide an example of strategy instruction using the SRSD model. Some tips and useful tools for implementing strategies are presented, along with a discussion of how differences between strategies affect implementation. In Chapter 5 we discuss self-regulation. The four major types of self-regulation strategies are defined and explained.

Chapter 6 includes examples of how each of the major self-regulation strategies can be implemented. In Chapter 7 we show how to combine strategies and self-regulation to enable students to become self-regulated strategy users. Chapter 8, a completely new chapter, shows how content-area strategies and self-regulation strategies can be integrated into lesson plans, and it includes sample lesson plans for two strategies. Chapter 9, another new chapter, deals with handwriting and spelling—two critical preskills for written composition. Chapters 10–14 cover strategies in major content areas or reading comprehension, written expression, math, study skills, and mnemonics. These chapters focus on well-validated strategies; we have added new strategies to each chapter. The end result is the second edition of *Strategy Instruction for Students with Learning Disabilities*.

Contents

CHAPTER 1

Why Use Strategy Instruction?

Students with learning disabilities (LD) constitute by far the largest group of students with special needs. According to the U.S. Department of Education, in 2010 there were more than 2,400,000 students from ages 6 to 21 served in federally supported programs for LD. Students with LD constitute 44.6% of the special education population and 4% of the total school enrollment, according to most recent figures (U.S. Department of Education, 2008). Although LD is by far the largest category of disability, the number of new students identified as having LD has shown a slight decrease over the last 4 years (U.S. Department of Education, 2010). Whether this is due to changes in the actual number of students with LD or to changes in identification procedures is still not clear.

A learning disability affects nearly every aspect of a child's life and is a lifelong challenge (Lerner, 2000). Students with LD are often caught in a vicious spiral of school failure. Their learning difficulties lead to a slower development of academic skills and abilities, which in turn impedes new learning (Stanovich, 1986). As a result of the repeated cycle of failure, these students fall further and further behind. According to the U.S. Department of Education (2008), students with LD are at greatly increased risk for dropping out: Nearly 40% of students with LD fail to graduate from high school with a standard diploma. The academic problems also result in a lower engagement rate in postsecondary schooling, employment, or both, compared to typically achieving students (Murray, Goldstein, & Edgar, 1997). Thus, the need to address the academic achievement of students with LD is critical in order to improve their academic outcomes.

The purpose of this chapter is to provide background information on LD, discuss those characteristics of students with LD that affect instruction in general and strategy instruction in particular, and provide a rationale for the use of strategy instruction. Readers who are interested in more in-depth information on these topics should refer to Swanson, Harris, and Graham (2003). In this chapter, we first present definitions of

1

LD and briefly discuss the history of this category. Next, we describe some important characteristics of students with LD and how our conceptualization of LD has changed over time. Finally we make a case for the use of strategy instruction with students with LD. Note that the use of strategy instruction is *not* limited to students with LD. Research clearly indicates that strategy instruction is effective for the great majority of students who struggle in academic areas.

WHAT IS A LEARNING DISABILITY?

LD has been recognized as a category of disability under federal law since 1975. The current legal definition of LD is written into the Individuals with Disabilities Education Act (IDEA); however, as Table 1.1 shows, other organizations have proposed their own definitions of LD that differ substantially, and exactly how to define LD has been, and continues to be, a controversial area. This controversy is due, in part, to the highly heterogeneous nature of the students who are defined as LD. Students with LD manifest a number of different problems in academic, behavioral, and social–emotional areas. Moreover, students with LD may exhibit vastly different profiles both within and across these areas. For example, some students may have serious problem with reading but will excel at mathematics. Others may have difficulties in mathematics, but not in reading. Table 1.2 shows examples of the subtypes of LD currently identified by researchers. Note that the problems of students with LD are not limited to academics. Some students will have serious problems with self-esteem or depression, whereas others have little or no problem in these areas but may exhibit serious behavior problems. Attention-deficit/ hyperactivity disorder (ADHD) also occurs in around 25% of students with LD (Reid & Johnson, 2012). Another factor that contributes to confusion in the area of LD is that the field cuts across a number of professional disciplines, such as education, psychology, medicine, and sociology. Each of these disciplines brings its own perspective to LD, and like the proverbial blind man and the elephant, each focuses on a different aspect of LD. As a result, there are differences across professional groups on the terminology that should be used to describe LD, and on which aspects of LD should and should not be included in the definition.

Although there is a lack of consensus on how to define LD, there is a practical consensus on how students with LD should be identified. Despite the fact that all of the definitions of LD contain references to its causes (e.g., disorders in basic psychological processes, neurological origins, central nervous system dysfunction) and that difficulties in academic areas are often described in medical language (e.g., *dyslexia*, *dyscalculia*, *dysgraphia*), these factors rarely, if ever, play a role in diagnosis. In practice, LD is a category of underachievement, and students with LD are identified by their chronic and severe academic difficulties. Until 2004, discrepancy formulas were commonly used to determine if a child should be labeled as LD. Mercer (1997) noted that over 90% of states include a discrepancy component in the identification process. These discrepancy formulas assessed the difference between ability, as determined by the results of intelligence tests, and academic achievement, as assessed by standardized tests. If the difference between the child's presumed ability and actual achievement was

TABLE 1.1. Definitions of Learning Disabilities

Individuals with Disabilities Education Act (1977)

The term "specific learning disability" means those children who have a disorder in one or more of the basic psychological processes involved in understanding or in using language, spoken or written, which disorder may manifest itself in imperfect ability to listen, think, speak, read, write, spell, or to do mathematical calculations. The term includes such conditions as perceptual handicaps, brain injury, minimal brain dysfunction, dyslexia, and developmental aphasia. The term does not include a learning problem that is primarily the result of visual, hearing, or motor handicaps; of mental retardation; of emotional disturbance; or of environmental, cultural, or economic disadvantage.

Association for Children with Learning Disabilities (1986)

Specific learning disabilities is a chronic condition of presumed neurological origin that selectively interferes with the development, integrations, and/or demonstration of verbal and/or nonverbal abilities. Specific Learning Disabilities exists as a distinct handicapping condition and varies in its manifestations and in degree of severity. Throughout life, the condition can affect self-esteem, education, vocation, socialization, and/or daily living activities.

Interagency Committee on Learning Disabilities (1987)

Learning disabilities is a generic term that refers to a heterogeneous groups of disorders manifested by significant difficulties in the acquisition and use of listening, speaking, reading, writing, reasoning, mathematical abilities, or social skills. These disorders are intrinsic to the individual and presumed to be due to central nervous system dysfunction. Even though a learning disability may occur concomitantly with other handicapping conditions (e.g., cultural differences, insufficient or inappropriate instruction, psychogenic factors), and especially attention-deficit disorder, all of which may cause learning problems, a learning disability is not the direct result of those conditions or influences.

National Joint Council on Learning Disabilities (1997)

Learning disabilities is a general term that refers to a heterogeneous group of disorders manifested by significant difficulties in the acquisition and use of listening, speaking, reading, writing, reasoning, or mathematical abilities. These disorders are intrinsic to the individual, are presumed to be due to central nervous system dysfunction, and may occur across the life span. Problems in self-regulatory behaviors, social perceptions, and social interactions may exist with learning disabilities but do not by themselves constitute a learning disability. Although a learning disability may occur concomitantly with other disabilities (e.g., sensory impairment, mental retardation, or serious emotional disturbance) or with extrinsic influences (such as cultural differences or insufficient/inappropriate instruction), it would not be a result of those conditions or influences.

large enough, the child could be identified as having a learning disability. Discrepancy formulas, though commonly used, came under scrutiny due to concerns pertaining to their validity and also because the use of discrepancy formulas required schools to wait until a student exhibited serious academic deficiencies before they could intervene (Fuchs, Fuchs, & Compton, 2004).

Because of concerns over the validity of discrepancy approaches and the "wait-to-fail" approach inherent in their use, the latest version of IDEA (2004) made a dramatic change in the approach that schools are allowed to use in identifying students with

TABLE 1.2. Subtypes of Learning Disability

Types of LD	Description
Reading— word level	• Problems with accurate and fluent decoding • Related to phonological processing, rapid naming abilities, and verbal short-term memory deficits
Reading— comprehension	• Problems with language comprehension, inferences, and abstraction • May have deficits in vocabulary and syntax • Problems with working memory • Phonological skills, short-term memory not affected • Problems parallel those of listening comprehension
Reading— fluency	• Excessively slow rate of reading • No decoding problems • Comprehension problems due to difficulty with rapidly processing information
Math	• Difficulty with learning, representing, and retrieving math facts • Difficulties in learning and using problem-solving strategies required for calculations • Normal reading/spelling
Reading and math	• Deficits in both reading and math • Memory-based deficit • Potentially related to working memory and long-term memory access
Written expression	• Problems with text generation • Problems with spelling • Poor handwriting

Note. Data from Fletcher et al. (2002); Fletcher, Morris, and Lyon (2003); and Lyon, Fletcher, and Barnes (2003).

LD. Schools are no longer required to determine whether any discrepancy exists. The approach now used in schools, response to intervention (RTI), is based on a principle of early intervention. In this approach, all students in a classroom receive effective instruction. If a student exhibits problems (e.g., fails to progress academically at an acceptable rate), the student is given additional instruction in an individual or small-group setting. For a student to be eligible for special education services related to LD requires only that the school document that a student continues to demonstrate significant academic underachievement when provided with instruction (based on scientifically supported principles) for a reasonable period of time.

CAUSES OF LEARNING DISABILITIES

The search for causes of LD has been the focus of research for more than 50 years. A number of possible causes have been put forward over the years with varying degrees of support. Table 1.3 presents some hypothesized causes of LD. No one has yet presented conclusive or compelling evidence to support any particular cause of LD, though researchers continue to make progress. In part this lack of clear etiology is due to the problems inherent in studying LD. Given the highly heterogeneous nature of LD, the differing theoretical orientations of researchers, and the problems with defining and accurately identifying a child as having an LD, this should not be too surprising. There are some clear trends in how LD has been approached that have direct implications for educators involved with instructional decision making for students with LD.

Medical Perspectives

Historically, LD have been viewed as brain-based disorders. That is, the learning problems evidenced by students were thought to be due to some specific neurologically based deficit or disorder. For example, James Hinshelwood (1917) coined the term *word blindness* to describe a child who had an inexplicable inability to learn to read, despite apparently normal intelligence and normal functioning in other areas. Hinshelwood speculated that the child's problem was due to a defect in the angular gyrus. Another early researcher, Samuel Orton (1937), noticed that many students who experienced difficulty in reading also tended to reverse letters such as *b* and *d*, or *p* and *q*. Orton termed this phenomenon *strephosymbolia* (twisted symbols) and attributed it to the failure of some individuals to develop "cerebral dominance" (i.e., neither of the brain's hemispheres was dominant). He hypothesized that reversals were due to mirror images of words or letters stored in the nondominant brain hemisphere.

TABLE 1.3. Hypothesized Causes of Learning Disabilities

Cause	Example
Central nervous system abnormality	Abnormal brain hemispheric symmetry; nerve cell anomalies in areas of the brain involved in language
Central nervous system damage	*Prenatal*: maternal drug use, smoking, fetal alcohol syndrome, fetal alcohol effects
	Perinatal: prematurity, anoxia, complications during labor, injury during delivery
	Postnatal: brain injury due to stroke, high fever, meningitis, encephalitis, or head trauma
Genetic	Evidence suggests that reading disabilities may have a strong genetic component. Conditions caused by chromosomal abnormalities, such as Klinefelter syndrome, Turner syndrome, or fragile X syndrome, can result in learning difficulties.
Environmental	Exposure to environmental toxins such as lead or other heavy metals
Biochemical abnormalities	Imbalances in neurotransmitters (e.g., dopamine, serotonin, acetylcholine)

This work was continued by researchers such as Kirk Goldstein (1936) and Alfred Strauss (Strauss & Lehtinen, 1947). Goldstein worked with soldiers who had suffered brain injuries during World War I. He noted that these soldiers commonly exhibited perceptual problems, impulsivity, distractibility, and hyperactivity. Strauss noted that students with mental retardation exhibited many of the same characteristics and theorized that the problems were due to brain injury. As a result, terms such as *brain-injured child* and *minimal brain dysfunction* were used to refer to students we would today call *learning disabled*. Strauss hypothesized that perhaps some extremely subtle brain damage was the root cause of a child's failure to learn. These labels were, understandably, unpopular with parents, and their relevance was also questioned. The medical influence on the field of LD is still strong. For example, use of medical terminology such as *dyslexia* or *dyscalculia* to refer to problems in reading and math is common. Current research on the brain and LD now uses extremely sophisticated tools and is beginning to shed further light on the relation between the brain and LD (e.g., Shaywitz, 2003).

Learning Disabilities as an Academic Problem

In 1963, a watershed event in the history of LD occurred at a meeting of concerned parents in Chicago (Mercer, 1997). The parents met to air their displeasure with medical practitioners who described their children as *brain-injured* or as having *minimal brain dysfunction*. Samuel Kirk, a psychologist with years of experience working with students with academic problems, coined the term *learning disabilities* to describe those students who had difficulty in learning to read. This relabeling shifted the prevailing perspective on learning problems. Rather than being attributed to organic damage to the brain, these problems were seen as related to underlying cognitive processes. That is, the students were neurologically intact but had difficulties with psychological processes (i.e., perceptual problems, as evidenced by difficulties with visual and auditory discrimination) that prevented them from receiving visual and/or auditory stimuli correctly and resulted in difficulty learning. This perceptual–motor approach shifted the focus from the medical aspects of LD to the academic, resulting in the creation of assessment instruments designed to measure underlying deficits, and of intervention programs designed to remediate them. The idea was that, if the hypothesized underlying deficit in perceptual processing were corrected, then the child would be able to progress academically in a normal fashion. Numerous programs were designed and implemented. Students learned to walk balance beams to improve motor skills, and to trace shapes to improve perceptual skills. Unfortunately, the training programs designed to remediate process deficits were found to be ineffective, and the assessment instruments were not reliable (Hammill & Larsen, 1974). However, the perspective on LD as a problem rooted at least in part in *instruction* remained and served to change LD practice.

Behavioral and Cognitive Approaches

During the 1960s, 1970s, and 1980s, new, influential perspectives on LD began to emerge. The first of these was behaviorism. This approach, developed by B. F. Skinner, was based on the theory that a functional relation exists between behavior (e.g., reading) and the environment. Behaviorists stressed direct observation and ongoing collection of objective (i.e., verifiable) information. Learning was viewed as a hierarchical process in which a child must master skills in a prescribed order. In this approach academic tasks were broken down into their component parts, and each part was taught in sequence. The application to LD lay in the notion that academic problems would be best addressed by effecting changes in the instructional environment. From the behaviorist perspective, a highly structured instructional environment that directly addressed the problem area was necessary for academic progress. Thus, if a child had reading problems, the solution was to directly teach the skills needed to read, by using appropriately sequenced, highly structured instruction. Several extremely effective instructional approaches, such as DISTAR (Engelman & Bruner, 1974) and Precision Teaching (Lindsley, 1964), were developed based on behavioral approaches.

In the 1970s, cognitive approaches to teaching and learning began to influence the LD field. The cognitive perspective focuses on the role of the individual in the learning process (Mercer, 1997). From this perspective, the key is the relation between demands of the learning environment (e.g., the task, instructional materials) and how the learner processes information. Learning problems may result from deficits in cognitive processes such as memory, failure to process information efficiently (e.g., failure to use an appropriate or effective strategy), or a combination of both. Metacognition (knowledge of one's own cognitive processes) also became important. During the 1980s, cognitive approaches became very influential, and a great deal of basic research was done to identify the cognitive characteristic of students with LD. Memory researchers developed new models for addressing how cognitive processes work. Perhaps the most important of these was the information-processing model, which envisioned cognitive processing as analogous to a computer with input, storage, and processing components. The information-processing model was extremely influential because it focused attention on the processes involved in memory and learning. Curriculum materials such as the University of Kansas learning strategies approach, which utilized cognitive approaches, were developed and implemented effectively. The work done on behavioral and cognitive approaches resulted in progress in our understanding of the nature of the problems encountered by students with LD and in the development of effective teaching techniques. The field of LD is still building on and refining the advances that occurred during this period.

CHARACTERISTICS OF STUDENTS WITH LEARNING DISABILITIES

It is important for educators to be knowledgeable about the characteristics of students with LD. Important characteristics of these students span emotional, behavioral, cognitive, and social domains of development. We focus on the information that is needed for teachers—whose job is to successfully educate students with LD. For this reason, the discussion of LD characteristics is limited to those that directly affect academic performance and that are thus relevant to strategy instruction.

Attention

Teachers who work with students with LD commonly note that "Things seem to go in one ear and out the other," or they remark on the need to "jog" students back after their attention has wandered. Attention is a critical aspect of successful learning. It is also a complex and multifaceted phenomenon. There are three important aspects of attention. First, there is task engagement. To succeed in school, students must be able persist at tasks. Students with LD are often off-task in the classroom. Research shows that, when left to their own devices, students with LD are on-task only around 30–60% of the time (Bryan & Wheeler, 1972; McKinney & Feagans, 1983). This has obvious educational implications. For example, students who do not complete practice tasks may fail to develop necessary fluency in important skills. Students who stop work when they encounter difficulty will learn less and are more likely to have negative classroom experiences. Maintaining focus is a common problem among students with LD (Hallahan, Kauffman, & Lloyd, 1996). Students with LD are often described as "spacey" or "not with it" or "distractible." Failure to maintain focus has serious consequences. Students whose minds wander while reading a passage will have difficulties remembering information. Students who are daydreaming and, as a result, don't attend to their teacher may not be aware of assignments or may miss important directions. Finally, difficulty with selective attention—the ability to identify important or meaningful information—is also common among students with LD (Brown & Wynne, 1984). As a result, students with LD may attend to unimportant components of a task and ignore relevant information. Exactly why students with LD experience these problems is still unclear, but we do know that much can be done as a part of strategy instruction to improve all aspects of attention.

Memory

One common concern among teachers who work with students with LD is that one day the child can readily remember important information—he or she "got it"—but the next day, for no apparent reason, it's gone. The ability to remember information is obviously critical to academic success. For example, if students cannot remember basic math facts, how commonly used words are spelled, or content-area facts (e.g., Civil War battles or the parts of an atom), they will have difficulty progressing academically. Students with LD exhibit just these types of problems. Research shows that students with LD do have more problems with memory than students without LD (e.g., Gettinger, 1991; Swanson, Cochran, & Ewers, 1990). Research also shows that memory deficits are linked to problems in academic areas (e.g., Ceci, Ringstrom, & Lea, 1981). Historically, these deficits were seen as due to a lack of innate capacity. To use an example, if we were to see memory as one of the "underlying psychological processes" with which students with LD exhibit deficiencies, we might use the metaphor of a bucket to describe the memory problems of these students. For these students it would seem, at least on the surface, as if their bucket were smaller (i.e., have less capacity) and very leaky (more forgetting, problems with retaining information). However, this is a case where appearances are deceiving.

Activate Prior Knowledge

Several factors affect how well a person can remember information. First, the amount of background knowledge, or the knowledge base, can affect memory. Individuals with background knowledge in an area will have an easier time remembering new material in that area than individuals without it. Being familiar with material can enhance memory (Swanson, 1996b). This is a problem for students with LD, as they generally tend to have lower levels of background knowledge. Second, the problem with recall exhibited by students with LD may not be related to a memory deficit, but rather may be a function of their failure to use processes that would allow them to remember. For example, if skilled learners were faced with the task of remembering a series of 10 random numbers, such as 3014056488, they would, almost automatically, use one of several methods for remembering. They might repeat the numbers to themselves several times (i.e., verbal elaboration). Or they might rearrange the information, using "chunking" to group the numbers into fewer components that would be easier to remember (e.g., 30, 14, 05, 64, 88). Both of these processes would improve ability to remember the 10 digits. In contrast, students with LD are unlikely to apply any sort of strategy spontaneously (Swanson, 1996b). In other words, students with LD may lack or not use strategies that would help them remember information. Strategies for improving memory are commonly part of strategy instruction.

Attributions

The term *attributions* refers to the manner in which students explain the cause of academic outcomes. For example, if we asked a successful student, "Why did you get an *A* on the science test?", the answer would probably be, "I got an *A* because I studied hard." In other words, the student attributed the cause of the good grade to his or her own effort to study hard—a controllable, internal factor. Attributions are extremely important because they can affect expectations for success, academic behaviors, and students' reactions to success or failure (Weiner, 1979). Students who attribute a good grade to studying hard have a healthy attribution pattern. Unfortunately, students with LD tend not to exhibit this pattern. These students often attribute success to external factors that they do not control, such as luck or the test being easy. Moreover, students with LD often attribute *failures* to internal, uncontrollable factors such as lack of ability or task difficulty (Chapman, 1988; Kistner, Osborn, & LeVerrier, 1988; Stipek, 1993). Think for a moment about the ramifications of this pattern of attributions. No credit is taken for academic success, only for failure. Any academic success is outside the student; in contrast, failure is internalized. This is an unhealthy or maladaptive pattern that can affect students' academic motivation and performance. Strategy instruction is sensitive to this problem and fosters the development of positive attributions.

Learned Helplessness

Learned helplessness refers to a belief that efforts are unlikely to lead to success. In other words, students believe that no matter how hard they try, they simply won't succeed, so there is no reason to try in the first place (Dweck, 1975). A previous history of school-related failure has led them to "know" they can't do it. As noted in the preceding section, for many of these students, the source of failure is perceived to be lack of ability ("I can't do this"). Even when they do succeed, these students are likely to attribute the success to outside factors ("The teacher was easy on me"). This pattern has a corrosive affect on academic motivation. Why strive for success if failure is inevitable? Research suggests that the problem of learned helplessness is common among students with LD. Kavale and Forness (1996) found that as many as 70% of students with LD may exhibit learned helplessness.

Lack of Coordinated Strategies

Imagine the following scenario. It's late at night and you are studying for an exam. You're reading a very difficult portion of your text, so you are reading much more slowly than normal. Suddenly you realize that you have no recollection of what you just read on the last two pages. You sigh and begin to carefully reread the section of the text. Though this vignette looks simple, there are several processes going on under the surface. First, you knew that the purpose of reading was to understand the text, so you adjusted your reading speed because you realized that in difficult sections, you need to read more slowly if you are going to remember important information. Second, you realized that you had experienced a lapse in concentration and had no recollection of what you had just read. This realization occurred because you were engaged in ongoing monitoring of your comprehension. Third, after you recognized the lapse, you realized that it was necessary to correct the situation because if you did not, you would miss important information. Finally, you used an appropriate method (going back to reread) to correct the problem.

This scenario has probably happened to you a number of times; it is common among skilled learners. In fact, there is good reason to believe that this sequence of events *describes* a skilled learner. However, this scenario is rare among students with LD; they are unlikely to respond appropriately to the demands of an academic task by using an effective set of cognitive strategies. For example, they will spend less time studying and will not realize that it is necessary to slow down for difficult sections (Bauer, 1987; Wong & Wilson, 1984). They may be unlikely to recognize that they have experienced a problem because they will not be actively monitoring their comprehension (Borkowski, Weyhing, & Carr, 1988; Harris, Graham, & Pressley, 1992). And if they do realize they need to correct the problem, they are unlikely to use an effective method to do so. Students with LD commonly exhibit problems in four areas (Swanson, 1993):

1. They have difficulty accessing, coordinating, and organizing mental activities that occur simultaneously or in close succession.
2. Even when they have an idea of appropriate strategies, students use them ineffectively.
3. They fail to engage in self-regulation of mental activity (e.g., planning, monitoring, revising).
4. They have a limited awareness of the usefulness of specific strategies for a given task.

In short, it seems as if students with LD neither do things spontaneously that would improve their learning, nor in some instances are even aware that such efforts are necessary or appropriate.

WHY A STRATEGY APPROACH?

The federal definition in the IDEA notes that LD is the result of a "disorder in one or more of the basic psychological processes," and the National Joint Council on Learning Disabilities definition states, "These disorders [learning problems] are intrinsic to the individual, [and] are presumed to be due to central nervous system dysfunction." As we noted earlier, the cause of LD has not yet been clearly proven; however, even if we accepted these conceptualizations, they would provide very little in the way of guidance for educators who are charged with teaching students with LD. For example, we can do very little about central nervous system dysfunction. However, at least in part the problems experienced by students with LD are due to difficulties with effective use of strategies. Swanson (1999a) noted that poor academic performances across all ages in students with LD can be seen as a problem in the use of efficient strategies. Students with LD tend to develop fewer strategies and to use strategies less often than typically achieving students (Stone & Conca, 1993). Exactly why this occurs is not certain at present. However, what is well known is that strategy instruction can meaningfully improve performance among students with LD and other struggling learners as well. Therefore, it makes sense to treat strategy use–disuse just like any other academic problem. If students with LD lack effective strategies for an academic task, then *we should teach them effective strategies*.

What about problems with maladaptive attributions or learned helplessness? Strategy instruction addresses these problems by directly using an approach advocated by Licht. In a very influential paper, Licht (1983) argued for a new definition of "ability" that was "incremental." From this perspective, what makes you "smart" is not some unchangeable entity such as intelligence, but rather "an accumulation of knowledge and skills that can be increased through effort. . . . The harder you try, the more you'll learn, and the smarter you'll get" (p. 487). From Licht's perspective, problems such as maladaptive attributions or learned helplessness can be addressed through instruction. If students have unhealthy patterns of attributions, they can be taught appropriate, positive attributions—failure and success depend on effort. If students have developed learned helplessness, they can learn that success can be obtained through the use of effective strategies.

Swanson (1996a) aptly summarized the advantages of the use of the strategy approach:

> A focus is placed on what is modifiable. That is, differences between ability groups are conceptualized in terms of cognitive processes that are susceptible to instruction, rather than to fundamental or general differences in ability. Thus, rather than focusing on isolated elementary memory processing deficiencies, the types of questions . . . are more educationally relevant. For example, a focus is placed on what students with LD can do without strategy

instruction, what they can do with strategy instruction, what can be done to modify existing strategy instruction, and what can be done to modify existing classroom materials to improve instruction. It [the strategy-oriented approach] allows for the child to be actively involved in the instruction. Students can participate in the analysis of which cognitive strategies work best for them . . . [and] . . . materials can be developed which maximize strategy use. (p. 301)

There are several significant advantages of the strategy approach. First, it assumes that many of the problems experienced by students with LD are due to the lack of, or failure to use, strategies. Thus, from this perspective, past academic problems were not due to an innate lack of ability or capacity, but rather to an ineffective use of abilities. Second, it assumes that if students learn effective strategies, there will be a significant increase in academic performance. Evidence for the strategy deficit hypothesis has been well documented. For example, in the area of memory, Torgesen (1984) found that when students with LD are directly taught memory strategies, there were no differences in recall between students with and without LD on selected tasks. Third, it assumes that strategies can be directly taught and effectively learned. There is now compelling evidence that students with LD can be taught to utilize strategies. Note that this approach *directly empowers* both students and educators; it places the control of learning in their hands. Students can always learn new strategies, and educators can always teach them. Finally, and most importantly, the strategy approach has a *30-year track record of success.* Students' performances can improve markedly as a result of strategy instruction (e.g., Graham & Harris, 2003; Graham & Perin, 2007a; Rogers & Graham, 2008). Furthermore, strategy instruction has also been used successfully within an RTI framework (e.g., Harris et al., 2012).

The last point is undoubtedly the most important. In a time when there are more and more demands for accountability, educators can no longer continue to adopt educational regimens that are not evidence based. Recall the perceptual–motor approach, which appeared logical but was also a complete failure in terms of helping students with LD progress academically. Given the number of students with LD who are at risk for academic failure, we simply cannot afford to use anything less than the best methods we have; and we have a very good idea of which methods are most effective at improving academic learning. Two studies (Swanson, 1999b; Swanson & Sachs-Lee, 2000) using meta-analysis evaluated the effectiveness of numerous teaching methods for students with LD. Meta-analysis allows researchers to combine the results of numerous studies and to test which instructional approach is the most effective. The two studies conducted by Swanson and his colleagues are the most comprehensive investigation of instructional methods for students with LD ever conducted. All told, Swanson's meta-analysis included a total of 163 separate studies with over 1,000 comparisons, encompassing all the basic skill areas: reading, math, and written language. The results were clear-cut. The most effective methods were those that incorporated most of the following elements:

- Explicit explanations, elaborations, and/or plans to direct task performance.
- Verbal modeling, questioning, and demonstration by teachers.

- Cueing, reminding, and/or teaching students to use strategies or procedures.
- Step-by-step prompts or multiprocess instructions.
- Teacher–student dialogue.
- Questioning by the teacher.
- Assistance provided only when necessary.

What instructional method typically incorporates most or all of these components? You have probably guessed. Students taught via the strategy instruction method showed the most improvement compared to other methods. Furthermore, the degree of improvement was impressive. In sum, we can say with confidence that strategy instruction approaches are highly effective for students with LD.

PUTTING STRATEGY INSTRUCTION INTO THE CLASSROOM

By now you may be wondering why strategy instruction isn't widespread. After all, if strategy instruction is effective, and we've known this for decades, shouldn't everybody be using it? Unfortunately it's not that simple for a number of reasons. Educators may choose to use one method over another based on a number of factors: (1) acceptability, (2) effectiveness, (3) time and resources, (4) theoretical orientation of the intervention, and (5) intrusiveness (Witt, 1986). Note that effectiveness is only one of the factors that influence what may be used in the classroom. Another factor could be termed *inertia*. In many cases, educational practices seem to develop a life of their own, independent of their effectiveness. As Heward (2002) noted, teachers sometimes become wedded to ineffective approaches and continue to use them, regardless of whether or not they are effective. Poor communication between researchers and classroom teachers is also a factor (Pressley & Woloshyn, 1995). Researchers often do a poor job of presenting the results of their research in a manner that teachers can grasp and, more importantly, immediately apply.

All of these factors have probably inhibited the use of strategy instruction, to some extent. However, we believe that there is an even more fundamental explanation. Few educators (either inservice or preservice) are provided with any degree of systematic professional development in strategy instruction approaches. This is a critical omission for two reasons. As Kauffman (1996) suggests, practices that are accompanied by systematic professional development are more likely to be adopted and used correctly. Unfortunately, few teachers are given more than a brief exposure to strategy instruction approaches. Training in strategy instruction may be limited to a video or one lecture in a methods course. Although strategy instruction is a very powerful tool, *effective* strategy instruction requires specialized knowledge on the part of the teacher, an investment of time and effort to acquire that knowledge, and an effective model for teaching strategies that addresses the cognitive, self-regulatory, and motivational problems of students with LD. In short, learning to use strategy instruction requires some work upfront. However, the time and effort are not exorbitant, and in our experience, teachers who invest in this training to learn how to effectively teach strategies find it time well spent.

The purpose of this book is to help teachers develop a practical, working knowledge of proven strategies and how to effectively implement strategy instruction in the classroom. Note that although we focus on students with LD, the same basic approach can be used with *any child* who needs help mastering a specific academic task (e.g., long division, writing an essay, comprehending a story). One particular group of students that can profit from strategy instruction is the subset with attention-deficit/hyperactivity disorder (ADHD). ADHD is particularly relevant in the case of LD because there is a considerable overlap (20–40% of students with ADHD also have LD) (Schnoes, Reid, Wagner, & Marder, 2006). For this reason we include information on strategy instruction for students with ADHD when appropriate. The strategy instruction model that we use—the Self-Regulated Strategy Development (SRSD) model—is based on well-established theory and has been validated in over 30 years of research. There are many models for strategy instruction. However, few are as well researched and "user-friendly," and few focus on both academic and motivational aspects of students' learning problems.

FINAL THOUGHTS

The approach that we use in this book mirrors the actual instructional model that we teach. We have discussed why strategy instruction is an important skill for you to learn. Next, we provide the necessary background knowledge to conduct strategy instruction and explicitly explain the components of the SRSD model. We then provide examples of how you might implement various steps in the strategy instruction process in general, and examples of specific, validated strategies for use in major content areas. Our intent is to provide teachers and teacher educators with detailed, practical, step-by-step information on strategy instruction. Moreover, the model contains many components that are useful, in and of themselves, aside from their use in strategy instruction. In closing we emphasize that the method we present is *not* the only way to instruct students with LD. No single method is that powerful. However, mastery of the techniques we present can improve instruction and academic achievement for all students.

CHAPTER 2

Building Background Knowledge

In Chapter 1 we noted that to effectively use strategy instruction in the classroom, teachers need specialized knowledge. Strategy instruction is a powerful tool, but to gain any value from a tool you must know how to properly use it, and what it is good for. For example, a hammer is great for driving nails, but a hammer only works if you know which end to grab and which end to hit with. And hammers are not much use if you need to tighten a screw. One of the most dangerous misconceptions about teaching is that "anyone can do it" and that no special knowledge or set of skills is necessary. This is half right. Anyone can do a poor job. But to do an optimal job of instructing students, especially students with special needs such as those with LD, you need to know how to use tools—such as strategy instruction—correctly and appropriately.

Strategy instruction may fail if teachers lack critical knowledge of the theory or process behind it—if, in other words, they don't understand the "why" behind the activities and steps used in the strategy instruction process. Understanding why you do a step in the strategy instruction process sensitizes you to the need to do the step and helps you to do it correctly. To do strategy instruction well, teachers need basic knowledge about how students learn because instruction will need to take this learning process into consideration. Additionally, effective strategy instruction goes beyond the academic realm. It involves affective components as well. Motivational problems such as maladaptive attributions or learned helplessness must also be addressed. The best strategy in the world is useless if students won't even try to use it. For these reasons, simply sharing strategies with students is unlikely to result in any real improvement.

In this chapter we provide you with some of the salient background knowledge that you will need to effectively implement strategy instruction for students with LD in the classroom. First, we provide both formal and practical definitions of the term "strategy" and discuss major aspects the definition. Second, we discuss the information-processing model, which is useful for understanding the rationale behind some steps in the SRSD instructional model. Third, we continue the discussion of attributions and provide more information on why attributions must be considered when using strategy instruction. Finally, we introduce the concept of metacognition (literally, thinking about thinking), which is critical to successful strategy instruction. We would stress that although gaining this background knowledge does require some time and effort, it is not a herculean task. In fact, in our experience, many teachers already have some or even most of the knowledge they need. What they don't have is a *framework* for the knowledge to help them apply it to instruction.

INTRODUCTION TO STRATEGY INSTRUCTION

What Is a Strategy?

Everyone uses strategies. Adults write themselves notes. Students are taught familiar spelling strategies: *i* before *e* except after *c*, or in words like *neighbor* or *weigh*. In fact, strategies are so integrated into our everyday life that we are usually not even aware that we are using them. This tendency toward strategy use is a critical component of academic success. Evidence suggests that the most effective learners possess a large repertoire of strategies that range from simple to complex, and that they can be combined to meet different task demands (Pressley & Woloshyn, 1995). Thus, the fact that you are reading this book suggests that you are an active strategy user. But what exactly is a strategy? The term "strategy" has been used in many ways. As with many terms, exactly what people mean by "strategy" may vary. In fact, there are several definitions of what constitutes a strategy. There are some differences across these definitions, but for the most part they are quite similar. Alexander, Graham, and Harris (1998) listed a number of important aspects of strategies.

First, strategies are facilitative and essential. The purpose of strategies is to improve—*facilitate*—performance. We use a strategy to do a task better, more easily, or more quickly. In this sense, a strategy is much like a tool. Tools help us accomplish tasks to a higher standard with much less effort. Strategies do the same. We would stress that it is important to understand that, like tools, strategies serve a purpose. We teach students strategies to improve their performance; *students don't learn strategies just to learn them. Essential* refers to the fact that strategy knowledge and use are what distinguish good students from the less competent students. Second, strategies are *willful* and *effortful*. Students must make a conscious decision to use a strategy, and must commit time and mental effort to do so. The fact that the use of a strategy is a conscious decision is important. If students could not be made aware that they were using a strategy and control its use so that the strategy could be employed when needed, then strategy instruction would have little practical use. To continue the tool analogy, if we can't learn how to properly use our hammer, or our hammer is never around when we need it, then it's not very useful. Finally, it is important to realize that strategies and task requirements are linked. Strategies must be matched to an appropriate task. For example, one strategy that many of us are familiar with is "ROY G. BIV," a simple mnemonic technique to help remember the order of colors in the rainbow. However, ROY G. BIV wouldn't be too useful if the task were to write a term paper. Again, strategies are like tools, and some tools have a very narrow range of uses.

The term "strategy" can also refer to cognitive processes that occur inside our head. For example, while driving in a strange city, you might mentally visualize a map to help you find your way (a visual imagery strategy). Or, if you had to remember an address, you might repeat it over and over to help maintain it in your memory (a verbal rehearsal strategy). The act of managing your activities or monitoring progress, attention, or understanding can also be called a strategy. For example, making sure that you have all the materials you need before starting a task would be a planning strategy. Stopping periodically while reading to ask yourself what you just read and how well you understood it would be a comprehension monitoring strategy. Strategies are typically used in combinations. For example, in the comprehension monitoring example, every time you stop to check comprehension, you might create brief summaries of what you just read and then write them down—thereby combining summarization and rehearsal strategies with a monitoring strategy.

For our purposes, we use a practical definition: A strategy is a series of ordered steps that helps a student perform a task. For example, Figure 2.1 shows a very simple strategy used for two-digit-by-one-digit multiplication with regrouping, with the handy acronym *MAMA*. It outlines a four-step process to follow to solve a multiplication problem. The strategy helps to structure the student's efforts (i.e., to do the steps in order) and to remind the student what to do at each stage of the process. Now look at Figure 2.2—we've added a new wrinkle. Now the student is asked to *track the use* of the strategy by placing a checkmark on the appropriate line. This step combines a self-monitoring strategy with the multiplication strategy. Note that strategies aren't limited to describing steps to use in performing a task. Strategies can also be used to cue students' cognitive processes. For example, the second step in MAMA serves to cue students to determine whether regrouping is needed, and requiring students to check the line after performing each step cues them to monitor whether they've performed the steps of the strategy.

This looks pretty simple and straightforward, doesn't it? If a strategy is just a series of steps, all you need to do is break down a task into its component parts and teach the steps directly to the student. This approach would actually be fairly effective for some

To multiply, remember MAMA:

Multiply—Multiply the 1's columns.

Across?—Is my number more than 9? If so, I regroup.

Multiply—Multiply the 10's column.

Add—If you regrouped, add the number to the 10's.

FIGURE 2.1. MAMA multiplication strategy. Developed by Robert Reid. Used with permission.

To multiply, remember MAMA:

Multiply—Multiply the 1's columns.

Across?—Is my number more than 9? If so, I regroup.

Multiply—Multiply the 10's column.

Add—If I regrouped, add the number to the 10's.

Remember to check off each step in MAMA as you do it.

____ Multiply 1's	____ Multiply 1's	____ Multiply 1's
____ Across?	____ Across?	____ Across?
____ Multiply 10's	____ Multiply 10's	____ Multiply 10's
____ Add	____ Add	____ Add

| 87 | 29 | 15 |
| × 5 | × 2 | × 7 |

FIGURE 2.2. MAMA multiplication strategy with self-monitoring. Developed by Robert Reid. Used with permission.

students. Unfortunately, as we will see in the next sections, the students who might profit from this approach are the ones who would need it the least because they are already good strategy users. For students with LD or other struggling learners, simply teaching the steps would be unlikely to have any meaningful effect because cognitive, metacognitive, and motivational problems of students with LD haven't been accounted for. In the next sections we provide additional information about these areas.

INFORMATION PROCESSING

One of the reasons the strategy instruction approach is so successful is that it incorporates knowledge about how our memory and cognitive processes work into the teaching process. The information-processing model uses the computer as a model of how our mind works on new information or attacks problems such as academic tasks. It's not an exact comparison for many reasons, not the least of which is that our minds are infinitely more complex than a computer! However, at a very basic level it is both useful and informative. In this section we discuss information processing and its implications for strategy instruction. We draw our discussion from Lerner (2000) and Swanson (1996a).

Figure 2.3 shows a simplified model of information processing. As Figure 2.3 shows, the information-processing model divides the flow of information into three stages. This division is analogous to how a computer is divided into different components that perform different operations:

Information processing

Sensory register—hearing, vision, touch.

Short-term memory—information from the sensory register is stored here for a brief interval. Unless the information is acted on in some way, it is lost forever.

Working memory—information is stored briefly and processed or manipulated in some manner. This store is limited and temporary. As soon as information is not being used, it disappears.

Long-term memory—information is stored permanently. Information stored here may be transferred to working memory when needed.

Executive functions—control how information is processed and stored.

Computer

Input devices—keyboard, mouse.

Random access memory (RAM)—temporary storage. Unless transferred to permanent memory, information is lost.

Random access memory (RAM)—the portion of memory used to process information.

Permanent memory—hard drive, optical disc. Information stored here is permanent. Information may be transferred to RAM.

Operating system—the code that tells the computer how to transfer information and allot memory for various functions.

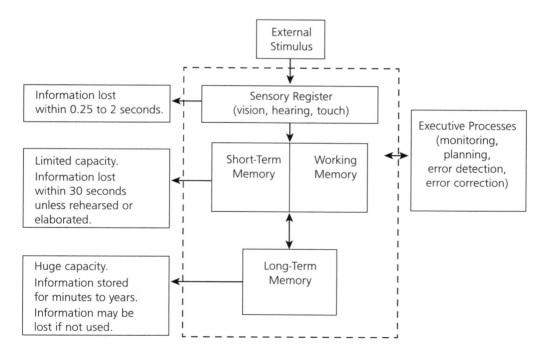

FIGURE 2.3. Simplified information-processing model.

Here is how it might work in practice. First, our senses perceive a stimulus. For example, we might see a printed word or hear a sentence. This information is stored in the sensory register. It is stored for only a very brief period of time—a fraction of a second. Our sensory register is bombarded with information, so information can't stay too long. From here, the information goes to short-term memory. There are two important aspects of short-term memory. First, short-term memory is quite limited. Estimates are that short-term memory can hold only around seven "chunks" of information at one time. Second, short-term memory is a temporary holding area. Information will remain in short-term memory for only a matter of seconds. When information is in short-term memory, we are consciously aware of it. For example, you are consciously aware of the sentence you just read. It's in your short-term memory, but it will be replaced with the next sentences you read and will fade from your memory. We want to remember information such as the sentence we just read, but it doesn't happen automatically. Our memory isn't like a videotape that faithfully records an exact representation of everything. If the information in our short-term memory isn't acted on (or processed), it will be lost (i.e., forgotten). Information that is processed in some manner, such as rehearsal (repeating the information to yourself), will then be transferred to long-term memory, where it can be stored permanently.

Once information is stored in long-term memory, the question becomes one of retrieval (remembering). Although the information has been stored, it may decay (i.e., decrease in strength) if not utilized. When information is utilized regularly, the strength of the memory increases. For example, you would have little trouble rattling off your present phone number or address. However, it would probably take you much longer to call up the address or phone number you had when you were in junior high school. And some information that was once strong may have faded almost entirely (can you recite the quadratic equation?). *Retrieval* also refers to being able to recall information when needed. It's entirely possible for information to be stored in long-term memory but not to be available on demand. For example, we have all had the experience of trying and failing to recall a name, only to suddenly remember it at a later time.

One of the important factors in how easily information can be retrieved is how the information is stored. Short-term memory has a number of "control processes" that are used to process information in a way that makes it easier to remember (Swanson, 1996a). These include:

- *Chunking*—grouping information into smaller units. For example, changing a series of 10 digits into a phone number, or taking a group of unrelated words and creating a sentence.
- *Clustering*—placing a information into meaningful categories. For example, grouping a list of words into animals, colors, or verbs.
- *Mnemonics*—organizing material in a manner that enhances recall. For example, ROY G. BIV forms an acronym that helps us to remember the colors of the spectrum in the correct order.
- *Relating information to known material*—using analogies to already existing

knowledge. For example, the game of cricket is much easier to understand if you have a working knowledge of baseball.

- *Tagging information*—setting up retrieval paths to help remember information. For example, to remember that *ranid* means frog, you might connect the term *ranid* with an image of a frog in the rain.

Another part of memory that is critical for information processing is called *working memory*. There are three components of working memory:

- *Phonological loop.* This deals with spoken or written verbal information. It has two subcomponents (1) the phonological store, which holds information in speech-based form (e.g., spoken words), and (2) the articulatory control process, which stores and rehearses information from the phonological store (e.g., inner voice).
- *Visuospatial sketch pad.* This stores spatial information (e.g., planning a route for a shopping trip).
- *Central executive.* This coordinates the actions of the phonological loop and the articulatory control process. It also deals with planning, organizing, and coordinating effort, and with problem solving.

Working memory is where information is temporarily *stored, processed*, and *manipulated*. It differs from short-term memory in that short-term memory involves only temporary storage of information. Here's an example of how short-term memory and working memory differ. Take a look at the numbers on the line below, then cover them with your finger.

$$6 \quad 4 \quad 9 \quad 7 \quad 2$$

Can you remember the order of the numbers? That is a short-term memory task. It only involves storing and retrieving the information. Now, add the first and last numbers together; when you are finished, subtract the second number from the sum. This is a working memory task because it requires you to process the information. Did you notice that this task was more difficult? In this task you had to maintain the order of the digits in memory while you selectively processed the digits (i.e., added and subtracted them).

Like short-term memory, working memory lasts for only a short while. For example, once you have used a math fact, it will disappear quickly because it is no longer needed. Additionally, if the teacher's instructions are lost from working memory, they are lost for good. Because they were unlikely to have been stored in long-term memory, they would not be retrievable. Like short-term memory, working memory is also limited. Thus, we couldn't call up all our math facts simultaneously. It would be impossible to maintain that much information in working memory. To return to the computer analogy, if we try to load a file that's too big for the available memory, the computer will either freeze up or give an error message. Similarly, if we try to hold too much information in working memory or have to process information in working memory because we can't apply it fluently, our ability to process information will suffer and our performance begin to decrease.

It's important to understand that even simple tasks can place heavy demands on working memory. Here is an example of the working memory tasks involved in a simple task that occurs frequently in the classroom: copying a sentence from the board.

Task	*Working memory component*
Maintain the words in the sentence in order in working memory while information is being processed and new information called up.	Phonological loop
Block out distractions that could cause the information stored in working memory to be lost.	Central executive
Call up the spelling for the first word from long-term memory.	Central executive
Maintain the spelling of the first word in working memory.	Phonological loop
Call up the orthography (form) of the letters in the first word.	Central executive
Maintain the orthography of the letters in the correct order in working memory	Visuospatial sketch pad
Write each letter of the word.	Visuospatial sketch pad
Monitor that the letters are formed correctly and written in the correct order.	Central executive
Call up the next word in the sentence from working memory and repeat the process.	Phonological loop

Note that all the components of working memory are called on for this simple task, and a breakdown in any of them will result in failure to complete the task.

How Knowledge of Information Processing Helps Strategy Instruction

Knowing how memory operates can help teachers. We need to teach in a manner that will help students process information efficiently and effectively. For example, to help students get new information into long-term memory you need to teach in ways that encourage them to process the information through elaboration, rehearsal techniques, or mnemonics. This is especially true for students with LD. Knowledge of working memory is particularly important. There is evidence to suggest that students with LD or ADHD have deficiencies in working memory (Alloway, Gathercole, Kirkwood, & Elliott, 2009; Martinussen & Tannock, 2006; Swanson, 1999a). If working memory is overloaded, then there is insufficient processing space for new information. We see examples of this insufficiency in the classroom every day. For example, every teacher has had experience with students who read a passage by painfully sounding out each word. At the end of the passage they can't remember anything they read because all their working memory processing was devoted to decoding—nothing was left to process information. To be able to read and comprehend, a student needs to be able to use decoding skills fluently so that working memory isn't overloaded.

Working memory also is associated with the ability to remember and follow directions (Martinussen & Major, 2011). Students with working memory deficits often can't follow directions because they cannot hold all the information in working memory and have literally forgotten the directions. They also may have difficulty because the processing demands of the task are too difficult for their working memory. For example, in the exercise above, imagine if you were required to multiply the first two numbers, then multiply the product times the third number and so on. Most people's working memory would quickly be overloaded. Thus it's important for teachers to consider the processing demands a task places on working memory. As the previous example illustrates, even a task as seemingly simple as copying a sentence from the board can place serious demands on working memory of some children. As we will see later, reducing demands on working memory is a critical aspect of strategy instruction.

THE IMPORTANCE OF ATTRIBUTIONS

In Chapter 1 we discussed the problem that many students with LD due to a maladaptive attribution style. Weiner (1979) developed a useful model of causal attributions that separates attributions into three dimensions:

1. *Internal versus external.* This dimension refers to whether students see the causes of success or failure as being inside or outside themselves. Examples of internal causes would be ability, effort, aptitude, or mood. External causes could be task difficulty or actions by another (e.g., "She helped me do it").
2. *Controllable versus uncontrollable.* This dimension refers to how strongly students believe that the causes for success or failure are under their direct control or influence. Examples of controllable causes are effort or strategy use. An example of uncontrollable causes is luck.
3. *Stable versus unstable.* This dimension refers to the extent to which the causes of success or failure have remained consistent or unchanging over time. Stable causes are those not likely to change. Unstable causes are those that are due to temporary factors or those that can be changed or modified.

Table 2.1 shows examples of possible attributions for each of the three dimensions.

TABLE 2.1. Examples of Attributions Classified by Weiner's Dimensions

Attribution	Dimensions	Comment
"I practiced what the coach told me for 3 weeks and my free-throw shooting got lots better."	Internal, controllable, stable	Success is due to effort and use of an effective technique.
"My free-throw shooting sucks. I'm just no good at basketball."	Internal, uncontrollable, stable	Failure is due to a lack of ability that will not change.
"I didn't really study enough for the test because I couldn't get organized."	Internal, controllable, unstable	Failure is due to a circumstance that could be corrected.
"I hurt my leg and couldn't practice for the game."	Internal, uncontrollable, unstable	Failure is due to a chance injury that is not permanent.
"Doctor Graham's tests are so hard I'll never pass them."	External, uncontrollable, stable	Failure is due to an external factor (difficult exam) that is not likely to change.
"I got an A on the test, but it was really easy."	External, uncontrollable, unstable	Success is due to an outside factor that may change.

How Knowledge of Attributions Helps Strategy Instruction

A knowledge of attributions is important for a number of reasons. Research shows that a student's attributional style can directly affect academic performance (Diener & Dweck, 1978; Dweck & Leggett, 1988). Students with maladaptive attributional styles often won't persist in, or even try, tasks that they perceive as difficult. Unfortunately, teachers tend to react negatively to this "won't even try" behavior (Weiner, 1992). In turn, these negative reactions make academic tasks even more threatening and aversive, making it more likely that the student will continue to avoid tasks. Students who have maladaptive attributional styles will tend to attribute failures to internal, uncontrollable factors ("I'm dumb") and success to uncontrollable, external factors ("I was lucky"). As a result these students are at risk for developing a negative attitude toward academics and anxiety when faced with academic tasks. They will make more negative statements to themselves ("I'll never get this done") and will develop the belief that they cannot succeed no matter how hard they may try. This in turn results in decreased effort, or in simply avoiding tasks that they perceive as difficult. As a result, their performance declines. This overall scenario captures what is referred to as the *helpless orientation*. In contrast, students who attribute success and failure to internal, controllable factors such as effort will remain positive in the face of a difficult task and will persist in their efforts much longer. They will not avoid challenging tasks and will actively work to improve their problem-solving skills. This is called the *mastery orientation*. The implications of these two orientations for classroom teachers are obvious. We want students to adopt a mastery orientation rather than maintain a helpless orientation.

Research shows that this approach of directly addressing attributional style can be effective for students. For example, Dweck (1975) taught students with learned helplessness to attribute failure to insufficient effort. These students then showed increased persistence. Other studies have provided students with verbal praise for attributing success and failure to effort (e.g., Andrews & Debus, 1978). These students also increased the time that they would persist at a task. Attribution training also combines well with strategy instruction. For example, Borkowski and colleagues (1988) found that attribution training in combination with strategy instruction resulted in a 50% gain on a reading task. The researchers also suggested that for strategy training to be effective with students who had maladaptive attributions or learned helplessness, it was necessary to teach them a healthy, mastery-oriented attributional style.

How do we go about instilling a positive attributional style in students? Simply put, we need to teach students to attribute success and failure to their *own efforts* and to the use of an *effective strategy*. To accomplish these two goals, it's necessary to shift students' attributions from an ability focus ("You succeed at tasks because you're smart") to a skill and effort focus ("You succeeded because you used an appropriate strategy and you tried hard"). The shift toward the skill and effort focus (or the incremental view of intelligence) is important. From this perspective our intelligence continues to develop as we gain new strategies and skills, *and we can always learn new strategies and skills*. Evidence shows that students who have this incremental perspective are more likely to adopt a mastery orientation.

To achieve this shift, there are two major tasks for the classroom teacher. First, changing instilled attribution patterns requires the teacher to be aware of why those attributions may occur and how to help students change to a healthier style. For example, one of the primary problems is that students often equate "trying hard" with having less ability. In other words, if you have to try hard to succeed at a task, then you must not be very smart. On the other hand, seemingly effortless success signals high ability. Another problem can be seeking help. Many students equate needing help with having low ability. Still another problem is the feedback we give students that may unwittingly reinforce the ability perspective. How many times have you praised a child's success with "You're a genius" or "You're so smart"? Second, teachers must systematically change their classroom behavior to help inculcate a healthy attributional style. This change entails systematically working to shift students' attributional styles from external and uncontrollable to internal and controllable. It also involves teaching the incremental perspective on intelligence.

Table 2.2 provides suggestions on how teachers can approach this task in the classroom. The effort to change attributional styles should be done on an ongoing basis as part of the strategy instruction process. Note that this process will require preparation and planning just as any other instructional activity. For example, Alderman (1999) suggested that teachers might actually write out examples of appropriate feedback or praise statements in advance.

TABLE 2.2. Tips for Changing Attributions

- *Provide students with feedback that stresses effort and/or strategy use.*

  Effort: "Johnny, all that extra spelling practice you did paid off. You got a 96% on your spelling test."

  Strategy: "Helen, you really learned the long-division strategy well! You followed all the steps and you got all the problems correct!"

- *If a student fails at a task, relate the failure to effort or strategy use.*

  Effort: "Well, Emma, your spelling score was only 52%. I noticed that this week you didn't spend as much time practicing your words. I think that you need to spend extra time practicing."

  Strategy: "Hepzibah, I noticed that you missed six problems on your worksheet because you didn't regroup correctly. If you remember the steps in the 4 B's strategy, you won't forget to regroup. Would you like go over it again?"

- *Teach children what it means to "really try."*

  Discuss the meaning of effort. *Effort* means sticking with it, not giving up. Stress that effort is important to success, and that you should always give your best effort. Teach the difference between productive effort and just getting by. For many children just handing in work, regardless of quality, is perceived as effort.

- *Show how effort can affect outcomes.*

  Link effort to success and learning. For example, have students chart the number of spelling practices and their weekly spelling scores. Show how increased practice relates to better spelling scores. Stress the relation between productive work and success. For example, children's social studies grades improve because they worked really hard at getting all their assignments done well.

- *Give students a strategy.*

  Give students a systematic means of completing a task—a strategy. Stress that using the strategy consistently and correctly will lead to success. Treat strategies like "tools"; stress that you can always add another "tool to your toolbox."

- *Make "smart" a skill.*

  Stress that what makes you "smart" is the number of skills and strategies you have. You can't change ability, but you can always learn more skills and strategies. You don't learn things because you are "smart"; you learn because of instruction, strategies, and effort, and these make you "smart."

- *Internalize responsibility for success and failure.*

  Through feedback and modeling, stress that the reasons for success and failure are inside us. We succeed because we try hard and use the right strategy. If we fail, we didn't put forth our best effort or use the right strategy. Note that to prevent failure, the teacher must ensure that child has the preskills to do the task and determine whether the child can do the task independently or with assistance.

METACOGNITION

What are you doing as you read this book? You almost certainly have a purpose in mind: You want to learn about strategy instruction. You might be underlining or highlighting what you believe are important passages. You may stop and verbally paraphrase a section to yourself or make notes in the margins or a notebook. You might make connections or relate information to your personal experience or other bits of knowledge about instruction. You may be reading some sections more slowly because the information is unfamiliar or difficult; however, you may breeze through others. While you read, you are probably aware of how well you understand the material. If you realize that you are confused about something you just read, you will probably stop and review the section. You may have actually done some planning before you even began to read, if you allotted time to read the chapter. If you are reading the book for a class, you may have scheduled a time to reread or look at notes. In summary, you are doing much more than simply decoding printed words on a page. You are actively engaged with the learning task at a number of levels.

Students with LD would likely have a much different experience. They may have no particular purpose in mind when they read. Their main goal would be to simply "get through" the task. They would be unlikely to effectively use the activities that would help them retain the information (e.g., highlighting or paraphrasing) or to be aware of their degree of comprehension, much less use error correction techniques such as rereading. This type of unengaged performance isn't limited to reading. It is typical of how students with LD or ADHD perform many academic tasks. Often they will make glaring mistakes or silly errors that seem so obvious that we wonder how they could be unaware of them.

One reason for these errors is that students are not actively involved in the learning task due, in large part, to a problem with metacognition. "Metacognition" is defined as one's knowledge of one's own cognitive processes and the products related to them (Flavell, 1979). Put more simply, metacognition means "thinking about thinking." What is the difference between *cognition* and *metacognition*? It is the difference between knowing something and understanding knowledge in terms of awareness and appropriate use (Flavell, 1979). To help understand the distinction we can use an the example of a hammer:

Cognitive	*Metacognitive*
"That's a hammer."	"A hammer is a tool I'd use to drive a nail. There are different kinds of hammers for different jobs. You need to practice a little before you can use a hammer well. You need to be careful using a hammer or you can hurt yourself."

As you can see, the metacognitive knowledge goes beyond the factual knowledge. It encompasses knowing (1) the purpose a hammer serves, (2) that it's necessary to match the correct hammer to a given task (you wouldn't use a sledge hammer to drive a nail), (3) that a skill set is needed to use a hammer successfully, and (4) that some monitoring is necessary when you use a hammer (if you don't pay attention, you might end up with a very sore thumb!). The hammer example illustrates the importance of metacognition. Students without a metacognitive understanding of a task will obviously not function as well as those who do have such an understanding. This lack of metacognitive knowledge also contributes to a student's frustration. There are three major components of metacognition: metacognitive knowledge, motivational beliefs, and the executive component, or self-regulation (Hacker, 1998).

Metacognitive knowledge refers to a person's (1) acquired knowledge and beliefs about him- or herself as a learner, (2) task demands and how they can be met, and (3) strategies that can or should be used to accomplish a task (Flavell, 1979). Metacognitive knowledge also includes the relation between task and strategy (i.e., which strategies are appropriate to a given task) and a knowledge of how, when, where, and why to use strategy. For example:

Type of knowledge	*Example*
Self as learner: This may include knowledge of your own capabilities, comparisons with others, and general knowledge of your cognition.	"I'm good at math, but my spelling is terrible." "If I don't write something down, I'll forget it." "My wife is better at math than I am."
Task demands: This may include knowledge of how different tasks place different demands, and how to approach a task appropriately.	Knowing that you read for detail differently than you would for the main idea. Knowing that when you read a very dense and complex passage, you need to slow down.
Strategy: This may include knowledge of what type of strategy (if any) is appropriate for a task, knowledge of how best to strategically attack a given task, and knowledge that strategies enhance performance.	"A paraphrasing strategy will help my comprehension, but a mnemonic would be better to remember a list." "To write a better story, I'll use my story grammar strategy." "Using a strategy helps me do better."

Motivational beliefs—which are related to attributions—also play a role in metacognition (Borkowski, Estrada, Milstead, & Hale, 1989). Students' beliefs about their competence and control over outcomes can directly affect their choice of strategies and how long they will persist at a task (Bandura, 1993). If students lack confidence in their skills, then they may not be able to use their skills effectively. In fact, some studies have shown that students' *belief* in their abilities was a better predictor of positive attitudes toward academic tasks than actual ability (Bandura, 1993). Components of motivational beliefs include:

- *General competency*—"How good am I as a learner overall?"
- *Competency in specific task*—"How good am I at this specific task?"
- *Control over outcomes*—"Do I have control over how well I do?"
- *Causes of failure*—"Why did I succeed or fail (internal or external)?"
- *Benefits of strategy*—Belief that a strategic approach is effective/superior.

Self-regulation refers to how learners regulate or manage cognitive and metacognitive processes. Self-regulation is critical for a number of reasons. First, effective learners are self-regulated learners (Butler & Winne, 1995). Students who actively regulate their cognition are more engaged in a task and typically perform better than those who don't. Although self-regulation is complex and there are numerous cognitive and metacognitive activities that can be monitored, there are four commonly recognized self-regulation activities that are important for strategy instruction (e.g., Hacker, 1998). These include:

- *Planning*—adopting a deliberate, organized approach to a task and planning next moves.
- *Monitoring*—checking comprehension and strategy effectiveness; testing, revising, and evaluating strategies; monitoring the effectiveness of attempts.
- *Failure detection*—"Are things going OK?"
- *Failure correction*—"Let's fix it."

Second, there is little use in teaching a strategy that students cannot use independently. For a strategy to be truly useful, students should be able to effectively use and *maintain it* without outside support or guidance. This level of self-regulation is concerned with maintaining effort and appropriate strategy use. It includes functions such as staying on task, blocking out or eliminating negative cognitions ("I can't do this"), and consistently and correctly using a strategy.

How Knowledge of Metacognition Helps Strategy Instruction

For strategy instruction to be effective, students—*especially those with LD*—must have a metacognitive knowledge of how, where, when, and why they are using a strategy, and the underlying reasons behind the components of the strategy (Pressley & Woloshyn, 1995). Students need this metacognitive understanding of a strategy in order to profit fully from strategy instruction (Hacker, 1998). Without this knowledge, there is little chance that a strategy will be maintained or generalized. For strategy instruction, metacognitive knowledge is literally like the mortar in a brick wall. Mortar serves to bind the individual bricks together to make a strong and durable structure. Metacognitive knowledge and self-regulation processes serve a similar function. Strategies are not intended to be performed mindlessly (Harris & Pressley, 1991). To derive maximum benefit from a strategy, students should have a deep understanding of how the strategy works and how it helps them perform better. Students also need to actively self-regulate their effort to help both with cognitive processes such as comprehension monitoring and to maintain that effort. Developing metacognitive knowledge and self-regulation skills is one of the most critical components of strategy instruction and is an integral part of the SRSD model.

The goal of the SRSD instruction process is to work with students until they have sufficient "ownership" of a strategy to successfully perform academic tasks. To do this, we need to help the child with LD become more like Pressley's "good strategy user"

(Pressley, Borkowski, & Schnieder, 1987). Specifically, we work with students until they are able to:

- Know where to use a strategy and why it should be used.
- Monitor the strategy to check whether it is effective.
- Shield themselves from maladaptive thoughts that could impair performance.
- Develop the strong belief that strategy use makes them better thinkers.
- Use a strategy fluently to the point where it becomes automatic.

The background knowledge we discussed relates specifically to these goals. Knowing where and why to use a strategy is an example of metacognitive knowledge. Monitoring the effectiveness of a strategy is also metacognitive—it is self-regulation. Finally, becoming a fluent strategy user depends on being able to process information (i.e., remember and use a strategy) effectively. As you can see, many of the components are interdependent. For example, fluent strategy use is unlikely to develop if a child cannot screen out negative thoughts ("You'll never get this right, so why try?"). Similarly, metacognitive knowledge and self-regulation are also prerequisites for effective and consistent strategy use.

FINAL THOUGHTS

As you can see by now, effective strategy instruction deals with much more than just academic content. For strategy instruction to be effective for students with LD or ADHD, it's necessary to attend to cognitive processes, motivational aspects, and information processing. In sum, strategy instruction deals with both cognition and emotional–motivational aspects of learning. It also requires teaching that is sensitive to the information-processing problems of students with LD or ADHD. Because effective strategy instruction requires attention to so many aspects of learning, it helps to have a teaching model that focuses attention on these aspects of strategy instruction as well as on teaching the actual strategy. And, that's just what the SRSD model was designed to do. It serves as a template for teachers to help them attend to all the steps in the strategy instruction process. In the next chapter we discuss the SRSD model in detail.

CHAPTER 3

The Self-Regulated
Strategy Development Model

In the previous chapters we presented a rationale for strategy instruction and provided some background knowledge about important characteristics of students with LD that affect strategy instruction. In this chapter we introduce a model for the strategy instruction process. The implementation model is based on Harris and Graham's (1996) Self-Regulated Strategy Development (SRSD) model. We chose this model for four reasons. First, it is based on years of research and, more importantly, has a well-demonstrated 30-year history of effectiveness (Harris, Santangelo, & Graham, 2010). Second, the SRSD model is a comprehensive approach to the strategy instruction process that takes into consideration critical cognitive, motivational, and academic characteristics of students with LD and other struggling learners. Students with LD have problems that go beyond academics, and these problems can adversely affect academic performance. The SRSD model stresses the need to provide students with essential metacognitive knowledge of the strategies, attends to the problem of maladaptive attributions that are common among students with LD, and stresses instruction that helps students process information more effectively. Third, the SRSD model is intended to be used in conjunction with different self-regulation strategies. This combination is particularly powerful for students with LD, who often benefit from strategies that help them maintain focus, effort, and motivation. Finally, the SRSD model is practical for the real-world classroom. Teachers won't use models that are unwieldy or impractical. The SRSD model was designed with the needs of students and teachers in mind and, as we noted in Chapter 1, has been used effectively by classroom teachers in the general education classroom, special education classroom, and in RTI. Its also been used effectively at elementary, middle, and secondary levels.

We cannot overemphasize how important it is to use an appropriate and effective model, such as SRSD, for strategy instruction. Following the SRSD model has two major advantages:

1. A good model gives you an instructional road map to follow so that you know how to teach the strategy in an *effective, systematic, step-by-step* fashion. This ensures that critical steps in the strategy instruction process are not omitted or shortchanged.
2. Strategy instruction involves a commitment of time and effort on the part of the teacher. To maximize the chances of a positive outcome (i.e., increased academic performance for students), it is crucial to use approaches that have been well validated. Teachers who approach strategy instruction without using a validated framework for instruction are unlikely to experience success.

You may be wondering why we have focused so much attention on the strategy instruction *process* and barely mentioned actual *strategies*. The reason for this is simple. Strategies are the easiest part of the process. In this book we introduce you to many powerful strategies that are effective for students with LD or ADHD. However, it is crucial to understand that *strategies are not magical*. Simply exposing a student with LD or ADHD to a strategy will not be effective. Strategies are *potentially* powerful, but, unless they are taught correctly, strategies are unlikely to result in improved academic performance. Therefore, for strategy instruction to succeed, teachers must adopt a systematic approach such as the one in the SRSD model. The goal of SRSD is to make the use of strategies habitual, flexible, and automatic. Getting to this level requires an investment of some time, practice, and effort. However, it is an investment that is likely to pay big dividends. When teachers use the strategy instruction process *correctly*, most students will markedly improve their academic performance.

In this chapter we first discuss the six stages of instruction in the SRSD model. For each stage we provide examples of activities and give examples of helpful tools. Second, we discuss evaluation of the SRSD process. Effective and ongoing classroom evaluation is important for student growth. Teachers must be able to accurately gauge how well SRSD is working. Students who are taught a strategy that does not work for them will not be enthusiastic about learning a second strategy. Finally, we conclude with general guidelines for strategy instruction.

THE SIX STAGES OF THE SRSD MODEL

The basic stages of the SRSD model are designed to ensure that all necessary aspects of strategy instruction are fully addressed. We present the stages in a commonly used sequence; however, the stages are flexible and can be reordered or combined as deemed appropriate or necessary. The model requires teachers to use their own professional judgment when employing it. Furthermore, the SRSD stages are intended to be recursive: Teachers loop back through stages, and activities are repeated as necessary. Revisiting stages helps students to rethink the process and develop metacognitive skills and abilities. In practice, it is common for a lesson to use components of two or three stages and to revisit stages. This recursive feature is discussed further in Chapter 8.

The time required to complete the SRSD process varies depending on the complexity of the strategy and the needs of students. Lessons typically last from 20 to 60 minutes (depending on factors such as grade level, class schedules, attention spans) and are taught at least three times a week. Most strategies can be taught fairly quickly. Harris suggested that in the elementary grades, eight to twelve 30- to 40-minute lessons are usually sufficient for students to complete the stages of the SRSD process (Harris, Graham, & Mason, 2003). In practice, we have taught students with LD or ADHD (ranging in grade level from elementary to secondary) strategies in written language and reading comprehension in from five to eight 30- to 40-minute sessions (Hagaman & Reid, 2008; Johnson, Reid, & Mason, 2012; Lienemann & Reid, 2008; Reid & Lienemann, 2006). However, we would stress that the instruction is highly individualized and the time needed depends on the students' progress through the instruction.

Stage 1: Developing and Activating Background Knowledge

Developing background knowledge sometimes seems so obvious, but in practice it is just this type of obvious task that is often overlooked. It is critical that students be able to perform prerequisite skills to effectively use a strategy. For example, trying to teach a long-division strategy to a student who has not mastered multiplication or subtraction would be a fruitless endeavor. Note also that *proficiency* at preskills may be important. If a student struggles to perform preskills, this degree of effort can place demands on working memory that could adversely impact the effectiveness of the strategy use. To return to the previous example, if a student struggled to remember multiplication facts, he or she might not be able to use a long-division strategy effectively because too much working memory would be used in the attempt to retrieve multiplication facts. At this stage there are two essential tasks: (1) Define the skills a child needs to perform a strategy and (2) assess the child's knowledge and/or ability to perform the skills.

Defining Skills

While developing background knowledge, it is necessary to initially define the basic skills needed to perform the strategy. For example, to learn a long-division strategy, students need to know basic subtraction, multiplication, and division facts, place value, and even so basic a skill as telling left from right, perhaps. It is also important to make certain that students understand the components of the strategy. For example, some reading comprehension strategies involve the use of text structures that may not be familiar to students. The best way to identify the basic skills and strategy components that are necessary is to break down the task in terms of the knowledge needed to successfully use the strategy. The task breakdown will help teachers determine what the students need to know to perform the strategy. The easiest way to break down a task is to make two columns. Label one column *Steps* and the second *Skills*. In the first column list the steps the student would need to perform to accomplish the task. In the second list the skills a child would need to know to perform these steps. Tables 3.1 and 3.2

TABLE 3.1. Example of Task Breakdown for Two-Digit by Two-Digit Multiplication

Steps	Skills required
Multiply 1's column.	Knowledge of place value Knowledge of multiplication facts
Bring down the 1's digit part of the answer.	Knowledge of place value Where to write answers to vertically written math problems
Carry the 10's digit part of the answer.	Knowledge of place value How to carry numbers
Multiply across, the bottom 1's digit to the top 10's digit.	Knowledge of place value Knowledge of multiplication facts
To that answer add the number that you carried and write that down.	Knowledge of addition facts Where to write answers to vertically written math problems
Under that answer write a 0 in the 1's column.	Knowledge of place value
Multiply the bottom 10's digit to the top 1's digit.	Knowledge of place value Knowledge of multiplication facts
Bring down the 1's digit part of the answer and put it in the 10's column.	Knowledge of place value Where to write answers to vertically written math problems
Carry the 10's digit part of the answer.	Knowledge of place value How to carry numbers
Multiply the 10's digit column.	Knowledge of place value Knowledge of multiplication facts
To that answer add the number that you carried and write that down.	Knowledge of addition facts Where to write answers to vertically written math problems
Add your two answers; the number that you get is *the* answer.	Knowledge of addition facts
Write it down.	Where to write answers to vertically written math problems

provide examples of a simple math task and a more involved writing task. The easiest way to break down a task is to actually do the task yourself, write down each step, and then ask yourself what you needed to know to perform the step.

Assessing Knowledge

There are many ways that teachers can check students' knowledge. For example, for the long-division strategy the teacher could simply use flash cards to assess a student's

TABLE 3.2. Example of Task Breakdown for Writing a Simple Research Paper

Steps	Skills required
Choose a topic.	Idea generation
Research that topic.	Ability to find source material, use card catalog or other references
Write down important and interesting information on note cards.	Ability to take notes effectively and to distinguish between relevant and irrelevant information
Sort note cards into categories with similar types of information.	Ability to group information according to similarities

Make an outline including:
  Introduction
  Body—using the two or three categories of note cards that have the most important and most interesting information
  Conclusion
	How to write an outline
	  What an introduction should contain
	  What a body should contain
	  What a conclusion should contain

Write a rough draft, making sure that you have:
  A complete introduction with a complete paragraph or two
  A body that is well supported and written in complete paragraphs, with complete sentences
  A conclusion that summarizes what you said and makes any points that you wanted to make
	Basic knowledge of writing mechanics:
	  Complete sentences
	  Complete paragraphs
	  Organized paragraphs
	  Paper components and how to write them
	    Introduction
	    Body
	    Conclusion

Type out your rough draft, using spelling and grammar check to make sure that your spelling and grammar are correct and to make any necessary changes.	Typing skills Knowledge of a basic word-processing program
Have a teacher or knowledgeable person proofread your paper and make any changes or give any suggestions that he or she might have.	Knowing who would be a knowledgeable person to ask for assistance
Rewrite your paper and make any necessary adjustments.	Knowing how to take criticism Knowing how to make corrections with the word-processing program
Look over your paper and make sure it looks good.	Knowledge of what a paper is supposed to look like

knowledge of basic multiplication and addition facts. Some commonly used methods include observing student performance, using curriculum-based measures, or simply asking students what they are doing (and how and why). Often, teachers will already be aware of a student's knowledge and deficit areas. Skill deficits should be addressed prior to introducing the new strategy. This means teaching the skill to a sufficient level of mastery for the student to perform the strategy successfully *or* providing a means for the student to compensate for a skill deficit. For example, if a student needed a long-division strategy but had difficulty with multiplication facts, the teacher could provide a times table for the student to use. Note that the teacher should still work on building up the student's skill at multiplication in the interim.

Stage 2: Discussing the Strategy

Discussion of the strategy is a more involved process than merely going through the steps of a strategy. There are three tasks that must be accomplished at this stage. First, teachers need to "sell" the strategy and get students to "buy in." Remember that one major goal of SRSD is to help students develop into self-regulated learners. In order for this goal to be achieved, students need to be actively involved in and take ownership of the SRSD process. Students need to believe that the strategy they are learning will help them perform better. This belief will enable them to be more actively involved, which is the first step in self-regulation. If a student does not want to use a strategy, it is fair to assume that he or she will not use it. Remember that motivational processes have significant effects on learning and effort. Throughout the SRSD process teachers need to be excited, committed, and energized so that students will be too. In practice, it's not hard for teachers to sell a strategy. After all, learning an effective, appropriate strategy will result in improved academic performance, which is an attractive outcome for students who are struggling. Teachers can provide students with examples of how this strategy or other strategies have improved student performance in the past, and even how strategies have helped them in the past. It is also helpful to know what motivates particular students. For example, if a student has lost recess time because he or she had to correct errors on a math worksheet, a strategy that will improve accuracy would be quite appealing.

Second, teachers should talk with students about their current level of performance and establish that it is a concern. For example, teachers can create graphs to show current performance levels and use the graphs to discuss performance goals. The teacher should also explain the benefits of using the strategy, and how learning and using the strategy can help the student reach performance goals. Note that the graphs can also be used to chart progress. We recommend the use of graphs if possible. Graphing can be used in conjunction with self-regulation strategies, and we have found that, in practice, it can help to motivate students as well.

The final step of this stage is introducing students to the steps of the strategy. The teacher explains what each step of the strategy is for, how it is used, and where it is useful. This is also where teachers begin to do some attribution retraining by stressing that good performance is the result of *effort* and *strategy use*.

During this stage, and those that follow, you will want to be sensitive to student feedback. Remember that strategies should be custom fit, not "off the rack." You *must* match the strategy to the student. Strategies that students dislike or that are too difficult are of little use. You should not hesitate to modify a strategy if a student doesn't understand it or is uncomfortable with part of it. Throughout this process, you should be closely monitoring students' understanding; ask questions on the steps and probe for comprehension. Remember that strategy instruction is not a one-way street. It is a reciprocal process. Students' aptitudes, deficits, and needs should inform the instruction process.

Stage 3: Modeling the Strategy

Modeling is one of the most crucial components of strategy instruction because it is the means by which teachers provide students with the metacognitive knowledge of strategy performance. Good modeling allows the student to see the thought processes of an "expert" learner employing the strategy. Typically, modeling incorporates the "think-aloud" process, wherein teachers or students verbalize their thought processes as they perform a strategy. The think-aloud process is analogous to opening the hood of a car to see how the engine is functioning. To do a good think-aloud, teachers must be able to "pop the top" to show students what a skilled strategy user is thinking. Just as an engine propels a car, thought processes propel effective strategy use and must be demonstrated to the student.

Modeling should improve students' cognitive and metacognitive knowledge of the strategy through exposure to the way a skilled learner implements and regulates strategy use. It also can help to increase students' knowledge of the steps of the strategy. Figure 3.1 shows an example of a think-aloud that was developed for the 4 *B*'s strategy (a subtraction strategy). Note that the think-aloud goes well beyond merely presenting the strategy steps—it provides students with the "why" and the "how" of various strategy steps (i.e., the metacognitive knowledge and the self-regulation processes associated with the performance of steps). This is critical. Research clearly shows that without this knowledge students will not fully benefit from the strategy. Note that good modeling also serves to teach students that using a strategy requires effort. It also addresses attributions (e.g., "OK, that was easy. I can do this!"), and stresses the value of strategy use—using the strategy results in better performance.

We have found that modeling is one of the more difficult components of the strategy instruction process for teachers. Constructing a good think-aloud is more complex than it may initially seem. The reason for this is twofold. First, there is a tendency for teachers to simply repeat the steps of a strategy or task. We call this *skill stepping*. This isn't a bad practice, but it's not sufficient, especially for students with LD, because skill stepping doesn't provide students with the metacognitive knowledge they need. Figure 3.2 shows an example of skill stepping, along with how the same task might be modeled using a think-aloud. The second reason teachers have problems with modeling is that for skilled learners, modeling involves making covert automatic processes overt. That is to say, when you model, you have to think about things you don't normally think about anymore. Think back to when you first learned to drive a car and how you were painfully aware of even the tiniest aspect of driving. You worried about the mirror, checked to see if the car was in park before turning the ignition key, thought about what should you should look over when going in reverse, and were painfully conscious of your speed. Compare this to your thought processes now when, in all likelihood, you are barely aware of many aspects of driving. The same thing happens with academic tasks. For example, in Figure 3.2 most of us would not even be conscious that we checked the sign to determine what operation we would use, and starting at the right is done automatically. Learning to be aware of and verbalize these automatic, unconscious processes may be difficult at first for some teachers.

46
−28

All right, what do I need to do here? Well, I know this is a two-digit by two-digit subtraction problem because each number has two digits, and I see the "minus" sign. So, what will I need to remember to do this problem? I will need to remember my basic subtraction facts, place value, and the steps for completing a two-digit by two-digit subtraction problem. Hmm . . . sometimes I have problems remembering the steps in a two-digit by two-digit subtraction problem, especially if there's regrouping. I know that getting the steps in the right order is important because if I don't get them in the right order I might get the wrong answer. How will I remember the steps? Oh, I know. Ms. Chaffin taught us a strategy the other day to help us remember the steps. It was the 4 *B*'s strategy; Begin, Bigger, Borrow, and Basic Facts. OK, I can do this, all I need to do is follow my strategy and try my hardest. Let's see, the first *B* stood for "Begin in the 1's column." That's simple. I know where the 1's column is. The 1's column is the one farthest to the right. That's right, with math problems we start in the right column; if I don't I might not get the values right. Great, what's next? Oh yeah, the next step is "Bigger. Which number is bigger, the bottom or the top?" I know that 8 is bigger than 6 because I know my number values. OK, 8 is bigger and it's on the bottom. Now what? The next step in my 4 *B*'s strategy is "Borrow. If the bottom number is bigger I must borrow." Well, since the bottom number is bigger I will need to borrow. Borrow?!? How do I do that? Well, I know if I don't have enough money to buy something that I want I can just borrow some money from my sister, but I need to make sure I keep track of how much I borrow so I can pay her back. Borrowing in subtraction is kind of like that. If the number in my 1's column isn't big enough I can just borrow from the 10's column, and I will need to keep track of what I borrow so I don't change the value of the original number. OK, so that means I borrow a 10 from the 10's column, and move it over to the 1's column to make it bigger; that makes 16, but since I borrowed a 10 from the 10's column I am taking 1 of my 4 10's, so I only have 3 left. I need to make sure I change that. OK, so now what do I need to do? Well, the last step in my strategy is "Basic Facts. I need to remember to use my math facts!" Wow, I'm up to the last step; now all I need to do is subtract. I'll start with my 1's column (16 − 8 = 8). I need to put that answer in my 1's answer column because I just subtracted the 1's column. Now, I need to go to the 10's column, I know to do that because I know my place value, and the 10's column is right next to the 1's column. OK, I have the 4 crossed out, and I wrote 3 above that. I need to remember to use the 3 because I changed that value when I borrowed to subtract the 1's column. All right, so 3 − 2 = 1; I need to put 1 in my 10's answer column. So that gives me an answer of 18. Yeah!!! I did it! My strategy really helped me remember all the steps in a two-digit by two-digit subtraction problem.

FIGURE 3.1. Example of a think-aloud.

Skill steps for two-digit addition	Think-aloud
First I'll add the 1's column. Now I'll write the 5 and carry the 1. Now I'll add the numbers in the 10's column. Finally, I'll write the answer.	What is it I have to do? OK, this is a two-digit addition problem; I know it's addition because of the "+" sign. That tells me to add. I know how to do this! I need to remember to follow the steps in my strategy and remember my basic facts.
	First I need to start in the 1's column and add those. If I don't start at the 1's column, I'll get the wrong answer! The 1's are on the right-hand side. I'll make a little mark to help me remember.
	OK, I'm ready to add the first two numbers. Did I get a two-digit number? Because if I did, I need to carry the 10's digit to the next column, to the 10's column. Yep, 15 has two digits. I need to remember to write the numbers down correctly too. I only write one digit down under the line. The one I write down is the 5 'cause that's the digit in the 1's column. I need to be careful to write the 5 down under the 1's column. If I don't, I can get my numbers messed up and get the wrong answer. Now what do I do with the 1? Oh, yes, I have to carry that number. I'll write it down above the 10's column of the problem. That way I'll remember that I've carried.
	Now, what do I do next? I know, I need to add all the 10's digits that I have—the two in the original problem, and the one that I carried. I'm almost done; now all I need to do is write down the answer. I need to remember to keep my numbers lined up. I'll write them carefully. I knew I could do it. I took my time, used my strategy, and tried hard, and I got the right answer.

FIGURE 3.2. Skill steps and modeling for adding 26 + 19.

There are several ways to make the process of creating good think-alouds easier. One of the tools teachers can use is a "metacognitive task breakdown." This is a straightforward process. For each step in the task, identify metacognitive knowledge or self-regulation processes by asking yourself "why," "how," and "what for" questions.

1. *"Why* am I doing this step in the task?"
2. *"How* did I know to do it?"
3. *"What* are the important actions, cues, or questions?"
4. *"What* knowledge do I need?"

Jot down your answers to the questions as you go through the task. Sometimes you may need to go over your answers and apply the same process. Try this process with simple tasks like math problems or simple everyday tasks (e.g., making a peanut butter and jelly sandwich). With practice you will be able to readily identify the metacognitive knowledge implicit in academic tasks, and it will be much easier to produce good think-alouds. Another way to elicit metacognitive information is to ask students who are effective at a task to talk themselves through the how and why of the steps in the task.

Stage 4: Memorizing the Strategy

In this stage students commit to memory the steps that constitute the strategy. This is probably the quickest and easiest of the six steps. The goal is for students to quickly and easily remember the steps of the strategy and use them automatically. As students have told us, "You can't use it if you can't remember it." Students must be able to focus their energy and attention on the task at hand—not on struggling to remember the strategy steps, per se. Remember that students with LD often have problems with working memory. Struggling to remember what to do next will likely impede performance. Note that this step may even be omitted for very simple strategies (e.g., the math strategy example used in Chapter 2) if students have no trouble remembering the steps. To help students memorize the strategy, many teachers make a game of practicing the steps by using round-robin activities or ball-toss games. For example, a teacher says the first step of the strategy and then tosses the ball to a student, who relates the second step, and so on. Students can go to the next stage in the process before they have reached automaticity if they are provided with prompts or other types of supports (e.g., a card listing the steps in order). However, before completing all stages, students must memorize the strategy steps. Note that memorizing a strategy goes well beyond parroting the steps of the strategy. Students need to *know* and *understand* what is involved with each step in the process. This knowledge and understanding are crucial if students are to use the strategy successfully.

Stage 5: Supporting the Strategy

Supporting the strategy is another critical step in the SRSD process. In this stage, the teacher and student(s) work together collaboratively and practice using the strategy until the student is able to perform it effectively and independently. During this stage, teachers and students repeatedly model strategy use and discuss how, when, and why to use the strategy. One key aspect of supporting the strategy is the *scaffolding* or *scaffolded instruction* process. The process of scaffolding is analogous to teaching a child to ride a bike. No one would put a child on his or her first bike, give a push, and expect the child to ride well. Instead, we normally use a process where we start with extensive supports (literally!), which are progressively removed. For example, we would typically start with training wheels and let the child practice with them. Then, we might move the training wheels up, for less support and more practice balancing and riding a little bit more independently. Next, we could take the training wheels off and run behind the child holding the seat. Finally, we would completely let go and let the child ride independently without any support, just our nearby supervision.

Scaffolding instruction works in much the same manner. Initially, teachers perform all or most of a task while modeling and soliciting student input. Over time, teachers increasingly shift responsibility for performance to students. As students gain experience with and confidence in using the strategy, teacher support is gradually withdrawn until students are able to use the strategy independently. Note that the transfer of strategy performance from teacher to student is *gradual*. It's not realistic to expect students to master a strategy the first time they try it. It's critically important for students to be given *adequate time* and *support* to master the strategy. Also note that if a student struggles, the teacher can provide additional support until the student becomes more comfortable or fluent with the strategy, and then the teacher would resume the gradual withdrawal process. Collaborative practice also gives the teacher an opportunity to check for student understanding, provide corrective feedback, and develop any necessary knowledge the student may be lacking. It's also useful in assessment. For example, through interacting with the student, the teacher may discover that the strategy should be modified or that earlier SRSD stages need to be revisited. It also gives the teacher another opportunity to make sure that students possess the skills necessary to complete the task successfully.

Exactly how the teacher goes about supporting strategy development through scaffolding and collaborative practice will depend on the strategies and the needs of the students. The following are some commonly used activities and supports used in the scaffolding process (Dickson, Collins, Simmons, & Kame'enui, 1998).

Content Scaffolding

There are three types of content scaffolding techniques:

1. Initially, teachers can use content material that is at an easy level. For example, for a reading comprehension strategy teachers might use text that was one grade below the students' current level.

2. Use content that the students are familiar with or interested in. Thus, content that featured cars or sports might be highly appropriate for adolescent males, and fashion-related material might be of interest to adolescent females.

3. Teach the easier steps of the strategy first, followed by the more difficult steps. Thus, during the initial practice sessions, the student would perform the easy steps while the teacher modeled how to perform the more difficult steps. The student gradually is given responsibility for the more difficult steps.

Task Scaffolding

Ownership of the strategy is gradually transferred by allowing the student to do more and more of the strategy during collaborative practice. For example, (1) the teacher asks the student to name the strategy step that should be performed, then the teacher describes the step and models its use; (2) the teacher asks the student to name the step and describe the step, then the teacher models it; and (3) the student names, describes, and models the step.

Material Scaffolding

This type of scaffolding uses prompts and cues to help students use a strategy (e.g., posters or help sheets that list strategy steps). Students can use these as a reference or if they get confused. Typically these prompts and aids are "faded"(i.e., gradually withdrawn) over time.

Teachers can also use cooperative groups or peers to help scaffold instruction. For example, a teacher might create heterogeneous groups and have each group go through the steps of a strategy. The group as a whole would be responsible for completing the strategy and for making sure that all group members understood each step of the strategy.

The goal of this stage is for students to be able to use the strategy effectively and independently. It's easy to make the mistake of assuming that because a student knows the steps in a strategy, she or he knows how to use the strategy. This is akin to thinking that because one of us (R. R.) knows all the parts of a jet plane, he could get in and pilot the plane to Chicago (he couldn't!). Remember that knowledge of the steps of the strategy is *not* synonymous with the ability to use a strategy. The time it takes for students to reach fluent strategy use may vary widely. This stage will probably last the longest of the six. That's normal and expectable. In our experience, when SRSD procedures are used with appropriate strategies, most students can master a strategy after two to four collaborative, scaffolded experiences. However, there are *no set timelines* that are appropriate for all students. The key is to allow students to progress at their own pace. Once again, this is a critical stage of the SRSD process. Skimping at this stage will likely mean that students will not fully master the strategy or may not reach mastery at all. This in turn means that both the teacher's and students' efforts have been for naught. Another problem that one teacher related to us is that, because of the pressures placed on teachers to cover curriculum rapidly, rather than scaffolding instruction, too often the PEE process is relied on. *PEE* is an acronym for Present the material, provide an Example, and Expect that students have mastered the material. The PEE process is unlikely to be effective for students who struggle and is not synonymous with scaffolding.

Stage 6: Independent Performance

At this stage a student should be ready to use the strategy independently. Your main task will be to monitor the student's performance and to check on proper and consistent strategy use. Monitoring academic performance is critical. Remember that the goal of strategy instruction is increased academic performance. The student's work should show a marked improvement, and it should also remain at a consistent level. There are a number of ways to monitor performance, which we elaborate on in the next section. Monitoring strategy use is also very important because students sometimes distort the strategy or skip steps when using them independently. However, teachers should always keep in mind that improved academic performance is the goal. If a student modifies a strategy but performance remains high, there is no cause for concern. Many students will adapt the strategy to meet their needs. This is acceptable as long as they are still successful in completing the task. Alternatively, if a student is performing the strategy correctly and consistently but a high level of performance is not attained (or maintained), then reteaching the strategy or considering a different strategy is probably in order.

EVALUATING SRSD

Evaluation is an important component of strategy instruction. Unless you systematically assess the outcomes, you will have no way of gauging the effect of strategy instruction.

SRSD facilitates meaningful assessment because the interactive, collaborative nature of the process allows teachers to easily assess changes in students' cognition, affect, and performance. Harris and Graham (1996) offered basic principles for evaluating the methods and procedures used in strategy instruction. The list is not exhaustive, but it does provide a working knowledge of how to accomplish effective strategy evaluation.

Including Students as Coevaluators

Students should be encouraged to become partners in the strategy evaluation process. This partnering increases their sense of ownership in the strategy, reinforces progress, and provides a practical way to reduce a teacher's load. Students can help in many ways, such as learning to evaluate their final products or deciding if the necessary criteria for each step of a strategy have been met. Helping students ask appropriate self-questions (e.g., "Am I ready to move on to the next step?") is another effective way to help students evaluate their own progress. Students can also graph or chart their progress.

Considering the Level of Evaluation Needed

Exactly how much time and effort should be expended on evaluation depends on a number of factors. At a minimum, teachers should know if students are actually using the strategy, the effect of the strategy on task performance, and whether students see the strategy as being valuable and easily used. Teachers may also find that evaluating their instruction may be useful. The type of strategy used and previous experience with a strategy are important factors in evaluation. For example, strategies, methods, and procedures that have been previously used and have demonstrated their effectiveness will need less scrutiny than a first-time strategy. As a general rule, the amount of time and effort you need to expend on evaluating the usefulness of a strategy depends on its established validity and your experience with it. However, even well-validated, frequently used strategies still require some evaluation.

Assessing Changes in Performance, Attitudes, and Cognition

Recall that motivation and emotion are important factors that are considered in SRSD. Changing a student's attitude toward a task and toward the possibility of success is a critical component of strategy instruction. As a result, the benefits of strategy instruction can go beyond improving academic performance; students' attitudes and cognition may also be affected. For example, after teaching a math strategy, a teacher might observe whether students' attitudes toward math and confidence in their abilities improve. The teacher might also check to see if a student performs the task outside the classroom. For example, after teaching a writing strategy, check the amount of writing the student does outside of school. Spontaneous statements are also pertinent. For example, one student we worked with on a math strategy, who had struggled previously, suddenly stopped in the middle of a problem and stated, "You know, this stuff is really easy!" Another student's mother called the teacher to report that the student was actually writing stories for fun in the evenings (as opposed to watching TV!). The use of open-ended questions such as "What is good writing?" or "What do you most like to say to yourself while you do history study questions?" also can help you determine if a strategy has changed students' perceptions of a task. It is important to remember that some changes (e.g., attitudinal improvements) take more time than others to obtain. It takes time to overcome years of previous frustration.

Assessing While Instruction Is in Progress

Most assessment occurs after instruction has occurred. However, strategy instruction depends on frequent and ongoing assessment. Assessment procedures for strategy instruction should reflect the developmental and ongoing process of learning to use a strategy. This means that teachers must evaluate success at learning the strategy. Establishing realistic performance criteria for each step of instruction is one way to facilitate this process. For example, if a student can tell you when and where it would be appropriate to use a strategy, then one of the goals of Stage 2 has been accomplished. When the student can list and explain steps of the strategy, then Stage 3 objectives have been met. When a student can quickly relate the steps in a strategy and tell what occurs at each step, the objective of Stage 4 has been met. By clearly defining what is expected at each stage of strategy instruction, both teachers and students know what needs to be accomplished and what standards will be used to measure progress.

Assessing How Students Actually Use the Strategy

Students will often modify their use of a strategy over time. Sometimes this is a natural and positive effect of becoming fluent with the strategy. Use of steps may become automatic and not readily observable (Alexander et al., 1998). However, students may also change things for the worse. Therefore, do not automatically assume that students are using a strategy as intended. Some modifications allow the strategy to meet a student's unique needs, but others, such as eliminating a necessary step, may be detrimental. The best way for teachers to monitor strategy usage is to directly observe what students do as they use the strategy. Ask the student to work through a strategy. While the student does this, ask questions and discuss how things are working. Looking for evidence of strategy use in students' work is often useful. Often, students will leave "tracks" that indicate they are using a strategy. For example, students will often write out mnemonics they use to remember a strategy.

Assessing Students' Use of the Strategy over Time and in New Situations

Teachers should not assume that students will continue to use a particular strategy or successfully adapt it to new situations. One of the common problems experienced by students with LD is that they do not automatically generalize skills or strategies to new situations. Karen Harris tells the story of the student who had learned a comprehension strategy and effectively used it in one class. When asked about using it in other classes, the child responded, "Was I supposed to?" If you wish for the strategy use to be maintained and generalized, you will need to include this point in your explicit instruction. In fact, it is beneficial to actively promote maintenance and generalization of strategy usage from the inception of strategy instruction. For example, to promote maintenance, teachers could periodically have students explain the purpose of a strategy or have them share ways they have used the strategy. Students also can keep a record of each time they use a strategy or how they modify it for other tasks. It's also useful to chart performance (which hopefully has improved), review it at regular intervals, and relate improvements to the use of the strategy. Generalization may be tougher. It will often be necessary to include other teachers who were not involved in the strategy instruction process. The teachers will need to be acquainted with the strategy and any procedures involved with its use (e.g., graphic organizers or prompt sheets) and, at a minimum, will need to remind the student to use the strategy and encourage its use. Remember that one major goal of strategy instruction is generalization. Thus, it is necessary to determine if students need additional support to consistently apply the strategy in all appropriate situations. Note that if other teachers are included, they should also be involved in evaluating strategy use and promoting its generalization

Utilizing Portfolio Assessment Procedures

Portfolio assessment is an excellent way to implement many of the recommendations we have presented for evaluation of strategy instruction. This type of assessment requires teachers to establish the credibility of, and become intimately involved in, the maintenance and evaluation of student portfolios. Portfolios offer many practical advantages. At a very basic level, portfolios can often help to graphically demonstrate progress. For example, collecting samples of writing over time can make improvements highly visible. They can also help to improve motivation and demonstrate the benefits of strategy use. For example, one junior high teacher kept pre- and poststrategy instruction examples of students' stories. Prestrategy stories were typically around one-half page long. Poststrategy stories averaged over three pages! Students were extremely proud of their obvious progress. Note that these examples can also be effective when trying to get future students to "buy into" using a strategy. Portfolios can also help students engage in reflective self-evaluation, understand that development is as important as achievement, and take greater responsibility for their own learning. Teachers will also gain new insights into and understanding about assessment, teaching, and their students' development and learning. As an aside, it important to note that *teachers* will also receive some reinforcement, since they can see that their instruction resulted in meaningful change.

PRACTICAL CONSIDERATIONS AND TIPS

As we noted, strategy instruction is one of the most effective methods for helping students with LD. The SRSD model is powerful and effective, but it only works if you do it correctly. There are some common pitfalls. In this section we present practical tips for teachers.

Take Your Time

Strategy instruction must be closely tailored to the needs of students. Individual students or groups must proceed at their own pace. For example, it is not possible to schedule 1 day for mastery of the strategy and 3 days for collaborative practice. With practice, a teacher may be able to closely estimate the time, but—though there are some exceptions—it is critical for students to attain mastery at each stage before proceeding. The SRSD model is scaffolded throughout. It assumes that responsibility for the use of the strategy will be transferred gradually, with increasing responsibility expected for strategy performance as competence and confidence are gained. There is sometimes a tendency to overestimate progress. Remember that "One swallow doesn't make a summer," and using a strategy well one time does not mean that the student has mastered it. Students need to use the strategy correctly and consistently and develop the metacognitive knowledge of "why" and "how" before they have truly mastered it.

Note also that the SRSD model assumes that teachers will "loop back" through some stages. In fact, it is common for lessons to include activities from different stages (this is discussed further in Chapter 8). For example, teachers should discuss how the strategy can be used during Stage 5, supporting the strategy. Practice with memorizing the steps of the strategy should also be repeated frequently. For strategy instruction to succeed, a teacher must commit to working with students for whatever amount of time is necessary for them to attain independent performance. Note also that instruction doesn't stop once independent performance is attained. Teachers should continually remind students of opportunities to use a strategy, expose them to modeling and examples of how the strategy can be used, prompt strategy generalization, and encourage verbalization and sharing of strategy use. Remember, the goal of transforming students with LD into active learners is not reached overnight.

Small Is Golden

Because strategy instruction is so powerful and practical, there's a natural tendency to want to use it as much as possible. If one strategy is good, two would be even better. At this point you might remember the old saying that you can have "too much of a good thing." The same is true of strategy instruction. We recommend using the "small is golden" principle advocated by Pressley (Pressley & Woloshyn, 1995). Teachers should focus on a small number of strategies and support their use over a sufficient period of time. There's no best number of strategies to teach during a school year; this decision depends on students' needs and abilities. There's also no set time limit for working on a strategy, although in general the more time spent, the better the result. It's much better to spend the time focusing on one or two strategies in depth than to teach half a dozen to a much lower level of mastery. Focusing on a limited number of strategies will allow students to develop a deeper understanding of the strategy and a realization of how strategy use can improve performance.

Generalization

It's worth repeating that generalization must be planned for—it won't occur on its own. Many students who could benefit the most from strategy instruction will not spontaneously generalize a strategy across settings. Teachers in other settings or grades must know what strategies students have learned and how to encourage their continued development. Note that getting another teacher to support the use of a strategy in his or her class may also involve a "buy-in" process. This will likely be new to the teacher and there will be an education process. In practice, one of the best ways to motivate other teachers to help in the generalization process is to show them (by using evaluation materials such as portfolios) how much the strategy has improved performance.

Pick Your Battles

Deciding which strategies to teach to which students is an important decision. There are two things to consider here. First, when starting out with strategy instruction, it is tempting to try it in the curriculum areas that cause the greatest difficulty or with students who are experiencing the most severe problems. This would be a mistake for teachers new to strategy instruction. If strategy instruction is relatively new to both you and your students, it is not fair to anyone to take on too much, too fast. The worst thing that a teacher could do is to attempt an ambitious program only to see it fail because of lack of experience. A better approach would be for teachers to begin with a relatively simple strategy in an area where they are comfortable and can reasonably anticipate success. This allows teachers to become more acquainted with the instructional process and hone their skills. It also helps to build confidence. Remember that teachers need to develop mastery just as students do. Second, be sensitive to what students already know and don't try to reinvent the wheel. Some students have developed strategies that are partially effective. It's better to build on what they already know and are accustomed to than to start from scratch. Additionally, because existing strategies look simple, many teachers think that it's easy to develop their own. This is decidedly not the case. Most effective strategies are the result of years of development. Rather than attempting to create an effective strategy from scratch, we would suggest that you find (or modify) an appropriate strategy that has already been developed and validated.

FINAL THOUGHTS

In this chapter we have presented the SRSD model for strategy instruction and provided examples of activities teachers could perform at each stage. We've also talked about evaluation and given practical tips for implementing strategy instruction. In closing, we want to stress three points. First, *strategy instruction should be seen as a process*. It is the process that is powerful. Strategies themselves are useless unless the teacher utilizes an effective strategy instruction process that attends to instilling the metacognitive knowledge students need and helps to change maladaptive motivational processes. Second, the *strategy instruction process depends on collaboration*. The teacher and students should work together to develop and evaluate new strategies. Remember that strategies are not "off the rack"; rather, they are custom made. Third, *teachers should collaborate with other teachers, as well as their students, during the strategy instruction process.* Professional cooperation allows teachers to share their personal triumphs and challenges and serves to facilitate supportive feedback and problem solving. Teachers who use strategy instruction gather powerful new knowledge about what works for students. Although this can be a demanding process, it is an exciting one that we hope you will try.

CHAPTER 4

How to Implement the SRSD Model

In Chapter 3 we introduced and explained the SRSD model. In this chapter we demonstrate how that instructional template can be used to help teachers implement strategy instruction. We provide two sample implementation plans involving a structured and an unstructured strategy: (1) the textbook reading comprehension strategy SCROL (Grant, 1993), and (2) the basic story comprehension strategy Story Grammar (Short & Ryan, 1984). The implementation plans illustrating these two strategy instruction processes present examples of activities for each of the six SRSD stages.

There are many different types of strategies. One of the most important differences among strategies lies in whether the strategy is structured or unstructured. We chose these two strategies to illustrate the difference between structured and unstructured strategies. Structured strategies provide an implicit sequence that allows the user (i.e., the student) to use the strategy in a step-by-step fashion. The structure provided also permits teachers to create an implementation plan that is easily sequenced. The SCROL strategy is a structured strategy.

In contrast, unstructured strategies do not provide an implicit guide to strategy performance. This kind of strategy requires the teacher to create a structure to guide students' use of it. This need for teacher input can actually allow for more flexibility. However, additional planning is necessary to create a set of steps to guide students and to design an implementation plan. The Story Grammar strategy is an example of an unstructured strategy. In our example we show how teachers can add structure to a strategy.

STRUCTURED STRATEGY EXAMPLE

SCROL is a reading comprehension strategy designed for students in middle and upper grades to help them read and understand textbooks and a variety of source books. The strategy encourages students to use text headings to aid their comprehension and help them find and remember important information. The SCROL strategy is composed of five steps. First, the students are instructed to *Survey* chapter headings. This provides students with an idea of what the chapter will be about and prompts them to recall what they already know about the subject, thus activating their prior knowledge. It also allows them to predict information that the writer may present. Next, students ask themselves how the headings relate to one another and write down any key words from the headings that might provide *Connections* between them. Third, students *Read* the text and look for words and phrases that express important information about the headings, mark the text, stop to make sure that they understand the major ideas and supporting details, and reread if necessary. Fourth, students *Outline* the text, using indentations to reflect text structure. Students are asked to write the heading and then try to outline each heading segment without looking back at the text. This encourages students to use their knowledge of the text to fill in the outline. Finally, students are prompted to *Look back* at the text and check the accuracy of the major ideas and details they wrote down, correct any inaccurate information in their outline, and use the text that they marked to help verify the accuracy of the outline.

Stage 1: Developing and Activating Background Knowledge

Prior to teaching the strategy, it is necessary to evaluate the students' background knowledge. Formal or informal assessments can be used to determine what knowledge and skills the students possess and what skills they lack; doing a task breakdown will provide the information for identifying the knowledge and skills necessary to successfully complete the strategy. Note that it is also important to assess students' motivational beliefs, goals, and metacognitive knowledge. Table 4.1 provides an example of a task breakdown for the SCROL strategy. Chapter 3 provided a task breakdown example that was divided into two parts. Here the task breakdown is divided down into three parts: (1) strategy, (2) skill/knowledge, and (3) assessment. Combining the assessment aspect with the skill and strategy is just another example of the flexibility of the SRSD model. Either method is acceptable.

The strategy section of the task analysis identifies what the students are asked to do as part of the SCROL strategy. The SCROL strategy is broken down into five steps; however, teachers need to be sensitive to skills that are prerequisites for strategy use. For example, SCROL requires that students possess basic literacy skills. It is critical that all necessary skills are identified prior to implementation of the strategy. The skills section details the skills that are necessary for the student to successfully complete each aspect of the strategy. Each skill is listed alongside its corresponding strategy step. Often the same skill is necessary at various steps in the strategy; however, it is not necessary to list it every time.

TABLE 4.1. Example of Task Breakdown for the SCROL Strategy

Strategy	Skills	Assessment
Basic reading skills	Ability to read content material with sufficient fluency	Informal reading assessment
Survey the headings	Knowledge of and ability to identify headings and subheadings	Students will be provided with a text and asked to identify the headings and subheadings.
	Knowledge of topics and how they are sometimes presented in texts	Given a short text, students will be asked to identify and explain the major topics in the text and how they knew what those topics were.
	Ability to generalize information and make predictions or inferences	Students will be given a short text and asked to verbally summarize what they have read and make any predictions or inferences that they can from the given text.
Connections	Ability to identify connecting words	Students will be given a list of words and asked to identify words that are often connecting words.
Read the text	Ability to identify key words or phrases as they relate to the topic	Given a passage, students will be asked to underline key words or phrases related to the given topic.
	Ability to check for understanding	Students will be given a short passage to read aloud and periodically stopped and asked to explain what the passage is about.
Outline	Knowledge of outlines	Students will be asked to outline a simple text using a standard outline form.
Look back	Ability to proofread	Students will be given a passage with spelling and grammatical errors and asked to find and correct those errors.
	Ability to compare original text with the outline for accuracy of information	Students will be asked to compare the outline that they produced earlier to the text for accuracy of information.

The assessment section explains how students will be assessed to determine whether or not they possess the prerequisite skills. If students do not possess the necessary skills, the skills will need to be taught or accommodations made. Accommodations for the SCROL strategy could include the use of texts that are at the students' independent reading level or premarked texts that have the headings, subheadings, and important points highlighted. Accommodations should help the students use the strategy independently; however, accommodations should be gradually faded as students reach mastery.

Each of the prerequisite skills can be assessed individually, or students can be given an overall assessment of skills. An example of this overall assessment is an informal student survey. Figure 4.1 provides an example of an informal survey for the SCROL strategy. An informal survey gives students an opportunity to evaluate their own mastery of necessary skills. Giving students an informal survey can be an effective way to gather information quickly. This kind of assessment can provide valuable insight into how students view their own learning and skills, although this should *not* be the sole means of evaluation. It is also necessary to acquire some data on students' actual performance. These data can also serve as a baseline prior to implementation of the strategy; they allow teachers to objectively evaluate the effectiveness of the strategy in improving students' performance. A teacher might collect data in the form of worksheets, quizzes, or homework that involved responding to questions from a text. This information can also be used in the next stage to establish a need for the strategy. Following the survey, teachers' observations, and any other information collecting necessary to determine if there are any deficits, instruction should be given to ensure the students' mastery of prerequisite skills.

Stage 2: Discussing the Strategy

This is the first stage in initiating the strategy. As discussed in Chapter 3, this stage requires more than merely going through the steps in the strategy. Students need to take ownership of the strategy; they need to recognize the value of the strategy and want to use it. The teacher must "sell" the strategy and get the students to "buy in." If students do not want to use the strategy, they are not likely to use it. Teachers must be excited, committed, and energetic throughout the whole process.

We have found that, in practice, it is not difficult to sell strategies to students. For the most part, students with LD or ADHD are willing, if not eager, to try anything that will help them become better learners, once they understand that they are having difficulty because no one has taught them the "tricks" for this task yet. The strategy should sell itself with the payoff of improved academic performance. However, that may not be enough for some students. It is often necessary to find out what motivates students. When do they see reading a text, understanding, and remembering it as important? It may be beneficial to brainstorm with students on situations where reading texts accurately is important. Teachers may want to come up with a "pitch" to the sell the students, providing examples of current performance, or examples of students who have been successful with the strategy in the past. Finding out when students view comprehending text as important is a good place to start. The teacher may pose a question such as "When would it be important for you to read a text accurately?" The teacher should have in mind a few responses, in case the students are reluctant to share or do not mention important times.

Here are some examples:

- When taking a test
- When doing an assignment

Name: _____ Date: _____

1 = Strongly agree   2 = Agree   3 = Not sure   4 = Disagree   5 = Strongly disagree

1. I am able to read and understand my textbooks.
   1   2   3   4   5

2. I can pick out headings and subheadings in my textbooks.
   1   2   3   4   5

3. I can pick out the topic or main idea in the passages of my textbooks.
   1   2   3   4   5

4. When I am done reading, I can paraphrase information from my textbooks.
   1   2   3   4   5

5. I am able to identify key words or phrases as they relate to the topic.
   1   2   3   4   5

6. I know if I understand what I have read or not.
   1   2   3   4   5

7. I am able to recall information that I have read.
   1   2   3   4   5

8. I am able to put my thoughts about text that I read into writing.
   1   2   3   4   5

9. I am able to create an outline.
   1   2   3   4   5

10. I am able to compare original text material with my outline to make sure it is right.
   1   2   3   4   5

11. I am able to proofread my own work.
   1   2   3   4   5

FIGURE 4.1. Sample survey for SCROL.

- When making an informed decision
- When learning more about something of interest to you
- When assembling something
- When operating equipment

If a student is uncertain or resistant to using a strategy, as a last resort the teacher may draw up a behavioral contract, stating that the student agrees to try learning and using the strategy for a set period (e.g., 1 week). At the end of this time the student will be given an agreed-upon reinforcer (e.g., lunch with the teacher).

It is important for students to understand the purpose of a strategy. When discussing this purpose, it is necessary to point out situations where students would need to understand and remember information that they read in a variety of source books. Such examples help students understand when, where, and why to use the strategy. This type of knowledge is very important for students with LD. It is also necessary to point out the obvious problems that could arise if they were not accurate in reading certain texts. For example, if students did not read a text accurately, they would do poorly on a test. Another practical example would be following directions to put something together. If students did not read accurately, it is not likely that they would be very successful.

During the discussion stage, it is also necessary to discuss students' current performance. One way to do this is to graph performance on completed tasks. We have found that, in practice, using graphs can also help with motivation because students can see progress. Graphs can also be used in conjunction with self-regulation strategies such as self-monitoring and goal setting. The teacher would stress that using the SCROL strategy will help students read their textbooks, take notes, and remember what they have read. The strategy will also help them later. If they have a good grasp of the material being read the first time they go through it, they will have to spend less time studying later. The outline and notes can serve as a quick review of the information. The outline highlights the important information in the text, and the notes explain that information, providing a nice overview of the information.

As we noted in the previous chapter, one important task in the discussion stage (Stage 2) is to get students to buy into using the strategy. For this reason, it is often useful for the teacher to prepare for selling the strategy. Here's an example of a teacher "selling" the SCROL strategy:

"We just came up with a list of situations when it would be important to read a text accurately [brainstorming]. There are several times that we decided this was important. Someone mentioned when learning and remembering information for a test. Let's take a look at some of our recent test scores [providing graphic representation of test scores would be a way for students to quickly examine their current performance]. It is obvious that we are doing some things well, but there is definitely room for improvement. I have a trick that we can use to boost those test scores and help us remember texts that we have read. It is a strategy called SCROL. The SCROL strategy can help us remember what we should do when we are reading text for information. . . . "

It is important to remember that students should make the commitment to learn and use the strategy. In practice, this isn't usually hard. Students want to do well. But remember also that there is often a history of failure that must be overcome.

The final step in this stage is introducing the strategy steps. Students are encouraged to take notes and express any ideas they have regarding the strategy. Note that teachers should be sensitive to student input. Students can offer many helpful insights. Remember that strategy instruction is a *dialogue*, not a monologue (Harris & Pressley, 1991). While explaining the strategy, it is important to begin any necessary attribution retraining, and to stress that improved performance is due to increased *effort* and *strategy use*. The strategy is just a tool to use to improve academic performance. The steps of the strategy are outlined in Figure 4.2. These steps can be placed on a wall chart to help students with the initial usage of the strategy.

Stage 3: Modeling the Strategy

Modeling the strategy is one of the most critical stages of strategy instruction. This is where the student is exposed to the thought processes of an expert learner. Through repeated exposure and practice, students gain metacognitive knowledge of the strategy, which allows them to profit maximally from using it. In our example, we use a wall chart (see Figure 4.2) to serve as a visual aid and help guide the modeling process. Cue cards or handouts matching the wall chart can also provide students with their own personal reminder of the strategy steps. During the modeling process the teacher uses a think-aloud to demonstrate the use of the strategy and expose students to the thought processes of a skilled learner. The purpose of this step is to instill metacognitive knowledge of the strategy. A think-aloud can be done using an outline of important points. Think-alouds are not easy for some teachers who are just beginning to use strategy instruction. Many teachers may find it helpful to make a detailed outline, or even write out their complete think-aloud at first. Writing out a think-aloud can help teachers organize their ideas and can also help them to remember the think-aloud. Teachers may also wish to emphasize certain steps in a strategy or even include tips on how to perform steps in a strategy that they believe might be difficult for students. Teachers also might spend less time on aspects of a strategy that their students already have a firm grasp on. The key point here is that a think-aloud should be tailored to students' needs. Here is an example of a think-aloud for the SCROL strategy using a science text about how our ears work.

"OK. What is it I have to do? I need to read this article about 'How Do You Hear?' To be a more effective reader I can use the SCROL strategy. Just to make sure I remember all the steps, I will use the wall chart or my cue card to help me. First is S. That stands for *Survey the headings and subheadings*. That is simple enough; I can do that. Let's see . . . how do I identify the headings? Well, headings are usually in bold and at the beginning of a section. I know that because most of our textbooks are broken up that way. OK, while I am looking at the headings and subheadings I need to ask myself a couple of questions: 'What do I already know about this topic?' and 'What information might the writer present?'

SCROL

Survey the headings
- In the assigned text selection, read each heading and subheading.
- For each heading and subheading, try to answer the following questions:
  - *What do I already know about this topic?*
  - *What information might the writer present?*

Connect
- Ask yourself, how do the headings relate to one another?
- Write down the key words from the headings that might provide connections between them.

Read the text
- As you read, look for words and phrases that express important information about the headings.
- Mark the text to point out important ideas and details.
- Stop to make sure that you understand the major ideas and supporting details.
- If you do not understand, reread.

Outline
- Using indentions to reflect structure, outline the major ideas and supporting details in the heading segment.
- Write the heading and then try to outline each heading segment without looking back at the text.

Look back
- Now, look back at the text and check the accuracy of the major ideas and details you wrote.
- Correct any inaccurate information in your outline.
- If you marked the text as you read, use this information to help you verify the accuracy of your outline.

FIGURE 4.2. Example of a wall chart for SCROL.

"OK, the first heading is 'The Outer Ear.' I just watched a show on *Discovery* about the way our ears work . . . cool. I bet that is what this article is about. I know that there are a couple different parts of the ear. How do I know that? I know that because that's what the show explained. The outer ear is one of those parts. OK, the subheading under that is 'The Middle Ear.' Yeah, that's right—outer ear, middle ear . . . what is the other one? I can't remember, but I do remember that the middle ear has some bones in it; they have funny names. I bet the next heading will tell me what the other part of the ear is. Let's see, 'The Inner Ear' . . . yep, that's it. I remember that the inner ear helps us with balance. The last heading is . . . 'Keeping Your Balance.' Look at that, I was right. Cool, I already know a lot about this. If I keep using the strategy, this will be a piece of cake.

"What is the next step? S . . . C. C stands for *Connect*. I need to ask myself how these headings relate to one another and write down the key words from the headings that might provide connections between them. All right, well, they are all about the ear. I think I should probably write down the title first, since that's what the whole article is about . . . 'How Do You Hear?' Then I think probably, *outer, middle, inner*, and *balance*, since those are the other major headings, and they all have to do with the ear, and how we hear. All right, what is next? S . . . C . . . R. R is for *Read the text*. This is the part that I used to start with. OK, as I read I need to remember to look for words and phrases that express important information about the headings. The strategy says to mark the text—usually in my textbook I can't, but my teacher said I could this time because this is just a photocopy and it's mine to keep.

"Let's see. I also need to stop every once in a while to make sure that I understand the major ideas and supporting details. If I don't understand then I need to reread. First paragraph [reads the paragraph]: I will mark that ears are organs—I think that is important—and ears receive sound waves and change them into signals that our brain can understand. I would mark that the ear is made up of three different parts, but I already know that. I already have it written down. Second paragraph [reads the paragraph]: I will mark *ear flap, ear canal, ear drum*, and *membrane* because they seem to be important terms. I know that because they are defined and explained. This whole paragraph is important.

[Teacher repeats the process with remaining paragraphs.]

"OK. Where am I now? Step 4 is *O*, which stands for *outline*. I know how to outline; we went over this. If I need to, I can use the wall chart as an example. My outline needs to include headings, major ideas, and supporting details. When I am writing my headings, I should try and outline them without looking back at the text. If I can remember it now, I will have a much better chance at remembering it later. Let's see, my first heading is the title 'How Do You Hear?'—I remember that the ear is an organ made up of three different parts, listed below. The ear converts sound vibrations to signals that the brain can understand. *Outer*—the outer ear has an ear flap and ear canal. *Middle*—the eardrum is made up of a sheet of skin and three bones: the hammer, anvil, and stirrup. The stirrup vibrates the oval membrane. *Inner*—the cochlea looks like a snail and has fluid and tiny hairs that vibrate when the oval window vibrates and that sends signals to the brain; then there is the vestibule and semicircular canals. *Balance*—the semicircular canals are filled with fluid and hairs that move with the movements of the head and send messages to our brain and help us balance. The vestibule has two sacs filled with fluid and chalky stuff that is pulled down by gravity and lets our brain know what position our body is in.

"The last step—I am almost finished!—*L. L* stands for *Look back*. Now I need to check my memory and look back to see if what I outlined was accurate. If I did write down something wrong, now is the time to change it. Since I marked my text, this should be easy. Let's see . . . wow, I really remembered well. I worded some things differently, but I have the same information. YIPPEE!!!!"

Stage 4: Memorizing the Strategy

In this stage students begin committing the steps of the strategy to memory. Memorization can continue into Stage 5. Memorizing the strategy steps is crucial. The idea is to reduce the demands on working memory. Teachers need to plan and prepare activities and monitor their effectiveness. For example, planning for the class to make their own cue cards would be a way to get students actively engaged with the strategy steps. Note that in this case *SCROL* is a mnemonic that can help memorization.

Memorization Activities

RECITING THE SCROL STEPS WITH A PARTNER. Students are paired up to recite the stages with a partner, explaining what needs to be done at each stage. Students use the mnemonic chart to check answers. Students who struggle are matched with peers who can help with memorization of the strategy.

MAKING CUE CARDS. Students make their own cue cards with the strategy steps on them. Each cue card has the mnemonic *SCROL* on it and the major parts of the strategy, as well as the prompting questions. Students are able to use these to ensure that all steps of the strategy are completed. They are also able to use the cards for classes in various content areas to assist them with their reading comprehension.

MEMORY CIRCLE. Students are asked to form a circle around one person. The person in the middle calls out letters in the mnemonic *SCROL* and points to someone. That person has 5 seconds to accurately state what the letter stands for. If the student chosen doesn't answer within the 5 seconds, then he or she goes to the middle.

Besides the various structured activities, students can be prompted during various times of the day to recite different steps in the SCROL strategy. Students need to understand the significance of memorizing the strategy and should be exposed to it as much as possible.

Stage 5: Supporting the Strategy

In this stage the teacher and students work together to practice using the strategy until the students are able to perform it fluently and independently. This is a critical part of the strategy instruction process: Students need to be given adequate time and support to master the strategy. Just as a scaffolding around a building is gradually removed when the building is strong enough to stand on its own, the teacher gradually transfers strategy performance to students.

There are two major pitfalls for teachers at this stage. First, teachers may confuse memorization of the strategy steps (from Stage 4) with facility in the use of a strategy. This is analogous to expecting someone who can name the parts of an airplane to be able to fly one. Second, teachers may be under pressure to "cover ground" and get through the curriculum. Thus, they may be tempted to end this stage as soon as students begin to demonstrate some success. This is a mistake because students need extensive practice before they *master* the use of a strategy. Unless the strategy is taught to mastery, students are unlikely to maintain its use. We provide examples of how a strategy can be supported through content, task, and material scaffolding.

Content Scaffolding

Students are given short passages to practice the strategy. The texts are relevant to the curriculum being introduced. The teacher and students then go over a passage using the SCROL strategy. The teacher directs the process, and the students will provide answers to teacher-directed questions (e.g., "What are some headings and subheadings?"; "What do you think they are talking about here?"; "Are there any key words that provide connections between them?").

Material Scaffolding

Students are given mnemonic prompt cards to be taken to various content-area classes with them. Initially, the cards list the steps of the strategy and describe what to do at each step. Over time these cards will provide less direction, first fading the descriptions, and eventually fading the mnemonic and steps altogether. At this point students should have reached mastery of the strategy and be able to work independently.

Task Scaffolding

During collaborative practice the teacher prompts students to name the step that should be performed, and then the teacher describes the step and models its use. In subsequent lessons the teacher asks students to name all the steps in the SCROL strategy and describe the step to be performed, and then the teacher will model the step. Finally, students name, describe, and model the steps of the SCROL strategy independently.

The students set individual goals with the teacher for reaching mastery of the strategy. These goals will help guide them to independent performance. If students are having difficulty reaching their goal, it may be necessary to reassess the situation.

Reteaching the strategy or clarifying uncertainties may be necessary. In other cases, readjusting the goal may be in order for a student to be successful.

Students need to show mastery of the strategy steps, as well as the ability to use the strategy with text. Each student needs to be able to demonstrate the use of the strategy by doing his or her own think-aloud. When students have successfully demonstrated their use of the strategy, they are ready to move on to independent practice.

Stage 6: Independent Performance

During this final stage, students are given a variety of texts along with their content-specific textbooks. They are required to use the strategy and turn in their notes for teacher review. The teacher's role has now changed; the main focus for the teacher is to monitor whether the students are using the strategy correctly and consistently and to evaluate their performance. The teacher intervenes only when students need clarification or reteaching if their performance is declining. Remember that evaluation of students' performance is crucial. The goal of strategy instruction is that students' academic performance should improve. Evaluations do not need be complicated; they can be as simple as grades. The important thing is to be clear that academic performance is improving. More involved forms of evaluation, such as portfolios, may provide more diagnostic information as well as academic improvement. Portfolios are a good way to see trends in students' performance and to determine any areas of deficit.

Students may modify or personalize the strategy for their own use. This is fine as long as they are still successful. Students may also use the strategy more automatically, making it appear as if they skipped steps or altered the strategy. Remember that at this point what matters is that the students can be successful at reading the given text, taking accurate notes, and recalling important information. If modifications to the strategy make the strategy less useful or inappropriate, then reteaching of the strategy is in order. Additionally, even when students are initially successful, it will be helpful to give booster sessions over time.

UNSTRUCTURED STRATEGY EXAMPLE

The Story Grammar strategy, an example of an unstructured strategy, is a beginning reading comprehension strategy that provides students with a plan for identifying important story information by asking themselves the five *w* and *h* questions (*who, what, when, where,* and *how*). The Story Grammar strategy is unstructured because procedural information is left out (i.e., exactly what steps the students will perform to use the strategy). This sample implementation plan demonstrates how teachers can create a structure for a strategy. This example focuses primarily on creating a structure.

Stage 1: Developing and Activating Background Knowledge

The process in this stage is identical to the previous example. An example of a task breakdown is provided in Table 4.2. Assessment of skills can either be formal or

TABLE 4.2. Example of Task Breakdown for the Story Grammar Strategy

Strategy	Skills
Basic reading skills	Ability to read content material with sufficient fluency
	Knowledge of and ability to identify story components
	Ability to check for understanding
	Ability to recall information that has been read
Who is the main character?	Knowledge of story characters and how they are sometimes presented in texts
Where and when did the story take place?	Knowledge of story setting
What did the main character do?	Knowledge of story actions
How did the main character feel?	Knowledge of emotions and how they are presented in text
How did the story end?	Knowledge of story endings/resolutions

informal, depending on the skills and the students. This is left up to the teacher's discretion. An example of an informal survey for the Story Grammar strategy is provided in Figure 4.3.

Stage 2: Discussing the Strategy

To explain the steps of the strategy, teachers will have to develop procedures prior to this stage. There are no hard and fast rules for creating a structure for a strategy. The most straightforward way to do this is to practice using the strategy yourself. In this example use the strategy with a simple narrative text. While using the strategy, bear in mind how students will keep track of the story information. Identify any useful cues or prompts. Then create a series of steps to help guide the use of the strategy. Remember to keep things *as simple and practical* as possible. Strategies that are cumbersome are unlikely to be accepted by students. Teachers also need to determine how they want students to use the strategy. For example, the Story Grammar strategy requires students to answer questions while they read text. This can be distracting for some students and interfere with their comprehension. If students are asked to stop while reading text and write down answers, this may be a sufficient distraction to prevent them from maintaining comprehension. We have chosen to structure the Story Grammar strategy to avoid this. Five steps have been developed to structure the strategy (Figure 4.4). This process is further illustrated during modeling of the strategy.

Name: _____ Date: _____

1 = Strongly agree   2 = Agree   3 = Not sure   4 = Disagree   5 = Strongly disagree

 1. I understand and am able to answer "wh" questions.

    1 2 3 4 5

 2. I am able to read and understand narrative texts.

    1 2 3 4 5

 3. I can pick out characters and identify the main character in stories.

    1 2 3 4 5

 4. I can describe/pick out settings (time and place) of stories.

    1 2 3 4 5

 5. I understand where a story ends and how it is finalized.

    1 2 3 4 5

 6. I can understand and describe character emotions/feelings from text that I read.

    1 2 3 4 5

 7. I can understand and describe the main characters' actions.

    1 2 3 4 5

 8. I am able to identify key words or phrases as they relate to the topic.

    1 2 3 4 5

 9. I know if I understand what I have read or not.

    1 2 3 4 5

10. I am able to recall information that I have read.

    1 2 3 4 5

11. I am able to put my thoughts about text that I read into writing.

    1 2 3 4 5

FIGURE 4.3. Sample survey for Story Grammar.

Step 1: *Read your Story Grammar questions*
- This reminds you what information you are looking for.

Step 2: *Read the story* and *mark information with the color-coded sticky tabs.*
- Mark the text that answers the Story Grammar questions.
- Use your cue card or wall chart for the color codes (Figure 4.5).
- Remember, you may have more than one answer for some of the questions.
- Mark everything that you think is appropriate.

Step 3: *Look back at the tabs and decide if what you have marked answers the Story Grammar questions.*

Step 4: *Fill in your Story Grammar graphic organizer (Figure 4.6).*
- Use the information that you have marked.
- The colors of the sticky tabs match the colors of the graphic organizer.

Step 5: *Read over the Story Grammar graphic organizer and decide if it accurately describes the story.*

FIGURE 4.4. Story Grammar steps.

From Robert Reid, Torri Ortiz Lienemann, and Jessica L. Hagaman (2013). Copyright by The Guilford Press. Permission to photocopy this figure is granted to purchasers of this book for personal use only (see copyright page for details). Purchasers can download a larger version of this figure from *www.guilford.com/reid-forms.*

Stage 3: Modeling the Strategy

Two wall charts serve as guides during the modeling process (Figures 4.4 and 4.5). Cue cards that mirror the wall charts are also provided so that each student has his or her own personal reminder of the strategy prompts. Students are also given graphic organizers to answer the questions once they are done reading the story (Figure 4.6). A sample script follows:

"OK. What is it I have to do? I need to read this book, *Arthur Meets the President.* To be a more effective reader, I can use my Story Grammar strategy. Just to make sure I remember all of the story part questions, I will use the wall chart or my cue card to help me. Let's see, Step 1 is to review the questions. That will help me remember. Who is the main character? Where and when did the story take place? What did the main character do? How did the story end? How did the main character feel? OK, I can do this!

"Step 2 is to read the text and mark it with my sticky tabs. I will start reading and keep referring back to my prompt card to make sure I am on track. [Reads

Who is the main character?

Where and when did the story take place?

What did the main character do?

How did the story end?

How did the main character feel?

FIGURE 4.5. Story Grammar questions.

Name _____ Date _____

Title _____

Author _____

Who is the main character?

When and where did the story take place?

What did the main character do?

How did the main character feel?

How did the story end?

FIGURE 4.6. Story Grammar Organizer.

page 1.] Hmm . . . a few characters were mentioned, but from what I already know about reading other books like this one, and by reading the title, I think Arthur is the main character. I will put a blue sticky tab by his name because I want to remind myself that he is the main character, and on my cue card the main character question is in blue. I'm sure Arthur is the main character, he always is. OK, that was easy, I can do this!

"What are the next questions? When and where did the story take place? What did the main character do? Well, from what I know now, the story takes place at Arthur's school, in his classroom. I'm not sure if this is the main setting in the book, but I will put a red sticky tab by that and come back to it after I have read some more. I put a red sticky tab there because my wall chart shows the where and when question in red. I'm not sure what he did. I better read on to find out. [Reads page 2.] Hmm . . . I was right. Right now the story is taking place in Arthur's classroom, but I'm still not sure if that is the main setting of the story, and it really doesn't say when it took place. I do know that it is during the school year, but I don't know exactly what day it is, or what time of the day it is. This isn't very specific, but I know it is a time and that answers the 'when' question. There really isn't a place for me to put my sticky note, so I will just jot that down on my Story Grammar organizer right here where it says 'when.'

"OK, the other question that I wasn't sure about was the 'what.' I now know that Arthur is writing a paper about 'How I Can Help Make America Great.' I'm going to put a pink sticky note by that because that's the color of my 'what' question. I better keep reading.

"[Reads pages 3 and 4.] Wow, this is getting exciting! The story is still taking place at school. I want to keep reading. [Reads pages 5 and 6.] Wow, Arthur won! His class is going to Washington, DC, to the White House. That's it; that is the setting, which really makes sense, since the title of the book is *Arthur Meets the President*, and I know that the president lives in the White House, which is in Washington, DC. I am going to mark that with a red sticky tab because that is a place and that fits my 'where' question.

"This is easy. I just need to read on, keeping in mind the last two questions, and make sure I was right about the action and setting. What are the last two questions again? Hmm . . . I know. How did the story end? How did the main character feel? OK, I should keep reading. [Reads pages 7 and 8.] Hmm . . . here is another action. Arthur needs to memorize the paper that he wrote so that he can recite it in front of the president. I think there is more than one action. Really, there is a kind of a chain of actions and reactions. I will mark them with pink sticky tabs. Let's see, first Arthur wrote a paper on how to make the world a better place—I already marked that—then he won the writing contest—I will mark that too. Then he had to memorize his paper to recite it for the president; I will mark that also. Ugh, this is getting long, and I have used a lot of sticky tabs. But I know this will help me later when I need to answer my comprehension questions.

"I should keep reading to see what else happens. [Reads pages 9, 10, and 11.] Another thing—Arthur was nervous and worried. Really, that is how he felt. I think I should mark that with a green sticky tab. I know this is a feeling that Arthur had because it says that he was too worried to sleep.

"I better keep reading and see what happens next. [Reads pages 12 through 20.] There was some more action. Arthur, his class, and his family flew to Washington, D.C., Arthur practiced reciting his paper, and the class toured Washington, D.C. I will mark all of those with pink sticky tabs. There was also more in there about how he felt. It said that he was very nervous about reciting his paper. That's the same feelings he had before. I will mark that again with a green sticky tab.

[Teacher repeats the process.]

"Oh, I am already to the last page—this is how the story ends. Arthur then recited his paper and felt really good because his whole paper was about helping others. D. W. helped him, and he was happy because of it. I will mark that with a purple sticky tab because the story-ending question on my Story Grammar strategy chart is in purple.

"Wow, I'm all done reading; that was easy! OK, I finished Step 2, now on to Step 3. Hmm . . . what is Step 3? Oh, yeah, I need to decide if what I have marked answers the Story Grammar questions. Let's see . . . yes, I think it does!

"OK, what's next? Step 4, what was Step 4? I need to fill in my graphic organizer. I can go back and fill in all of my questions on my Story Grammar organizer by looking at what I marked with my sticky tabs. They should be easy to find.

"I will start with 'who'—I know those are the blue tabs . . . then I will go to the red ones because I know those are the 'where' and 'when' or setting ones. . . . Next, I will do the pink ones, which are the action ones or the 'what' question. . . . Then I will go to my purple tab and write down how it ended. . . . Last, I will look at my green tabs and write down how the main character felt.

"OK, Step 5: I need to read what I have written down and see if I've answered all the questions correctly. . . . Yes, I think I did answer all the questions right. Yippee, I'm done! That really did help. I was able to answer all of my Story Grammar questions."

Stage 4: Memorizing the Strategy

Memorization activities for an unstructured strategy are similar to those for a structured strategy. The activities for the Story Grammar strategy could be the same as those for the SCROL strategy. Students simply follow the structure or steps that the teacher has established. Following our example, students would need to state the color of sticky tab that they would use to mark their text.

Stage 5: Supporting the Strategy

Scaffolding procedures in this stage are similar to those described in the SCROL implementation plan. For the Story Grammar strategy we have added a new type of activity; a graph for students to monitor their progress (Figure 4.7). Students are given a sheet of Story Grammar Rockets and instructed to color in a square on one rocket for every box in the Story Grammar Organizer that they have filled in correctly. This graph serves

FIGURE 4.7. Story Grammar Rockets.

two purposes. First, it serves to help motivate students; they can see their progress by how many parts of the rocket they have colored in. Additionally, students are allowed to "bust out" their rocket if they have more than one correct answer for each question.

The second function is self-regulation. The rockets help students self-monitor how many of the Story Grammar questions they have answered. Initially, the teacher needs to make the determination of whether or not the Story Grammar Organizer is filled in correctly and tell students how many squares in the rocket they can color in. After students have shown that they can use the Rockets independently, they are allowed to work with a partner or in a small group assigned by the teacher to check their answers. After students have shown the ability to work effectively with their peers on performance assessment, they can be allowed to work independently. The eventual goal is that students are able to check the accuracy of their performance independently. Note that as with any other activity, the use of the Rockets needs to be modeled:

"OK, I have my Story Grammar Organizer all filled out and the teacher has put stars by the boxes that I have filled in correctly. Now I can use these cool rockets to graph my progress. Let's see . . . 'Who is the main character?' Right, that's Arthur. I know that because I got a star. I get to color in the bottom square of the rocket. I also got a star by the second question, 'When and where did the story take place?' because I got that one right too. I can color in another square on my rocket. Right here, I will color in this one, above the last one I colored. It looks like I also got 'What did the main character do?' right because there is a star by that one too. I will color in another box. My rocket is half filled in; this is cool! Uh-oh, it looks like I missed something on 'How did the main character feel?' because there is no star by that box. I will need to go back and look at the story again to find the right answer. That way I'll know what to do next time to have a full rocket. I'm up to the last question, 'How did the story end?' I know I got that one right because I see another star next to my box. I get to fill in another box. Wow, look at that—I almost have a full rocket. That is so cool! I need to be really careful when I answer my questions so I can have a full colored-in rocket. Kids who have full colored-in rockets get to put them up on the wall. I want to get mine put up too!"

Initially teachers will need to monitor students' use of the self-regulation component. This is to ensure that students are consistent in their use of the rockets, and to make sure that they do not have any difficulty filling them in. If they have trouble, prompting, modeling, or reteaching may be necessary. When students demonstrate fluent and independent use of the strategy multiple times, they are ready to move on to independent practice.

Stage 6: Independent Performance

Teaching for this stage can follow procedures similar to those for the SCROL strategy. Variations on strategy use should be noted. Evaluation should focus on how well the student can answer questions pertaining to story components (e.g., "Who were three characters in the story?").

FINAL THOUGHTS

Once teachers have an SRSD plan completed, it can be used many times, allowing for improvements and tailoring to the needs of individual students. Moreover, after teachers have taught one strategy using this model, it is much easier to teach a different strategy because they have gained experience in the process. In closing we would stress the following points:

- When teachers design SRSD instructional plans, their job is to fit the instruction to the student, rather than vice versa. Strategy instruction is tailored to the student, not "off the rack."

- Don't rush the modeling or support stages. It's far better to overteach a strategy than to underteach it. Remember also that students will progress through this stage at different rates. Some students will grasp a strategy quickly, whereas others may need a few more practice sessions. This is especially true for students with LD or ADHD. The key point for teachers to remember is that students need to develop *facility* with the strategy and understand where, how, and why it should be used. If teachers don't spend enough time at this stage, then all their work may go for nothing.

- If one goal of strategy instruction is for students to generalize strategy use across academic areas (e.g., the student might use the SCROL strategy in science and history classes), then collaboration between teachers is necessary. Students with LD typically need support to generalize strategy use. Teachers must actively plan for generalization with students and all other teachers. Prompts or reminders to help the student remember to use the strategy will often be necessary.

CHAPTER 5

Self-Regulation Strategies

Self-regulation has long been important in research and intervention in LD and ADHD (Reid, Harris, Graham, & Rock, 2012). Self-regulation strategies are important for struggling learners because there is good reason to believe that the academic difficulties of these students are due, at least in part, to problems in the self-regulation of organized, strategic behaviors (Reid et al., 2012). Recall that in previous chapters we stressed that often problems of students with LD were due to lack of effective strategies as opposed to deficits in specific abilities. The same perspective holds for the area of self-regulation. Many students with LD or ADHD lack effective self-regulation strategies. We firmly believe that teachers should consider self-regulation as a skill that can be taught and should actively teach students effective self-regulation strategies. Research also supports this perspective; there is clear and compelling evidence that students with LD or ADHD (and other struggling learners) can be taught self-regulation strategies, and that the use of these strategies can have a meaningful impact on their school functioning (Reid, 1996; Reid, Trout, & Schartz, 2005).

There are a number of self-regulation strategies that can be effectively taught to students with LD or ADHD. The major ones are self-monitoring (also called *self-assessment* or *self-recording*), self-evaluation (which is closely related to self-monitoring), self-instruction, goal setting, and self-reinforcement. All of these self-regulation strategies have been thoroughly researched and classroom tested and have demonstrated efficacy for students with LD and ADHD (Mace, Belfiore, & Hutchinson, 2001; Reid, 1996, 1999; Reid et al., 2012). Though we discuss each separately, we stress that these self-regulation procedures are commonly and effectively combined in practice. The strategies we introduce can be extremely useful as stand-alone interventions. However, self-regulation strategies become even more powerful when used in conjunction with effective content-area strategies. Recall that the *SR* in SRSD stands for *self-regulated*. One of the major goals of the SRSD model is to *develop self-regulated learners*. To do this, *effective content-area strategies should be combined with appropriate self-regulation strategies.*

We discuss the major self-regulation techniques listed above, focusing primarily on self-monitoring and self-instruction because they are both powerful and are the ones most commonly used. Goal setting, self-evaluation, and self-reinforcement are also effective, but they are most commonly used in conjunction with other self-regulation strategies. For each strategy, we provide background information, discuss its uses, and provide a step-by-step guide to implementing it.

SELF-MONITORING

Self-monitoring is one of the most thoroughly researched self-regulation strategies (Reid, 1996; Reid et al., 2012). It was originally developed as an assessment procedure designed to allow psychologists to gather information from patients in order to evaluate effectiveness of interventions (Kanfer, 1977). Psychologists would ask patients to self-monitor the frequency of a behavior (e.g., the number of cigarettes smoked or the number of times they opened the refrigerator for a snack). This monitoring allowed the psychologists to collect baseline data on the behavior. However, much to their surprise, the psychologists discovered that the act of self-monitoring a behavior caused changes in the behavior. This led to the use of self-monitoring as an intervention.

Self-monitoring occurs when an individual self-assesses whether or not a target behavior has occurred and then self-records the occurrence, frequency, or duration of the target behavior (Nelson & Hayes, 1981). For example, in one of the earliest self-monitoring studies, researchers taught a student to periodically ask herself whether or not she was working or paying attention in class and to then self-record the results (Broden, Hall, & Mitts, 1971). In contrast to behavioral approaches, self-monitoring usually does not involve the use of external reinforcers; however, in some cases, such as with students with ADHD, self-monitoring has been effectively combined with external reinforcers (e.g., Barkley, Copeland, & Sivage, 1980).

Self-monitoring can be used with a broad variety of behaviors. For our purposes, we focus on areas that most directly concern strategy instruction: on-task behavior and academic responding. There are two major types of self-monitoring interventions: self-monitoring of attention (SMA) and self-monitoring of performance (SMP). In SMA students self-assess whether or not they are paying attention when cued (typically, cueing is provided via randomly presented taped tones) and self-record the results. In SMP students self-assess some aspect of academic performance (e.g., number of correct practices) and self-record the results (Reid, 1993; Reid & Harris, 1989). There are many types of SMP. For example, students may self-assess their productivity (e.g., the number of math problems they attempted), accuracy (e.g., the number of math problems completed correctly), or strategy use (e.g., whether or not steps in a strategy were performed). Self-assessments can occur during a work session (sometimes using taped tones as cues) or after a work session (without cueing). SMP also typically involves the use of charting or graphing.

Exactly how self-monitoring works is not fully understood; however, the basic processes involved are fairly straightforward. Figure 5.1 shows a simplified version of the self-monitoring cycle. First, a behavior occurs. Next, students self-assess whether the behavior they performed was the target behavior or not, and then self-record the results in some manner. Note that so far all the steps are a part of the self-monitoring process. Students then internally evaluate whether they performed the target behavior or not (e.g., was I paying attention). If they were successful, they reinforce themselves for performing the target behavior. It's sort of a mental "high five" awarded for performing the target behavior. If not, there is a mild admonishment ("Darn it!") that serves as negative reinforcement. The resulting reinforcement, in turn, affects the likelihood that the target behavior will be performed in the future.

Teaching a student to use self-monitoring is straightforward. Reid (1993) outlined the following steps.

Step 1: Selecting a Target Variable

The teacher must first determine what behavior will be self-monitored. Though the behavior targeted for change and the behavior that is self-monitored are often the same, they are not necessarily *always* the same. Thus a student might, for example, self-monitor the amount of on-task behavior, even though the teacher was actually concerned with increasing the amount of seatwork that was completed. A good target behavior is specific, observable, appropriate, and a personal match.

Specific

The teacher must be able to *exactly* define the target behavior. Because the self-monitoring process begins with self-assessment, students must be able to easily and accurately determine whether or not a target behavior has occurred. If students are unable to determine whether or not they are performing the target behavior, self-monitoring will not be effective. Target behaviors such as "better reading" or "being

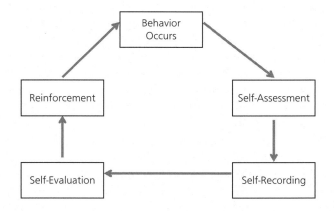

FIGURE 5.1. The self-monitoring cycle.

good" are not appropriate; instead, use behaviors such as "number of math problems correctly answered" or "listening to the teacher," which are easily understandable and readily assessed by the student. Note that a number of behaviors can be targeted (e.g., being in my seat, having my work on my desk) so long as they are all well specified. It's also possible to target a behavior that is complex, such as "paying attention," if the component behaviors that constitute paying attention are specified. For example, any of the following—looking at the teacher, listening to the teacher, doing work, or raising a hand for help—would constitute *paying attention.*

Observable

Students must be *aware* of the occurrence of a target behavior. Students who engage in a behavior impulsively and/or unconsciously may be unaware of the occurrence of the behavior and thus be unable to self-assess the behavior. For example, students who impulsively talk out of turn may be unaware of the behavior. The lack of awareness would preclude effective self-monitoring. In the case of students who talk out of turn, the teacher might ask them to self-monitor the number of times they raised their hand to speak, as this might be more observable for them.

Appropriate

For a behavior to be appropriate for self-monitoring, it must meet three criteria. First, it must be a behavior that is already in the student's repertoire (i.e., the student can already perform the behavior). Remember that self-monitoring does not create new behaviors; it simply alters *existing behaviors* in terms of frequency, intensity, duration, and so forth. For example, Reid (1993) noted that if the goal of a self-monitoring intervention was to increase the amount of time a student spent in his or her seat, the student would have to be able to spend at least some time in the seat. Note that the same concern holds true for academic behaviors. Self-monitoring alone does not produce new learning or academic skills (Reid, 1993). Second, it must be a behavior that is *under the student's control.* For example, self-monitoring would not be effective in improving the handwriting of a student with cerebral palsy because fine motor tremors are not under the student's control. Third, the behavior must occur with sufficient frequency (Rafferty, 2011). Behaviors that occur very infrequently (e.g., once a week) are not appropriate target behaviors. Students will not have sufficient opportunities for reinforcement to effect behavior change. It's also important to know that there are some behaviors that are not appropriate for self-monitoring (or self-regulation interventions in general). A student who is totally out of control, who is a danger to self or others, or is exhibiting severe problems is not a good candidate for self-monitoring.

When selecting a target behavior, teachers should also be sensitive to the environment in which self-monitoring will take place. Although self-monitoring has been used effectively in whole-class, small-group, and individualized settings (Reid, 1996), it is advisable to try to visualize possible problems that could arise. Avoid procedures that could cause a student to be embarrassed or that could disturb other students. For example, if SMA, which typically uses taped tones to cue students to self-assess, were used in a group setting and a student felt as though he or she were being singled out, it would be inappropriate. The fit between self-monitoring procedures and academic tasks should also be closely examined. In some cases, self-monitoring procedures can be intrusive and detract from successful performance (Reid, 1996). For example, using SMA procedures that require students to self-assess and self-record frequently would probably be inappropriate during a small-group reading lesson. There are no established guidelines to help select the most appropriate target behavior for any given combination of environment and task. One practical method might be to simply expose students to a variety of target behaviors and allow them to choose the behavior they feel is the most appropriate or effective for them to self-monitor. Research has shown (Maag, Reid, & DiGangi, 1993) that students are capable of selecting the most effective target behavior when given a choice between several alternatives.

Personal Match

Self-monitoring may not be appropriate for students who are very young or are immature because they must be able to understand the connection between self-monitoring procedures and the target behavior (Graham, Harris, & Reid, 1992). If this connection is not made in the mind of the student, reactivity will not occur. For example, imagine a student who self-monitored the number of arithmetic problems completed and graphed the results. For self-monitoring to be effective, the student must be able to relate the graph to the work completed (i.e., be able to comprehend that the graph represented the amount of work completed). Unless the student can meaningfully connect the work done with the graphic portrayal of results, reactivity (in the form of increased number of problems worked) will probably not occur. Teachers should also be sensitive to developmental factors. Students' developmental level may affect how they perceive the value or salience of target behaviors. Although developmental effects on self-monitoring are only beginning to be addressed, there is evidence of differential effectiveness of target variables across age levels (Maag et al., 1993).

Step 2: Collecting Baseline Data

At this stage, baseline data should be gathered and recorded. This should not be a strenuous or time-consuming procedure. The teacher should first identify when and where the self-monitoring intervention will take place. Next, he or she should determine how to collect data. For example, if the intervention were to be directed at out-of-seat behavior, the teacher would simply count the number of times the student was out of his or her seat during the period of time when the intervention occurred. In the case of interventions directed at academic accuracy or productivity, baseline data collection could be as simple as collecting work samples. Collecting baseline data is important for two reasons. First, the data provide an objective benchmark against which to evaluate the success of the intervention. Second, collecting objective data on the extent of the problem may obviate the need for an intervention! Practitioners sometimes find that the problem was not nearly as serious as they believed—or they may discover that they have targeted the wrong behavior.

Step 3: Obtaining Willing Cooperation

The *self* is the active ingredient in self-monitoring. This means that the teacher will need active and willing cooperation on the part of the student. Teachers should schedule a conference with the student and address problem areas frankly. Discuss the benefits to the student (e.g., "Staying in your seat means you don't lose recess"; "Doing all your arithmetic problems means you'll do better on the test"). Don't promise the moon; students are unlikely to respond to inflated or exaggerated claims (Reid & Harris, 1989). Be optimistic, but realistic; describe self-monitoring as "something that has helped a lot of students like you with the same kind problem." If students are unsure, try using a contingency contract. This means that if students commit to trying self-monitoring for a specified period of time, they will receive a reinforcer. Typically the improvements will sell themselves very quickly. After you have enlisted students' cooperation, establish when and where the self-monitoring will be used.

Step 4: Instruction in Self-Monitoring Procedures

During this stage teachers are not only teaching skills, they are also "selling" the self-monitoring. It is important to go through each step in succession; however, the time spent at any one step may vary widely depending on the student and the choice of target variables. Students should master each step in turn before proceeding to the next step. Note that although there are a number of steps, students typically can learn to self-monitor quickly and easily, with total training time typically well under 1 hour.

Defining the Target Behavior

Explain to the student exactly what constitutes the target behavior. For most types of self-monitoring, this is quite simple to do. For example in SMP defining the target variable may involve little more than telling the student to count correct answers. For other types of self-monitoring, defining the target variable may be more complex. For example in SMA interventions the student must understand what it means to *pay attention*. Here the teacher must teach the student a list of specific behaviors that constitute paying attention, such as looking at the teacher or one's work, writing answers, listening to the teacher, or asking a question. Remember that students must understand the target behavior before they will be able to proceed.

Discrimination of Target Behavior

The student should be able to discriminate between the target behavior and other behaviors. One simple way to teach discrimination is for the teacher to model examples and nonexamples of the target behavior and ask the student to determine if each behavior is, or is not, an example of the target behavior. This whole process may take only a few minutes, but it provides reinforcement of the knowledge of the target variable gained in the previous stage and also provides evaluative feedback for the teacher. Note that modeling would not be necessary for some types of self-monitoring (e.g., self-monitoring the number of practice items completed).

Explanation of Self-Monitoring Procedures

In this stage the teacher explains where and when self-monitoring will be used and teaches the actual procedures of the particular self-monitoring intervention. First, the teacher directly explains the procedures involved in self-assessing and self-recording. Next, the teacher models proper performance while verbalizing the steps. The student is then asked to verbalize the steps as the teacher performs them. Following this, the student is asked to model and verbalize the procedures. It is extremely important that the student attain a high degree of mastery (Mace & Kratochwill, 1988). Self-monitoring procedures should be minimally distracting for the student; thus a high degree of automaticity is necessary for effectiveness. After the student is able to demonstrate the procedures correctly, provide a brief period of guided practice to provide structured experience for the student and also allow the teacher to assess mastery. Again, this entire procedure can be done very quickly.

Independent Performance

At this stage the student is ready to use self-monitoring. Before the student begins self-monitoring for the first time, it is wise to prompt him or her to use the procedures and/or to check for knowledge of the target variable. During the first few sessions, make sure that the self-monitoring procedures are used consistently and properly. If any problems are evident, reteach the procedures. Remember that self-monitoring procedures must be used properly and consistently if self-monitoring is to be effective. If a student appears to be having problems there are several options available to the teacher. In some instances, additional training may be indicated. For less serious problems simply providing students with prompts, such as reminders of what constitutes the target behavior or cues to self-assess or self-record, may be all that is required. However, if students consistently experience problems, it may be best to rethink whether self-monitoring is appropriate.

Evaluation

After the student has begun to self-monitor independently, the teacher should continue to collect data in order to assess the effectiveness of the intervention. If the intervention is effective, research suggests that improvement should occur rapidly. The teacher should also conduct periodic probes to assess maintenance. In practice, students have been able to maintain increased performance levels for considerable periods of time in the classroom (e.g., Harris, 1986b). However, if the student's performance begins to deteriorate, additional "booster sessions" in self-monitoring procedures may be necessary.

Frequently Asked Questions

Teachers new to self-monitoring regularly ask a number of questions. In this section we address some of these frequently asked questions (FAQs).

How Accurate Are Students' Self-Recordings?

Many teachers are concerned about the accuracy of students' self-recordings—or, to be more precise, about what to do if students willfully misrepresent their behavior when self-recording (i.e., they cheat). Accuracy of self-recording does not seem to be a critical factor in behavior change (Hallahan & Sapona, 1983). In fact, it is common to see meaningful change when self-recording accuracy is quite low (e.g., Broden et al., 1971; Reid & Harris, 1993). Remember that the goal is improvement of behavior, not accurate self-recording. There is one instance when inaccuracy is important: when students are inaccurate because they cannot consistently discriminate the target behavior from other behaviors. If this is a problem, retraining is indicated. In this case teachers need to reexplain the target behavior and provide examples and nonexamples to give the child practice in discriminating the target behavior.

What If Procedures Are Not Followed?

For self-monitoring to be effective, procedures should be used properly and *consistently*. For example, if a teacher used SMA, it would be a good idea to see if the student was self-recording at every cue. Sometimes students need to be reminded to use self-monitoring consistently. One technique that has been used effectively in these situations is to reinforce students for properly and consistently using self-monitoring procedures. For example, Rooney, Hallahan, and Lloyd (1984) reinforced students if their number of self-recorded tallies closely matched the number of taped tones used to cue self-recording (e.g., if there were 18 tones and students had from 16 to 20 tallies, they were rewarded). This reinforcement resulted in students using the procedures more consistently, and it increased the amount of on-task behavior.

What Are Some Problems with Self-Recording Procedures?

Sometimes the procedures used to self-record can pose problems. This is most often the case in SMP interventions, where it is fairly common for some students to exhibit problems accurately counting up work or properly graphing. In situations like this aids such as paper with numbered lines or simplified graphs can be used to overcome problems.

What Is the "Best" Target Behavior for Self-Monitoring?

We can't answer this question at this point in time. There is no way to predict whether any specific target behavior is the most effective in any given situation. Both SMA and SMP interventions are effective at increasing on-task behavior and academic productivity. There appear to be few, if any, differences between the two interventions in terms of their effects on on-task behaviors (Lloyd, Bateman, Landrum, & Hallahan, 1989; Reid & Harris, 1993). We would recommend that you simply try the method that you judge best fits the student and task as well as the classroom environment. We would also note that combing SMA and SMP can also be quite effective in practice (Rock, 2005; Rock & Thead, 2007).

How Long Should I Use Self-Monitoring?

Self-monitoring interventions have been used effectively for prolonged periods of time in classroom environments (e.g., Harris, 1986b; Rock & Thead, 2007). There does not appear to be an upper limit on the amount of time that these interventions can be used effectively. However, for SMA interventions there is an effective procedure to "wean" students from the procedures (Hallahan, Marshall, & Lloyd, 1981). First, students are asked to self-assess without self-recording the results. If the target behavior is maintained, the taped cues are eliminated and students are asked to self-assess whenever they think of it. Self-praise may also be effective during the weaning procedure (Hallahan, Lloyd, Kosiewicz, Kauffman, & Graves, 1979).

SELF-EVALUATION

Self-evaluation is closely related to self-monitoring in that both require students to self-assess some aspect of their behavior and self-record the results. Self-evaluation typically involves the use of self-monitoring in that it requires students to of self-assess and self-record their rating of a behavior at set intervals (Shapiro & Cole, 1994). For example, students might rate their behavior on a scale of 1 (stayed in seat, was quiet, and finished work) to 5 (did not stay in seat, was noisy, and did not finish all work) during seatwork and record the results. Figure 5.2 shows an example self-evaluation rating sheet. Self-evaluation differs from self-monitoring in two ways: (1) student self-assessments are compared to an external standard or criterion, and (2) students typically receive reinforcement based on the accuracy of their self-assessments (Mace et al., 2001). Thus, in self-evaluation, reinforcement depends on *accurate* self-assessment of behavior. Self-evaluation interventions also commonly use goal setting (discussed later in this chapter).

Procedures for implementing self-evaluation interventions are well established (Shapiro, DuPaul, & Bradley-Klug, 1998). Note that the same concerns discussed previously regarding well-specified target behavior and teaching procedures also apply to self-evaluation. In the first stage, the teacher collects baseline data. The teacher defines the behavior(s) to be targeted (e.g., raising hand to be called on, finishing seatwork, following teacher directives) and establishes the time and place when the intervention will be in effect (e.g., during second-period math class). Next, the teacher rates the student's performance using a Likert-type scale (e.g., 1 = poor, 5 = acceptable, and 10 = excellent; or 1 = poor, 5 = very good) at set intervals during the period (e.g., every 15 minutes). These ratings are graphed and will be shared later with the student. In the next stage, the teacher meets with the student and talks with him or her about the ratings system. The teacher tells the student that he or she will be rated at regular intervals. Points will be awarded based on the ratings, which can later be redeemed for reinforcement. The teacher then shares the graphed baseline data with the student and discusses this information. During the time self-evaluation is in effect (e.g., second-period math), the teacher again rates the student's behavior at set intervals and informs him or her of the ratings. Once again ratings are graphed and the teacher and student discuss the results.

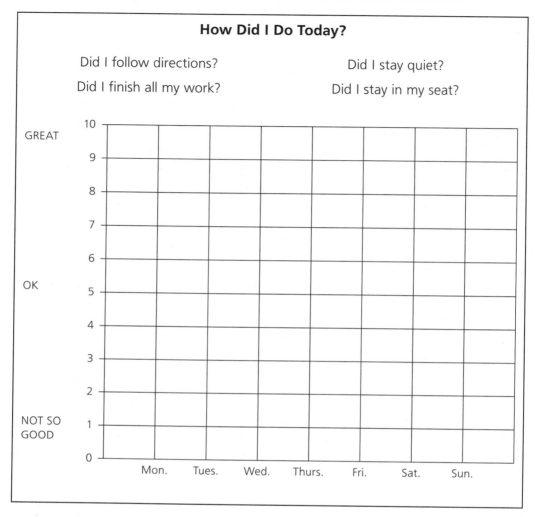

FIGURE 5.2. Example of a self-evaluation chart.

This process continues until the student receives acceptable ratings for several consecutive days.

In the next stage, both the teacher and the student rate behavior. The purpose of this phase is to enable the student to become aware of and accurately assess his or her behavior. After each rating period, the teacher and student compare ratings. Points are awarded based on the accuracy of the ratings. If ratings are close (e.g., within 1 point), the student receives points for accurately self-assessing. The teacher and student should, however, discuss why the discrepancy in the ratings occurred. If the ratings match exactly, the student receives points equal to the rating (e.g., if the student rating was a 5, 5 points would be awarded) plus a bonus point. If ratings exceed a set limit (e.g., differ by 2 or more points), no points would be awarded for that rating period.

In the next stage, matching is gradually faded. For example, if the teacher and student had five chances to match ratings, the teacher would first match four times, then three, and so on until none occurred. In periods when matching did occur, points are awarded solely on the basis of the student's rating. At the same time the length of the rating period is gradually increased (e.g., from 15 minutes to 20 minutes, and so on). Fading should take place gradually and only after the student's behavior has remained stable and at an acceptable level for a period of time. After the student has shown stable and improved behavior, he or she moves to the final stage. Here, the student gradually shifts to oral assessments (as opposed to written) of behavior, given to the teacher at the end of a class period, and external reinforcement is also gradually faded.

SELF-INSTRUCTION

If you've ever watched young children at play, you probably noticed that they often talk to themselves. This is termed *self-talk* or *private speech*. Private speech is used by students to help self-regulate and guide behavior, and it is a part of the normal developmental process (Harris, 1986a, 1990). Self-instruction techniques take advantage of the fact that language is often used to self-regulate behavior. Self-instruction interventions involve the use of *induced* self-statements to direct or self-regulate behavior (Graham, Harris, & Reid, 1992). Put simply, with self-instructions students quite literally learn to talk themselves through a task or activity. There are two levels of self-instructions: (1) task approach, which is general and appropriate for a wide range of situations, and (2) task specific, which is aimed a particular situation and would not generalize. Both types are useful. Self-instructions can serve many functions. Table 5.1 lists the six basic functions of self-instructions identified by Graham, Harris, and Reid (1992) and provides examples of each.

Self-instruction techniques are both powerful and flexible. They have a well-demonstrated record of effectiveness for students with LD (e.g., Swanson, 1999b). They are also commonly used as a component in strategy instruction interventions (e.g., Graham & Harris, 1996). Note that self-instructions can also work on motivational processes, and that error detection and correction are also useful areas for self-instructions. Many times teachers incorporate self-instructions that deal with coping or with continuing a task that is difficult. An example of how this was done in one classroom is Karen Harris's classic story of "The Little Professor" (Graham, Harris, & Reid, 1992).

Dr. Harris was studying private speech among students with and without LD, using a rigged puzzle that could not be successfully completed. The non-LD children often used helpful self-speech. In contrast, the children with LD commonly used irrelevant and often negative self-statements. Near the end of the study, a dapper young man with a crewcut, horn-rimmed glasses, wearing a coat and bow tie, came to work on the puzzle. He quickly got to work and, as was the case with the other students with LD, appeared to become frustrated quickly. However, rather than stop working,

TABLE 5.1. Examples of Self-Statements Associated with Six Functions of Self-Instruction

Type of self-instruction	Examples
Problem definition—defining the nature and demands of a task	"OK, what do I need to do now?" "What's my next step?"
Focusing attention/planning—attending to task and generating plans	"I need to take my time and concentrate." "What's the best way to do this problem?"
Strategy related—engaging and using a strategy	"I need to remember to use my strategy." "OK, what I need to do is remember my MAMA strategy."
Self-evaluation—error detection and correction	"I need to check and see how I'm doing." "Does this answer make sense?" "Oops, this isn't right. I need to fix it."
Coping—dealing with difficulties/ failures	"I can do this if I keep at it." "This isn't rocket science. I know I can do it." "Take a deep breath and relax."
Self-reinforcement—rewarding oneself	"I did it! Great job!" "I worked hard and I got it right!"

he pushed himself back from the table, folded his hands, took a deep breath, and said, "I'm not going to get mad; mad makes me do bad." The "Little Professor" used this self-instruction several times, and he was able to fit more pieces and worked longer than any of the other children with LD. He had learned this intervention from his classroom teacher, who was not aware of research on concepts such as self-statements, but believed (correctly) that what we say to ourselves affects what we do and think. Her students met regularly to help one another identify problem areas and develop self-statements to deal with the problems. The Little Professor had identified getting mad as a problem that kept him from doing his best. Together the class had worked out the procedure of pushing back his chair, taking a deep breath, folding his hands, and using the self-statement "I'm not going to get mad; mad makes me do bad."

Teaching students to use self-instructions involves a simple, four-step process (Graham, Harris, & Reid, 1992). *Step 1* involves discussing the importance of verbalizations. The teacher explains how what we say to ourselves can help or hurt us. This is very important because students with LD often exhibit high rates of very negative self-statements (e.g., "I'm stupid—I'll never get this"). The teacher stresses the need to use words to help oneself. In *Step 2* the teacher and student develop meaningful, individualized, task-appropriate self-statements together. It's important to remember that self-instruction is not simply parroting back statements provided by the teacher. To reiterate our comment about strategy instruction, self-instruction training is a *dialogue*, not a monologue. If self-instruction is to be successful, then the self-statements must be meaningful to the student. And, the most meaningful statements often are those that the student develops. Note, however, that this does *not* mean that a student should not use an example provided by a teacher. If students like a teacher's example, it's perfectly appropriate for them to use it. In *Step 3* the teacher and student model the use of self-statements and discuss how and when they would use them. At this stage it is very useful for the student to see a peer use self-instructions (if possible). Peer examples are extremely powerful motivators. Some teachers actually videotape students who have successfully mastered a self-instruction technique. The videotapes are a motivator for the student and useful as examples when teaching self-instructions to new students. Finally, in *Step 4* the teacher provides opportunities for collaborative practice in the use of self-instructions to perform the task. This would include modeling the self-statements and discussing how and when to use them. The ultimate goal is for students to progress from the use of modeled, overt self-statements (i.e., talking aloud to oneself) to covert, internalized speech (Harris, 1990).

GOAL SETTING

Effective learners are goal-oriented (Winne, 1997), and goal setting is viewed as an important aspect of self-regulation (Bandura, 1986). Goals serve extremely useful functions for learners (Schunk, 1990):

1. Goals structure effort by providing a target for our efforts (e.g., "I'm going to lose 10 pounds on the diet"). This target, in turn, determines what we need to do to accomplish the goal (e.g., cut down on calories, increase exercise).
2. Goals provide information on progress. To continue the previous example, we could track our weight loss to monitor how close we had come to meeting the goal.
3. Finally, goals serve to motivate performance and achieving goals serves to reinforce effort. To put it plainly, it feels good to accomplish our goals.

There are three important dimensions of effective goals: specificity, proximity, and difficulty (Bandura, 1988). *Specificity* refers to how well a goal is defined. Goals that are vague (e.g., "Do your best on the test") are not as effective as those that are well specified (e.g., "Achieve at least 80% correct on the test"). *Proximity* refers to temporal aspects of goals. Proximal goals can be completed in the near term (e.g., "Copy my spelling words three times by the end of class") and are generally more effective than distal goals, which can only be completed in the far future (e.g., "Learn 100 new spelling words by the end of the year"). Note, however, that it is possible to use a series of proximal goals to accomplish a distal goal. *Difficulty* refers to how challenging a goal is. Goals that are easily attained do not serve to enhance or maintain effort (Johnson & Graham, 1990). The most effective goals are those that are moderately challenging. That is, those that are neither too easy nor too difficult.

There is also a distinction to make in assessing whether or not a goal is met. Goals may be either absolute (i.e., with a fixed standard, such as completing 20 math problems correctly in 6 minutes) or normative (i.e., doing as well as another student on the math problems). There is some evidence that the most appropriate goals for students with LD might be normative, as these types of goals may enhance self-efficacy and motivation (Schunk, 1987). That is, students believe that if Joe Smith can do it, then they can do it too. However, there are no hard-and-fast rules here. Teachers should pick the standard that best fits the student and the situation. Also remember that monitoring progress is a key to success. Students who see satisfactory progress toward a goal are more likely to sustain effort (Bandura, 1986). Alternatively, students who do not perceive progress (even though there may indeed be progress) are not likely to sustain effort.

Just as with self-monitoring, goal setting often involves a self-evaluative process that consists of comparing current performance with a goal (Schunk, 2001). This is the source of motivation. Note that for goal setting to affect behavior, goals *must be valued*. If a goal has little or no importance to the student, then it is unlikely to improve performance or maintain motivation or effort. Thus, teachers may need to point out the benefits of accomplishing a goal (e.g., getting homework completed prevents students from being grounded and improves social life). Additionally, attributions (the perceived cause of an outcome) must be considered (Schunk, 2001). Students should see that progress toward a goal is the result of *their own* efforts rather than simply luck or factors outside their control (e.g., "The teacher helped me").

Goal setting is a straightforward process. The teacher and student meet and discuss performance in an area (e.g., spelling test results). Together the teacher and student decide on an appropriate goal, determine a timeline for meeting the goal, and establish how progress toward the goal could be monitored. Initially, it's best for the teacher to help with setting the goal to ensure that it is realistic and attainable. Many students with LD will set goals that are either much too high or much too easy. As we noted previously, goals should be moderately challenging. It is also important for students to be aware of progress toward their goals. This knowledge of progress provides them with self-evaluative feedback that increases motivation. Self-monitoring can be used to help provide performance feedback. Some students may choose to focus on a distal goal (e.g., "Getting an A in spelling"). This is perfectly understandable. In such cases, the teacher should establish more proximal (and attainable) goals (e.g., "Getting a C on this week's spelling test"). Note that the teacher needs to establish procedures to help the student attain the goal. For example, to extend the spelling example, the teacher might suggest daily 10-minute spelling practice sessions. The teacher would teach the student an effective spelling practice strategy (see Chapter 9) and would establish a practice schedule. The student would self-monitor the number of words practiced during each session to ensure that the amount of practice was adequate. This consistent practice would provide the student with the means to achieve the goal.

SELF-REINFORCEMENT

Self-reinforcement occurs when an individual identifies a reinforcer and self-awards it when a predetermined criterion is reached or exceeded (e.g., "If I study for 2 hours, then I get to watch my favorite TV show") (Graham, Harris, & Reid, 1992). For example, one writer we know will treat himself to a very decadent dessert when he meets his weekly writing goal. This process mirrors the natural developmental process wherein a child learns that meeting expectations typically results in positive reinforcement (e.g., praise, attention), while the opposite typically results in no response or perhaps a negative response (Mace et al., 2001). As a result of this environmental shaping, students learn to self-reinforce (or self-punish) their own behavior.

Implementing self-reinforcement involves a four-step process. First, teachers should determine the standard that must be met for receiving rewards. Standards should be clear and objective. For example, "Getting better at spelling" would not be a good standard; "Getting 80% on my weekly test" would be more appropriate. Second, the teacher should select a reinforcer. If possible, involve the student in this process—strictly pragmatic reasons. Students know what is rewarding to them. Third, determine how students will evaluate their work. For example, they may self-correct or bring the work to you to check. Finally, if students meet or exceed the criterion, they may award themselves the reinforcer. The reinforcement step does not need to be totally independent. For example, students could be taught to check with you before self-awarding reinforcement. Self-reinforcement is often combined with other self-regulation techniques. For example, self-reinforcement and goal setting can work very well together since they have so much in common. Self-reinforcement has also been combined with self-monitoring. We should note that the notion that individuals can actually engage in self-reinforcement may be seen by some as counter to a strict behavioral perspective on self-regulation (see Mace et al., 2001, for a detailed critique); regardless, the technique itself is quite effective.

THE CASE FOR SELF-REGULATION

Self-regulation strategies are not only effective but also provide two distinct advantages over other possible choices. First, self-regulation strategies avoid the "hidden curriculum" that is implicit in more behavioral approaches. With self-regulation, students are the agent of change rather than the teacher or another adult figure. The lesson here is one of empowerment—students can independently make changes in their behavior (Graham, Harris, & Reid, 1992). For students with learned helplessness and other motivational problems, this is an important consideration. Second, and equally important, self-regulation strategies offer a distinct practical advantage over many other approaches. After the initial data collection and instruction, the teacher's involvement is minimal because the child is literally running the intervention. The savings in time can be considerable in contrast to other approaches. For example, self-regulation strategies do not require teachers to take the time to constantly reinforce behaviors or track points earned through token economies; instead teachers are free to perform other instructional duties.

We would stress that although self-regulation strategies are powerful, they are *not a panacea*. No intervention can claim to be 100% effective for every student. Furthermore, as Reid (1993) noted, it is important for teachers to realize that to effectively implement self-regulation, they must follow both the "letter" and the "spirit" of the procedures outlined above. However, with these caveats in mind, we should emphasize that because self-regulation strategies can be easily implemented in the classroom and have a demonstrated track record, educators should strongly consider using self-regulation strategies in their classrooms. Additionally, as we noted earlier, self-regulation strategies are useful in their own right, but they are even more powerful when combined with content-area strategies as a part of the SRSD process.

FINAL THOUGHTS

In closing, we stress that self-regulation does not take place in a vacuum. The environment is a significant factor in enabling or impeding self-regulation (e.g., Mace et al., 2001; Schunk, 2001). Changing the environment can enhance or enable self-regulation (e.g., taking a limited amount of cash prevents overspending; Mace et al., 2001). Students also may self-regulate their environment to help themselves complete tasks (e.g., finding a place to study that is quiet and free of outside distractions). Providing students with a structured environment and predictable, stable routines is an important prerequisite for self-regulation. Additionally, a stable environment can increase the likelihood of effective self-regulation.

Note also that even in the *best possible* environment, students with LD will probably have some problem with self-regulation. In an environment that is disordered or chaotic, successful self-regulation is unlikely to occur. Luckily, there are numerous simple, practical, environmental changes that can enhance self-regulation, such as providing students with folders to serve as organizers for assignments, taping prompts to lockers ("Did you remember to bring your book?"), or using prompt cards that list the steps for a task and serve to cue performance. The major point that teachers need to remember is to attend to both self-regulation strategies and to the provision of supportive environments.

CHAPTER 6

Implementing Self-Regulation Strategies

In the previous chapter we presented five self-regulation strategies: self-monitoring, self-evaluation, self-instruction, goal setting, and self-reinforcement. In this chapter we provide examples of how these self-regulation strategies can be implemented in practice. We also provide examples of support materials (e.g., self-monitoring graphs, examples of self-statements) that teachers can use to implement self-regulation strategies. Note that the steps in implementing self-regulation interventions have much in common with the SRSD model. For example, both involve discussing the strategies and enlisting willing cooperation. Note also that although we discuss each strategy separately, they can also be combined (e.g., self-monitoring could be used with goal setting).

IMPLEMENTING SELF-MONITORING

In this section we present examples of how commonly used self-monitoring strategies can be implemented in the classroom. The focus is on the practical activities involved in implementing self-monitoring interventions in the classroom. We present two examples: self-monitoring of attention (SMA), wherein students are cued to self-assess and self-record via tones, and self-monitoring of performance (SMP), wherein students self-assess by counting the number of correct practices and self-record via graphing.

Example 1: Self-Monitoring of Attention

SMA is an excellent way to increase the time students spend on task because SMA helps them maintain effort and focus. Increasing time on task results in increased engagement with a task and improved academic performance. SMA can also serve to inhibit inappropriate behavior. Having to self-assess and self-record can interrupt inappropriate behaviors. For example, if Emma is playing with her pencil, she will need to stop this behavior to self-assess and self-record. In this example we use a hypothetical student, Steve. Steve has a great deal of difficulty staying on task. His main problem is that he becomes distracted very easily and engages in impulsive behaviors. He daydreams or wanders around the room, sometimes shooting make-believe jump shots. When he stays on task, however, he has no difficulty doing the work. The problem seems to occur frequently during seatwork when he is required to sit at his desk and focus on a task for a period of time. Spelling practice is a particular problem. Here's an example of how SMA instruction for Steve might go.

Step 1: Defining the Target Behavior

Steve's teacher, Mrs. Barrett, wants to reduce the time Steve spends daydreaming or wandering around the room. To do this she will try to increase the time Steve spends in his seat doing his work. The behaviors she will target for self-monitoring are (1) writing spelling words, (2) raising his hand for help, (3) watching/listening to the teacher, and (4) staying in his seat.

Step 2: Collecting Baseline Data

To collect baseline data, Mrs. Barrett counts the number of times that Steve gets up from his seat during spelling practice time over a period of 3 or 4 days. She makes a tally mark on a 3" × 5" card each time the behavior occurs. At the end of the period she graphs the data for each day.

Step 3: Obtaining Willing Cooperation

At this stage Mrs. Barrett meets with Steve to discuss the problem and get him to buy into trying SMA. Here's an example:

> "Steve, I wanted to talk with you today about some problems you've been having. You are really having problems paying attention to your work, and this has been going on for a while. Last week you missed recess three times because you didn't get your spelling practice done. But I've noticed that when you finish all your practice, your spelling is great. I know a way to help you out with the problem you're having. I've done this with kids just like you, and it worked really well. I think it would really help you to pay attention better. That way you won't miss out on playing basketball at recess. Would you like to try it?"

In practice, most students will be happy to try self-monitoring. If, however, there is resistance, set up a contract with the student. For example, if Steve were uncertain, tell him that if he tries self-monitoring for 1 week, he will get a reinforcer (e.g., extra computer time, a sticker) for each day he tries it. After the buy-in, it's time to explain the procedures.

Step 4: Instruction in Self-Monitoring Procedures

In this step Mrs. Barrett (a) defines the behavior Steve student will self-monitor, (b) ensures that he can discriminate the behavior, and (c) explains the self-monitoring procedures.

> "OK, Steve, let's talk about paying attention. Why is it important to pay attention?"

Mrs. Barrett discusses the benefits of paying attention (e.g., get work finished, learn more, don't miss recess, get better grades). Next, she discusses the specific behaviors involved in paying attention.

> "Now, Steve, can you tell me some things you do when you're paying attention? Let's make a list."

She makes a list of the behaviors and discusses each one briefly, focusing on the behaviors that she wants Steve to self-monitor (e.g., looking at the teacher, staying in his seat, listening to the teacher, doing work, raising his hand to ask for help). Next, she discusses behaviors that happen when Steve is *not* paying attention.

> "You did a really good job with what you do when you pay attention. Now let's talk about what you do when you're not paying attention."

As before, she makes a list and discusses the behaviors (e.g., looking out the window, walking around the room, playing with his pencil, shooting imaginary jump shots). Then she asks Steve to demonstrate behaviors that show paying attention and not paying attention, in order to ensure that he can discriminate the behaviors that indicate he is paying attention from those that show he is not paying attention. Mrs. Barrett then models some behaviors and asks Steve to tell her whether they were behaviors that show paying attention or not.

Next, she introduces the "beeper" used to cue students to self-assess and the self-recording sheet. Figure 6.1 gives instructions on how to make a beeper. Figures 6.2 and 6.3 show examples of self-recording sheets. Note that these sheets can be very simple. However, it's a good idea to include reminders on the sheets (i.e., the specific behaviors that indicate paying attention). Here's how Mrs. Barrett instructs the student in the procedures.

> "Now, Steve, I'm going to show you how to help yourself pay attention. In a minute I'm going to start a tape. On the tape, every once in a while, you will hear a beep. When you hear the beep, you should ask yourself, 'Was I paying attention?' What do you do when you hear the beep? [Steve responds.] That's right. You ask yourself, 'Was I paying attention?' Then you use this sheet [introduces recording sheet] and mark 'yes' if you were paying attention or 'no' if you were not paying attention. Look at the top of the sheet. It has a list of what it means to pay attention. Let's practice a little. I'll pretend to be the student and you tell me what to do."

By far the easiest way to implement SMA in the classroom is to use a "beep" file. A beep file is simply a computer audio file on which you have recorded some type of auditory cue (e.g., a beep, chime, click, or an oral reminder to self-assess). Many computers come with the capability to create audio files, and commercially available software (e.g., Garageband) can also be used.

Research suggests that the cues should be random, with intervals of from 10 to 90 seconds between them (Reid, 1996). It's important for the cues to be *random*. If cues are set at regular intervals, students will quickly sense the rhythm and will know when they will be asked to self-assess. Making a beep file is simple:

1. Find a source of random numbers. One good source is your old statistics books (which often have tables of random numbers in the back). Another readily available source is a phone book. We'll use the phone book example here, but the random numbers table works the same way.

2. Pick a page in the phone book randomly. Then randomly pick a starting point (e.g., halfway down the middle column).

3. Ignore the first three digits in the number. Break the last four digits into pairs of two-digit numbers (e.g., the number 2466 would be broken into 24 and 66). Ignore number pairs that are less that 10 or greater than 90. Write down each number separately.

4. Using a calculator, enter the numbers and sum them. You need to sum the numbers to make sure that the file will be long enough. For example, to make a 30-minute beep file, you need to sum to around 1,800.

5. Repeat Steps 3 and 4 until you have sufficient numbers.

6. Find a suitable cue. This could be a sound from the computer program (e.g., a note on the piano synthesizer or any other sound that could serve as a cue). If you are using an external microphone, anything that is easily audible will work. Teachers have used buzzers, beeps, chimes (from a toy xylophone), and other sources.

7. Find a quiet room. Lay out your list of numbers where it's easy to see. These numbers are the intervals between beeps (e.g., 44, 19, 84). Use a watch or a clock with sweep second hand to time intervals. Start the file. Wait the appropriate time (e.g., in the example above, 44 seconds), then record the cue. Repeat until you've made the entire file. Don't worry if your timing isn't exact. A few seconds either way are not critical.

When you are ready to use the beep file, just start the program. You may also wish to transfer the file to another device, such as an iPod or an iPad, which is more portable and less obtrusive.

There are also small unobtrusive devices that can deliver tactile cues to students at random intervals. One such device, the MotivAider®, has been used successfully in self-monitoring interventions. There is also a cell phone application from MotivAider.

FIGURE 6.1. Creating a "beep" file.

Was I Paying Attention?

When you hear the beep, ask yourself if you are:

- Writing spelling words
- Raising my hand
- Watching the teacher
- In my seat

If the answer is yes to any of these things, then place a check in the "Yes" column. If the answer is no, than place a check in the "No" column.

	YES	NO			YES	NO
1				11		
2				12		
3				13		
4				14		
5				15		
6				16		
7				17		
8				18		
9				19		
10				20		

FIGURE 6.2. Example of a self-recording sheet.

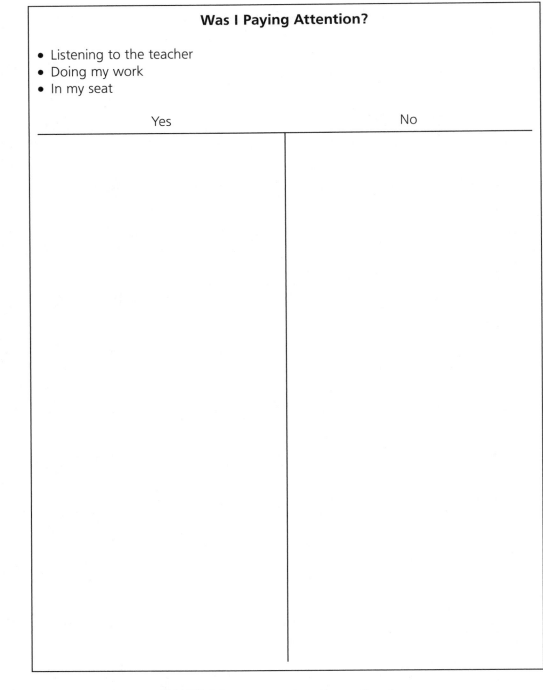

FIGURE 6.3. Example of a self-recording sheet.

Mrs. Barrett starts the tape. When he hears the beep, Steve should be able to tell Mrs. Barrett that she should ask if he was paying attention and mark the sheet. Mrs. Barrett may also wish to model paying attention and not paying attention and marking the sheet accordingly. She may also ask Steve how she should mark the sheet.

Steve appears to grasp the procedures, so he is ready to try them himself.

> "OK, Steve, now it's your turn to practice. Let's do some spelling practice. Do it just like you normally would. Remember to listen for the beeps. When you hear the beep, ask yourself, 'Was I paying attention?' and mark your sheet. Let's try it."

Mrs. Barrett starts the tape and lets Steve use the procedure for 2 or 3 minutes to make sure he can do it properly. Finally, she establishes when and where the self-monitoring procedures will be used.

> "Now, Steve, tomorrow when you do your spelling work, we will use the beeps to help you pay attention and do your work better. We will do it just like we practiced today."

Step 5: Independent Performance

The next day, Mrs. Barrett gives Steve the self-monitoring sheet, then adds a brief reminder.

> "OK, Steve, remember to listen for the beeps. Every time you hear a beep, ask yourself, 'Was I paying attention?' and mark your sheet."

Now Mrs. Barrett starts the tape. The first few times students use the self-monitoring procedure, it's a good idea to monitor them unobtrusively to make sure that they are following procedures correctly and consistently. Most students have no trouble mastering these procedures. Total time to train the student in procedures should be less than half an hour.

Step 6: Evaluation

To evaluate the effects of SMA, Mrs. Barrett repeats the procedure used to collect baseline data. She counts the number of times that Steve gets up from his seat and graphs the daily results. Typically there will be a marked improvement in behavior very quickly (e.g., within 1 or 2 days).

Example 2: Self-Monitoring of Performance

Self-monitoring of performance (SMP) is an excellent intervention for children who need to improve the rate at which they work or who have problems finishing work. It is especially useful for drill-and-practice or seatwork situations when building fluency is important. SMP typically uses graphs for self-recording. The graphs provide visual feedback on performance and can be quite motivating. For this example we use another hypothetical student, Karen, to see how self-monitoring of performance could be used with spelling. Karen hates spelling; she'd much rather think about riding her horse. During the time when she is supposed to practice spelling, she does very little practicing, which in turn means that her scores on the weekly spelling tests are poor. Her teacher, Mr. Graham, decides to use SMP along with a simple spelling practice strategy (the cover–copy–compare method described in Chapter 9) to help improve her spelling. Note that self-monitoring will *not*, in and of itself, create new skills or knowledge. However, increasing the amount a child practices *can* help improve fluency or retention. Here's how training in SMP might look.

Step 1: Defining the Target Behavior

The target behavior here is the number of spelling practices. Each word written out correctly counts as one practice.

Step 2: Collecting Baseline Data

To collect baseline data, Mr. Graham collects Karen's spelling practice work for 3 days. Each day Mr. Graham counts up the number of practices and graphs the number.

Step 3: Obtaining Willing Cooperation

Mr. Graham sets up a conference with Karen.

> "Karen, I want to talk to you about your spelling. I know that you don't like spelling and that you've had some problems on your spelling tests. On your last report card your grade was a D, and I know you didn't like that. I think that one problem is that you need to practice your words more so that you can remember their spelling. You know that old saying 'Practice makes perfect.' Well, it's true for spelling. I know a way to help you practice more. I used it with Bobby last year, and now he does much better on spelling tests. Plus it helps in your writing class. It's a lot easier to write when you can spell the words. I'd like you to try it for 2 weeks and see if it helps. How about it?"

After Karen agrees, he explains the procedures.

Step 4: Instruction in Self-Monitoring Procedures

Here is how instruction in procedures might look. Note that because the target behavior—spelling practices—is familiar to Karen, Mr. Graham doesn't need to discuss or define it.

"OK, Karen, we'll use our regular spelling list. You will practice the words for 10 minutes a day. On Friday you'll take the test just like we always do. Now, the first thing we're going to do is to show you a good way to study your words. Here's how we'll do it. First, you look at the word and say the word. Then you cover the word with your finger and practice writing it three times. After you write it, you check to see if you spelled it correctly. That's important because you don't want to practice a wrong spelling. If you got it right, then you can go on to the next word. Now let me show you how you'll do it. [Models and verbalizes the steps.] Your turn. Show me how you'll do your practice. Tell me what you do at each step. [Karen models and verbalizes the steps correctly.] You'll keep doing this for the whole 10 minutes. If you get to the end of the list, then you can go back and practice any hard words or just start at the beginning of the list.

"We'll set a timer for 10 minutes so you'll know how long to practice. When the timer goes off you need to check to see how many practices you did. To help you see how much you've practiced, we'll use this graph [shown in Figure 6.4]. What you do is count up the number of practices and then put them on this graph. [The student examines the graph briefly.] Now let's practice what you'll do. Here's your spelling list. I'll set the timer for 3 minutes. Remember to look at the word, say the word, cover the word, and copy it three times. Ready? OK, let's go."

He starts the timer. After 3 minutes he cues Karen to count up the number of practices and graph them.

"Good job, Karen. Now tomorrow we'll start doing this for real. Would you like to decorate your graph now? Maybe you could draw a horse and see how high it could jump? The bars on the graph could be like fences that the horse could jump over."

Letting the student personalize the graph increases the sense of ownership and makes the process more enjoyable.

Step 5: Independent Performance

Before starting self-monitoring, it's a good idea to briefly review the procedures. Mr. Graham reminds Karen how to practice and to count up and graph her words at the end of 10 minutes. After Karen graphs her words, he checks to see that she is counting and graphing correctly.

Step 6: Evaluation

To evaluate the effects of SMP, Mr. Graham compares the graphs that Karen made to the baseline data. This technique can be very helpful at increasing effective practices and improving weekly spelling test scores. We used it with one class and raised the average score on weekly spelling tests to 100%.

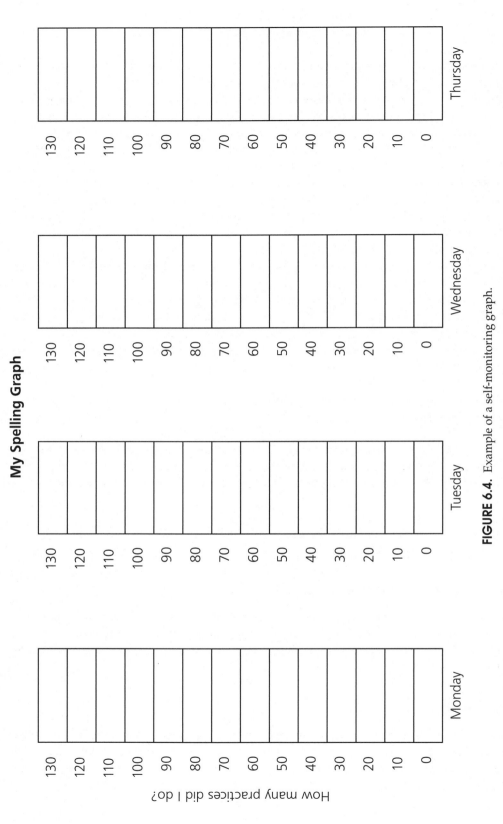

My Spelling Graph

	Monday	Tuesday	Wednesday	Thursday
130				
120				
110				
100				
90				
80				
70				
60				
50				
40				
30				
20				
10				
0				

How many practices did I do?

FIGURE 6.4. Example of a self-monitoring graph.

IMPLEMENTING SELF-EVALUATION

Self-evaluation is a powerful and practical self-regulation strategy. It has demonstrated effectiveness in improving problem behaviors in the classroom (e.g., talking out, out-of-seat behavior) as well as academic problems (e.g., coming to class prepared, completing homework) with students with LD and ADHD (DuPaul & Stoner, 2003; Reid et al., 2012). To illustrate how self-evaluation might be used in the classroom, we show how it could be used with Steve, the student in a previous example.

Step 1: Collect Baseline Data

In Step 1, the teacher defines the problem behaviors and collects baseline data. It is important to explicitly define the behaviors because Steve will be called upon to rate himself on these behaviors in a later step, and the teacher must rate his performance during this step. In the case of Steve, the teacher will focus on four behaviors: staying in seat, following directions, staying quiet, and doing assigned work. The teacher will also create a self-evaluation sheet like Figure 5.2. The teacher will use this sheet to record baseline information, and Steve will use it when self-evaluation is in effect. Next, the teacher rates Steve's behavior during spelling practice over 3 of 4 days and records the rating on the self-evaluation sheet. The spelling practice period is 15 minutes in length, so the teacher will make a rating every 5 minutes. This will result in three ratings for each period.

Step 2: Teacher Rating

In Step 2 the teacher meets with the student to explain the procedures. The teacher establishes that there is a problem and notes the behaviors that are inappropriate. Next, the rating sheet is introduced. The teacher tells Steve that, in the future, she will be rating his behavior at 5-minute intervals during spelling practice. The teacher explains the behaviors that the ratings will be based on and provides examples (e.g., to get the top rating of 10 in a period, Steve would need to remain at his desk, follow instructions, remain quiet, and work on his spelling practice for the entire 5 minutes). The teacher then shares the baseline ratings with the student and discusses them. The teacher should note intervals when ratings were low and discuss the problems that caused the low ratings. The teacher should also point out ratings that were higher and note the desired behaviors that occurred. The student is then told to do his spelling work and is reminded that the teacher will rate his behavior at 5-minute intervals. The teacher sets a timer. When the timer goes off, the teachers records the rating, shares it with the student, and briefly notes the reason for the rating (i.e., specific behaviors that resulted in the rating). Teacher rating continues until the behavior is stable and at an acceptable level.

Step 3: Matching

In this stage the student also rates behavior and compares it with the teacher's rating. It's at this step that the student actually self-evaluates and learns to accurately rate his or her behavior. The teacher again meets with the student. In our example the teacher informs Steve that now he will also rate his behavior and that his rating and the teacher's rating will be compared. Points, which can be redeemed for reinforcers, will be awarded for accurate rating. If Steve's rating is within 2 points of the teacher's ratings, he will receive points equal to his rating (e.g., if the teacher rated Steve's behavior as a 3 and Steve rated it as a 5, he would receive 5 points). If the ratings match exactly, Steve will receive an additional bonus point. However, if the ratings differ by more than 2 points, Steve will not receive any points. Remember that the purpose is to help the student accurately assess his or her behavior. Note that the teacher would need to determine in advance suitable reinforcers and the number of points needed to redeem them (e.g., 10 points = 5 minutes of extra computer time). There should be a mix of smaller (and less expensive) and larger (and more expensive) reinforcers.

Step 4: Fading

After the student has maintained the desired behavior at an acceptable level, a fading process begins. In this process the number of times that the student's and teacher's ratings are matched is gradually decreased, and the time interval between matches is increased. In our example the teacher would meet with Steve and tell him that the next spelling practice there would be two matches rather than three. The teacher would set the timer for 7 minutes and 30 seconds (half of the spelling practice period), perform the initial match, and then repeat the process. If the student's behavior remained improved after three or four sessions, the teacher could then decrease the number of matches to one. Finally, the written ratings are faded and the student orally rates behavior at the end of the period with the teacher. External reinforcers are also gradually diminished during this step. The teacher should be sure to provide ample social reinforcement (e.g., praise) during this phase as the external reinforcement is withdrawn.

IMPLEMENTING SELF-INSTRUCTION

Self-instruction strategies are powerful and extremely flexible tools for the classroom teacher. Self-instruction strategies have been used successfully with a wide range of children, including children with traumatic brain injury, cognitive deficits, behavior disorders, and LD (e.g., Browder & Minarovic, 2000; Hux, Reid, & Luggert, 1994; Smith & Sugai, 2000). The range of application is very broad. Self-instructions can be used to help a child use a strategy; focus on important aspects of a problem; or cope with a situation that provokes anxiety, frustration, anger, or other emotions. In this section we provide examples of how self-instruction strategies can be implemented in the classroom.

Example 1: Self-Instructions for Coping with Anxiety

As we noted earlier, motivational aspects of academic performance are very important for children with LD. This is an important use for strategy instruction. In the previous chapter we gave the example of the "Little Professor" who used self-instructions to help him deal with frustration. Dealing with frustration is particularly relevant for students with LD as they commonly have problems with negative self-statements and thoughts that impede learning (Harris, 1982; Wong, Harris, & Graham, 1991). In fact, self-instructions were designed in part exactly for situations such as this (Meichanbaum, 1977). In this example, we show how two researchers (Kamann & Wong, 1993) helped students with LD reduce their math anxiety. Note that although math is used in this example, the same technique could be used for any situation.

Step 1: Discussing Importance of Verbalizations

Here is how a teacher might discuss this concern with a student.

> "I've noticed that you really had a lot of problems with the math test last week. You also had some problems finishing your homework. Now we've worked together at a lot of the skills you use, like borrowing and math facts, so I don't think that's the problem. I was watching you do some math work the other day and I heard you saying things to yourself like 'I'll never get this right' or 'I'm dumb at math.' I'd like to talk to you about something we can work on that might make it easier for you to do your math work. It might seem silly, but what you say to yourself can make a difference in what you do. Do you remember the old story about the little engine that could? Remember how the little engine had to pull a heavy load up a big hill? The engine told himself over and over again, 'I think I can.' That helped the engine to keep trying, and sure enough, he was able to make it up the hill. You know I did the same thing when I was in school. I had one course that was really tough. I would say to myself, 'This isn't rocket science. I can do this.' It really helped me. But you know what, if you say negative things to yourself, it can actually hurt you. If you tell yourself 'I can't do this,' then pretty soon you start believing it and you quit trying."

Discuss other examples. Try to bring out examples of positive self-statements.

Step 2: Developing Self-Statements

Here the teacher and student need to generate statements to help deal with problems encountered during math work. In this stage, they work together to generate appropriate self-statements. Table 6.1 presents examples of types of self-statements that might be appropriate for the problem. The first type of statement deals with defining the problem, the second with approaching math tasks, the third with recognizing negative thoughts, the next with coping with controlling response when feeling stressed, and the last is about reinforcing. Note that all types of self-statements may not be appropriate. For example, self-statements dealing with error detection and error correction aren't necessary for this situation.

Here's how you might generate self-statements.

> "We need to think of some positive things to say to help with math. First we need to think about what to say when we get ready to do math. Let's think about what

TABLE 6.1. Examples of Self-Statements for Math Problems

Type of statement	Examples
Problem definition	"OK, what do I need to do now?" "What's my next step?"
Approaching task	"I can do this." "I need to pay attention and remember my math facts." "I'll take my time and be careful and I can do it."
Recognition	"OK, now I'm getting scared." "Uh-oh. I'm saying bad things to myself. I need to think positive."
Coping/controlling	"It's all right. I'm doing OK. Just keep on working." "Be calm and relax." "You can do this. Just keep trying hard."
Reinforcing	"Sweet!" "I did it!" "Outstanding!"

we can say to ourselves when we start doing math work. Remember that it needs to be positive to help us get through the work. Sometimes I like to start by asking myself what I need to do or remember about doing problems. I might ask myself, 'OK, what's the first thing I need to do?' or I might say, 'Pay attention and remember your math facts.' "

Discuss possible problem definition and approaching task statements. Then go on to the coping statements.

"You know, it is really important not to let yourself get frustrated or scared. You don't want to start thinking negative thoughts. I remember what I like to tell myself: 'This isn't rocket science.' That really helps me. If I feel myself getting upset, I tell myself something positive too. Sometimes I tell myself 'Just settle down.' Here are some examples of things you could say to yourself."

Present a cue card with examples and brainstorm possible statements with the student. Write out a list and let the child choose which ones he or she likes. It's fine if the student likes one from the list or one that you've modeled. It's best if students generate their own statements. These are typically the most meaningful self-statements. However, it's not absolutely necessary. After this, move on to statements that acknowledge negative thoughts.

"The first thing to think about is that after we get started, we need to be ready if we start thinking negative thoughts. This is like the weather report. We need to look for black clouds that might sneak up on us. That way, we'll know when we're saying things that can keep us from doing our best."

Show examples. As before, generate self-statements and discuss them.

> "After we know that we're thinking negative thoughts, then we need to be ready to say good things to ourselves. These good things are like umbrellas. They keep off the bad thoughts, and they help us keep going. If we tell ourselves that we can do it, then lots of the time we really can. We just keep saying *we can do it*, and then we do it! We talk ourselves through the negative moments. Here are some things some kids have used."

Again, show examples and generate and discuss self-statements for the student. If the student mentions specific problems he or she encounters (e.g., while working on one problem, worrying about other math problems; feeling panicky; feeling rushed), then work on statements that address the problems. Finally, work on developing a reinforcing statement.

> "After we get done with our math and we did our best job, then we need to say something nice to ourselves. We kept telling ourselves we could do it, and we did do it, so we deserve to feel good about that. Here are some things you might say."

Again, show the cue card. Next, give the student a sheet to write down the self-statements (see Figure 6.5). The student can use this sheet to help remember the self-statements and for practice. Exactly how many and what types of self-statements are generated should be decided by the student and teacher together (Harris & Graham, 1996). Too many self-statements may be confusing to the student. And, the student should decide what type (e.g., coping) should be used initially.

Step 3: Modeling Self-Statements and Discussing When to Use Them

During this stage the teacher and the student model the self-statements and discuss when and how they might be used. For example, the teacher might model a moment when coping is needed in this manner.

> "Man, this problem is hard. Ohhh. I don't think I can do this. OK. That's a black cloud. OK, I need to stop and take a deep breath. Now, just keep cool. If I keep cool, I can do this problem."

The teacher and student should discuss each situation where the self-statements might be needed and how the student can remember to use them.

Step 4: Collaborative Practice

The final step is to work together collaboratively with the student to practice using the self-instructions. For example, the teacher might model a math task using the previously generated self-statements during the task. The student could prompt the teacher

Before I start, I say . . .

When I see rain clouds, I say . . .

To help me keep going, I say . . .

When I'm done, I say . . .

FIGURE 6.5. Example of a self-instruction sheet.

to use the self-instructions. Then the student would model the use of the instructions. Remember that one of the keys to using self-instruction successfully is to make sure that the student understands why the self-statements are useful, and that these statements are developmentally appropriate and meaningful to the student (Graham, Harris, & Reid, 1992).

Example 2: Self-Instructions for Number Writing

In the previous example we saw how self-instructions could help with coping. Self-instructions can also help guide students through a task. This guidance can be achieved in several ways. For example, self-instructions can step them through a task (i.e., the students literally talk their way through a task). Or, self-instructions can help students call up and store information in memory to aid them with a task. Here's an example of how self-instructions could be used to help students perform a task. The task is writing numbers correctly. Self-instructions are used for two purposes. The first purpose is to provide a structure for students (i.e., to help step them through the task). The self-instruction actually functions as a simple strategy. The second purpose is to help them remember how to correctly write a number (i.e., call up information from memory to aid them with a task). The strategy is called STAR (Boom & Fine, 1995):

S = *Stop* and ask myself what I am expected to do (e.g., write the number that the teacher is saying).
T = *Think* of using a saying to help in forming the number.
A = *Ask* myself which saying should be used for this number.
R = *Recite* the saying while I write the number.

The letters in STAR are a mnemonic to help students remember self-instructions. The first letter, *S*, serves to orient the student to the task (i.e., writing a number). The last three letters remind students to identify the appropriate self-instructions (see Figure 6.6) and retrieve information to help them with the task. Here's how it might work in practice.

Step 1: Discussing the Importance of Verbalizations

The teacher meets with the student and explains exactly how the strategy works (e.g., "It helps you remember what to do," "You talk yourself through a task") and what the student would use it for (i.e., helping to write numbers).

Step 2: Developing Self-Statements

In this case there is no need to generate self-statements because they have already been developed. The teacher goes over the self-instructions in Figure 6.6. During this process, the teacher should be sensitive to the match between the student and the self-statements. If the student does not understand a self-statement, then it would need to be explained or modified. Additionally, if the student independently developed one or

> To make 0: The boy walked all the way around the circle.
>
> To make 1: The girl jumped straight down.
>
> To make 2: The boy circled up and right, slid down to the left, then went straight right.
>
> To make 3: The girl made a half circle and then another.
>
> To make 4: The boy slid down the slide, then went right, then he made a stick.
>
> To make 5: The girl walked around the corner, then made a half-circle back.
>
> To make 6: The boy slid down and circled round back.
>
> To make 7: The girl ran right to the slide, then slid down.
>
> To make 8: The boy made a snowman with one line.
>
> To make 9: The girl made a balloon on a stick.

FIGURE 6.6. Example of self-instructions for forming numerals.

more self-statements, they should be substituted as these would be more meaningful to the student.

Step 3: Modeling Self-Statements and Discussing When to Use Them

Next, the teacher would model the strategy. For example:

"OK, I have to write a 7. I get mad when I write it backwards. I want to do it right. I'm going to use my new STAR strategy. The first thing I have to do is <u>S</u>top and ask myself what I have to do. OK, I have to write a good seven on this line. Now I have to <u>T</u>hink. Let's see, to remember which way the seven goes, I can use one of the sayings. Now I have to <u>A</u>sk myself which saying to use. Which one is it? I know. Seven is the one with the man who made a line at the top. Now I have to <u>R</u>ecite the saying while I do it. Here's my pencil. The girl ran right to the slide then slid down. That's a good seven. I know it's facing the right way. I'll check it with the card to make sure. Outstanding!"

Step 4: Collaborative Practice

The teacher should model other numerals, this time stopping after the varying STAR steps to ask students, "What should I tell myself to do next?"—thus giving students practice in using the self-statements. Next, students would memorize the steps in STAR and the self-instructions for each number. Note that the teacher would probably work most closely on the numbers with which students had difficulty. Next, the teacher would practice using controlled materials. Some good ways to do this would be to practice one number at a time by dictating numbers, doing simple math, or asking questions that require a given number as the answer. The teacher should provide immediate feedback on the elements of the strategy that are being done correctly and point out any steps that are done improperly. Again note that if a child changes a self-instruction (e.g., changes the saying for 9 to "a circle on a stick"), this is fine. Self-instruction must be meaningful to the child to be effective.

IMPLEMENTING GOAL SETTING

Goals can be powerful sources of motivation. Goal setting has been successfully implemented in a number of different manners. However, there are some commonalities across studies. We present recommendations suggested by Alderman (1999) and Licht (1993).

Step 1: Establishing the Goals

The first step in the process is to establish the goals. The teacher and student can work together to set the goal, or it may be desirable for the student to set goals independently. Whether or not student-created goals are superior to those developed by others (e.g., teachers) isn't yet clear (e.g., Locke & Latham, 1990). What does seem to be important is that students accept the goals, as this seems to be an important element in success (Locke & Latham, 1990). This is understandable. Goals that we accept and want to accomplish are those that most inspire effort. It's possible that jointly set goals (i.e., goals collaboratively developed by the student and teacher) may actually help increase the extent to which students accept goals (Alderman, 1999).

Step 2: Ensuring That Goals Are Appropriate

The second step is to work with the student to ensure that the goals that are set are appropriate. Many students do not know how to set goals that are realistic or measurable. Thus, as with any other skill, this must be taught. Note that this is important whether the student sets the goal independently or jointly with the teacher. Here the teacher will explain how to recognize a good goal (i.e., specific, proximal, and moderately challenging). Alderman (1999) suggested that it is also useful to present student examples of poor goals (e.g., "I will be a good speller") and let students identify problems and correct them to create an appropriate goal (e.g., "I will raise my spelling test score to 80% on weekly tests"). In the discussion, the teacher should be sure that the student understands why some goals are inappropriate (e.g., poorly defined, too ambitious). Then ask the students to independently create two or three appropriate goals.

Next, the teacher and the student can discuss product goals and process goals (Graham, MacArthur, et al., 1992). *Product goals* refer to an end stage. For example, the previous goal to raise spelling test scores to 80% would be a product goal. *Process goals* refer to the means to accomplish the end stage. To continue with the spelling example, process goals might include: (1) "I will practice my spelling words 20 minutes a week"; (2) "I will use my spelling strategy"; (3) "I will use my self-monitoring graph to increase my amount of practicing." After realistic goals have been created, the teacher and student may wish to make the goals public by posting them. There is evidence to suggest that public goals are more effective than private goals (Martin & Pear, 2003). However, teachers should use discretion. Public goals may be threatening to students with a history of failure. A reasonable compromise might be to let the initial goal be private, but after it has been met, make subsequent goals public.

Step 3: Establishing Feedback and Monitoring Procedures

As we noted in the previous chapter, one of the important aspects of goals is that they can provide feedback on progress. Teachers should be sensitive to this during goal setting (or any other intervention, for that matter). The type of feedback teachers provide can directly affect student effort and progress toward meeting goals. Feedback should stress progress or comparison with prior performance, rather than comparison with normative standards or with peers (Bandura, 1993; Licht, 1993). To continue the spelling example, if the child got 70% on a spelling test, a good comment might be one such as "Good job on the test. You went from 60% to 70%. You're halfway to your goal!" This feedback emphasized progress and noted specific progress to the goal of 80%. Feedback on specific errors could focus on areas of strength and those that need improvement (e.g., "You got all the *ie* words correct, but a few of the *ei* words fooled you. We can work on a trick to help you with those"). The teacher should stress effort and correct use of strategies.

Progress monitoring is an important factor in the success of goals. Remember that one of the characteristics of goals is that they provide information on progress, which is, in turn, motivating. Thus, ongoing progress monitoring should be built into the goal-setting process. Progress should be evaluated frequently. Evaluation should be done at least weekly and at best daily (assuming that this is appropriate). This frequency is very easily accomplished. One possibility is to use logs or journals (Alderman, Klein, Seeley, & Sanders, 1993) in which the student narrates progress toward the goal and reflects on problems and successes. (This method would likely be more appropriate for middle school or high school students.) Another suggestion is to use goal cards (Smolen, Newman, Walthen, & Lee, 1995) that list a student's goals for a period of time (e.g., today or this week). At the end of the period the student writes a brief note to show progress toward the goal. This note may even include a brief evaluation. Figure 6.7 shows an example of a goal card for the spelling example.

Step 4: Starting Up

At this point the appropriate goals have been established, and monitoring and feedback procedures have been established. Now the student should work toward attaining the goals. Teachers should be careful to *monitor progress carefully*. If goals were too difficult or would take too long to reach, they should be adjusted. Teachers should provide

---

My Goals This Week

Goal 1: I will practice my spelling words 30 minutes a week

How Did I Do? I did 20 minutes of practice

Goal 2: I will use my spelling strategy

How Did I Do? I did it!

Goal 3: I will use my self-monitoring graph to help me practice more

How Did I Do? I did 16 more practices

Can I Do Anything Better? Next week I will try to do all 30 minutes of practice

---

FIGURE 6.7. Example of a completed goal card.

frequent targeted feedback on progress toward the goals. This feedback can enhance motivation.

IMPLEMENTING SELF-REINFORCEMENT

Self-reinforcement is a powerful intervention that has been demonstrated to be effective in increasing academic productivity. Some studies have suggested that self-reinforcement may even be superior to teacher-awarded reinforcement (Lovitt & Curtis, 1969). The procedure for self-reinforcement follows.

Step 1: Setting Explicit Standards for Reinforcement

The teacher or the teacher and student can work together to set explicit reinforcement standards. It is probably best to set standards jointly because allowing students to set standards for reinforcement independently often results in very lenient standards. It is important to set the standards for reinforcement at an appropriate level of difficulty. Harris and Graham (1996) suggest that standards should be stringent because stringent standards produce better results. Note that *stringent* is a relative term. What is stringent for one student might be lenient for another. If students set overly lenient standards, teachers may prompt them to make the standards more stringent or allow initial lenient standards and then work toward making standards more challenging. In contrast, some students may suggest standards that are much too difficult. This is a problem because if the standards are too high, the student will not receive any reinforcement. The teacher should take pains to set standards that ensure the student will earn at least *some* reinforcement. Otherwise, the intervention will not be effective.

Step 2: Selecting the Reinforcer

One of the best ways to select a reinforcer is to use a reinforcement menu (Maag, 2004; see Figure 6.8). Note that this selection process involves determining both the reinforcer itself and the amount of behavior needed to earn it (e.g., "For every 10 spelling practices, you get 1 minute of free time"). It is important that the amount of reinforcement that can be earned be *explicitly defined* and *stated*. It is also important that the amount of reinforcement to be awarded be carefully considered. Too little may not provide sufficient motivation to change behavior. For example, 1 minute of computer time for 1,000 spelling practices would obviously be inappropriate, as the amount of effort the student would expend would far outstrip the reward. Similarly, 50 minutes of computer time for each practice would be equally inappropriate. The key is to find a fair balance.

Step 3: Determining How Students Will Evaluate Their Work

For self-reinforcement to succeed, students must be able to accurately self-evaluate their work. For example, students may self-correct or bring the work to the teacher to check, and then determine the amount of reinforcement earned. It is best if explicit, objective criteria for evaluation are determined in advance. When evaluation criteria are subjective, students may be too hard or too easy on themselves. In cases where explicit, objective criteria may be difficult to define (e.g., overall quality of a writing assignment), teachers and students should collaborate on evaluations.

Step 4: Self-Award Reinforcement

If the student met the criteria, he or she may be awarded the reinforcer. In theory (Bandura, 1997) the student should control access to the reinforcer and administer it. In practice, teachers may be uncomfortable with this arrangement. A good middle ground is for students to show the teacher the work and state the amount of reinforcement they

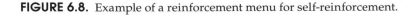

Lynn's Spelling Rewards		
Daily Rewards		
Good match		2 minutes of computer time
For every 10 correct practices		1 minute of computer time
100 practices in one session		10 extra minutes of computer time
Weekly Reward		
Spelling test score of	70–75	1 sticker
	76–79	2 stickers
	80–90	A soft drink
	91 or more	Lunch with Mr. Fuchs!

FIGURE 6.8. Example of a reinforcement menu for self-reinforcement.

believe they should self-award. One good way to involve the teacher is to award students extra reinforcement for accurately determining how much they have earned. For example, if a student accurately counted up the number of practices and determined the correct amount of reinforcement, he or she would receive a bonus. Note that self-reinforcement *does not mean* that the teacher should refrain from, or reduce, other forms of reinforcement. Teachers should continue to provide social reinforcement (e.g., a wink, a "Good job," a pat on the back). Over time, teachers should encourage children to move from tangible or activity reinforcers to self-praise (Harris & Graham, 1996).

Here is how you might teach a student to use self-reinforcement.

> "Hi, Lynn, I wanted to talk with you today about your spelling. I know you don't like spelling much and that you don't really like to practice it. On the last report card your average was only 64%, and your mom was really upset. Well, guess what? We're going to treat spelling practice just like a real job! When you do a real job, you get paid, don't you? Of course they don't pay you for nothing, do they? Right, you have to work for your pay and do a good job. Well, from now on we are going to pay you for doing your spelling. Let's figure out how we could pay you. We'll make a list of some rewards you could earn."

At this point the teacher and student confer about the possible rewards.

> "OK, Lynn, you seem to like extra computer time, so let's make that the everyday award. Now let's decide how many practices you should do to earn extra computer time."

Now the teacher and student negotiate the number of practices necessary to earn rewards. Note that it's a good idea to track the amount of the behavior that the student would normally produce (i.e., in this case, how many practices the student normally would do daily). You can use this amount as a baseline for setting reinforcement levels. For example, if Lynn normally did 30 practices in a session, then 35 or 40 might be an appropriate level. Also note that reinforcement levels can and should change when performance improves.

> "Well, Lynn, I think we decided what you can earn. Let's write it down so we can remember it, then later I will make a card for you. You'll keep the card in your spelling folder. It will help you remember what you can earn. Now let me show you how your job will work. Every day you will have 10 minutes to practice your spelling. You can use the spelling strategy we always use to help you. When 10 minutes are up, I want you to count the number of practices you did and write the number on the top of the sheet. Then, I want you decide how much computer time you earned and write it on the top of the sheet. After you've done that, come to me. I'll check it. If you counted correctly and figured out what you earned right, I will give you a bonus! You'll get 2 extra minutes of computer time. Now, on Friday you take your spelling test. We'll do pretty much the same thing. You'll check your test, just like always. Put your percent correct at the top. Then figure out the

reward and write it at the top. I'll check it just like we do every day. Now let's go over how we do this."

Walk the student through the steps once and model the process. Then ask the student to tell you in his or her own words how he or she will do it.

COMBINING STRATEGIES

In the previous sections we treated each self-regulation strategy separately. However, self-regulation strategies can be very effectively *combined*. For example, in the goal-setting example, we really combined goal setting with self-monitoring because the student actually self-monitored progress. This is a natural and very powerful combination. In fact, it's not unusual for students to spontaneously engage in goal setting when using self-monitoring of performance if graphing is involved. For example, a child might do 35 practices on Monday. After counting the practices and coloring in the bar graph, he or she might look at the next day and draw a line at 50. If this occurs, the teacher should briefly discuss what the student did when drawing that line and explain how setting goals is a very positive thing and praise the student for doing so. Then the next day the teacher can note whether the student met the goal and set a new goal for the next day. Another example of how self-regulation strategies could be combined would be to use self-instruction with self-reinforcement. In the previous number-writing example, students could reinforce themselves for the number of correctly formed letters. Note that it is not necessary, or even desirable, to combine *all* the self-regulation strategies. This could easily result in procedures that are cumbersome, confusing, or even aversive.

FINAL THOUGHTS

In this chapter we provided examples of how self-regulation strategies might be implemented. We would stress that these examples should be considered as guidelines. So long as the implementation process is followed, the materials or the exact language teachers might use to explain steps or model processes can vary considerably (e.g., teachers would approach the process much differently for a kindergartner than for a high school student). We should also stress that these strategies can be used on a stand-alone basis. Self-regulation strategies do not have to be combined with content-area strategies. For example, self-monitoring is quite effective at increasing time on task or the amount of seatwork. And, self-instructions can help students cope with stressful situations or talk their way through tasks. Finally we would note that self-regulation strategies can be easily and fruitfully combined. In closing, we would caution that self-regulation strategies are not appropriate for some tasks. For example, overt self-instruction may interfere with behaviors that require speedy, reflexive performance or that require complex processing (e.g., sounding out a word) (Harris, 1982).

CHAPTER 7

Integrating Strategies and Self-Regulation

O ne of the major strengths of the SRSD model is the stress placed on creating independent learners. A strategy that can only be used with a teacher's help, that requires constant prompting to use, or that won't be maintained is not desirable. As we noted earlier, students with LD or ADHD (and other struggling learners) commonly have problems remembering to use strategies, using strategies successfully, and generalizing their use. Problems of this sort are at the heart of the academic difficulties of these students. Thus, for these students, self-regulation is crucial. As shown in the last chapter, self-regulation strategies can be very useful alone or in combination. However, they can be even more powerful when combined with strategy instruction. Self-regulation strategies can be used in conjunction with content-area strategies in many beneficial ways. They can (1) cue the student to use the content strategy, (2) help students remember the steps of a content strategy, (3) ensure that the content strategy steps are used correctly, (4) guide content strategy use, and (5) help the student screen out outside distractions, improve motivation, and maintain effort.

Until now we have treated content strategies and self-regulation strategies separately. In our experience, teachers sometimes have problems combining content strategies and self-regulation strategies. This difficulty is due in part to the fact that teachers often perceive content strategies and self-regulation strategies as separate. There is a tendency to see self-regulation as directed toward problem behavior and content strategies as academic activities. As a result, some teachers may treat them separately when planning for strategy implementation. This, in turn, can lead to problems with integrating self-regulation strategies and strategy instruction. It's important to remember that self-regulation strategies should be an integral part of the strategy instruction process. As we noted in our discussion of the SRSD model, strategies are explicitly taught and modeled by teachers and memorized and practiced by students. The same principle applies to self-regulation. In our experience, we have found that well integrated self-regulation strategies are very effective and desirable components of strategy instruction. They can improve performance, enhance motivation, and help to maintain strategy use.

Just as students need scaffolding when learning a new strategy, teachers who wish to master the SRSD model often need examples of how content strategies and self-regulation strategies can be combined. As we noted above, self-regulation strategies can serve many functions. There are also many ways in which content strategies and self-regulation strategies can be integrated. In this chapter we present examples of how they can be combined. These examples are drawn from research and practice in real-world classrooms. In these examples we do not provide full-blown lesson plans for either the content strategies or self-regulation strategies—these lesson plans are provided in Chapter 8. Instead we focus on how self-regulation strategies have been used and combined with content strategies.

SELF-MONITORING, GOAL SETTING, AND A SPELLING STRATEGY

Problems with spelling are common among students with LD or ADHD. These problems can have negative effects on both written language and reading (Graham & Harris, 2000). Some educators place an emphasis on acquired spelling skills, whereby a student learns to spell through reading and written-language activities (e.g., writing stories or compositions) (Graham, 2000). Unfortunately, this approach poses problems for students with LD or ADHD, who do not typically benefit from this approach, and most teachers believe that explicit instruction in spelling is necessary (Graham, 2000). One important factor in learning new spelling words is the decidedly old-fashioned practice of simply writing the word down on paper. Elaborating on information (writing a word, in this case) helps to store it in long-term memory. However, practicing spelling words in this manner may be difficult for some students because of the need to maintain focus and effort on a highly repetitive task.

We recently worked with a team of teachers in a sixth-grade class who had problems with poor spelling performance. Students were given weekly spelling lists on Monday and were told to practice the words at home in preparation for the test on Friday. Unfortunately, many of the students did little or no practice at home, and spelling performance overall was not at the level the teachers had hoped for. Based on the situation, we decided that two related actions were needed: (1) students needed to use an effective spelling practice strategy, and (2) students needed to increase the amount of spelling practice. To address the first problem, we used a well-validated spelling strategy (Harris, Graham, & Freeman, 1988) that consists of the following steps: (1) Look at the word, (2) say the word, (3) cover the word, (4) write the word three times, and (5) check to see if the word is correct. If it's not, repeat Steps 1–5; if it is, go on to another word. Teaching the strategy was quite simple. First we told the students that we were going to show them something that would help them do better on their weekly spelling test. We wrote the steps of the strategy on the board and went over them with the entire class. Then we modeled the steps before the class. Next, we asked selected students to model the steps in the process aloud for the class. We then told all the students that they would be practicing spelling for 10 minutes a day from Monday through Thursday. The spelling test would be on Friday, as usual.

After the spelling practice session was done, we introduced the self-monitoring strategy. Using self-monitoring of performance (SMP), we had students count and graph the number of daily practices. This was a simple, nonintrusive method intended to increase the number of practices in the daily session. To introduce the self-monitoring, we passed out Spelling Rockets graphs. These were simple bar graphs in the shape of rockets. Each page had four separate bars (one for each practice day). We then told the students that we would like them to count up the number of practices they had done and fill in their graph for Monday. During this time, we circulated through the class to check whether students could correctly fill out their graphs. After the students had filled in their graphs, we explained that the reason for the graphs was to help them keep track of the number of practices they did every day. Next, we asked the students why it was important to practice and emphasized the fact that the more they practiced, the better they would remember their spelling words and the better they would do on the weekly test. Finally, we asked the students to set a goal for the number of practices that they would do for the next day by marking a line across the bar for Tuesday.

The total time needed to teach this strategy was around half an hour. The results were immediately evident. The number of practices increased dramatically over the course of the week. Most students doubled or tripled their number of practices. Some students actually completed over 100 practices in the 10-minute period. In fact, students were doing so many practices that they complained that it took too long to count up their practices. It's important for procedures not to be cumbersome or aversive to students, so we made the counting process easier by giving them 3" × 11" slips of paper to use for practice. Each slip had lines for 20 words and was numbered. Using this method, students only had to add up the number of practices. Before each session, we would pass out slips to students and ask them how many they thought they wanted. This step had the added effect of making them focus on their daily goals. The effects on spelling were also dramatic. For most weeks, the class spelling average was 100%. The teachers were pleased with the intervention. It improved the spelling performance of the class and did not require any additional time commitment on their part. In fact, because the students worked independently during the spelling practice sessions, the teachers actually had 10 minutes to use for other purposes. This is an example of how self-regulation can help students improve performance through maintaining effort. It also illustrates how it may be necessary to change procedures to tailor the intervention to students.

SELF-MONITORING AND A MATH STRATEGY

Many students with LD have difficulties with math. Although the types of difficulties vary, one aspect of math that frequently causes students with LD difficulties is following the procedures needed to solve problems involving multiple steps, such as long division or subtraction with regrouping. These types of problems pose difficulties because the child must be able to correctly recall the steps and understand what is involved in each step, all the while maintaining and utilizing the necessary basic math facts in working memory. One group of researchers (Dunlap & Dunlap, 1989) used a simple and straightforward self-monitoring checklist (which served as a strategy) to help students solve subtraction problems with regrouping.

None of the students had problems with basic math facts, which obviously constituted a critical preskill. However, the students all had problems with subtraction that involved regrouping. The first step in the intervention was to develop an individualized strategy for each student. To do this, the researchers analyzed the types of errors each student committed. This involved looking at each student's past work and compiling a list of each type of error the student made. The next step was to compile an individualized checklist for each student. This checklist was based on the errors the student typically made. Figure 7.1 shows an example of what a math checklist could look like. The checklist provided the steps in the strategy. Each checklist used "I" statements that served as specific reminders (Harris, 1986a) for operations that the student

---

Subtraction Example

1. I copied the problem correctly.

2. I underlined all the top numbers that were smaller than the bottom.

3. I put a 1 next to each underlined number.

4. I borrowed correctly (number crossed out is one bigger).

5. I subtracted all the numbers.

6. I subtracted correctly.

Multiplication Example

1. I started in the 1's column.

2. If the product was more than 9, I remembered to regroup.

3. I wrote the regrouped number above the next column.

4. I remembered to check my multiplication facts.

FIGURE 7.1. Example of a self-monitoring checklist for math.

had problems with (e.g., copying the problem correctly, crossing out and changing regrouped numbers).

Students were given the checklists and told that they were to use them while they worked their math problems. After they worked each problem, students were told to go through each item on their checklist. If they had performed the item, they were to put a plus sign by the item. If not, they were to put a minus sign by the item. The minus sign served to emphasize that the student had omitted a step. If students recorded a minus sign, they were to rework the problem and attend to the step they omitted. When the students completed their worksheet, the teacher had a brief conference with each student to discuss the results. The teacher awarded points (redeemable for reinforcers) for each correct answer and an additional point for problems in which the student self-monitored all the steps on his or her checklist. Any errors were also discussed, and the teacher provided corrective feedback. After each child had demonstrated improvement and performance had stabilized, the checklists were removed to assess whether the improvements would be maintained. The results of the study were dramatic. The use of the checklists increased accuracy levels from 30 to 50% across the class. More important, the high levels of performance were maintained after the checklists were removed. This finding suggested that the students were able to independently perform the strategy.

There are several instructive aspects to this study. First, the strategy was constructed individually for each student. This was possible, in large part, because math is a highly procedural subject. The steps in solving math problems are well specified, so it's easy to identify and isolate the specific problems of each student. Though we would not recommend that teachers attempt to develop their own strategies as a general rule, in some areas (such as math) it may be possible and desirable for teachers to create strategies that are individualized for their students. In this case, a simple task breakdown was used to identify the steps that each student had difficulty performing correctly. Second, the researchers *directly linked* the strategy and the self-regulation technique. That is, they used self-monitoring to ensure that the student performed the steps of the strategy consistently. Recall that the strategy steps were the operations (in the form of a checklist) that the students tended to forget. The self-monitoring ensured that crucial steps in the subtraction (or multiplication) procedure would not be omitted. Thus, it is not surprising that the students' accuracy improved. Finally, this study utilized reinforcement in addition to the strategy and self-regulation technique. It's not absolutely necessary to combine strategy instruction with outside reinforcement. In many cases, simple verbal praise and awareness of improved performance will be sufficient reinforcement. However, it's also not forbidden to use external reinforcement in the SRSD model. Teachers should use their best judgment. It's quite possible that judicious use of reinforcers would be appropriate in many cases. For example, for some students, such as those with ADHD, it may be preferable to use external reinforcers at least initially. If you choose to use reinforcement, however, don't forget the attribution pattern that you want to stress. It is important that the students be aware that the reinforcement is in response to improved performance due to *their* effort and the use of the strategy.

SELF-INSTRUCTION AND A WRITING STRATEGY

The writing process poses many challenges for students with LD or ADHD. Many students lack knowledge of basic text structures (e.g., the parts of a story or the methods of organizing expository text). They must deal with mechanics (e.g., transcription skills, spelling, sentence structure), planning, organization, and revising. They must also monitor their written product on an ongoing basis (e.g., does it make sense—is it clear?). Dealing with these processes, often simultaneously, can be both cognitively demanding and emotionally stressful. One very effective strategy to help students learn to write narrative text (i.e., stories) is the WWW, What = 2, How = 2 strategy. Table 7.1 shows the strategy. This strategy is unusual in that it was designed to integrate self-instructions and a content strategy. Thus the self-regulation component is literally built into the strategy. In this case, the self-instructions are designed to ensure that the student focuses on important tasks in the writing process and deploys and uses the content strategy. Each step of the strategy is a self-instruction directed toward an important aspect in the writing process. The self-instructions serve to focus the student on important aspects of the task, to cope with possible anxiety, to deploy a content strategy (i.e., the story parts), to use the content strategy, and to self-monitor the quality of the story that is written.

When teaching strategies that have both content and self-regulation strategies, such as WWW, What = 2, How = 2, it's important to explicitly teach and model both the content and the self-regulation strategies. Figure 7.2 shows how a teacher might model the strategy. Note that the design of this strategy is intended to let students "talk themselves through" the story-writing process. Students quite literally tell themselves what to do at each step in the process.

There is another important aspect of self-instructions that teachers should understand. Self-instructions can be used effectively to help students with motivational problems. As a part of the strategy process, students can be taught specific self-statements

---

TABLE 7.1. Self-Instruction Strategy for WWW, What = 2, How = 2

Step 1. Think of a story to share with others.

Step 2. Let your mind be free.

Step 3. Write down the story part reminder: WWW, What = 2, How = 2

- *Who* is the main character? *Who* else is in the story?
- *When* does the story take place?
- *Where* does the story take place?
- *What* does the main character do?
- *What* happens when they try to do it?
- *How* does the story end?
- *How* does the main character feel?

Step 4. Write down story part ideas for each part.

Step 5. Write your story. Use good parts and make sense.

Note. Based on Graham, Harris, and Sawyer (1987).

"What am I being asked to do?" Mrs. Parde said that I am going to use the WWW, What = 2, How = 2 strategy to write a story. I need to remember the parts that go into a story, and this strategy will help me.

Now STEP 1 of WWW, What = 2, How = 2 says to think of a story. Mrs. Parde showed us a picture of this bird flying into a deli shop window and a man feeding the bird. I think I will use this for my story. OK, Step 1 is done. This picture will be fun to write a story about.

On to STEP 2, "Let your mind be free." Well, I know it always helps me if I clear all the distractions from my workspace. I better put these books away and clear those papers off my desk. OK, now I'll take some deep breaths and begin my work. It is important to do this so I'm not distracted and can focus on my writing. My mind is free. I'm ready and excited to start writing.

Now STEP 3. This is a big step, but very important. I see lots of questions. Hey, I bet this is where the WWW, What = 2, How = 2 mnemonic helps me remember all the questions I must answer to write my story. Why are these so important? Oh yeah, they help me to make sure I have all the important parts of my story. OK, so I think I should write the mnemonic on my paper so I'll commit this to my memory. I know I have Mrs. Parde's sheet here to help me, but just so I can become better at this strategy, I better try writing the questions out on my own.

Now how will I remember the exact questions that must go with all these *W*'s? And why is it important that I do? Well, it's important to remember all these "W" questions so I do the strategy correctly. We always ask *who, what, when, why*, and *where* when we read and write other stories, so I think that will help me remember these. We need to know "*Who* is the main character?" and along with that "*Who* else is in the story?" I have characters, now I need a setting and time, so a *when* and *where*. So "*When* does the story take place?" and "*Where* does the story take place?" I now have a *who, when*, and *where*. There's two *whats*. I remember that stories must have a plot or a problem. So maybe one question is "*What* does the main character do?" and "*What* happens when they try to do it?" The *whats* are now answered, now on to the *hows*. I bet the *hows* have to do with "*How* the story ends" and how everything is tied up and ended. I also know it's important to know "*How* the main character feels." OK, so now I've determined all the questions, and now I must answer them. I know I have them all correct, as I look back on the sheet Mrs. Parde gave me to remember the strategy.

Now I need to look at the picture again and begin answering the questions. The picture shows a man and a bird. I think my main character will be the man, and I think I'll name him *Fred*. Other characters will be the bird and other customers at the deli. *When* does the story take place? Well, it looks like the middle of a beautiful Sunday afternoon. *Where* does it take place? At Freddy's, because I think Fred, the main character, owns the deli. *What* does the main character do? Well, Fred looks to have made friends with a beautiful blue bird, and it looks like the bird has stopped by Freddy's for the Sunday afternoon special. *What* happens when Fred tries to feed the bird? I think the bird is a regular, and Fred often feeds the friendly bird. The story ends with this event happening several times, and the deli earns a new name, the "Bird Café." How does the main character feel? I think Fred feels very happy and looks forward to seeing the bird every day. OK, so now I've answered all the WWW, What = 2, How = 2 questions. Now on to Step 4.

(cont.)

FIGURE 7.2. Example of a think-aloud for WWW, What = 2, How = 2. This think-aloud was developed by Aimee Parde and is used by permission.

STEP 4. "Write down the story part ideas for each part." Well, I've already done that as I was trying to think of the answers to the questions to help create my story. Yeah, that was really easy to work into Step 3, so I can move on to Step 5.

STEP 5. "Write your story. Use good parts and make sense." Well, what do I do to write a story? We've been writing lots of stories. There must be a beginning—this is where you "set the stage." I like this part because you can create the setting and let the reader see exactly where the story is taking place. The beginning must be catchy too so the reader stays interested and wants to read more. I know my mom would really like to read a story I wrote and probably Mrs. Parde too. Since she assigned us to write a story, she'll want to read it too. I know she likes humor and excitement. I think that will be easy because the picture is funny. The middle is where the story builds to a climax with the plot or the problem developing. And the end ties it all together, solving the problem. So now I can begin writing my story. I remember that Mrs. Parde always says to skip lines when you write, but why? Oh yeah, that's so when I go back and reread my story and proofread and revise, I can make changes. Just so I remember that I better put a little dash along the side of my paper on every other line, or I could get some of Mrs. Parde's colored paper with every other line grayed out. That would be good to do. It's important to remember to use paragraphs when writing. Paragraphs are good for helping to organize ideas and to keep like topics together. OK, here I go . . .

FIGURE 7.2. *(continued)*

designed to help them cope with negative thoughts or feelings that may occur. Students can also be taught to self-reinforce. Note that self-reinforcement does not have to be tangible. Positive self-statements can be quite effective. The following are some examples of self-statements that can be used for self-reinforcement:

"Awesome!"	"Sweet!"
"Nice job!"	"Outstanding!"
"That was my best!"	"Score!"
"I can do this!"	"Super!"
"I did it!"	"Excellent!"

GOAL SETTING AND A READING COMPREHENSION STRATEGY

Students with LD or ADHD often experience problems remembering what they read. In some cases this is due to problems with decoding. For these students, deciphering the words is so demanding that the meaning of text is lost along the way. However, there are also instances where students with LD fail to remember what they read because they do not know what elements of text are important. Johnson and Graham (1997) used a combination of a reading comprehension strategy and goal setting to help improve students' recall of stories. The first step in the process was to teach students the important parts of a story, based on the Story Grammar strategy of Short and Ryan (1984). Table 7.2 shows the story parts used. The students were also given a graphic reminder

TABLE 7.2. Story Parts and Graphic Symbols

Story part	Symbol
Characters	Stick figure
When the story took place	Clock
Where the story occurred	Picture of a room
The story problem	Question mark
Characters' goals	An arrow
How the characters achieved the goals	The numbers *1, 2, 3* for sequence of events to accomplish goals
The ending	Checkered flag
How the characters felt	A heart

Note. Based on Johnson and Graham (1997).

for each story part. These visual cues were placed on a prompt card and could also be used by students as a part of the strategy. The reading comprehension strategy was a four-step process:

1. *Write and say the story parts* (prompts students to write down the story parts, which focuses attention on the story parts and activates prior knowledge before reading the story).
2. *Read and think* (prompts students to look for story elements while reading).
3. *Remember and write* (reminds students to write notes about each story part).
4. *Look back and check* (prompts students to go back through the story to check their work and add information if they wish).

These steps were designed to focus students' attention on the important elements of a story and to prompt them to locate and write them down.

Goal setting was used to help improve motivation and increase the likelihood that students would use the strategy correctly and consistently. Students were taught to make two types of goals: a performance goal and a process goal. The performance goal related to overall improvement in remembering the elements of a story. As noted previously, a performance goal is analogous to a product goal. The process goal involved the identification of the steps the student would take to meet the performance goal. For example, the students' process goals might be to use the strategy, try hard, concentrate, and so forth. The students were also taught specific procedures to determine the progress they had made toward their performance goals. In this case progress was monitored by counting the number of story elements students could recall when asked to retell a story they had read, and by assessing the extent to which they had followed their process goals. Steps for goal setting and monitoring were practiced and committed to memory. Note that this is an important aspect of training. Just as the steps for a strategy must be committed to memory, so must self-regulation strategies.

SELF-MONITORING AND A MAIN IDEA COMPREHENSION STRATEGY

As we noted in the previous example, many students with LD or ADHD have difficulty identifying the important details in text. Another common problem experienced by students with LD is difficulty finding the main idea of a passage. The ability to locate the main idea is an essential skill that affects students' ability to study effectively, draw inferences, and read critically (Williams, 1988). There is good evidence that strategy instruction can improve students' ability to locate the main idea in text (e.g., see Carnine, Silbert, Kame'enui, & Tarver, 2004; Hagaman, Casey, & Reid, 2012). However, it's also important to remember that students with LD or ADHD will need help to activate and correctly use a strategy that would help them identify the main idea.

With this point in mind, Jitendra and colleagues (Jitendra, Hoppes, & Xin, 2000) developed a main idea comprehension strategy that used self-monitoring to help students learn how to self-regulate the correct use of the strategy. An eight-step instruction process was used:

1. Students were taught the rule "Name the person and tell the main thing the person did in all the sentences."

2. Students were taught to generate a group name and tell the main things the group did.

3. Students were given practice in discriminating main ideas by selecting a sentence that best described a sample passage.

4. At this point distracter sentences (i.e., sentences not related to the main idea) were introduced. Students were taught to find the distracter and then to create a main idea sentence that reflected most of the sentences in a passage. Note how the process in Steps 1–4 was carefully scaffolded by gradually increasing the difficulty of the task.

5.–8. The remainder of the lessons focused on creating main idea sentences for passages that described where, when, why, or how something looked or was done. For each lesson, students were given a prompt sheet that helped cue them to activate the strategy. The prompt sheet reminded students to ask themselves who or what was the subject of action, why something happened, where and when something happened, how an action was done, and also reminded them that some sentences may not concern the main idea.

To help ensure that students used the strategy, the researchers used self-monitoring. Students were given a card to help them check if they had used each step of the strategy. As they performed the strategy, students were supposed to place a checkmark by each of four steps as they performed them:

- "I read the paragraph."
- "I used the prompt card to recall the strategy steps."

- "I applied the strategy to identify the main idea and construct a main idea sentence."
- "I wrote out the main idea sentence."

This self-monitoring procedure was used throughout the instruction process and was modeled and discussed as teachers would do for any other SRSD component. This example is similar to the math strategy (Dunlap & Dunlap, 1989) discussed earlier. Once again the students are self-monitoring the use of the strategy in order to ensure that the strategy is used correctly and consistently. This is an important consideration because as we noted earlier, students with LD or ADHD will often skip steps or forget to use a strategy. Including a self-monitoring component helps to focus attention on the steps of the strategy. Note also that the skills involved in the strategy are at a higher cognitive level than those required for the math strategy.

INTEGRATING STRATEGIES TO SOLVE MATH WORD PROBLEMS

Research has consistently shown that students with LD or ADHD have difficulty solving arithmetic word problems (Case, Harris, & Graham, 1992; Parmar, Cawley, & Miller, 1994). One of the difficulties encountered is translating written problems into math sentences. Apart from any problem caused by reading difficulties, word problems pose special problems because students must (1) understand what question is being asked, (2) locate the relevant information within the problem, (3) set up the problem correctly, and (4) determine what arithmetic operations will be used to solve the problem.

Cassel and Reid (1996) used the FAST DRAW strategy with students with LD to teach them how to successfully solve word problems. FAST DRAW combines a content strategy with a self-instruction strategy, self-monitoring, and self-reinforcement. The strategy is designed to help students find the important information in word problems, set up the problem properly (i.e., use the correct operations), and solve the problem. The steps of the FAST DRAW strategy are shown in Table 7.3.

After the strategy has been discussed, the teacher can emphasize the importance of self-speech and how what we say can affect what we do and how we feel. The student

---

TABLE 7.3. FAST DRAW Strategy

- Find and highlight the question, then write the label.
- Ask "What are the parts of the problem?" then circle the numbers needed.
- Set up the problem by writing and labeling the numbers.
- Tie down the sign (i.e., decide whether to use addition or subtraction).
- Discover the sign (recheck the previous step).
- Read the number problem.
- Answer the number problem.
- Write the answer and check to see if the answer makes sense.

Note. Based on Cassel and Reid (1996).

and teacher then work together to generate statements he or she could say to help use the strategy and record the self-statements on a strategy check-off sheet. The check-off sheet is used to self-monitor whether the self-statements were used, which helps to remind the student to use the steps of the strategy. Some examples of these statements follow: (1) To find the question, look for the sentence ending with a question mark. (2) When setting up the problem, remember to write the larger number on top. (3) To tie down the sign, ask, "Am I *putting together,* so my answer will be larger than the other numbers?" (if *yes,* use addition), or "Am I *taking apart,* so my answer will be smaller than the largest number?" (if *yes,* use subtraction).

The instructor models the use of the strategy using the following self-instructions:

- Problem definition: "What is it I have to do?"
- Planning: "How can I solve this problem?"
- Strategy use: "FAST DRAW will help me organize my problem solving and remember all the things I need to do in order to successfully complete a word problem."
- Self-monitor: "To help me remember what I have done, I can check off the steps of the strategy as they are completed."
- Self-evaluation: "How am I doing? Does what I am doing make sense? Did I complete all the steps?"
- Self-reinforcement: "Great, I'm halfway through the strategy. Oops, I made a mistake, but that's OK because I can correct it. Fantastic!"

Following the modeling, the teacher and student discuss how self-statements helped the teacher use the strategy. Next, the student generates and records examples of statements for each of the six categories on his or her strategy check-off sheet. The teacher and student discuss how self-instructions do not always have to be spoken aloud, but can be whispered or thought to oneself. The instructor and student review the assessment and recording process for self-monitoring strategy use (i.e., using the check-off sheet to record strategy steps and self-instructions). During the support stage, the instructor uses collaborative practice to support the student as he or she moves toward independently solving word problems while using the strategy and self-instructions. The instructor prompts and facilitates the student's strategy use. Corrective feedback and positive reinforcement are initially provided by the instructor to facilitate correct use of the strategy and self-instructions.

FINAL THOUGHTS

In this chapter we presented examples of how self-regulation procedures (i.e., self-monitoring, self-instruction, self-reinforcement, and goal setting) can be combined with strategy instruction. The combination of self-regulation and strategies is a powerful instructional tool. To reemphasize some of the points made in the chapter: First, it is important that teachers *integrate* the strategy and the self-regulation procedures. This entails making the self-regulation mesh with the strategy. Self-regulation procedures should enhance students' ability to use strategies consistently and correctly. It should not interfere with strategy use (i.e., the procedures should not be cumbersome, time-consuming, or aversive to students). For example, in the spelling vignette, procedures were altered to make the self-monitoring procedure simpler for students. Remember that if procedures are cumbersome or aversive, students are unlikely to use them. Some strategies (e.g., WWW, What = 2, How = 2) have already integrated self-regulation with a powerful strategy. However, this kind of synthesis tends to be the exception. In most cases, teachers will need to develop appropriate self-regulation procedures and integrate them. Note that research suggests that sometimes simply teaching a strategy can enhance self-regulation (e.g., Reid & Harris, 1993).

Second, self-regulation strategy procedures must be included in the instructional process. Examples of how this can be done are provided in Chapter 8. The self-regulation procedure must be discussed and modeled by the teacher, committed to memory by the student, and practiced collaboratively, just as you would a content-area strategy. Teachers cannot assume that students will simply "pick up" the self-regulation strategy.

Third, there is no "best way" to self-regulate. Teachers frequently ask, "What is the best self-regulation strategy?" They need to consider the match between the student, the strategy, the task, and the environment. For example, we have worked with some students who had a great deal of difficulty with self-monitoring. However, they could use self-instructions quite easily and effectively. Conversely, we have also worked with students who resisted using self-instructions, but were able to successfully use self-monitoring and goal setting. Sometimes there may be a mismatch between the task and the self-regulation method. For example, SMA may interrupt students while they are performing a task. Some students dislike this and prefer SMP because they don't need to stop to self-record at frequent intervals. Alternatively, some students dislike SMP because it requires counting up practices.

Finally, several examples used multiple self-regulation strategies. This can lead to the impression that if using one self-regulation strategy is good, using two must be even better, and so on. That would be wonderful if true, but in practice you can overload students with self-regulation strategies. Resist the temptation to load up every self-regulation procedure you can fit. It can literally be too much of a good thing. When procedures become time-consuming and unwieldy, students resist using them, and resistance defeats the purpose of strategy instruction. The idea is to use just as much self-regulation as necessary and no more. The self-regulation strategies should serve to enhance the content strategy, not distract from it. Remember that the purpose of self-regulation is to make students effective, independent strategy users.

CHAPTER 8

Creating Lesson Plans
Using the SRSD Model

In the previous chapters we presented three major topics. First, we discussed critical components of strategy instruction, such as the role that information processing, attributions, working memory, and metacognition play in learning. Next, we introduced the SRSD model for teaching strategies. The model includes a series of six stages to ensure that a strategy is taught systematically using a step-by-step process. Finally, we discussed self-regulation strategies, such as self-instructions and goal setting, that can and should be incorporated into strategy instruction. Until now, we have talked about the different components of strategy instruction in isolation. However, it is important to note that, in practice, the actual lessons used in strategy instruction will typically combine, reorder, or even omit stages, depending on the strategy being taught or the students for whom the strategy will be used. In this chapter we discuss how to create detailed lesson plans when teaching a strategy and provide sample lesson plans to guide you in the creation of your own lesson plans.

SRSD LESSONS

In Chapter 4 we illustrated how to implement structured and unstructured strategies by illustrating the six stages of the SRSD model. Here again we noted that the six stages can be reordered, combined, and in some instances, even omitted. However, we have found that, in practice, it can sometimes be difficult for teachers to visualize how to reorder or combine the SRSD stages into workable lesson plans to implement in classrooms. In part, this is due to the fact that we present the SRSD model in a linear fashion (i.e., Stage 1, Stage 2) so it seems natural that actual lessons would follow the same order. However, in practice this may not be the case. Additionally, teachers' lack of experience with strategy instruction also plays a part—sometimes teachers just don't have a feel for what stages of strategy instruction go together. To help teachers better understand how to create their own lessons to teach strategies using SRSD, this chapter provides two sets of sample lesson plans. One set of lessons (Porath, 2012) is for a simple math strategy, LAMPS, which helps students with computation of multidigit addition problems (Reetz & Rasmussen, 1988). The second set of lessons is for a reading comprehension strategy, PARS, which helps students identify and remember important information in reading passages (Cheek & Cheek, 1983). We use a format for these lessons that was developed and implemented for strategy instruction (see Harris, Graham, Mason, & Friedlander, 2008; Mason, Reid, & Hagaman, 2012) and that has been proven to be effective. Please note that although this is *a format* for SRSD instruction, it is *not* the only way to create lesson plans using the SRSD model.

Scripting Lessons

In the lesson plans we provide, you will notice that in some places we provide scripted examples of what the teacher could say and the responses expected from students. This scripting helps to illustrate how teachers can approach teaching some of the stages of strategy instruction (e.g., providing metacognitive knowledge to students, attributing success to effort and strategy use, self-reinforcing statements). However, scripting out some parts of a lesson is also useful in the process of creating lesson plans for strategy instruction. We recommend that teachers self-script portions of lessons when creating lesson plans. In our experience, we have found that both preservice and practicing teachers alike find the process of self-scripting lesson plans to be a very useful in planning and creating lessons. Self-scripting can help ensure that all the necessary components of strategy instruction (e.g., buy-in) are included and that the actual way that information will be presented (e.g., examples, self-statements) has been planned. It also makes it easier for teachers to remember how they wish to present information. Remember that in practice, teachers may not be able to work directly off a lesson plan. Scripting can also be especially helpful for the think-aloud in modeling; few teachers can improvise an effective think-aloud without considerable experience. Note, however, that we are *not advocating that entire lessons be scripted*. Teachers should only script out the portions that they believe are most demanding or new to them and critical for their students. Additionally, it's not necessary for the scripted portions to be repeated exactly; it's fine if the scripted portions are changed or paraphrased so long as the gist of the information the teacher is trying to convey is included.

Developing Checklists

In addition to self-scripting lessons, we recommend that teachers develop checklists for each lesson. A lesson checklist consists of a simple list of tasks that should be done in the course of the lesson and the order in which they should occur (e.g., review the steps of the strategy, model self-statements). There are several reasons for using checklists. First, if a teacher loses his or her place or gets off track, the checklist serves as a quick reminder for what he or she should be teaching and when. Second, the checklist provides a simple, step-by-step "roadmap" to follow. Having a short checklist helps to keep the lesson on track and ensures that critical steps or stages of instruction are not missed. Third, a checklist can be used easily by an outside observer (e.g., co-teacher, principal) as a checklist for fidelity of implementation. In this case, an outside observer could provide a teacher with critical information about teaching behaviors (e.g., pacing, enthusiasm, clarity of instructions) in addition to the steps of strategy instruction. This feedback can be very useful for teachers who are using SRSD for the first time. A sample checklist for the LAMPS strategy is provided in Figure 8.1.

The remainder of this chapter provides sample lesson plans. Throughout the lesson plans we highlight important aspects of each lesson (e.g., when a teacher provides metacognitive knowledge during a think-aloud) using sidebars and thought bubbles. We also highlight the stages of the SRSD model used in each lesson and note where we combine or reorder the stages of instruction, and how and why we chose different types of scaffolding (e.g., content, task). These lessons may also be reproduced, as needed, for educational purposes.

Here are a few points to note as you read through the lesson plans:

- It's possible for stages to be presented "out of order," depending on teacher and student characteristics. For example, the first sample lesson for LAMPS begins with the Discuss It stage, rather than the Develop Background Knowledge stage. This reordering should be done only when the teacher determines that students already have the background knowledge needed, or when the teacher prefers to develop background knowledge after discussing the strategy (or the two can be done in combination).
- Stages can be repeated in multiple lessons (e.g., memorization in LAMPS); note also that stages can be recursive, returned to as necessary when the whole class or individual students need to do so.
- There is much more involved in teaching a more complex strategy such as PARS (e.g., activities, modeling, self-regulation) than there is in a simple strategy such as LAMPS.
- Lesson plans are guides. They are not written in stone. For example, if students quickly memorized strategy steps, memorization activities in later lessons might be curtailed or even skipped.
- Once again, the format we present is only one of many possible ways to prepare SRSD lessons.

LAMPS LESSONS

Lesson 1: Introducing LAMPS

Lesson Overview

The purpose of the first LAMPS lesson is to introduce and describe the strategy, discuss current performance, obtain student commitment to learn and use the strategy, and set an initial performance goal.

Lesson Components	Yes	No
Set context for student learning		
Discussed why it is important to be able to add by hand		
Introduced students to their current performance in adding		
Develop background knowledge		
Addressed why it is good to use strategies		
Acquired "buy-in"		
Introduced steps of the LAMPS strategy		
Discuss LAMPS steps		
Described each step		
Gave examples of how to complete each step		
Memorization		
Worked on memorization		
Allowed students time to practice memorizing		
Obtain commitment		
Encouraged students to use the LAMPS strategy		
Discussed when it would be a good time to use the strategy		
Obtained verbal commitment		
Set a goal		
Discussed why it is important to set goals		
Prompted students to set a goal		
Assisted students in creating realistic goals		
Wrap-up/generalization		
Reminded to practice		
Reminded to memorize		
Teacher behaviors		
Materials ready for each activity		
Instruction delivered with enthusiasm		
Maintained appropriate pace during instruction		
Monitored and checked for understanding		

FIGURE 8.1. LAMPS Lesson 1 checklist.

Student Objectives

The students will commit to learn the LAMPS strategy and establish goals for LAMPS.

Materials

Poster/PowerPoint with LAMP steps (Figure 8.2) and flash cards; for each student provide marker board markers, matching worksheets, and a blank graph (goal chart) (Figure 8.3).

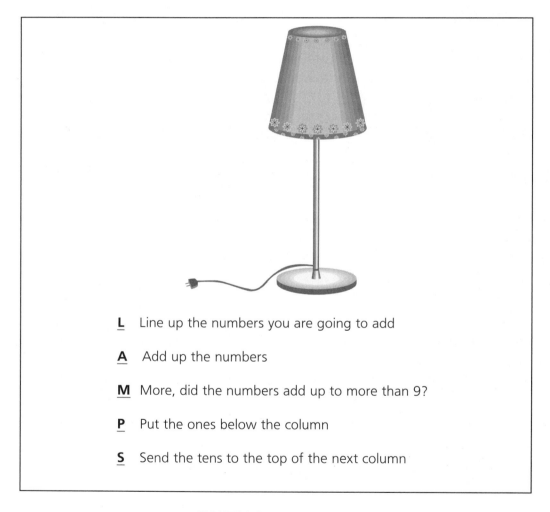

L   Line up the numbers you are going to add

A   Add up the numbers

M   More, did the numbers add up to more than 9?

P   Put the ones below the column

S   Send the tens to the top of the next column

FIGURE 8.2. LAMPS poster.

My Math Goal!

No. of Problems Correct	Baseline	Worksheet 1	Worksheet 2	Worksheet 3	Worksheet 4	Worksheet 5
20						
19						
18						
17						
16						
15						
14						
13						
12						
11						
10						
9						
8						
7						
6						
5						
4						
3						
2						
1						

 Draw a line to show your goal. After you finish your math, color your chart to show your progress.

FIGURE 8.3. LAMPS goal sheet.

SET THE CONTEXT FOR STUDENT LEARNING

At first, the LAMPS strategy and steps should not be displayed.

1. SAY, *"I want to talk with you today about why it's important to add numbers by hand."* Discuss why it is important to be able to add by hand. Solicit specific instances when it is important to add without the use of a calculator. Ask for examples (e.g., for a test or quiz, doing homework, grocery store).

2. SAY, *"I am concerned that you may have a problem adding numbers by hand."* Hand out graph of last assignment (quiz) or other sources. Discuss the results and consequences (e.g., low grades on assignments or tests).

3. SAY, *"How many of you are happy with how well you can add numbers by hand? How many of you would like to do better? Today I am going to teach you about a strategy to help you add numbers by hand, including numbers with decimals. This strategy has been used with lots of kids just like you, and it really helped them get much better at adding numbers."*

The teacher begins by "selling" the importance of math and adding numbers by hand.

Note: These lessons begin with components from Stage 2 of the SRSD model: student buy-in and why math is important. Stage 1 (develop background knowledge) could be assessed before teaching LAMPS (e.g., determine whether students have the necessary skills to use LAMPS) or discussed after students "buy in" to the strategy.

DEVELOP THE STRATEGY AND SELF-REGULATION

Step 1: Develop Background Knowledge

1. SAY, *"The strategy is called LAMPS. Each letter stands for a different step we will take when adding up complicated numbers. It's easy to remember because when you get confused or feel like you are <u>in the dark</u>, all you have to do is turn on the LAMPS!"* Show the LAMPS poster.

2. Put out the mnemonic chart/poster so that only the heading "LAMPS" shows. Uncover each step of the strategy as you introduce and discuss it.

Material scaffolding (i.e., poster with strategy steps).

SAY, *"It's important for you to learn the steps really well. It will help you use the strategy more effectively and that will help you remember what you read. There are five steps to the LAMPS strategy. If you use the LAMPS strategy, it will make it much easier to add!"*

Step 2: Discuss LAMPS Steps

1. *Line up the numbers you are going to add.*
   SAY, *"The first step in LAMPS is to look at the problem and line up the numbers so all the same-place values are on top of each other, and all the decimal points are on top of each other. We have to be careful to do that or we won't get the correct answer. So let's look at a quick*

Note: The teacher explains the steps in detail, but this is not modeling.

example. If I had the problem '12 + 18,' I would want to start by lining up the numbers, which means I should stack these two numbers so that one number is on top of the other. Doing this makes it easier to add the numbers. When I line up the numbers, I am also going to look to see if there are any decimal points—and in this problem there are not. So, I should line up the numbers like this":

The teacher includes metacognitive knowledge for each step.

$$\begin{array}{r} 12 \\ +18 \\ \hline \end{array}$$

2. *Add up the numbers.*

   SAY, *"When you are done lining up the numbers, you <u>a</u>dd up the numbers. You start with the farthest right column of numbers. It's important to remember that you start on the right because it is the opposite of reading where you start on the left. If we look at our sample problem, starting on the right means that we would add <u>2</u> and <u>8</u> first because they are in the right-hand column (the 1's column)."*

3. *More—did the numbers add up to more than 9?*

   SAY, *"Next, you need to ask yourself, did the numbers add up to <u>m</u>ore than 9? If the farthest right-hand column of numbers adds up to more than 9, then go to the next step, <u>P</u>. If the numbers don't add up to more than 9, you write down the number and then move to the next column and start back over with <u>AMPS</u>. We don't have to do the <u>L</u> step again because the problem is already lined up. Let's look at our sample problem again. If we add our right-hand column, 2 plus 8 is 10. Is that more than 9? Yes. So that means we can go to the next step in LAMPS, <u>P</u>."*

4. *Put the 1's below the column.*

   SAY, *"If the number is more than 9, we need to put the 1's below the column we just added. We got 10 when we added our 1's column, so I am going to write 0 below the 8 and 2 because I remember that the number 10 means that there is 1 ten and 0 ones."*

$$\begin{array}{r} 12 \\ +18 \\ \hline 0 \end{array}$$

5. *Send the 10's to the top of the next column.*

   SAY, *"After you place the 1's below the column. You <u>s</u>end the 10's to the top of the next column by writing it on top of the next column. That means I have to take my 1 from my 10 and put it on top of the other two 1's in the problem:*

$$\begin{array}{r} 1 \\ 12 \\ +18 \\ \hline 0 \end{array}$$

Once you finish, LAMPS for the farthest right-hand column, you start on the next column of numbers and begin again with AMPS until there are no more columns to add! I can see that this is my last column, so I'm almost done. So, if I use my A step again, I need to add up the numbers in this column. And I get 3 when I add 1, 1, and 1. Then the M step means I ask 'more than 9?'—and I know that 3 is less than 9. So I can go to my P step, which tells me to put the number below the column—so I will write 3. And I'm done!"

```
    1
   12
 +18
   30
```

Step 3: Review and Making Flash Cards

1. SAY, *"That's it! That's all it is; five easy steps that will make it so much easier for you to add complicated numbers by hand. Let's review. Who can tell me what the L stands for in LAMPS?"* Wait for 50% of hands to be raised and then call on a student. Continue this process for the rest of the letters.

2. SAY, *"Excellent job, everybody! You are on the right track to knowing LAMPS by heart. Now, can I have a volunteer to please hand out five note cards to each student?"* While the note cards are being handed out, explain that students will be making flash cards. Discuss how flash cards are a great tool to help memorize terms and facts.

   Creating flash cards will help students commit strategy steps to memory.

3. SAY, *"We are all going to make out own set of flash cards, but we're going to do it together as a group. On your first note card write the first letter in LAMPS. Once you are done, hold up your note card for me to see."* Wait for students to write and hold up their cards.

4. SAY, *"Great! Now on the backside of that card, write what L stands for and then hold it up for me to see."* Continue this pattern for all of LAMPS. Check for student understanding. Make sure that students have the correct definition for each step.

Step 4: Practice Memorizing

1. SAY, *"I would like everybody to take their flash cards with them and find a partner. With your partner I want you to quiz each other on the steps in LAMPS."*

2. SAY, *"One person should hold up the letter side of the card and the other person will say the definition of that letter. Once you have gone through all the flash cards, switch jobs so that the other person is being quizzed. You should try to quiz each other at least twice."* Monitor students while they practice. Do not offer help unless a student(s) asks for it. Once students are done, give them a matching worksheet.

Step 5: Obtaining Commitment

1. SAY, *"Now that we've practiced memorizing our LAMPS strategy, I want your commitment to learn and use the strategy. I want you to try using the LAMPS strategy because it can help you add numbers by hand. If you learn the strategy and use it, you will start getting better grades on your assignments and quizzes or tests."*

2. SAY, *"The LAMPS strategy works, but it's going to require some effort and practice on your part. I will work with you and help you learn the strategy, but I need you to promise to learn the strategy and try your hardest."* Obtain students' commitment.

> *Note: Stage 4 (memorization) came before obtaining student commitment, which is part of Stage 2. Note also that the memorization activities will occur multiple times throughout these lessons.*
>
> *Attribute success to effort and use of strategy.*

Step 6: Set a Goal

1. Show graph (Figure 8.3). SAY, *"Each time we work problems using the LAMPS strategy, we will graph the results. This will show you how much better you are getting at solving math problems by hand. Let's set a goal for our next practice."* Discuss why goal setting is important and the reasons/situations for which we might set goals.

2. SAY, *"Look at your last score from your worksheet and decide what you want your goal to be. Then draw a line on the graph to show what your first goal will be."* Help students set realistic goals that are not too high and can easily be met with effort. Be sure all students are setting goals and writing their goals on the goal chart. It may be appropriate for the teacher to give an example of an appropriate goal (e.g., "somewhere between _____ and _____."). SAY, *"OK, I see a lot of very good goals, and if you use the LAMPS strategy, you are more likely to meet your goals. You might even go higher than your goal on the first day!"*

> *Goal setting, a self-regulation strategy, is a powerful way to motivate students to use the LAMPS strategy.*

Step 7: Wrap-Up

SAY, *"For next time, I want you to be thinking about some situations in which you might use the LAMPS strategy. Think about the steps I taught you and how you can use the strategy. Tomorrow I am going to ask you for some situations in which you might use the strategy. Also, I am going to quiz you on the steps of LAMPS. I want you to be able to tell me the steps of LAMPS and what you do at each step."*

> *Asking students to think of situations in which to use the strategy helps them to generalize the strategy to other settings.*

Lesson 2: Modeling LAMPS

Lesson Overview

In this lesson the teacher and students discuss the strategy, the teacher models its use, and students continue to work on memorizing the strategy.

Student Objectives

Students will be able to line up numbers and supporting decimals. Students will be able to state the steps of LAMPS and the actions at each step.

Materials

Poster board, markers of different colors; for each student provide worksheets with 20 addition problems and a goal chart.

SET THE CONTEXT FOR STUDENT LEARNING

1. SAY, *"Who remembers the name of the trick we learned yesterday to help us add large numbers with decimals? (Wait for 50% of hands and call on a student.) Yes, it was called LAMPS. At the end of class yesterday you all worked so hard to memorize the steps of LAMPS. I don't know about you, but I even have a hard time remembering all the steps from day to day."*

2. SAY, *"What we're going to do this morning to review as a class is to make a poster that we can hang up in the room to remind us of the steps. Someone, tell me again the name of our trick."* As a class, make a LAMPS poster. See Figure 8.2 for an example.

Making a poster as a class is material scaffolding and it assists with memorization.

DEVELOP THE STRATEGY AND SELF-REGULATION

Step 1: Think-Aloud: Model Use of LAMPS and Thought Process

1. Write the problem on the board: 7.0 + 13.8 + 21.6 + 3.0

2. SAY, *"Now I want to show you how I use the LAMPS strategy. I am going to use the strategy on the math problem I have written on the board and then I am going to ask you to try using the strategy."* Start by using some self-statements such as *"Wow, math always makes me nervous—but that's OK. I have my LAMPS strategy!"*

3. SAY, *"LAMPS will help me set up my problem correctly and help me remember each step. Now what did L stand for again? L . . . L . . . oh, yeah, line! I have to line up the numbers so all the decimal points are on top of each other. OK, I can do that, that's easy."* Write the numbers in a vertical setup on the board.

   $$7.0$$
   $$13.8$$
   $$21.6$$
   $$\underline{3.0}$$

4. SAY, *"Hey, when I line up the decimals, all the place values are on top of each other. All the 1's are in a column, all the 10's are too, and so are the 10ths and 100ths. That's nice; it looks so neat and tidy now. This will make sure that I am adding the right numbers together because*

Plan which math problem(s) will be modeled during the think-aloud.

Notice the different types of self-statements: problem definition, approaching task, and coping.

all the place values are lined up with each other. OK, focus. I'm adding numbers and I lined them up. That was L.

5. SAY, *"So that means I have to do <u>A</u> next because it's the next letter in LAMPS. <u>A</u> is easy because it stands for <u>a</u>dd, which is what we're doing—how convenient! Do I start on the right or left column? Oh, I remember, I start with the right-hand column because it's the opposite of when you read. OK, so 8 and 6 are the only numbers in the far right column, and they equal 14 when you add them together. Man, that's so easy, a second grader could do that."*

6. SAY, *"Now I'm on a roll, so let's keep going. What's next? LAMPS, L-A-... <u>M</u>! What was <u>M</u> again? I remember it had something to do with 9. Hmmm ... oh, yeah—<u>m</u>ore than 9. If it's more than 9, I have to keep going. 14 is more than 9, so I guess I have to keep going."*

Reinforcing self-statements.

7. SAY, *"OK, I need to focus so I will get all the steps in LAMPS. I just did <u>M</u> for <u>m</u>ore, so there's only two steps left. I can do this. Now I have 14, but I can't write it down as my answer yet. If I don't write it down soon, I'm going to forget it and have to start all over. OK, L ... A ... M ... <u>P</u>—put! Because I have this sum of 14 floating around, I have to put the 4 from 14 below the column because it's in the 1's column of 14. I have to remember to put only one number down in the answer place for each column. Each column can only have a one-number answer below it. Yes! But wait, I have the 1 left still. What do I do with it, just throw it out? No, that can't be it because I still have one step left: S."*

The teacher might model a particular step or process that he or she knows students struggle with. In this case, knowing how to carry when adding might be an issue for students in the class.

8. SAY, *"Awesome, I'm already on the last step—that wasn't so hard. But I'm not done yet, just keep going, finish it out. <u>S</u> ... OK, well I've already put something below, so now I have to <u>s</u>end the 1 to the top to even it out. Put one number below, send the 1 to the top. All right, so now I have the 1 on top of the next column over. Sweet, that was LAMPS! That trick was pretty easy. And now I've got it down, so it's going to be easy to finish out this problem."*

9. SAY, *"Now I start back at <u>A</u> in LAMPS, so it's <u>AMPS</u> with the second column. <u>A</u> stands for <u>a</u>dd—this is too easy. I have to add the second column now: 7 + 3 + 3—and oh, yeah, I can't forget the 1 that I sent to the top. So that equals 14 again. I just did <u>A</u> so <u>M</u> is next. <u>M</u> is for <u>m</u>ore than 9. 14 is more than 9, so I have to keep going. I've added and now have this number and I have to write it down before I forget. Oh, shoot, what was next? Uhhh, I know ... it starts with a <u>P</u>, but what was the trick? Oh, duh, it was <u>p</u>ut the 1's below and move the 10's to the top! But don't get ahead of yourself now, just do <u>P</u>. I put the 4 from the 1's place below, and I send the 1 from the 10's place to the top—that's the <u>S</u>. Sweet, so my answer so far is 4.4."*

Modeling confusion and/or frustration during the think-aloud can help students see that it's not the end of the world if they get confused.

10. SAY, *"One column left. I can see home base—I'm doing great! I finished AMPS with the second column, so now I start again with AMPS on the third column. <u>A</u>—<u>a</u>dd. I love this step; it's so quick and easy. 1 + 2 + the 1 I sent up from the last column. Easy! That equals 4. AMPS: so <u>M</u> is next. Is it more than 9? Nope it's not, so I'm done! All I have to do is write down the 4 below the column. My answer is 44.4. Yay! I did it without a calculator! Thank you, LAMPS!"*

Step 2: Review

After the students have watched the teacher model the strategy for a few problems, he or she should involve the students by reviewing the modeled problems.

1. SAY, *"See how useful LAMPS can be! All right, let's go back through the same problem I just worked with all of you as a class. What do I do first with LAMPS?"* Wait for 50% of hands and call on a student. Students should be very accurate at this point. If errors occur, stop and review the steps in LAMPS. *"Right! We line up the numbers using the decimal points."*

2. SAY, *"What's next?"* Wait for hands. *"Yes, we add the right-hand column."* While going through the steps, point to the problem you worked on the board, emphasizing each step.

3. SAY, *"Next is M. What did I do at that step?"* Wait for hands. *"Remember, M means you ask yourself, more than 9? 8 + 6 equals 14, so you're right—that is more than 9 so we move to the next step. Someone explain to me what I did next."* Wait for hands. *"I put the 4 below the column, not above. Remember, the 1's place goes below the column. What did I do next?"* Wait for hands. *"Good! I sent the 1 to the top of the next column. Good work, class!"*

Step 3: Guided Practice and Monitoring

1. SAY, *"Now that you have seen me use the LAMPS strategy, it's your turn to try using it. Let's work on some problems together on the board."*

2. Write a two-digit by two-digit addition problem on the board horizontally. Call on a student and have him or her come to the board.

3. SAY, *"What should we do first?"* The student should be able to give the step and write the problem in a vertical format. Go through each of the steps in LAMPS. Call on different students for each step. If a student is confused, allow the other students to help or provide the answer and briefly reteach the step.

Note: Transfer of strategy ownership (Stage 5) should begin after the think-aloud.

This is task scaffolding.

INDEPENDENT PRACTICE

1. SAY, *"Great job, class! Now I want to see how well you can use the strategy on your own. I am going to hand out a worksheet with five problems on it."* Ask for volunteers to hand out the worksheet.

2. SAY, *"You will see that I have already completed four of the math problems for you! But, I may have made some mistakes. I want you to look at my answers and circle the problems that I answered correctly. If you get stuck, you can look at the poster we made for a hint."*

3. SAY, *"For an extra challenge, solve the fifth problem on your own!"*

This is content and task scaffolding. The students only need to complete one problem on their own—as students practice the strategy, they will complete more problems on their own.

4. Walk around the room, checking to see that students are using/checking the strategy steps. Do not help students unless they ask for it.

5. Once all students have completed the worksheet, go over the questions as a class.

WRAP-UP

SAY, *"Today we spent some time practicing the LAMPS strategy that will help us do better in math. Tonight, I want you to be thinking about some situations in which you might use the LAMPS strategy and I want you to think about the goal you set yesterday. Tomorrow we are going to see if we met our goals!"*

Lesson 3: Guided Practice

Lesson Overview

The purpose of this lesson is to provide guided practice for students and for the teacher to begin transfer of strategy ownership by gradually lessening support.

Student Objectives

The students will use LAMPS on two-digit math problems with teacher support.

Materials

Flash cards; for each student provide worksheet, graphs, marker boards, markers.

SET THE CONTEXT FOR STUDENT LEARNING

1. SAY, *"Hello, everybody! Have you been thinking about LAMPS all night? I sure have. You did great on your worksheets yesterday— I'm very impressed. Has anyone been quizzing themselves with their flash cards? We are all going to play a game using them as a warm-up today; this will get our minds focused on LAMPS again. I am going to split the class into two groups. Once I am done, I want group 1 students to bring their chairs and set them up in a circle on this side of the classroom. Group 2, do the same on the other side of the classroom."*

   Beginning each lesson with a quick memorization activity is an easy way to ensure that students are working toward memorizing the strategy.

2. The groups should be split up based on grades from the worksheets from the previous lesson. The higher grades will all in one group and the lower grades in the other. This will ensure that all students will benefit from this activity and that a few students aren't continually winning.

3. SAY, *"Now that we're all set up, we're going to play Around the World with our flash cards."* Designate one student from each group to grab his or her flash cards.

4. A student in the higher grade group will be told that he or she is going to be the facilitator of the game for that group. This student will be the one with the highest grade on the worksheet from yesterday. The teacher is the facilitator of the lower-grade group. Designate one student from each group to begin standing behind the chairs. Play Around the World for approximately 5 minutes.

SUPPORT THE STRATEGY AND SELF-REGULATION

Step 1: Guided Practice

1. SAY, *"Today I am going to give you a worksheet with 20 math problems. I want you to use your LAMPS strategy to solve all of the problems. While you are working on this worksheet, I want you to be thinking about the goal that you set a few days ago."*

2. SAY, *"Everyone should take out your graphs and look to see what your goal is. If you use the LAMPS strategy on every math problem, you will get more problems right and you will be closer to your goal— you might even do better than your goal!"*

3. Hand out the worksheet. Walk around the room and guide students through strategy use as needed. It is best to intervene only if students are struggling.

4. As students finish, check their work and show them how to graph their performance.

5. Ask students if they met their goals. Praise them and remind them that using the LAMPS strategy will make them better at math and help them to continue meeting their goals.

6. Students who exceeded their goals can set new goals. You may want to check on students who did not meet their goals to make sure the goals they set were realistic; help them to lower their goals if necessary.

Step 2: Modeling and Generalization

1. SAY, *"Yesterday and today we've been practicing adding numbers with only two digits—and many of you already saw how much LAMPS can help you because you met your goals! Today we are going to add numbers with three or four digits. LAMPS can help us add larger numbers, and it will be just as easy as adding smaller numbers. LAMPS helps us organize our numbers and then walks us through each step. So as long as we follow the steps, we'll be fine."*

2. SAY, *"Let's start with just two numbers with three digits each: 10.5 + 27.9."*

3. Write the numbers on the board. As you work through this

Student performance on this worksheet will be used to monitor progress toward the goals set in Lesson 1.

Remember: A good goal is specific, proximal, and challenging.

This is task scaffolding and generalization. The teacher is helping students to generalize the LAMPS strategy to larger numbers.

problem, continue to show your work on the board so everyone can see. Prompt students to suggest each step of the strategy (e.g., *"What's the first step? What's next?"*)

4. After completing the strategy once (i.e., the first right-hand column), spend a little time discussing what comes next. SAY, *"We made it all the way through LAMPS for the first column. We have to start back over for the next column—but, remember, we start at A instead of L. A for add up the numbers is where we will start for the next column."*

5. Continue on through the problem. SAY, *"We are going to add 1 + 0 + 7. Remember, we always have to add the numbers we move to the top of the column, so don't forget about it once you send it to the top. 1 + 0 + 7 equals 8. That was A for add, so now we move to the next step, M. What do we ask ourselves? We ask ourselves, more than 9? 8 is not more than 9, so do not go on with the rest of the steps in LAMPS. This is because we do not have a number to send to the top of the next column. 8 is only a one-digit number, you see. So all we do with the 8 is put it below the sum line."*

The teacher briefly models a problem.

6. SAY, *"Our answer so far is 8.4, but we're not done yet; we still have one more column to add. Where do we start at now? We don't start at L because we already have our numbers lined up. We start at A again. Remember, after the first column one we always start at A—A for add—so in our final column we are adding 1 + 2, which equals 3. What do we ask ourselves next? We ask ourselves, more than 9? Is 3 more than 9? No, it is not, so we do not have to continue with the rest of our steps. We just place 3 below the sum line and we are done because we have no more columns to add. Our answer is 38.4. Good work, everybody, we just used LAMPS to help us add three-digit numbers!"*

Step 3: Guided Practice

1. SAY, *"Now I want us to practice using LAMPS on larger numbers because tomorrow we will try to meet our goals again. Practicing our strategy will make us better at math and more likely to meet our goals!"*

After the teacher models how to use LAMPS on larger numbers, students should practice as soon as possible, while the modeling is still fresh in their minds.

2. Pass out marker boards and markers to each student (or small groups of students).

3. SAY, *"I want you all to add these numbers: 54.98 + 643.1. I want you all to do the L step of LAMPS and hold up your board when you are done."* If students are correct, praise them. If they are incorrect, ask them to try again. If they still get it wrong the second time, model it for them. *"Excellent, everyone was able to line the numbers up by the decimals. Now, everybody do the A step of LAMPS."* Continue with this process all the way through the problem. Make sure to keep complimenting, correcting, and modeling as needed. Repeat with several problems. The problems should have multiple digits and decimal places.

Note that the complexity was increased.

Here the two addends have a different number of decimal places.

WRAP-UP

SAY, *"Today we spent more time practicing the LAMPS strategy that will help us do better in math. Tonight, I want you to be thinking about some situations in which you might use the LAMPS strategy and I want you to think about your goals. Tomorrow I am going to challenge you with all different types of addition problems—some with only two digits and some with four digits! I bet if you practice and use your LAMPS strategy, you will continue to meet your goals!"*

Lesson 4: Independent Practice

Lesson Overview

The teacher provides the students with independent practice in using LAMPS.

Student Objective

The students will use LAMPS independently.

Materials

Small ball, sales flyer from a local business; for each student provide worksheet and graphs.

SET THE CONTEXT FOR STUDENT LEARNING

1. SAY, *"Good morning, class! Has anyone been reminded of our LAMPS trick when they've turned on a light at home? I sure have—I started whispering the steps to myself last night when I turned on my reading lamp! To start today, we are going to play a little game to review the steps of LAMPS. Everybody stand in a circle over in our reading area."* As students move around the room, grab the ball from your desk. *"We are going to softly toss this ball around the circle. When you catch the ball, you have to say the next step in LAMPS or what it stands for. You can't toss the ball to someone who has already had it. Toss it to a new person. Ready, I'll start. The first step in LAMPS is L for line."*

   This lesson begins with another memorization activity (Stage 4).

2. Toss the ball to a student. Hopefully, he or she will say that L means to line up all the decimals points. If the student does not say this, prompt him or her toward the right answer. After you have gone through the strategy once, time students the second time and on the third time, motivate them to beat their previous time. Make sure that all the students get the ball at least twice.

GUIDED PRACTICE AND GENERALIZATION

This is task and content scaffolding and generalization.

1. SAY, *"We've been using LAMPS the last couple days to help us add large numbers with decimals points. But we don't only add large numbers at school or on worksheets. When you buy items at a store, their prices have three or more numbers, and they always have decimals points! If you only have so much money you can spend, you need to add up your purchases so you don't spend more than you have. I bet LAMPS can help us with that!"* Turn the Elmo on, projecting it on the board, and place a grocery store ad on the Elmo.

2. SAY, *"I need to choose five items from this ad to buy. The only problem is, I only have $25 to spend. Can I have five volunteers to come up and circle items for us to buy?"* Call on five students and have each circle an item.

3. SAY, *"Interesting choices! So now we need to add all these prices up and see if we are under $25."*

4. Write down all your work for the students to see. However, have the students walk *you* through the steps. Prompt for each step. SAY, *"What do I do first when using the LAMPS strategy?"* or, *"Now that I have put a number below the sum line, that is a cue for me to do what?"* Check for understanding by having the students walk you through the problem by using the strategy.

5. Once you have gone through all the steps and have your answer, SAY *"Good work, you guys made that look like a breeze, you told me all the right steps to do. Now we have our answer. Did we stay under $25?"* If it is under $25, congratulate the students on being frugal. If you are over $25, tell the students, *"We'll have to switch out some items so that we do stay under our budget."* Once the items to be removed are selected, have the students walk you through LAMPS again.

SUPPORT THE STRATEGY AND SELF-REGULATION

Note that, again, the difficultly level is increased gradually. Results from this worksheet will be used to graph progress toward goals.

1. SAY, *"Now that we have spent some time getting better at using our LAMPS strategy in other situations, today I have another worksheet with 20 math problems on it. This time you will notice that it's not just two-digit math problems. This time there are two-, three-, and four-digit problems all mixed up. Your job is to use your LAMPS strategy to solve all these math problems and meet your goal."*

2. Have students take out their goal sheets and remind themselves of their goal.

3. Pass out worksheets and walk around the room. Assist and intervene only if students are struggling.

4. As students finish, have them check their work (or allow a peer to check their work) and graph the results.

5. Ask students if they met their goals. Praise them and remind them that using the LAMPS strategy will make them better at math and help them to continue meeting their goals. Students who exceeded their goals can set new ones.

WRAP-UP

SAY, *"Can somebody raise your hand and tell me why LAMPS is an important strategy to know?"* Call on students and make sure they state these points: organization, less mistakes, and don't forget steps. *"Good job. When else will we use LAMPS other than when we're in math class?"* Call on students and look for answers such as planning budgets for trips, balancing checkbooks, when adding scores to figure out your average, etc. *"Those are all great examples. We can use LAMPS with lots of things in life. So remember, if you ever feel in the dark when adding, just remember to turn on the LAMPS!"*

The teacher is helping students with some of the metacognitive knowledge important to using strategies—specifically, why and where to use the LAMPS strategy.

Note: This lesson can be repeated until students have the strategy memorized and can successfully use the LAMPS strategy to solve multiple types of problems (e.g., two-digit, four-digit) on their own. After teaching the strategy once, it may be helpful to create a checklist to follow. See Figure 8.1 for an example of a checklist.

PARS LESSONS

Lesson 1: Introducing PARS

Lesson Overview

The purpose of the first lesson is to introduce and describe the strategy, discuss current performance, obtain student(s) commitment to learn the strategy, and set performance goals.

Student Objectives

The students will commit to learn the PARS strategy, set goals for using PARS, and work on memorizing the strategy.

Materials

Poster/presentation with PARS steps (Figure 8.4), previous quizzes/tests for each student, blank graph (Figure 8.5).

Preview	Preview the material to identify main ideas by scanning the chapter/passage and surveying: • The title • The introductory statement • Headings • Graphic aids • Chapter summary
Ask	Ask questions that relate to the main ideas discovered when surveying the chapter.
Read	Read the chapter to answer the questions developed.
Summarize	Summarize the main ideas in the chapter.

FIGURE 8.4. PARS poster.

SET THE CONTEXT FOR STUDENT LEARNING

1. SAY, *"Today we are going to talk about reading your textbooks and understanding what you read. The first thing I want to do is come up with situations where it is important for you to read and understand information in a textbook. Let's do a little brainstorming. I am going to write our ideas on the board as we go. Does anyone have an idea of a time when it would be important to read and understand your textbooks?"*

   • Studying for tests

2. SAY, *"Great! This is a perfect example of when it is really important for us to read our textbooks and understand what we're reading. Why is that important? Because the better you understand what you're reading, the better you will remember it, and the better you will do on tests! When else is it important to understand texts?"*

   • Quizzes, completing assignments, to gain information, to be able to get homework done more quickly so you can do something fun, making an informed decision

3. SAY, *"These are all great ideas of when it is important for you to read and understand your textbooks. I think two very important times to understand what you are reading is when you're reading for tests and*

Note: These lessons begin with Stage 2 of the SRSD model: "selling" the strategy and why it is important to understand what you read.

Prerequisite knowledge for using the PARS strategy includes the ability to read independently and fluently, a basic understanding of different types of text (e.g., textbooks vs. novels) and the structures of textbooks (e.g., headings, graphics).

How much can I remember?

Goal								
10								
9								
8								
7								
6								
5								
4								
3								
2								
1								
	Baseline	Quiz 2	Quiz 3	Quiz 4	Quiz 5	Quiz 6	Quiz 7	Quiz 8

Write your goal at the top. Draw a line to show your goal.

After you read, fill in your chart to show how much you remembered.

FIGURE 8.5. PARS goal sheet.

quizzes. You all want to do well on the tests and quizzes you take, right? Well, you know what? I have a simple trick, called PARS, that will help you read and better understand what you are reading, and that will help you remember what you read too!"

DEVELOP THE STRATEGY AND SELF-REGULATION

Step 1: Discuss PARS Steps

1. Put out the mnemonic chart/poster so that only PARS shows. Uncover each step of the strategy as you discuss it. See Figure 8.4 for an example of a chart/poster.

2. SAY, *"Each of the letters in PARS stands for something you do to help you to remember what you read."*

3. Preview the chapter. SAY, *"The P in PARS stands for preview the chapter, which is the first step you will do when you are using this strategy. You will preview the chapter to identify main ideas by scanning it and reading some of the main points in the chapter, such as the title, introductory statement, any headings, looking at some of the graphics (e.g., tables, graphs, pictures), and reading the chapter summary at the end of the chapter. Then you will identify the main ideas of the chapter from what you previewed. Doing this is going to help you access any information you already know about the topic and get you ready to learn more!"*

   Teachers can supply metacognitive information on the strategy at any stage. Here the teacher provides it in several places while discussing the strategy.

4. Ask. SAY, *"The second step in PARS is the A, which stands for ask. You're going to ask questions related to the chapter's main ideas, which you discovered when you were previewing. You might want to ask general questions about the main idea—for example, you could ask 'What new information will I learn about bugs?'—or you might want to ask specific questions related to the headings you read or the pictures you saw. Asking questions before you read will help guide your reading and organize any new information you learn."*

   Again, the teacher provides metacognitive information about the strategy.

5. Read the chapter. SAY, *"The third step in PARS is the R, which stands for read the chapter. While you are reading the chapter, you are going to be looking for the answers to the questions you asked about the main ideas in the chapter. In some cases you might want to write down your answers or take notes."*

6. Summarize. SAY, *"And the last step in PARS is the S, which stands for summarize. After reading the chapter and answering all your questions about the main ideas, you will summarize the main ideas in a few sentences. When you summarize, you should say the main ideas in your own words. This is a way to make sure you truly understood what you read, and it also helps you to remember what you read!"*

   Following the explanation for each step of the strategy, the teacher provides metacognitive information (e.g., why the step is helpful).

Step 2: Obtaining Commitment

1. SAY, *"So that is how PARS works, and we're going to learn even more about it so you can do really well on your quizzes and tests. If you work really hard and use this strategy, you will improve your scores. Right now, I want to look at some of your old quizzes, so that you can see how you have been doing before using PARS. I'm going to give each of you a blank graph. Then I'm going to give you your old quizzes, and you're going to graph your scores so you can see how you have been doing up until now. We're going to learn this awesome trick, PARS, and once you start using PARS, you're going to graph your new scores next to your old scores to show how much you have improved!"*

2. Hand out graphs and previous quizzes.

Showing current performance and establishing a need for improvement is a great way to "sell" the strategy and gain student commitment. Note that the teacher attributes success to effort and use of the strategy.

Step 3: Set a Goal

1. Hold up a copy of the graphs. SAY, *"When we practice using PARS, we will graph the results. This will show you how much better you are getting at understanding what you read. Let's set a goal for our next practice."* Discuss why goal setting is important and reasons or places where students might set goals (e.g., gives you something to work toward, can help to motivate you).

2. SAY, *"Look at what your last scores were and decide what you want your goal to be. Then draw a line on the graph to show what your first goal will be."* Help students set realistic goals. Set a goal that is not too high and can be met with effort. Stress that students will be more likely to meet their goals if they work hard and use the PARS strategy.

WRAP-UP

1. SAY, *"For next time, I want you to be thinking about some situations in which you might use the PARS strategy. Think about the steps we discussed and how you can use the strategy on almost anything you read—especially on textbooks. Tomorrow I will ask you if you thought of some more situations you could use the PARS strategy."*

2. SAY, *"Tomorrow I will also quiz you on the PARS strategy. Your assignment for tonight is to learn the steps in PARS and be ready for the quiz tomorrow. I want you to be able to tell me the steps in PARS and what you do at each step."*

Lesson 2: Modeling PARS

Lesson Overview

In this lesson the teacher and students will discuss the strategy. The teacher will model strategy use, and students will begin to memorize the strategy.

Student Objectives

Students will be able to state the steps of PARS and the actions performed at each step.

Materials

For each student provide reading passage, graph, self-monitoring checklist (Figure 8.6), self-statement worksheet (Figure 8.7).

☐ Preview	Preview the material to identify main ideas by scanning the chapter/passage and surveying: ☐ The title ☐ The introductory statement ☐ Headings ☐ Graphics ☐ Chapter summary ☐ Highlight, use stickies, or write the main ideas.
☐ Ask	☐ Use the main ideas identified to ask questions. ☐ Questions use *who, what, when, where, why.* ☐ Write down the questions.
☐ Read	☐ Read the chapter to answer the questions developed. ☐ Check to see if all your questions were answered.
☐ Summarize	☐ Summarize the main ideas in the chapter. ☐ Write or say your summary in your own words.

FIGURE 8.6. PARS checklist.

My Self-Statements

Here are some things I can say to myself *before* I read:

_____

_____

_____

_____

Here are some things I can say to myself *while* I read:

_____

_____

_____

_____

Here are some things I can say to myself *after* I read:

_____

_____

_____

_____

FIGURE 8.7. PARS self-statements.

SET THE CONTEXT FOR STUDENT LEARNING

1. SAY, *"Yesterday I taught you about a trick to help you understand more of what you read. Who can tell me the name of the strategy?"* Pause for responses. *"Yes! PARS! Now who can tell me the steps of that strategy?"* Pause for responses. *"Wow, you all remembered most of the steps of the strategy and it's only the second day! Tomorrow I am going to ask you to write the steps of the strategy from memory."*

2. SAY, *"Today, we are going to practice using the strategy. But first, did you think of some situations in which you could use the strategy?"* Solicit responses and add some of your own as appropriate (e.g., social studies textbook, reading for homework).

3. SAY, *"There are lots of places you could try using the PARS strategy. I'm noticing that almost anything I read to understand, I can try the PARS strategy!"*

After Lesson 1, each PARS lesson begins with Stage 4, memorization.

DEVELOP THE STRATEGY AND SELF-REGULATION

Step 1: Discuss Previewing Text and Asking Questions (Prerequisite for Strategy Use)

1. SAY, *"One really important step in PARS is previewing a chapter or section before we read it to find the main ideas and asking questions about those main ideas."*

2. Discuss why it's important to spend time predicting and previewing text (e.g., predictions help students think about what they already know about a topic and access this prior knowledge; previewing can help to create a "map" of what information will be included in a chapter). Discuss text elements that are helpful in previewing (e.g., chapter title, headings, pictures, tables, charts).

3. Give students 5 minutes to do a quick activity with text elements. First, organize students into small groups or pairs. Give each group or pair a stack of sticky notes or page markers (e.g., sticky flags), preferably with several colors. Hand out a short chapter or use a current textbook (e.g., social studies). Ask students to identify different text elements by sticking notes on different pages. For example, headings could be pink, graphics/tables could be green, and chapter summaries could be yellow. After 5 minutes, go through the text as a class.

4. Then discuss prediction questions that could be generated based on previewed text.

   - Questions should start with words such as *who, what, when, where, why, how.* These words make it easier to generate questions and help to focus student attention on important information in a chapter (e.g., important people, dates).

   - Provide sample questions—for example: *"What might this chapter tell me about animal cells? Why is it important to learn about animal cells?"*

   - Make sure students understand that predicting and generating questions should be "educated guesses" based on information previewed (e.g., questions should relate directly to possible information in text). However, the teacher should also note that not every question generated can be answered in a passage/chapter. Using the text elements to generate good questions can increase the likelihood that the question can be answered.

5. Have students get back into their groups or pairs. Ask groups to go back through the text and generate questions using the post-it notes as a guide. For example, if a group put a post-it next to a heading, they should create a question using the

Note: Previewing text and self-questioning is part of Stage 1, background knowledge. In some cases, important prerequisite knowledge can be incorporated into strategy instruction rather than simply assessing for it. For these lessons, the teacher explicitly teaches how to preview text, important text structures, and how to "self-question." Some students may already have this knowledge—in this case, this instruction serves as a critical review.

Note: How and why questions are generally more difficult to answer because answering them requires going beyond literal comprehension and possibly making inferences.

heading. After groups have generated three to five questions, go over questions as a class.

Step 2: Think-Aloud: Model Use of PARS and Thought Process

1. SAY, *"Now I want to show you how to use the PARS strategy. I am going to use the PARS strategy on this chapter from a science text and then I am going to ask you to try using the strategy!"*

2. Introduce the checklist (Figure 8.6). Show the students the self-monitoring checklist that you will use while reading the passage. Tell the students that you will show them how to use the checklist and then ask them to try using the checklist on another passage. Explain that using the checklist will remind them of the steps and also ensure that they don't forget a step in PARS.

3. Start by using self-statements such as *"Ugh—it's time to do my homework. It always takes me so long and I have to reread my textbook over and over to remember what the chapter is about."*

4. SAY, *"I'm going to get started on reading the chapter. Oh man, this chapter is so long, and it looks really hard! Wait, I remember that if I have a chapter in a textbook I need to read, then I should use the trick we learned in class, the PARS strategy, because it will help me to read and understand the information in the chapter, and then I will remember it better for the quiz!"*

5. Begin by stating the first step of the PARS strategy. SAY, *"The first step in PARS is P, which means preview. In this step, I need to preview the chapter by scanning it for the introductory statement, any headings, visuals, pictures, or the chapter summary. Looking over these items in the chapter will help me to figure out the main idea and important details about the main idea. Knowing the main idea of the chapter will help me to understand what I am reading and then I will be more likely to remember it for the quiz and I will hopefully meet my goal! OK! I can do this!*

   "I know when I scan the chapter I just look over the material without actually reading the paragraphs. However, I do want to read some things—such as the introductory statement, headings, and chapter summary—so that I can get an idea of the main ideas before I really read the chapter. OK, I'm going to start by looking at the first page of this chapter . . . I see that there is a title to this chapter. Actually, I think the title of the chapter is important because it gives me a really good idea of what the chapter is going to be about. The title of the chapter is 'Geology.' Under the title, the first sentence, which is sometimes called the introductory statement, says, 'Geology is more than the study of rocks.' I think I will put a sticky note next to that sentence so that I can remember to look at it when I'm figuring out

Note: This scripted think-aloud includes a number of self-statements. These will serve as a basis for introducing self-instructions later in the lesson.

Any chapter, passage, or text could be used to perform the think-aloud for PARS.

The checklist serves as both a self-regulation technique and as scaffolding. During the think-aloud the teacher also models how to use the checklist.

what the main ideas in this chapter are. I could highlight that sentence, but this isn't my book, so it's best to just use sticky notes.

"I'm already feeling pretty good about this—I think the chapter is about geology. The next thing I need to do is look at headings in the chapter. Headings are usually bold and all by themselves—and there can be several headings throughout the chapter, so I need to make sure that I look through the whole chapter. I don't want to miss any because then I might miss something important about the main ideas of the chapter. OK, so I start at the beginning of the chapter and look for bold statements above the paragraphs. The first heading I see is 'History of Geology.' I'm going to put another sticky note by the heading because it will remind me to look back at it when I'm figuring out main ideas. OK, I have to keep going.*

"So now I'm scanning down the page, but there aren't any more headings, so I'm going to keep going. . . . OK, several pages later there is another bold heading. I'll put a sticky note next to the heading, 'Geologic Materials,' as a reminder. I need to keep going through each page until I get to the end of the chapter, and mark each heading in the chapter because they all give me an overview of what the main ideas of the chapter are."

Continue on through the remaining headings of the chapter. Next, model checking off your self-monitoring sheet. SAY, *"I'm going to look at my strategy checklist to make sure I'm doing this right. . . . OK. Well, I can check 'title' because I already previewed that. I can also check 'headings' because I went through the whole chapter and looked at all the headings! Awesome! I am right on track!*

"What else am I supposed to look for when I'm previewing the chapter? Hmmmm. I looked at the title, the first sentence, and the headings. . . . Oh, right, I need to look for tables and graphics! I remember that pictures, charts, or graphs can help me better understand what I'm going to read. Just like I did when I was looking at headings, I'm going to start at the beginning of the chapter and go through each page looking at all the graphics. It's really easy to find the graphic aids because they're not in the paragraphs—they're always off to the side and have something written below them explaining what the picture or graph is. Cool—it looks like there are lots of pictures and a timeline to help me understand geology . . . OK, done with that." Check off your self-monitoring sheet.

SAY, *"But wait, there's one more thing I need to look for when I preview the chapter—the chapter summary. Reading the chapter summary can give me a good idea of what the main ideas of the chapter are. And that's the next thing that I need to do—come up with the main ideas of the chapter based on the information I found previewing the chapter! The main ideas tell me what the chapter is going to be about so I have an idea before I start reading. Having an idea before I start reading helps me better understand when I'm actually reading the chapter. And the better I understand, the better I will remember the information, and the better I will do on my quiz!*

"So, when I'm trying to come up with main ideas about the chapter, I need to make sure they're not too specific because then they would be more like a detail and not a main idea. A main idea should tell me what something is about very generally. How do I think of a main idea? Wait! You know what, as part of the PARS strategy, I'm supposed to use the information I previewed—the introductory statement, headings, graphics, and chapter summary—to come up with the main ideas of the chapter. OK, so I am going to look back at my chapter and find the sticky notes I put in there. The sticky notes make it so easy to find the things I previewed in the chapter—I'm sure glad I used them! OK, I think I know what the main ideas of the chapter are. I am going to write them down so I can remember them. It will be important to remember the main ideas for the next step in PARS. These are the main ideas of the chapter."

6. Write the main ideas for the chapter/passage on the SMART board. Check off that step on the self-monitoring sheet.

7. SAY, *"OK, I think I am finished with the first step in PARS. Wow! I feel like I've already learned a lot and I haven't even read the chapter yet! The second step in PARS is the A, which stands for ask. In this step, I need to ask questions related to the main ideas that I will hopefully be able to answer by reading the chapter. When I ask myself questions about the chapter, I get really interested in finding the answers to my questions, and then I understand what I read better. So, I will create some questions using the main ideas I wrote down. I need to focus—this is really important. It's a good thing I wrote down my main ideas so I can remember them when I'm asking my questions—I knew it would be a good idea to write them down! I think I will write down my questions too because then I can remember the questions I want to answer while I am reading. I am going to come up with a question about each main idea I found because that way I will have questions for more than just one section of the chapter. And, all of the main ideas are important, not just one. I also need to remember the kinds of words you use to ask questions, such as who, what, when, where, why, and how. So, I think these will be my questions for each main idea"*:

8. Use the main ideas from the previous step to create questions. Write the questions down. Check off this step on your self-monitoring sheet.

9. SAY, *"All right, so now I created my questions about the main ideas in this chapter. That really got me thinking about what I might learn, and now I'm really excited to find out the answers to my questions. OK, the next step in PARS is the R, which stands for read. Now I need to read the chapter to try to answer the questions that I asked myself!*

I am going to keep my list of questions right next to my book, so that I can look at my questions as I read. If I forget my questions, then I won't be able to answer them, and I won't understand the information in the chapter as well. It's really important for me to understand the chapter because then I will do well on my quiz and meet my goal. I really want to meet my goal. If I keep at it and use PARS, I know I can do it! I am going to start reading and see if I can answer all of my questions. When I find an answer to a question, I will write down the answer under the question, so I can remember the answer after I get done reading."

Read through the chapter, searching for answers to the questions, and continue to use self-statements throughout. When you've read through the passage, check off this step on your self-monitoring checklist.

SAY, *"Hmmm . . . I found all the answers to my questions except my question about _____. I wonder if I just missed it when I was reading. I think what I'll do is go back and look for a heading about _____, and then I will reread that section to see if I can find the answer. Yep, there it is! It's a good thing I went back to check! I will write that down so I can remember it, and now I'm done with that step of PARS. I found out some really interesting answers to my questions when I was reading that chapter! But, before I move on, I should double-check to make sure all my questions were answered. . . . I did! Great!*

"OK, the last step of PARS is the <u>S</u>, which stands for <u>s</u>ummarize. In this step I write down a summary of the chapter in my own words. I remember that it needs to be in my own words because that will help me understand the information better than if I just copy it down from the chapter summary. And I'm going to try to summarize the chapter without using the book or anything I wrote down. That way, I will have a good idea of whether or not I really understood what the chapter was about. I need to keep in mind all of the really important information when I write my summary, but I remember that it can be pretty general too and it shouldn't be more than a few sentences."

Write a brief summary of the chapter. Check off this step on your self-monitoring sheet.

SAY, *"Now, I'm going to look back at the main ideas I wrote down when I did the first step in PARS to make sure my summary includes all of the main ideas. Yep, it does. Wow, I think I really understood that chapter about geology! I did a great job! The PARS strategy really helped me to understand what I was reading, and then I remembered so much of what I read when I was finished. I know that my hard work and using PARS will help me to do well on the quiz tomorrow because I understood the chapter, and I can remember what I read about!!"*

The teacher would have previously identified some important areas or areas of difficulty (e.g., coping, persisting with the task, staying focused) and developed sample self-statements to use in the think-aloud.

Here the teacher models making a mistake and then going back to fix it.

The teacher continues to include self-statements. In this case, the teacher uses self-reinforcement statements.

Step 3: Reinforce Performance

Review the PARS checklist with students. Answer any questions students may have and check that all steps of the PARS strategy were performed (and checked off on the self-monitoring checklist, Figure 8.6).

Step 4: Develop Self-Instructions

1. Give each student a blank copy of the self-instruction worksheet (Figure 8.7). Explain that they will use the worksheet to write things that they can say to themselves when reading and using PARS. Discuss the self-statements the teacher used while modeling (e.g., what was said, when self-statements were used, how self-statements helped).

   Self-statements can help to keep students motivated while using a strategy or help students deal with confusion or frustration.

2. As a class, brainstorm some self-statements that could be used before reading, during reading, and after reading.

3. Have students independently write one or two statements that they could say to themselves when reading a passage. Tell the students that these are statements they can say to themselves, inside their heads, when they use the PARS strategy.

   Note: If students resist creating their own statements, they can use statements from a peer or statements that the teacher used during the think-aloud.

WRAP-UP

SAY, *"Tonight, I want you to think about situations in which you would use the PARS strategy. Think about the steps I taught you and how you can use the strategy on most things you read. Tomorrow I am going to ask you to write whatever you can remember from the strategy. Tomorrow we will also practice using the strategy and see if we met our goals!"*

Lesson 3: Guided Practice

Lesson Overview

The purpose of this lesson is to provide guided practice on the PARS strategy. The teacher should facilitate transfer of ownership by lessening support.

Student Objectives

The students will use the PARS strategy with peer and teacher support.

Materials

For each student provide reading passage, self-monitoring checklist, quiz, graph.

SET THE CONTEXT FOR STUDENT LEARNING

1. SAY, *"Yesterday we talked about PARS and I showed you how I use the strategy. Right now, I want you to write down everything you can remember from the PARS strategy. If you can, I also want you to write down what you <u>do</u> at each step."* Provide enough time for students to write. Praise students for remembering and support them when necessary.

2. SAY, *"Today we are going to continue to practice our PARS strategy. Before we practice, did any of you think of more situations you could use the strategy?"* Solicit student responses. *"Did any of you try to use the strategy on your own last night? I encourage you to try using the strategy on your own—the more you use the strategy, the better you will be at it and the closer you will be to your goal!"*

SUPPORT THE STRATEGY AND SELF-REGULATION

Step 1: Guided Practice

1. Hand out a short reading passage and a PARS checklist. Ask students to get out their self-statement worksheet (from previous lesson). Remind students that they can refer to the self-statements while they use the PARS strategy, especially if they have difficulty or feel frustrated.

2. Tell the students that you will complete the steps of PARS together and that the goal is to use all the PARS steps. They are expected to use the PARS checklist to monitor their strategy use. Remind them that the more they practice the strategy, the better they will get and the more likely they will meet their goals.

In this lesson, students practice the PARS strategy with guidance from the teacher and the self-monitoring checklist (task and material scaffolding). For additional scaffolding (i.e., content scaffolding), the reading passage could be shorter in length, written at a lower grade level, or on a topic of interest to the class.

3. SAY, *"I just gave you a passage to read—what is the first step of the PARS strategy?"* Students should respond, "Preview." *"And what do you do when you preview?"* Prompt students for responses (e.g., look at the title, look for headings, look at graphics and pictures). Praise students as they respond correctly. Guide students through the first step as necessary (e.g., *"What do you notice about the headings in this passage? Are there a lot of tables/ graphics in this passage?"*). Check off the self-monitoring checklist.

4. SAY, *"Now that we've done the first step in PARS, what should we do next?"* Prompt students for the next step (Ask). *"What kinds of questions should we ask ourselves?"* Students should respond with *who, what, when, where, why, how,* etc. Have students generate questions on their own or in pairs. Then ask for volunteers to share their questions and write the questions on the board. Check off the self-monitoring checklist.

5. SAY, *"Now that we have some good questions to guide us as we read, what do we do next? What is the next step in PARS?"* Wait for student responses (i.e., read). Praise them for knowing the steps of the strategy.

6. Allow students time to read—this can be done in pairs or individually. Remind students to think of the questions they generated and find answers. When students are finished reading, ask them if they were able to find the answers to their questions.

Note: They may not find all the answers to their questions. Remind them that this is OK. Sometimes we might generate questions that we can't answer in one chapter or passage.

7. Prompt students for the final step in PARS (summarize). As a class, create a summary of the passage. Discuss what makes it a good summary (e.g., "It's in our own words, it mentions the main ideas of the passage, it includes important details about the main ideas"). Praise students and remind them of the goals they set.

Step 2: Comprehension Quiz

1. SAY, *"You used the PARS strategy on that entire passage! Now I want to see how much you can remember and what you learned from that passage."* Hand out a short 10-question quiz about the passage they just read. Remind students that the quiz is just for practice—but that results will be graphed to see if they met their goals. Students can work with a partner to complete the quiz (if necessary).

2. Once students have finished the quiz, go through the answers and have students add up their results. Show students how to graph their scores.

3. Praise students for effort and strategy use (and meeting their goals). Remind students that using the PARS strategy will make them better readers and help them to continue meeting their goals.

WRAP-UP

SAY, *"Tonight, I want you to practice using the PARS strategy on any homework you have. Tomorrow I am going to quiz you again on the steps of PARS and we will try meeting our goals!"*

Lesson 4: Peer Practice

Lesson Overview

The purpose of this lesson is to provide additional guided practice on the PARS strategy. The teacher should facilitate transfer of ownership by lessening support.

Student Objective

Pairs of students will collaboratively practice PARS.

Materials

For each student provide reading passage, self-monitoring checklist, quiz, graph.

SET THE CONTEXT FOR STUDENT LEARNING

1. Make sure any posters or visual reminders are removed or covered for testing of memorization.

2. SAY, *"Yesterday we talked about PARS and we practiced using the strategy. Right now, I want you to write down everything you can remember from the PARS strategy. If you can, I also want you to write down what you <u>do</u> at each step."* Provide enough time for students to write. Praise students for remembering and support them when necessary.

3. SAY, *"Today we are going to continue to practice our PARS strategy. Before we practice, did any of you think of more situations in which you could use the strategy?"* Solicit student responses. *"Did any of you try to use the strategy on your own last night? I encourage you to try using the strategy on your own—the more you use the strategy, the better you will be at it and the close you will be to your goal!"*

SUPPORT THE STRATEGY AND SELF-REGULATION

Step 1: Guided Practice

1. SAY, *"Today I have another reading passage for you. I want you to read this passage with a partner."* Allow students time to find a partner. *"Remember to use all the steps of PARS to help you remember and understand what you are reading."*

2. SAY, *"While you are using the PARS strategy with your partner, I want you to remember to check each step of the strategy on your self-monitoring sheet. I also want you to remember that you each set a goal."* Encourage students to take out their graphs and look at their goals.

3. Give students a few minutes, in pairs, to preview the passage together. Then solicit student responses (e.g., *"What did you notice about this passage?"*). Remind students (as necessary) to check off each step as it is completed.

4. Guide students to the next step of PARS (Ask). Give the pairs a few minutes to generate questions about the passage. Encourage each pair to create three questions. Review the questions as a class. Praise students for their effort and strategy use (e.g.,

In this lesson, the teacher's role should be reduced. Students should work with peers while using the self-monitoring checklist.

The reading passage used could slightly increase in length, readability, or difficulty (e.g., fewer headings, no graphics). This increase provides an opportunity for the teacher to assist students as they assume more responsibility for the strategy and aids in generalization of strategy use.

"I can tell that you have been practicing your strategy, and I like that you used words like who, what, *and* when *to create your questions"*).

5. Prompt students for the next step of the strategy. Allow them to read the passage individually. As they finish reading, encourage students to check with the partner to see how many questions were answered. Remind students to use the checklist.

6. Ask students to create a summary of the passage with their partner. As a class, ask for volunteers to share their summary.

Step 2: Comprehension Quiz

1. SAY, *"You and your partner used the PARS strategy on that entire passage! Now I want to see how much you can remember and what you learned from that passage."* Hand out a short 10-question quiz. Remind students that the quiz is just for practice—but that results will be graphed to see if they met their goals. Students should work individually to complete the quiz.

2. Once students have finished the quiz, go through the answers and have students add up their results. Ask students to graph their results.

3. Praise students for effort and strategy use (and meeting their goals). Remind students that using the PARS strategy will make them better readers and help them to continue meeting their goals.

WRAP-UP

SAY, *"Tonight, I want you to practice using the PARS strategy on any homework you have. I also want you to think of some situations in which you could use the PARS strategy—maybe you could use the strategy in other classes! Tomorrow I am going to quiz you on the steps of PARS one more time and we will try to meet our goals again!"*

Note: This lesson should be repeated if students struggled with using the strategy.

Lesson 5: Independent Practice (Fading Instructional Supports)

Lesson Overview

The teacher provides the students with independent practice in using PARS.

Student Objective

The students will use PARS independently.

Materials

For each student provide reading passage, short quiz, graph.

SET THE CONTEXT FOR STUDENT LEARNING

1. Review the steps of PARS. Call on students to help explain what should be done at each step of the strategy.

2. SAY, *"Today we will continue to practice our PARS strategy and we will see if we meet our goals!"*

Make sure any visuals are hidden or removed while you test for memorization.

SUPPORT THE STRATEGY AND SELF-REGULATION

Step 1: Guided Practice

1. SAY, *"Today I have a different passage for you to read. This time, I want you to read it on your own and try to remember all the steps of PARS without our self-monitoring checklist. While you are using the PARS strategy, I also want you to remember the goal you set!"*

2. Encourage students to use the strategy independently. Walk around the room and guide students only as needed.

For this lesson, the reading passage should be at grade level. Students should work independently and without the self-monitoring checklist.

Step 2: Comprehension Quiz

1. SAY, *"You used the PARS strategy on that entire passage all by yourself—and without any reminders of the strategy steps! Now I want to see how much you can remember and what you learned from that passage."* Hand out a short 10-question quiz. Remind students that the quiz is just for practice—but that results will be graphed to see if they met their goals.

2. Once students have finished the quiz, go through the answers and have students add up their results. Show students how to graph their scores.

3. Praise students for effort and strategy use (and meeting their goals). Remind students that using the PARS strategy will make them better readers and help them to continue meeting their goals.

WRAP-UP

1. Discuss how the passages that students have been reading might look different from other types of reading they do in school (e.g., there might be more or fewer headings, no pictures, chapter books).

2. Explain that the PARS strategy can be modified to fit the type

This discussion can help students to generalize the strategy to other settings or types of text.

of text being read. For example, if they are reading a novel, they can use the PARS strategy on chapters by still previewing and asking questions related to the title of the chapter.

Note: This lesson can be repeated with different reading passages until students are able to successfully use the PARS strategy independently and fluently. In addition, the fading of instructional supports can be changed to meet the needs of students. For example, the first time the lesson is taught, the students could use the self-monitoring checklist but work independently (or vice versa). The second time the lesson is taught, both supports should be removed (i.e., students should work independently and without the checklist).

CHAPTER 9

Strategies for Handwriting and Spelling

Writing is a complex task that requires the ability to generate, organize, and express ideas. Generally, the process of writing can be divided into two primary areas: *mechanics* and *content* (Richards, 2008). *Mechanics* includes knowledge of grammar, punctuation, and spelling. It also includes the ability to use the muscles in the hands and fingers to physically form words, letter by letter, on paper (Tompkins, 2002). *Content* involves conveying meaning through writing (e.g., vocabulary use, elaboration of detail, organization of ideas) and higher-level cognitive processes such as planning and revision of writing (Spear-Swerling, 2006). Mechanics and content are both necessary to produce written products such as essays and narratives. For example, the more efficient and automatic students are with writing mechanics (e.g., spelling, letter formation), the easier it will be to focus on content: the generation, expression, and organization of ideas (Richards, 2008). This chapter focuses on the *mechanics* of writing. Specifically, this chapter discusses handwriting and spelling. Higher-level writing skills, such as content generation and organization, are discussed further in Chapter 10.

Handwriting and spelling are two major prerequisite skills in the writing process. These skills are typically taught in the early years of school. If students fail to develop these essential prerequisites, they are likely to experience several long-term negative consequences. First, illegibility of written text and misspelled words can negatively influence perceptions about a student's competence as a writer (Graham, 1999; Graham et al., 2008; Graham, Harris, & Hebert, 2011). For example, when teachers were asked to rate the quality of several papers that differed only on legibility of handwriting and number of misspelled words, the papers that were neatly written with fewer spelling errors were rated much higher than those containing multiple spelling errors and poor legibility (see Chase, 1986). Second, difficulty with forming letters and with spelling may overtax a student's working memory, leaving him or her with fewer mental resources for higher-order skills such as content generation and planning (Graham, 1990, 1999). When students must frequently stop to think about letter formation or how to spell a word, they are interrupting planning and idea generation, which can lead to lost ideas, frustration, and disjointed writing. Several studies have found that explicit instruction in handwriting and spelling can result in increases in the completeness (e.g., number of genre elements) and length of written work (e.g., Graham, McKeown, Kiuhara, & Harris, 2012). Finally, difficulties with handwriting and spelling may cause avoidance of writing tasks, which can lead to a delay in writing development (Berninger, Mizokawa, & Bragg, 1991; Graham, 1999). For example, Berninger and colleagues (1991) noted that young students who experienced difficulties with handwriting were more likely to avoid writing tasks altogether and to develop a belief that they could not write. In summary, teachers must understand that if handwriting and spelling do not become automatic, these skills can substantially limit the writing process, causing students to have shorter, less complete writing that is perceived as qualitatively poor.

PROBLEMS FOR STUDENTS WITH LEARNING DISABILITIES AND ATTENTION-DEFICIT/HYPERACTIVITY DISORDER

Students with LD and ADHD often experience more difficulty with handwriting and spelling than their typically developing peers (Barkley, 2006; Graham & Weintraub, 1996). These difficulties are evident early on and often persist well into later grades. As we noted previously, these problems may influence students' ability to attend to higher-level skills such as planning and organizing text.

Handwriting

For some students with LD and ADHD, the physical act of producing text is extremely laborious. Students with LD often have difficulty with their rate of text production, producing letters and words slowly even when asked to write as quickly as possible (Isaacson & Gleason, 1997). In many cases, teachers may notice overt physical signs of a student struggling with writing, such as a tight and awkward pencil grip, awkward or unstable body position (e.g., crouched over the paper, not anchoring elbow and forearm on a table when writing), or tiring quickly during writing tasks (e.g., complaining of hand-cramping; National Center for Learning Disabilities [NCLD], 2010). One of the biggest handwriting issues for students with LD and ADHD is legibility of written text. Students with LD or ADHD commonly exhibit problems such as poor letter formation, inconsistent letter size, issues with letter and word spacing, and incorrect use of lowercase and capital letters. Difficulty with letter formation is the most frequent cause of illegibility. Research suggests that six letters (*q, j, z, u, n,* and, *k*) account for roughly 48% of the problems in letter formation (Graham, Weintraub, & Berninger, 1998). In some cases, the struggles students encounter with letter formation and text legibility are related to neatness and spacing of letters. For other students, text and letter legibility may be related to motor control and fine motor skills (see Graham, 1999).

Spelling

Students with LD and ADHD typically experience persistent problems with spelling, which can be especially difficult for these students for several reasons. First, the deficits in reading that many students with LD and ADHD experience typically involve difficulty with decoding. Many of the same weaknesses that impact decoding (e.g., poor phonemic awareness, poor knowledge of letter–sound relationships) also influence spelling (Moats, 1995; Shankweiler & Lundquist, 1993). Poor spellers commonly have weaknesses in their ability to analyze and remember the individual sounds (i.e., phonemes) in the words, such as the sounds associated with *j* or *ch* (International Dyslexia Association [IDA], 2008). Second, poor spellers frequently have trouble remembering the letters in words because they may have trouble noticing or recalling features of those words, such as the syllables in words, and the meaningful parts (i.e., morphemes) of longer words, such as *un-*, *-pect*, or *-able* (International Dyslexia Association, 2008). Finally, many educators have noted that students who struggle with spelling experience difficulty with recalling previously learned words or parts of words (Moats, 1995). For example, a student may be able to sound out and read a word with little effort, but unable to spell that same word correctly.

PREREQUISITE SKILLS

Handwriting

The prerequisites for handwriting fall into four general categories: motor/muscle development, foundational knowledge, establishment of a dominant hand, and posture and pencil grip. First, to form letters fluently (i.e., correctly and quickly), students must have sufficient small muscle development and eye–hand coordination. Otherwise they will be unable to manipulate writing utensils. Second, students need to have foundational skills such as basic stroke formation (e.g., ability to make lines and circles with a pencil), letter recognition, and orientation to written language (e.g., writing from left to right, starting at the top left of a page) to developing fluent handwriting (Polloway, Miller, & Smith, 2003). Third, students must have established a dominant hand (Benbow, Hanft, & Marsh, 1992). If both hands get equal practice at developing fine motor skills (e.g., cutting with scissors, handwriting), students may end up with two mediocre hands rather than one strong, specialized hand. In order for students to do well at forming letters, there should be a dominant hand that becomes specialized at controlling a pencil (Marr, Windsor, & Cermak, 2001).

Another ability related to establishment of a dominant hand is crossing the midline (i.e., imaginary line that runs down the body, separating the right and left halves) with the dominant hand. This means that one hand should be able to move from one side of the body to the other side of the body. Crossing the midline of the body is an important prerequisite skill required for the appropriate development of a number of motor skills, including handwriting. Midline crossing ability emerges as students develop bilateral coordination skills (e.g., ability to use both sides of the body). As students learn to coordinate a strong hand that is doing something skilled (e.g., cutting, coloring) and an assisting hand that is helping (e.g., holding the paper), the ability to spontaneously cross the midline develops. Young children who have difficultly crossing the body's midline are more likely to have difficulty with writing because it requires coordination of the two halves of the body (e.g., hands doing different tasks) and cross-lateral motion (e.g., dominant hand crossing to the nondominant half of the body).

Finally, proper posture and pencil grip are essential prerequisites to handwriting (see Benbow et al., 1992; Marr et al., 2001). For posture, both feet should be on the floor and the body should be slightly turned to one side. For right-handed writers the body should be angled slightly to the left, and for left-handed writers the body should be angled to the right. In addition, the elbow and forearm of the writing hand should be anchored on the desk. Ideally, the chair should be high enough that when the forearm is extended, the elbow will be at about a 90-degree angle (with the forearm parallel to the floor). For pencil grip, students should hold a pencil with three fingers. The index finger and thumb should hold the pencil while the middle finger provides support for the pencil.

Spelling

Prerequisite skills in spelling are similar to those for early reading skills (e.g., alphabetic principle, phonemic awareness). For example, students should understand that there are systematic and predictable relationships between written letters (graphemes) and spoken sounds (phonemes) and that those sounds can be represented by letters and letter combinations (Armbruster, Lehr, & Osborn, 2001). Phonemes are the smallest unit of sound (e.g., there are three phonemes in the word *cat*: /c/ /a/ /t/). Graphemes are the letters or letter combinations that make up a phoneme (e.g., /k/ sound of the *c* in *cat*). There are more than 40 distinctive phonemes in the English language, but more than 70 letters or letter combinations to symbolize those phonemes. For example, the /ee/ sound can be produced with the graphemes *ee* (e.g., *see, feel*), *ea* (e.g., *each, peach*), and *ie* (e.g., *piece*). Good spellers have a strong understanding of the relationship between phonemes and graphemes. Knowing the different combinations or patterns of graphemes to represent phonemes is a critical prerequisite for good spelling. Students who have an understanding of patterns and combinations of graphemes are able to spell more words correctly and approach spelling more strategically (e.g., they consider the combinations of graphemes that can make the long-*a* sound before attempting to spell a word). In addition, understanding patterns and frequent combinations of graphemes is helpful to students when spelling because the patterns within words are largely predictable (Moats, 2005). For example, half of all English words can be spelled accurately based on only sound–symbol correspondence (Hanna, Hanna, Hodges, & Rudorf, 1966). This means that the letters used to spell these words also predictably represent their sound patterns (Moats, 2005) and if students are taught these patterns (e.g., when the /k/

sound will be spelled with a *k*, as in *look*, or with *ck*, as in *lack*), they can successfully spell more words.

INSTRUCTION IN HANDWRITING AND SPELLING

In order to improve students' fluency in handwriting and spelling, teachers should directly address these problems. In the sections that follow, we present examples of instructional strategies for teaching and/or remediating handwriting and spelling problems.

Handwriting

Effective handwriting instruction should include four basic components (Troia & Graham, 2003). First, letter and word formation, pencil grip, and paper positioning should be explicitly taught, modeled, practiced, and reviewed. For example, before beginning a writing activity, the teacher should tell students which letters or words are to be learned in the lesson and explicitly show how each letter or word should look, while also highlighting proper pencil grip and paper positioning using "think-aloud" procedures (e.g., "I know I should hold my pencil between my thumb, index finger, and middle finger and make sure my paper is angled toward the left so that my letters and words will look as neat as possible"). However, please note that the use of self-instructions and self-statements should be used only during the acquisition phases of handwriting (e.g., to model how to form a particular letter) and should not be used when students are working toward increasing handwriting fluency. Second, students should be given supports for attaining legible handwriting. For example, teachers might provide pencil tripod grip molds, paper with raised lines, or hand-over-hand assistance in forming letters.

Third, students should be taught to evaluate and improve their own handwriting. For example, if a teacher notices that a student consistently struggles with forming a particular letter or series of letters, the teacher should explain how the letter(s) should look and prompt the student to be aware when writing the letter. The teacher should remind the student that he or she should always go back and reread written work for legibility and correct letters and words that are difficult to read or incorrectly formed. Teachers also play an important role in evaluating handwriting by helping students keep track of their handwriting performance, setting goals for improvement, and correcting poor handwriting when it is noticed. Finally, teachers must stress that students need to be able to produce handwriting fluently, and they must explain why fluent text production is important (e.g., lets the student focus on the content of writing). Teachers can help students increase fluency by providing many opportunities to practice handwriting and by administering speed trials for which students set a goal of copying text 5–10% faster with each trial. There are several commercially available programs for teaching handwriting. Some of these programs are briefly described in Figure 9.1.

Handwriting without Tears
Handwriting without Tears, conceived by Jan Olsen, is a comprehensive program for kindergarten through fifth-grade students that encourages active involvement in the writing process. Incorporates instruction on posture, grip, and paper positioning in addition to instruction on different scripts (e.g., cursive). *www.hwtears.com/hwt*
Zaner–Bloser Handwriting (Hackney & Lucas, 1993)
The Zaner–Bloser Handwriting program teaches vertical manuscript/print (as opposed to slanted) using step-by-step instructions and self-evaluation, meaningful practice, and application through engaging activities. *www.zaner-bloser.com*
D'Nealian Handwriting Program (Thurber, 1993)
The D'Nealian Handwriting Program teaches a specific type of script that has shared characteristics with print and cursive letters. *www.dnealian.com/index.html*
Write-on Handwriting
The Write-on Handwriting program teaches children motor movements needed for text production through multiple instructional tools (e.g., paper- and computer-based exercises). The program includes print and cursive handwriting. *www.writeonhandwriting.com/home.htm*

FIGURE 9.1. Commercially available handwriting programs.

Scripts: Manuscript, Cursive, D'Nealian

One of the common issues in teaching handwriting involves the script(s) that are taught in school (e.g., the style or type of writing). In the United States students are typically taught two scripts (e.g., manuscript/printing and cursive). Generally, manuscript is introduced in kindergarten or first grade whereas cursive is introduced in later grades (e.g., second or third grade). The D'Nealian Handwriting Program (Thurber, 1993), a commercially available program, is meant to make the transition between manuscript and cursive easier (Graham, 1999) by having students produce manuscript letters using a continuous stroke without lifting the pencil. Despite the fact that most students learn both manuscript and cursive, some educators have recommended that only one script be taught to students who struggle with handwriting (Graham, 2010). The recommendation has been to teach traditional manuscript letters because most children come to school already knowing how to write some manuscript letters and there is evidence to suggest that the use of traditional manuscript in early grades may facilitate reading development (see Graham & Miller, 1980).

Although the specific script taught to students may seem like an important decision, the impact of specific programs and scripts on students' handwriting is still unknown. There is little evidence to support one program or script over another (see Polloway et al., 2012; Wood, Webster, Gullickson, & Walker, 1987). What is clear is that handwriting can be difficult for some students regardless of the script used, and teachers should be prepared to address any deficiencies as they arise. Several suggestions for remediation have been suggested.

Guidelines for Teaching Handwriting

Vaughn and Bos (2012, p. 312) recommended several guidelines for teaching and remediating handwriting:

1. Teach handwriting explicitly, including how to form letters. Teachers should not assume that students will develop insights into letter formation on their own. Instead, teachers should voice the steps in writing letters (e.g., "Start with your pencil on the top line and draw a straight line down to the bottom line").

2. Provide modeling and frequent feedback.

3. Initially focus on the motor pattern and then increasingly focus on legibility. The first step in learning a new letter or word should be to practice forming the letter or word. Once the motor pattern is established, the student should repeatedly form the letter or word while focusing on neatness and accuracy.

4. Teach handwriting several times a week (e.g., 5 days a week for 15 minutes at a time).

5. In addition to short lessons on letter formation, provide handwriting instruction in the context of writing assignments. For example, if students are working on narrative writing, provide feedback on handwriting in the context of the student's narrative. In addition, if a teacher knows that a student or group of students is struggling with a particular aspect of handwriting (e.g., neatness and legibility), the teacher should imbed instruction and modeling about these aspects in lessons related to narrative writing.

6. Handwriting skills should be overlearned in isolation and then applied in context. This means that students should practice letters or words in isolation (e.g., write the letter *m* 10 times) until they become more fluent. Once the motor pattern associated with the letter or word is learned, students can begin to practice the letter in the context of words and sentences.

7. Ask students to evaluate their own handwriting and the handwriting of others, when appropriate. If students are able to critique the handwriting of peers, it can be a useful exercise in critical evaluation of handwriting skills. However, peer evaluation is not always possible or appropriate. In this case, teachers should encourage students to critically evaluate their own handwriting for clarity and neatness. In some cases, teachers may want to provide students with a checklist or guide for evaluating their own handwriting (e.g., "Are there spaces between each word?," "Can I identify individual letters within each word?," "Can I read all the words in the passage?").

8. Teachers should ensure that their own handwriting is a model for the neatness and legibility that are expected of the students. In addition, teachers can use frequent,

short "think-alouds" to highlight their own thought processes related to handwriting (e.g., "Oh, wow! I can't even read my own writing here. I guess I should erase and write it again so that my letters are neatly written and easy for anyone to read and understand").

9. In the beginning stages of letter formation, letter writing and letter naming should be integrated into instruction. Specifically, teachers should encourage students to voice the names of the letters that are being written. For example, if students were practicing the letter *m*, they would be expected to say *m* each time they wrote the letter.

10. Once students are proficient in letter formation, fluency should be increased. Students need to work toward writing neatly and quickly. Teachers can encourage this by asking students to write as quickly and legibly as possible.

Self-Instructional Strategy

The following six-step self-instructional strategy (Graham, 1983b) has resulted in improved handwriting when taught to students.

1. The teacher models the writing of a target letter and describes how to form the letter. Students then describe the formation of the letter. *This step is repeated three times.*
2. The teacher writes the letter *while* describing the process. This continues until students can describe the process for writing the letter.
3. Students trace the letter while the teacher and students describe the process of letter formation together.
4. The teacher writes the letter, traces it, and then discusses the process while including any corrections (e.g., "My letter is too slanted") and self-reinforcement (e.g., "That looks a lot better!"). This step continues, with and without errors, until students can model the process.
5. The teacher writes the letter, and the students copy the letter while describing the process and self-correcting as necessary. Students should complete this step successfully three times before moving to Step 6.
6. Students write the letter from memory.

Spelling

Spelling is typically taught in most classrooms through the use of word lists and weekly spelling tests or through an integrated reading and writing approach. The first approach includes a prescribed list of weekly words that should be learned by all students in a classroom or group (Polloway et al., 2012). A typical classroom procedure might entail the following:

1. New spelling words for the week are introduced on Monday, by providing students with a list of new words to be practiced and learned. In some cases, the weekly words might follow a theme (e.g., homophones, *ou* words). For example,

a weekly spelling list might include homophones such as *to, too, two, be, bee, dew, due,* and *do.*

2. A spelling pretest of new words is administered the same day.

3. On Tuesday, Wednesday, and Thursday students practice the spelling words through independent activities such as using spelling words in sentences, finding words in the dictionary, or writing the words several times.

4. On Friday a posttest is given to determine which spelling words were learned.

Although not every classroom uses these exact procedures, most classrooms follow a procedure similar to this to teach the spelling of words.

The second approach involves immersing students in literacy-rich environments and providing giving them multiple opportunities to read and write for authentic purposes (Graham, 1999, 2000). According to this view, students "catch" most of their spelling skills through engaging in reading and writing activities. For example, students may be exposed to spelling through the teacher's modeling of correct spelling while writing in class, by sharing their own writing with peers, or through reading different texts. In addition, teachers use mini-lessons and teachable moments to explicitly instruct students on a particular skill, as the need arises (e.g., if a student is struggling to notice a spelling pattern in a particular word). For students with LD, however, there is little evidence to support the efficacy of this approach for teaching spelling (Graham, 1999). Research suggests that students with LD and those who find reading and spelling challenging will learn to spell only a small proportion of the words they encounter and are less likely than their typically developing peers to learn the correct spelling of a word by encountering it in reading material (Graham, 1999; Ormrod, 1985). As a result, it is important for teachers to explicitly teach spelling skills to students with LD.

Guidelines for Teaching Spelling

Generally, spelling instruction should include four components (Graham, 1999). First, students should be explicitly taught how to spell words they frequently use in their writing. Second, students should learn how to generate plausible spellings for unknown words. This can be done through strategies such as *spelling by analogy* (further explained below). Third, students need to know how to detect and correct spelling miscues when they occur. This can include learning how to appropriately use resources such as spell checkers, help from peers, and using dictionaries. Finally, students need to recognize the importance of good spelling and develop a desire to spell correctly (Graham, 1999). Teachers can foster this desire by consistently modeling correct spelling and providing opportunities for students to engage in activities where correct spelling is an expectation (e.g., homework assignments, school/classroom newspaper/blog).

Spelling Strategies

There is no shortcut for becoming better at spelling. To spell better, a student must spend time practicing spelling and generating text using newly practiced words. As a result, in many of the strategies and techniques presented below, students are expected to write and rewrite a spelling word several times. For example, most of the spelling strategies below require students to look at a correctly spelled word (e.g., list of spelling words), write the word from memory, check the word to ensure that it is spelled correctly, identify any errors, and rewrite the word correctly.

TEST–STUDY–TEST. This technique is commonly used in schools and has been successful with both good and poor spellers (Graham, 1983a; Graham & Miller, 1979). With this technique, students are given a test to determine which spelling words are already known and which words still need to be learned. A new list of words is constructed from the words that were spelled incorrectly on the pretest. These words are studied and the test is readministered to determine which words were mastered (Graham, 1999).

CORRECTED–TEST. With this technique, students correct specific spelling errors, under the teacher's direction, immediately after being tested or whenever errors are detected while studying (Graham, 1983a). When using this technique, the teacher would administer a test and immediately show students which words were spelled incorrectly. The teacher would then prompt students to correct any errors and carefully monitor them as they practice writing the words correctly. These procedures enable students to identify which words are difficult for them, identify parts of words that may be particularly difficulty, and correct errors as soon as they occur and under the supervision of a teacher.

MNEMONIC DEVICES. The use of mnemonic devices has been found useful in teaching students rules associated with spelling (e.g., "*i* before *e* except after *c*") or in memorizing the spelling of specific words. Examples of spelling mnemonics can be found in Figure 9.2. In addition, *acrostics* (further explained in Chapter 14) are mnemonic devices that can help students remember how to spell tricky words. For example, students can create their own "silly sentences" (i.e., acrostic) to help them remember how to spell a word (e.g., "*F*rieda *r*eally *i*sn't *e*ven *n*eeding *d*ucks" to remember how to spell the word *friend*).

COVER–COPY–COMPARE. This simple, three-step strategy promotes acquisition of spelling words by engaging students in a step-by-step practice routine. This method

---

"*i* before *e* except after *c*, unless it sounds like an *a* as in *neighbor* and *weigh*."

They went *together* to-get-her.

The *principal* is your pal.

An *island* is land surrounded by water.

That liar looks *familiar*.

I lost an *e* in an *argument*.

FIGURE 9.2. Examples of mnemonic devices for spelling.

has been used effectively with students with LD and ADHD (Moser, Fishley, Konrad, & Hessler, 2012; Murphy, Hern, McLaughlin, & Williams, 1990; Skinner, McLaughlin, & Logan, 1997). Students are given a spelling sheet with the target words correctly spelled (i.e., a spelling list). Students look at each correctly spelled word, cover the word, and then write the word from memory. Finally, students compare the copied word to the original word. If students determine that they spelled the word correctly, they progress to the next word. If students determine that the response was incorrect, they write the correct response a set number of times. Correction procedures may involve copying the incorrect word only once or copying the word multiple times (e.g., three times). The correction procedures to be used should be determined by the teacher prior to implementing the strategy with students.

FIVE-STEP WORD STUDY STRATEGY. The five-step word study strategy, developed by Harris, Graham, and Freeman (1988; see also Graham & Freeman, 1986) is a variation on the cover–copy–compare strategy and was previously discussed in Chapter 7. The strategy has five recursive steps: (1) Look at the word; (2) say the word aloud; (3) cover the word; (4) write the word three times; and (5) check to see if the word is spelled correctly. If mistakes were made in spelling the word, Steps 1–5 should be repeated. If the word was spelled correctly, the student(s) can move to the next word on the list. Several studies have shown that this strategy, when combined with self-monitoring, is effective for students with LD and ADHD (e.g., Harris et al., 1988; Reid & Harris, 1993).

GENERATE AND TEST. Wong (1986) developed a self-instruction strategy that has been used successfully with students with LD.

1. "Do I know the word?"
2. "How many syllables do I hear in the word (write the number down)?"
3. "Spell out the word."
4. "Do I have the correct number of syllables in my word?"
5. "If yes, is there any part of the word I'm not sure of? Underline that part and try spelling the word again."
6. "Now does the word look right? If so, leave it alone. If it still doesn't look right, underline the part I'm unsure of and try again. *If the word I spelled does not have the correct number of syllables, I should try to hear the word in my head again and find the missing syllable. Then go through Steps 5 and 6 again.*"
7. "When I finish spelling, I should tell myself, 'Good job, I worked hard.' "

SPELLING BY ANALOGY. Spelling by analogy, sometimes referred to as a *word family approach*, teaches students to use common rimes (e.g., *are*) to help spell unfamiliar words. Englert, Hiebert, and Stewart (1985) taught students with LD an analogy strategy based on the spelling rule that parts of words that rhyme are often spelled the same. These students first learned to spell banks of words that contained a specific spelling pattern (e.g., *an*) and then used their knowledge of these words (e.g., *ran, can, fan*) to help them spell new words that rhymed (e.g., *ban, pan, tan*). For some examples of word families, see Figure 9.3.

at family	op family	un family	an family	ay family	it family	ot family
at	hop	run	an	day	it	tot
bat	mop	sun	can	may	fit	rot
cat	top	bun	tan	bay	sit	pot
fat	cop	fun	ran	pay	lit	lot
mat	lop	gun	pan	ray	hit	dot
sat	chop	stun	man	lay	pit	got
pat	plop	shun	fan	clay	wit	cot
rat	crop		ban	stray	quit	blot
chat			than	play	flit	not
that			plan			trot
brat			clan			plot

ill family	all family	ate family	eat family	oil family	ink family	ook family
ill	all	ate	eat	oil	ink	look
pill	call	date	meat	spoil	sink	took
mill	tall	fate	beat	toil	mink	book
will	mall	late	heat	coil	pink	nook
dill	fall	mate	seat	foil	link	cook
drill	hall	bate	treat	broil	wink	hook
trill	wall	plate	pleat		rink	shook
grill	ball	skate			think	crook
thrill	stall				drink	
	small					

FIGURE 9.3. Examples of common word families. Note: This list is not exhaustive.

Editing

In addition to instruction and strategies that explicitly teach students how to generate possible spellings for words or practice new spelling words, some editing and revision strategies include steps that prompt students to check for legibility of text and spelling errors in written work. Two such strategies are discussed in the following section.

COPS

The University of Kansas Institute for Research in Learning Disabilities developed a strategy called *COPS* to assist students in making mechanical revisions (Table 9.1). Through a series of questions students are prompted to monitor and revise any

---

TABLE 9.1. COPS Revision Strategy

C—Have I capitalized the first word and proper names?

O—How is the overall appearance?

P—Have I put in commas and end punctuation?

S—Have I spelled all the words right?

Note. Based on Schumaker, Deshler, Nolan, Clark, Alley, and Warner (1981).

mechanical errors in their papers. Students follow the mnemonic *COPS*. The *C* reminds them to ask themselves if they have capitalized the first words and proper names. The *O* stands for overall appearance: Students ask themselves, "How is the overall appearance?" This is when students check their handwriting and the general neatness of the paper. The *P* stands for punctuation. Students are prompted to ask themselves, "Have I put in commas and end punctuation?" This component addresses basic mechanics; it helps students attend to end punctuation, as well as punctuation within sentences. The final step in the strategy is the *S*, which stands for spell. Students ask themselves, "Have I spelled all words right?" Students should be encouraged to identify any words that they suspect are spelled incorrectly. Those words need to be checked for accuracy in the same manner that other material in the text is corrected.

Mechanical revisions, or transcription revisions, are essential to composition; too many mechanical errors are distracting to the reader and take away from the intent of the composition. It is also essential for young authors to understand the purpose of writing and to be aware that revisions should not only clean up their writing, but clarify their thoughts.

Detecting and Correcting Errors

Students with LD can be taught to detect and correct errors in their own written language. Graham and Miller (1980) suggested several activities for teaching proofreading and editing skills:

1. Provide a list of words that includes misspelled words to be found.
2. Provide a short passage with spelling errors, including easily recognized errors and misspelling with which the student may currently struggle (e.g., spelling demons).
3. List the number of purposefully misspelled words in a passage and have students locate them.
4. Have students identify the correctly spelled words from several alternative spellings.
5. Provide a passage with words that may be spelled incorrectly and have students identify misspelled words.

Technology and Word Processing

The use of technology, especially word processing, can be helpful for students who struggle with handwriting and spelling for several reasons (Graham, Harris, & MacArthur, 2004). First, using word processing produces neat, legible text. Second, it allows students to add, delete, and move text easily (e.g., without erasing and rewriting). Third, for struggling writers, typed text can be produced more quickly than handwritten text. As a result, more attention can be paid to other aspects of the writing process, such as planning and editing. Finally, a major advantage of using word processing is the support provided for mechanical demands such as spelling (e.g., spell-check), capitalization, and punctuation. In addition to these benefits, research suggests that the use of word processing has positive effects on the writing quality of struggling writers (see Graham & Perin, 2007a, 2007b).

IMPLEMENTATION PLANS

In this section, we provide partial examples of implementation plans for each of the strategies previously discussed. Please note that when teaching spelling strategies, it may not be necessary to develop a complete implementation plan (i.e., one that includes all stages). In most cases, only some of the SRSD stages are used.

Stage 1 for COPS: Developing and Activating Background Knowledge

Prior to teaching a spelling strategy, it is necessary to evaluate the students' background knowledge, attitudes, and beliefs about spelling. Formal and informal assessments can be used to determine which skills the students already possess and which skills they still need to develop. Doing a task analysis can provide valuable information about the skills that are required for a given strategy and help to determine whether the students

TABLE 9.2. Sample Task Breakdown for COPS Revision Strategy

Strategy	Skills	Assessment
Have I capitalized the first word and proper names?	Knowledge of capital and lowercase letters	Given an informal assessment, the student will correctly produce capital and lowercase letters.
	Knowledge of first word of sentence	Given a paragraph, the student will be able to identify all first letters of sentences and proper names.
	Knowledge of proper names	
How is the overall appearance?	Understanding of neatness of writing (e.g., letter spacing)	Given an informal assessment, the student will write a short paragraph as neatly as possible.
	Ability to write neatly (if a student is unable to write neatly, he or she can type)	Given a paragraph or short narrative written by the student, the student will determine whether the narrative should be rewritten for neatness or whether the narrative will need to be typed.
Have I put in commas and end punctuation?	Knowledge of punctuation	Given text with mechanical errors, the student will be able to satisfactorily correct those errors.
Have I spelled all the words right?	Knowledge of spelling	Provided with a spelling test on common words, the student will be able to write and spell words correctly.

already possess those skills. Table 9.2 shows an example of a task analysis for the COPS strategy.

Stage 2 for Cover–Copy–Compare: Discussing the Strategy

This is the first stage in initiating the strategy when it is important to stress its relevance. During an initial conference the teacher discusses the student's current performance. In order for students to be successful and able to self-regulate the strategy, they need to make a commitment to use the strategy; they need to "buy into" the value of the strategy. Thus, it is important for the teacher to stress this value. Brainstorm with the students on situations wherein using a strategy or completing a given task accurately is important. For example, the following might be appropriate brainstorming ideas in response to the question "When would it be important for you to spell correctly?":

- Writing papers or essays in class
- Completing homework assignments
- Writing e-mails or letters
- Filling out job applications

A sample script for "selling" the strategy is as follows:

"The reason I wanted to talk with you is that we have been working on some new spelling words over these past few weeks. When I was looking at your weekly spelling tests, I noticed that you were making some careless spelling errors that might be because you. . . . Let's look at your last three spelling tests. You really did a nice job with _____. [Point out a few positives; focus on any letter patterns within words or vowel combinations that might have been tricky.] However, I also see that there are several misspelled words and that some of these words were spelled correctly one week and not the following week. This tells me that maybe you didn't spend enough time practicing your spelling words. Remember when we were just talking about why it is important to spell words correctly and you said _____? [Refer back to reasons why spelling is important.] Well, knowing these spelling words will help you to complete your assignments more accurately and earn more points because when I grade your writing in class, I look at how well you spell in addition to the great ideas you think of. Well, I have a strategy that will help you be more efficient with how you study your spelling words. This means that you are going to waste less time and you will be more likely to learn the correct spelling so you can consistently spell the words correctly (on your test, on your assignment, in your papers). The strategy only has three steps, and it's pretty easy to remember because each step tells you exactly what to do when studying spelling words! Cover–copy–compare!"

In this stage we would also introduce the steps of the strategy and any prompts or materials that may be given (Table 9.1).

Stage 3 for COPS: Modeling the Strategy

Here is an example of a think-aloud for the COPS strategy.

"OK, what is it I have to do here? I know, I have to edit my paper. Editing is hard for me, but I know that using my COPS strategy will help me do a good job. I can remember *COPS* because police clean up the neighborhood, and I need to 'police up,' or clean up my paper by editing and making sure that I don't leave any errors (rule breakers). The COPS strategy can help me remember what to do when I am editing. OK, I can do this if I try my best and use my strategy. I should write down the steps of my strategy so I don't forget any of them. OK, *C* stands for *capitalize*—have I capitalized the first word and proper names? Next is *O*. What does *O* stand for? I can't remember. I know, I can just look at the wall chart . . . let's see . . . the chart says, 'Overall appearance—How is the overall appearance?' Oh yeah, I remember that now; I better write it down. Let's see, then *P* is for *punctuation*—have I put in commas and end punctuation? Good, I'm remembering most of this; I can do this! Finally comes *S*, which stands for *spelling*—have I spelled all the words right? Great, I got them all written down; I'm really doing well.

"OK, what do I do now? I need to start with the *C* and ask myself, 'Have I capitalized the first word and proper names?' Let's see . . . oops, here's a sentence that needs a capital letter at the beginning, and oooh, I forgot to capitalize the name of this town. Good thing I'm going over this! OK, that seems to be all of them. What's next? I have written down *O*. I need to ask myself, 'How is the overall appearance?' Well, I should clean up some of my handwriting; I can barely read it, and if I can't read it I'm sure no one else will either! Oh, there are quite a few extra marks, too. I need to erase those and clean up my paper; I want it to look good when I hand it in so maybe I will get a gold star. I would really like one of those gold stars on my paper! OK, all clean; it looks good.

"Now, what do I need to do? What's after *O*? *O* . . . *P*; I need to ask myself, 'Have I put in commas and end punctuation?' I need to remember where to use commas. OK, I use commas when I am listing things; here's a list . . . I remembered to use commas. Way to go! When else do I use commas? I use commas to break up sentences, when I want a pause. Let's see, do I have any long sentences? Yep, here's one that could use a comma! Are there any others? No, I don't see any; looks good! How about that end punctuation? Oops, forgot a period at the end of a sentence, and I really should change that to a question mark. That's an asking sentence, not a telling sentence. The rest of it looks really good. Wow, this is going really well! I like using this strategy—it's kind of fun. I can't believe it, but I'm almost done!

"I'm up to the *S*, the last letter! I need ask myself, 'Have I spelled all the words right?' This is kind of tough for me, but I know I can do it; I've come this far. I can't quit now! OK, let me see . . . most of it looks OK, but there are a few words that I'm just not sure about. I better look those up in the dictionary. That's what we're supposed to do first if we're not sure how to spell a word. . . . OK, all done! I did a great job. Using that strategy and sticking with it really helped me remember what to look for when I'm editing my paper."

Stage 4 for COPS: Memorizing the Strategy

Memorizing the strategy is extremely important! We want students to be able to focus on the task at hand and not on trying to remember the steps of a strategy. The specific activities for encouraging memorization are not nearly as important. There are many appropriate activities. The important aspect of the activities is whether or not they facilitate memorization. You will need to plan and prepare the activities and monitor their effectiveness. Here are some examples of memorization activities for the COPS strategy.

Reciting the Strategy with a Partner

Students are matched up with peers and given a checklist/handout with the COPS strategy. Each student takes a turn "quizzing" his or her partner, using the handout. For example, Student A would have the COPS handout and ask Student B what the *O* in COPS stands for. Once all steps of the strategy have been discussed, the students will switch roles.

Creating a Poster

Students create their own posters (either on a blank piece of paper or on a small note card). The posters should include the steps of the COPS strategy and a picture or reminder of each step. Students can then share their individually made posters with the whole class or in small groups.

Stage 5 for Cover–Copy–Compare: Supporting the Strategy

In this stage, scaffolding the strategy is important. With scaffolding it is possible to gradually transfer strategy ownership from teacher to student. Students need to be given adequate time and support to master the strategy. Here are examples of how to use content, task, and material scaffolding with the cover–copy–compare strategy.

Content

Students are given a spelling list of fewer words with a mixture of unknown and known words. The teacher and students should go through the list together and the teacher should direct the process (e.g., "I think I already know this word, but I should still use my strategy to make sure I learn and practice it correctly"). Next, students receive a spelling list that they have already worked with (e.g., one from the previous week). Students should use the cover–copy–compare strategy to practice each of the words. The teacher can provide a chart, poster, or checklist to ensure that every step is completed.

Task

During collaborative practice the teacher prompts students (or class) by asking them to identify the first step to be completed (i.e., cover); then the teacher describes and models the step. In subsequent lessons the teacher asks the students to name and describe the steps, and the teacher models the steps. Finally, the students are able to name, describe, and complete the steps on their own.

Materials

Provide students with a mnemonic prompt card to be placed on their desks (see Figure 9.4 for an example). Initially, this card should list the steps of the strategy and what to do at each step. Over time, the card will provide less direction, first fading the descriptions and eventually fading the mnemonic and steps altogether. At this point students should have reached mastery of the strategy and be able to work independently.

Stage 6 for Cover–Copy–Compare: Independent Performance

At this stage students are ready to use the strategy independently. The teacher's main task is to monitor student performance and check on consistent and correct strategy use. Remember that students can make some idiosyncratic changes to the strategy as long as their performance remains high. However, if a student begins making changes to a strategy (e.g., skipping steps, reordering steps) and his or her performance decreases, the teacher may need to reteach certain steps of the strategy or model strategy use again.

---

1. To get ready, get out your list of spelling words, a piece of paper, and a pencil.

2. Look at the first word you want to learn. Notice any letter patterns in the word.

Cover
- Cover the word after you study it.

Copy
- Write the word from memory on your piece of paper.

Compare
- Uncover the sample word and compare it to what you wrote.

Continue until all words on the spelling list have been spelled and checked.

FIGURE 9.4. Cover–copy–compare poster.

FINAL THOUGHTS

Writing is a complex task that involves the automatic use of basic skills such as handwriting, spelling, and proper grammar usage, in combination with more complex skills such as thought generation, word choice, idea organization, and audience awareness. Students who struggle with the basic skills of writing (e.g., spelling) are more likely to struggle with the complex skills (e.g., idea generation). For example, poor spellers may restrict what they write about to the words they can spell or may lose their thought process (and subsequently their ideas) when they frequently stop to consider the spelling of a word. However, there is good evidence that time spent improving a student's handwriting and spelling skills can result in increases in length of writing and in the number of story or essay elements (e.g., characters, problem, solution). As a result, it is important that students receive explicit instruction in handwriting and spelling early to reduce the likelihood of struggles later on. In addition, explicit instruction in these basic writing skills should be provided to older students who continue to struggle with these skills as they progress through school. Remember that handwriting and spelling are two *critical* prerequisites for acquiring later writing skills—a topic that is discussed further in the following chapter.

CHAPTER 10

Strategies for Written Language

Proficiency at written communication is a critical skill in society today. Student learning in the schools is evaluated, to a great extent, on the basis of written products such as essay tests, reports, and written homework answers (Graham, 2006). Writing also can enhance students learning; writing about a topic can actually improve students' comprehension (Graham & Hebert, 2010). Additionally, more and more states now require students to pass a writing proficiency test to graduate from high school (Zabala et al., 2007). Proficient writing skills are also critical for entry into the job market and success after entry regardless of whether the job is blue collar or white collar (Graham & Harris, 2011). There is now compelling evidence (Salahu-Din, Persky, & Miller, 2008) that a majority of American students need to improve their writing skills, so improving writing skills is a critical concern. The situation is even more serious for students with disabilities. Graham and Harris (2011) noted that among these students 19 of 20 do not acquire sufficient written fluency for success in school. Thus many students with LD and ADHD are at an immediate academic disadvantage and a longer-range risk for difficulty in gaining employment due to problems with written expression.

There are three likely reasons for why these students experience difficulties with writing. First, writing is a difficult and demanding task requiring attention to multiple processes. Not only do students need to learn to attend to the mechanics of text production (as discussed in the previous chapter), they also need to develop effective and efficient composition skills (Graham & Harris, 2003). Negotiating and coordinating basic skills, knowledge, and conventions of written language is often difficult for skilled writers; for students with LD or ADHD it may be overwhelming. Second, skilled writers use strategies to plan, write, and revise their compositions, whereas students with

180

LD or ADHD often lack effective strategies. Moreover, writing requires constant self-regulation and attention control. The ability to regulate and monitor one's own composing process is an important part of writing (Graham & Harris, 2003). Finally, as Graham and Harris (2011) note, many teachers are simply not well prepared to teach writing because few teacher preparation courses provide instruction in evidenced-based writing practices.

PROBLEMS FOR STUDENTS WITH LEARNING DISABILITIES

Students with LD often experience greater difficulties with writing than their nondisabled peers. It is well documented that the writing of students with LD is less polished, coherent, expansive, and effective (Englert & Raphael, 1988; Graham, 1990; Graham & Harris, 1989; Montague, Graves, & Leavell, 1991; Newcomer & Barenbaum, 1991; Wong, Wong, & Blenkinsop, 1989). Although students with LD represent a heterogeneous population, there are some commonalties that can be noted. Wong (2000) identified five areas in which students with LD differ significantly from their nondisabled peers:

1. Students with LD have difficulty expressing their ideas in writing.
2. Students with LD tend to have a warped conception of what constitutes good writing. They focus on the mechanics of writing (spelling, punctuation, etc.) versus clarification and organization.
3. Students with LD use unproductive strategies to make up for their limited vocabularies. When they are unable to find or spell the appropriate word to express their thoughts, they tend to substitute another, simpler word that does not fully communicate what is intended.
4. Students with LD make quantitatively more mechanical errors.
5. Students with LD require more practice to achieve mastery of a writing strategy.

Students with LD typically do not see writing as a purposeful way to communicate and control the world around them, and even if they do, they are often not equipped with appropriate strategies to facilitate their ability to produce effective written communication. Writing instruction should help students develop a more sophisticated approach to composing (Graham, Harris, & McKeown, in press). Students with LD must learn that creating composition is a process involving mastery of three critical recursive elements—(1) planning, (2) organizing, and (3) revising—as well as attention to mechanical aspects of composition (Wong, 2000).

Planning

For students with LD, planning for writing involves, at best, minimal effort. These students often choose a single composition approach: the solitary act of generating written content (Graham & Harris, 2003). They tend to jump right into writing before doing any sort of planning; Scardamalia and Bereiter (1987) termed this behavior *knowledge telling*.

Any information relevant to the topic is written down without regard to organization, goals, or audience; there is minimal metacognitive control (Graham & Harris, 1997). Little attention is directed toward the goal of the composition, which is to express an idea or thought through written communication.

A main objective of writing strategy instruction for students with LD is to enable them to become more planful. Students must be taught to integrate some of the same types of planning strategies, or schemas, that skilled writers utilize. One of the most effective ways to do this is through direct instruction of planning strategies such as brainstorming or semantic webbing. The strategy *STOP and LIST* prompts students to be more planful. STOP and LIST (s̲top, t̲hink o̲f purpose, and l̲ist i̲deas, s̲equence t̲hem) encourages students to identify the purpose of their paper, brainstorm ideas, and organize those ideas (Troia & Graham, 2002). The use of such a strategy prior to writing can lead to more planful, organized compositions.

Organizing

Englert and Mariage (1991b) noted two kinds of organizational knowledge that influence skilled writers' performance:

1. *Understanding and recognizing recurring patterns or text structures.* A writer's ability to recognize and appreciate that text has structures and to use cues related to those structures is crucial to successful composition and comprehension of texts. One of the first text structures to which students are exposed is narrative text structure. Students often understand and recognize narrative or story structure first.

Unfortunately, students with LD are often unaware of patterns or structures in text. They do not analyze text or recognize recurring patterns in text that they read or to which they are exposed. Therefore, they do not utilize these patterns while generating their own compositions. When given a topic, they simply start writing what they know about it, letting each thought prompt the next; minimal effort is made to assess what is written or to regard the constraints of the topic, audience needs, or text organization (Graham & Harris, 2003). Instruction for students with LD must address these issues.

2. *Employing strategies specific to the writing domain.* Organization of written compositions is largely a strategic task. Instructing students to utilize appropriate organizational strategies will help them to be understood by others, as well as improve their ability to interpret and negotiate the meaning of text (Englert & Mariage, 1991b). While composing, students with LD often fail to employ effective or efficient writing strategies to guide composition generation; as a result written work is often difficult and discouraging for both students with LD and their teachers. Directly teaching organizational patterns and strategies to guide composition has proven to be highly effective in improving academic performance of students with LD (Harris & Graham, 1992). Enabling students to utilize appropriate organizational strategies will help them to interpret and negotiate the meaning of their texts, as well as make themselves understood by others (Englert & Mariage, 1991a).

Revision and Mechanics

Revision skills for students with LD often emphasize the mechanics of writing, including handwriting, spelling, grammar, punctuation, and format, rather than revising for clarity of meaning. This is understandable considering that the writing of students with LD is often laden with mechanical errors, including malformed letters, misspelled words, and errors in punctuation and capitalization (Graham & Harris, 2003). These errors inevitably affect students' written compositions, as well as their execution of the writing process. Having to attend to obstacles such as how to spell a word or write a letter can interfere with students' writing flow, leading them to forget writing plans or ideas being held in their working memory. Students who have difficulty with handwriting can likewise lose ideas or plans because their handwriting is not fast enough to keep up with their thought processes (Graham & Harris, 2003).

Students with LD tend to focus their revision efforts on these mechanical errors. They employ a "thesaurus" approach, focusing on word substitutions when trying to enrich their compositions, as well as attempting to "clean up" spelling, grammar, punctuation, format, and other mechanical errors. They are focused on the overall appearance of the composition. These changes are only partly effective; the quality of the composition or clarity of meaning generally remains unchanged (Graham & Harris, 2003).

PREREQUISITE SKILLS

As we noted in the previous chapter, it is essential to consider the prerequisite skills necessary for a student to be a successful writer, not the least of those being transcription skills. These are basic skills that include handwriting and spelling. Proficient writing requires mastery of these basic transcription skills in order for attentional resources to be focused on the greater task at hand: writing a composition for meaning. If students have not yet mastered the mechanics of writing and need to concentrate on putting their language onto paper, they are unable to attend to higher-level skills, such as planning and organizing. For young writers these basic transcription skills can be so demanding it may be necessary to minimize writing tasks (Graham & Harris, 2000).

Graham and Harris (2003, p. 325) cited three sources of information supporting the effect of mechanical difficulties on writing output.

1. Handwriting fluency and spelling account for 66% and 41% of the variability in writing output of primary and intermediate grade students, respectively (Graham et al., 1997).
2. Removal of mechanical demands through dictation usually results in a corresponding increase in written output (De La Paz & Graham, 1995). For instance, the length of stories produced by fifth- and sixth-grade students with LD tripled when they were asked to dictate rather than write or type their compositions (MacArthur & Graham, 1987).
3. Providing extra handwriting instruction for poor writers has a positive impact on their writing output (Berninger et al., 1997, 1998).

It may be necessary to adjust demands on students' transcription skills in order to promote effective and efficient composition skills.

INSTRUCTION IN THE WRITING PROCESS

The process of writing requires frequent reexamination and reworking of text, as well as multiple opportunities for practice. Research suggests that effective writing instruction involves scaffolded writing activities that teach students common structures of composition, as well as actively involving them in the writing process. In the sections that follow, we provide examples of strategies for teaching narrative and expository text structures, as well as strategies for editing and revising.

Narrative Text Structure Strategies

Narrative text structure is one of the first structures to which students are exposed; not surprisingly it is also one of the earliest composition structures acquired by students. Stories follow a pattern that is easily understood by students: setting, episode, and conclusion. Often narrative texts are structured around a main character, a conflict presented to the main character, the action or goal of the main character for solving the problem, outcomes of the actions, and the story conclusion (Englert & Mariage, 1991a). Utilizing students' knowledge of story structure to teach them composition skills is highly beneficial. Students who are aware of the basic parts of a narrative text are often more successful at writing stories as well as understanding stories that they have read.

WWW, What = 2, How = 2

Narrative compositions require students to possess a basic understanding of story structure. Although story structure may be familiar to students, they still may be unclear about how to use it to compose a complete story. Graham and Harris (1989) utilized Story Grammar elements, prompting students, through five steps and a series of questions, to generate narrative prose. These steps and questions encourage students to include all necessary components of a complete narrative composition.

A series of five steps is used to assist students in the composition process. The third step includes the mnemonic WWW, What = 2, How = 2 to help students remember the critical questions of that step (see Table 7.1 in Chapter 7). In Step 1 students are initially prompted to *think of a story that they would like to share with others*. Considering their audience and what their audience's needs and wants are is important. Most of the time, these factors set the tone for the composition. Students are then reminded, in Step 2, to *let their mind be free*. This instruction is intended to increase students' focus on the task of composing by encouraging them to free their minds of distractions and focus on their story.

The third step of the strategy prompts students to *write down the story part reminder: WWW, What = 2, How = 2*. This mnemonic-aided step helps students start to plan and organize their stories, keeping in mind the essential components of a narrative. Having students write down the questions before they start writing down their ideas ensures that they will attend to each of the essential components, not just start writing without consideration of these crucial elements. In the fourth step students are asked to *write down story part ideas for each story part*. This is where the students get to add their ideas.

Answering the story part questions help students with the initial generation of content for their own stories. In the final step, students put together all of their ideas into a complete story. Students are reminded to *use good parts* and *make sense*. After all of the steps are completed, students should have a narrative composition that is (1) interesting to their audience, (2) easy to follow, and (3) possesses all the essential components of a good story. Detailed lesson plans for WWW, What = 2, How = 2 are commercially available (see Harris et al., 2008).

C-SPACE

The C-SPACE strategy (MacArthur, Schwartz, & Graham, 1991) is another strategy based on Story Grammar elements. C-SPACE is an acronym for character, setting, problem, action, conclusion, and emotion. It can also be used to help students learn to write personnel narratives, which are stressed in many elementary curriculums. Organizational strategies to help students plan and write narratives or stories are typically included in instruction of C-SPACE. Detailed lesson plans for using C-SPACE for personal narratives and story writing are commercially available (see Harris et al., 2008; Mason et al., 2012).

Story Map

Knowledge of text structure can provide a map for students to produce well-developed compositions. A graphic organizer (Figure 10.1), such as the one created by Englert, Raphael, and Anderson (1985), can provide a template for student composition. Such an organizer can prompt students to consider which ideas to include, how to organize those ideas, and when the composition is complete (Englert & Mariage, 1991b). This organizer can be used for both composition generation and reading comprehension.

Expository Text Structure Strategies

The concept of using a schema or plan, such as WWW, What = 2, How = 2 or a story map, to produce narrative prose can also be utilized with various expository compositions. The use of strategies or schemas for composing single-genre essays is a good place to start with emergent writers. Teaching students one form of writing enables them to concentrate on basic structural concepts. We started with narrative compositions because of the familiarity of that form of text to young writers. However, various expository text structures can be similarly taught.

Understanding and utilizing text structure are essential to composition. Different text structures can be used for planning, organizing, and drafting various types of expository text. It is important to understand that each type of expository text structure answers different questions, such as these: What is alike? What is different? How are they the same? What is being explained? The answers to these questions are indicated by a range of meaning and sentence structure systems. Certain key word indicators can be found in either topic sentences or concluding sentences. For example, "Fresh water and salt water fish are similar in many ways, yet they are very different in others."

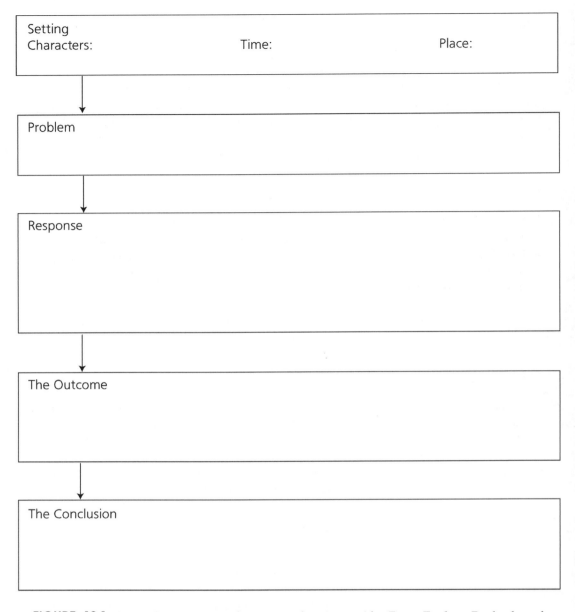

FIGURE 10.1. Story Grammar map/narrative planning guide. From Englert, Raphael, and Anderson (1985).

The structure of this topic sentence and the key words (*similar, yet different*) are indicators of a compare–contrast composition (Englert & Mariage, 1991a). Students with LD often have difficulty picking up on these cues in text. They may understand that a text is explaining what is similar or different about two entities; however, they are often unaware of how the piece is structured. Explicit instruction about various text structures is necessary.

POW + TREE

The TREE strategy (Graham et al., 1987) can be used to guide students' composition of opinion essays. The TREE strategy is composed of four self-directional prompts used to guide the fundamental form of an opinion essay. To most effectively use the TREE strategy, students are taught to use it within a general three-step planning strategy: POW (Table 10.1). The POW strategy is used to frame the writing process; TREE is used to organize the written prose. First, students are asked to <u>p</u>ick an idea. Picking an idea helps students narrow their focus and begin to conceptualize what they will be writing about. Then students are prompted to <u>o</u>rganize their notes using TREE. Students organize their thoughts and ideas in the fashion of a typical opinion essay, starting with a <u>t</u>opic sentence, which is the first step in TREE. Students are taught that a topic sentence <u>t</u>ells readers what they believe clearly and concisely. The topic sentence makes the author's opinion clear.

Students are then asked to provide three or more <u>r</u>easons to support their opinion. These reasons should then be supported with <u>e</u>xamples. Students are prompted to ask themselves, "Why do I believe this?" and "Will my readers believe this?" These questions not only help students to elaborate and support their opinions, they also prompt them to consider the audience's thoughts on their rationale. The final step in the TREE strategy is the <u>e</u>nding. Students need to write a concluding statement that wraps up their thoughts and opinions. The final or ending statement should let the reader know that the essay is complete. This statement ends the paper and usually reiterates the opinion. The final step in POW is to <u>w</u>rite and say more. Students are prompted to

TABLE 10.1. The POW + TREE Strategy

<u>P</u>	Pick my idea.	
<u>O</u>	Organize my notes using TREE.	
	<u>T</u>opic Sentence	Tell what I believe.
	<u>R</u>easons	Three or more.
	<u>E</u>xamples	Why do I believe this? Will my readers believe this?
	<u>E</u>nding	Wrap it up right!
<u>W</u>	Write and say more.	

Note. Based on Graham, Harris, and Mason (2005).

check over their compositions for completeness. If any areas are found that need further development, students should work on them until the composition is complete and fully expresses their opinion.

POWER

Englert and colleagues (1985; Englert & Raphael, 1988; Englert, Raphael, & Anderson, 1985) developed an organizational writing strategy called *POWER* that organizes all the steps in the writing process and teaches students different organizational structures for composition. The POWER strategy can be used with various text structures and in combination with pattern guides for writing. These pattern guides include the compare–contrast structure (Figure 10.2), the explanation structure (Figure 10.3), and the narrative or story structure (Figure 10.1). The example provided in Figure 10.1 can be used for the narrative or story structure pattern guide. The first step in the POWER strategy is planning. Students are encouraged to focus on three areas: (1) the audience for the paper, (2) the purpose of the paper, and (3) the background knowledge that is necessary to write the paper. These areas provide students with a solid foundation to build their composition. The second step is organizing: Students complete a pattern guide to help them organize their papers. A pattern guide is an organizing think sheet and represents the text structure being studied. Students follow this pattern guide to ensure that essential components are included in their written compositions.

The third step is writing. This step involves taking the information from the planning guide and generating a first draft. Students must understand that this is a *first* draft and that the process of writing is recursive. The next step is editing. This step teaches students to critique their own writing and to identify areas in which they need clarification or assistance—an important self-evaluation skill. The editing process is a two-step one involving student self-evaluation and peer editing. During the self-evaluation students reread and evaluate their own drafts, starring sections of the paper they like best and putting question marks in the margins by passages they think may be unclear. Then they think of two questions to ask their peer editors. During peer editing, students read their papers to peer editors, who then summarize the content. Next, the peer editors evaluate the papers, giving an analysis of salient features of the writing that might guide revisions or lead to improvement. For example, a peer editor might suggest that the writer add key words or reorganize the paper for clarity. These suggestions are shared with the writer. Then the peer editor and the writer brainstorm ways to improve the paper.

The final step is revising. During the revising step students decide on changes to make, using their self-evaluation sheet and peer feedback. Teacher modeling on how to insert new text or change the order of information is suggested. Another part of the revision process is a teacher–student conference, wherein changes in writing mechanics are suggested. This way, if a student is still having difficulty with clarity or errors have gone undetected through the other two evaluations, the teacher will be able to make suggestions. A final draft is then composed on a clean sheet of paper. Students can use the checklist in Figure 10.4 to ensure that all steps in the process are followed.

What is being compared–contrasted?	

On what?	

Alike?	Different?

On what?	

Alike?	Different?

On what?	

Alike?	Different?

FIGURE 10.2. POWER planning guide: Comparison–contrast organization form. From Englert, Raphael, and Anderson (1985).

What is being explained?

Materials/things you need?

Setting?

What are the steps?

First,

Next,

Third,

Then,

Last,

FIGURE 10.3. POWER planning guide: Explanation organization form. From Englert, Raphael, and Anderson (1985).

Planning

- ☐ Who will read my paper?
- ☐ Why am I writing this?
- ☐ What do I know about this topic?
- ☐ How can I group/label my facts?

Organizing

- ☐ Which pattern guide do I use (why am I writing this)?
- ☐ Have I filled in the pattern guide completely and answered the questions being asked?

Writing

- ☐ I need to write a paper using the information from the pattern guide, using complete sentences.
- ☐ Have I followed the flow or organization of the pattern guide?

Editing

Self-evaluation

Did I . . .

- ☐ Tell what was being explained?
- ☐ Tell what things you need?
- ☐ Make the steps clear?
- ☐ Use key words?
- ☐ Make it interesting to the reader?
- ☐ Star the parts I like?
- ☐ Put question marks in the margins by things that are unclear?
- ☐ Prepare two questions for my peer editor?

Peer evaluation

- ☐ I need to summarize the paper.
- ☐ Can I pick out, and do I understand, the most important features of the paper?

(continued)

FIGURE 10.4. Example of a checklist for the POWER strategy. From Englert, Raphael, and Anderson (1985).

Did the author . . .

- ☐ Tell what was being explained?
- ☐ Tell what things you need?
- ☐ Make the steps clear?
- ☐ Use key words?
- ☐ Make it interesting to the reader?

☐ Would revisions improve the quality or clarity of the paper? Where?

☐ I need to share suggestions with the writer.

Collaborative conference

☐ Have we decided on ways to make the paper better?

Revising

☐ Have I made the changes to improve my paper using my self-evaluation?

☐ Have I made changes to improve my paper using my peer's evaluation?

☐ Have I made the changes that we decided upon in our collaborative conference?

☐ Is my final draft clean and free of errors?

FIGURE 10.4. *(continued)*

STOP and DARE

The planning and essay writing strategies STOP and DARE were developed by De La Paz and Graham (1997) to help students write better persuasive essays. They have been used effectively with students with LD or ADHD (Jacobson & Reid, 2010). STOP and DARE contains a planning strategy, STOP, and a writing strategy, DARE. First, the planning mnemonic *STOP* is used to help students plan their persuasive essays in an effective manner. *STOP* stands for "Suspend judgment" (consider both sides and think of ideas for and against the topic); "Take a side" (take a position based on the ideas generated and mark the side of the argument the writer will support); "Organize my idea" (mark the strongest ideas and decide how to arrange or sequence them); and finally, "Plan more as I write" (continue to evaluate and revise). These statements help students to brainstorm ideas and organize them for an effective, persuasive essay. As we noted earlier, one problem with students who have ADHD or LD is that they leap into writing without engaging in any planning. To actually write the composition, students use DARE. This essay writing mnemonic prompts students to "Develop a topic sentence," "Add supporting ideas," "Reject possible arguments for the other side," and "End with a conclusion." DARE ensures that students will include all the necessary essay components and also serves as reminder for students to include the ideas developed in planning.

Quick Writes

The Quick Write technique has been recommended to help students write to learn (Fisher & Frey, 2008). It is not a strategy, per se; however, Quick Write can be combined effectively with the strategies discussed previously, such as POW + TREE (Mason, Benedek-Wood, & Valasa, 2009). As the name implies, the Quick Write strategy requires students to plan and write a composition in a brief period of time (i.e., 10 or 15 minutes). Quick Writes can be used at the beginning, middle, or end of instructional units to assess students' understanding and to encourage them to reflect on new knowledge, make connections between topics, summarize knowledge, or react to a topic (Mason, Benedek-Wood, et al., 2009). Quick Writes have been effectively combined with SRSD instruction with students with LD and ADHD (Mason, Kubina, & Taft, 2009). To use Quick Writes in conjunction with a writing strategy is quite straightforward (Mason, Kubina, & Taft, 2009). The strategy (e.g., POW + TREE) is first taught to mastery (i.e., students can use the strategy independently and fluently). Then the teacher discusses how it is important to be able to complete assignments or tasks quickly, and that the more students practice a task, the faster they perform it. The teacher then notes that students can use the strategy to plan and write a composition in a brief period of time. Next, the teacher models using the strategy to quickly write a composition and discusses the process with students. Students then write independently. Note that Quick Writes should not be graded and that the focus should be on getting ideas down on paper as opposed to getting all mechanics (e.g., grammar, punctuation, spelling) correct (Daniels & Bizar, 2005). Detailed lesson plans for using Quick Writes for personal narratives and informative and persuasive essays are available (see Mason et al., 2012).

Editing and Revising Strategies

With students with LD or ADHD, revising during the writing process tends to receive the least amount of time and effort; revisions are generally limited to proofreading for errors (Graham, Harris, & McKeown, 2013). The focus is on appearance (e.g., does the paper look neat?) rather than on content, and fewer than 20% of revisions made actually affect the meaning of compositions. Mechanical revisions, or transcription revisions, are certainly essential to composition; too many mechanical errors are distracting to the reader and take away from the intent of the composition. However, it is also essential for young authors to understand the purpose of writing and to be aware that revisions should not only clean up their writing, but clarify their thoughts. The revision process can be very difficult for many students with LD or ADHD. These students typically have greater difficulty than their nondisabled peers monitoring the content of their writing, and traditionally are not even encouraged to do so. Emphasis in instruction is often placed on the mechanics of writing—handwriting, grammar, and spelling—rather than on developing meaning. As a result they may be unable to detect instances where their writing is unclear, or they may even delete text that is critical to conveying important information in the composition (Graham et al., 2013). Moreover, even when a student locates a problem in text (e.g., a section that is unclear, ambiguous, or that lacks important information), there is no guarantee that he or she will be able to make a revision that remedies the problem. Research suggests that teaching students to make effective revisions involves using problem-solving activities that encourage students to focus their attention on strategies for gathering, analyzing, and structuring information (Reynolds, Hill, Swassing, & Ward, 1988). Unfortunately, revision strategies have received much less attention than planning and organizing strategies, and there are few revision strategies for struggling writers that are supported by research (Graham et al., 2013).

SCAN

Graham and MacArthur (1988) developed the SCAN revision strategy (Table 10.2). Although this strategy was developed for use with a word processor, it can be used on hard copy (without a computer) as well. The SCAN strategy facilitates students' ability to examine written compositions in terms of clarity and cohesiveness, add material where necessary, and correct mechanical errors (Harris & Graham, 1999). The SCAN strategy consists of five steps. Step 1 is to "read your essay." Students need to read the first draft of their essay to reacquaint themselves with the substance of their paper. Step 2 is to "find the sentence that tells what you believe—is it clear?" This step encourages writers to reexamine their topic sentence and make sure it is stated clearly and accurately. Students also check the topic sentence to ensure that it reflects the desired intent. If it does not, then it needs to be revised. Step 3 is to "add two more reasons why you can believe it." This step helps the writer provide enough support to adequately defend his or her position. Step 4 is where the SCAN mnemonic comes in: Students are to "*SCAN* each sentence" and ask themselves: "Does it make sense?", "Is it connected to my belief?", and "Can I add more?" Then students note any errors. Each sentence is "scanned" to make sure that the essay is (1) clear—will the reader understand it?; (2) useful—does it directly support the development of the argument?; (3) complete—do more details need to be added to make the sentence better?; and (4) error free—are there any mechanical errors that need to be corrected? During Step 5, the final step, students make any necessary changes on either the computer or on a hard copy.

TABLE 10.2. SCAN Content Revision Strategy

Step 1:   Read your essay.

Step 2:   Find the sentence that tells what you believe—is it clear?

Step 3:   Add two more reasons why you can believe it.

Step 4:   *SCAN* each sentence and ask yourself:
"Does it make sense?"
"Is it connected to my belief?"
"Can I add more?"

Step 5:   Make your changes on the computer and/or on a hard copy.

Note. Based on Graham and MacArthur (1988).

IMPLEMENTATION PLANS

In this section we provide partial examples of implementation plans for each of the writing strategies previously mentioned.

Stage 1 for WWW, What = 2, How = 2: Developing and Activating Background Knowledge

Prior to teaching the strategy, it is necessary to evaluate students' background knowledge, attitudes, and beliefs about writing. Formal or informal assessments can be used to determine which skills the students possess and which skills they lack; doing a task breakdown will provide the information for identifying the skills necessary to successfully complete the strategy. Table 10.3 shows a sample task breakdown for the WWW, What = 2, How = 2 strategy.

Stage 2 for POW + TREE: Discussing the Strategy

This is the first stage in initiating the strategy when it is important to stress its relevance. During an initial conference the teacher discusses the student's current performance. In order for students to be successful and able to self-regulate, they need to make a commitment to use the strategy; they need to "buy into" the value of the strategy. Thus, it is important for the teacher to stress this value. Brainstorm with the students on situations wherein using this strategy or completing a given task accurately is important. For example, the following might be appropriate brainstorming ideas in response to the question "When would it be important for you to write a persuasive opinion paper?":

- Complaining to a company
- Debating or defending a position
- Writing a letter to the editor
- Campaigning
- Trying to change someone's mind

A sample script for "selling" the strategy follows:

"The reason I wanted to talk with you is that we have been doing a lot of writing this year, and I know sometimes writing can be a difficult thing to do. Let's take a look at some of the papers that you wrote this month. You really did a nice job [point out positives; focusing on topic sentences, reasons, explanations, and endings]. However, if I try and understand what your opinion is on [topic of the paper], it is difficult for me. Earlier you had said that it would be important to make your opinion clear if you were [focus on when the student felt it would be important to write a persuasive opinion paper]. Right now your opinion is not as clear or persuasive as it could be. I have an idea about how we can make your opinion clearer in your writing. You know how you use tools in shop class to make your projects

TABLE 10.3. Sample Task Breakdown for WWW, W = 2, H = 2

Strategy	Skills	Assessment
Basic writing skills	Ability to write (print)	Given an informal assessment, the student will correctly produce letters.
	Ability to spell	Provided with a spelling test on common words in narrative prose, the student will be able to write and spell words correctly.
	Knowledge of basic grammar and punctuation	Given text with grammatical and mechanical errors, the student will be able to satisfactorily detect and correct those errors.
Who is the main character? Who else is in the story?	Knowledge of story elements	Given a story, the student will be able to identify all major story elements.
	Knowledge of main character and how to develop a main character	
	Knowledge of other characters	
When does the story take place?	Knowledge of setting	
What does the main character do?	Knowledge of action	
What happens when he or she tries to do it?	Knowledge of consequence of action	
How does the story end?	Knowledge of story endings/resolutions	
How does the main character feel?	Knowledge of emotions and how to present them in text	

better? I have a tool for you to use in writing that will make your papers better. The tool is a strategy called POW + TREE. The POW part of this strategy gives you power when you write, and the TREE part helps you remember all the parts to a good opinion essay."

In this stage we also introduce the strategy steps and any prompts that will be given (Figure 10.5).

Stage 3 for STOP and DARE: Modeling the Strategy

The teacher will need to use a think-aloud to demonstrate the use of the strategy. Here is an example of a think-aloud for the STOP and DARE strategy.

"Well, my teacher assigned us to write an essay about our opinion on whether teenagers should be allowed to work part-time jobs during the school year. I can do this because she taught us that STOP and DARE would help us to write a good essay. OK, what do I need to do first? I think I will write down the STOP and DARE parts. I'll use those parts to plan and organize my paper. Writing out the steps will keep me from accidentally skipping any important parts. OK, that's done, so now I'm ready to plan out my essay. The first step is 'Suspend judgment.' I need to carefully think about both sides of the issue and write down my ideas. I'll draw a line down the middle of my page and label one side *yes* and one side *no*. Then I will write my ideas for and against in the columns. That will help me keep organized. OK, that looks like a pretty good list.

"All right, what's the next step? I'll check the steps I wrote on the top of my paper. Good thing I wrote them down. OK. *T* is 'Take a side.' I know what side I think is best. Students absolutely should be allowed to work part-time jobs. Wait. I need to check the ideas I wrote down to make sure that is a good choice. OK. I think I have a bunch of good ideas for why they should be allowed to work. I'll put a star on the *yes* side to remind me that this is the side I chose. Now I need to 'Organize my idea,' so I have to pick the ideas that I think are best and decide on the order I will write about. Well, my teacher always says to use your best idea first, so I will

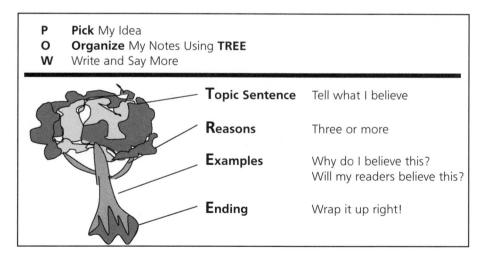

FIGURE 10.5. Example of a mnemonic chart for POW + TREE.

pick 'A job teaches students responsibility' as my first idea. Now I can just put the others in order. I think that is a great argument. Wow. It didn't take long at all to plan this essay.

"OK, now I'm ready to start to 'Plan more as I write.' What do I do first? I remember. I 'Develop a topic sentence.' That's really important because it tells readers my position. I need to make the topic sentence really clear. I'll try to be really clear: 'I believe that students should be allowed to work part-time jobs during the school year.' That sounds pretty clear to me. Now I have to 'Add supporting ideas.' Hey, I've already developed them when I used STOP. Boy, this strategy really helps. I will go through and put each one in my essay. I need to remember to add more details to the ideas to really make a strong argument. I'm on the home stretch now. If I keep going, I'll be done in no time. I remember that my next step is to 'Reject possible arguments for the other side.' OK, I think the best argument on the other side is that working could hurt a student's schoolwork. How do I reject that? I know, I will say that students should only work on the weekends when it won't affect their schoolwork. Almost done now and I really like my essay so far. Just one more thing. I need to 'End with a conclusion' that says why students should be allowed to work part time. I did a good job!"

Stage 4 for POWER: Memorizing the Strategy

Memorizing the strategy is extremely important! We want the students to be able to focus on the task and not on trying to remember the steps of the strategy. The specific activities used to help students memorize a strategy are not nearly as important. There are many appropriate activities. The important aspect of the activities is whether or not they facilitate memorization. You will need to plan and prepare the activities and monitor their effectiveness. Here are some examples of memorization activities for the POWER strategy.

Ball Toss Game

The teacher starts off with the ball and tosses it to a student. That student starts off and says, "P—P stands for planning. We need to plan what to write, remembering the audience for the paper, the purpose, and the background information necessary to write the paper." Then that student tosses the ball to another student of their choice. That student needs to say, "O—O stands for . . .," and so on. It is important that the students not only say the letter and what the letter stands for, but also what that means. That is, they need to know what to do at each step in the strategy.

Reciting the Strategy with a Partner

Students are matched up in pairs. A student who struggles should be matched with a peer who can help with memorization of the strategy. Prior to the activity these peers are instructed on how to help their partners. The students recite the POWER mnemonic and what they need to do at each step in the strategy. Students then take turns using the mnemonic chart to check if their partner can recite the steps of the strategy and what must be done at each step.

Making Student Checklists

Students are given a checklist for the POWER strategy (Figure 10.4). The checklist lists the steps of the strategy and what must be done at each step. Students are able to use their lists to ensure that they complete all steps of the strategy. The checklists should be laminated for multiple uses and placed on students' desks to be readily accessible.

Stage 5 for SCAN: Supporting the Strategy

Scaffolding is important in this stage. With scaffolding it is possible to gradually transfer strategy ownership from teacher to student. Students need to be given adequate time and support to master the strategy. Here are examples of how to use content, task, and material scaffolding with the SCAN strategy.

Content Scaffolding

Provide students with a simple passage. The teacher and students then go over the passage and SCAN for revisions. The teacher directs the process and the students provide answers to teacher-directed questions (i.e., "Is this a complete sentence?", "Does this make sense here?", "Are the author's feelings clear?"). Next, students are given a passage that they had written during their baseline probes. They can use the SCAN strategy to evaluate and revise their compositions. Provide a chart to ensure that every step is included.

Task Scaffolding

During collaborative practice the teacher prompts students to name the step that should be performed; then the teacher describes the step and models its use. In subsequent lessons the teacher asks students to name the steps in the SCAN strategy and describe each step, and then the teacher models the steps. Finally, the students name, describe, and model the steps of the SCAN strategy.

Material Scaffolding

Provide students with a mnemonic prompt card to be placed on their desk. Initially, this card lists the steps of the strategy and describes what to do at each step. Over time these cards provide less direction, first fading the descriptions, and eventually fading the mnemonic and steps altogether. At this point students should have reached mastery of the strategy and be able to work independently.

Stage 6 for POWER: Independent Performance

At this stage students are ready to use the strategy independently. The teacher's main task is to monitor students' performance and check on proper and consistent use of the strategy. If students deviate from the given POWER strategy, their performance should be evaluated and action taken only if performance is no longer improving.

Teachers also must evaluate whether or not the strategy is being generalized to other appropriate situations. Students do not always generalize strategies to appropriate situations; they often need to be prompted and encouraged to do so. To promote generalization, students should be encouraged to use the strategy in other content areas where they are required to write expository papers. All team teachers should be informed about the use of the strategy, the prompts, and what is required at each step. All team teachers are given a wall chart to hang up in their room as a reminder for students to use the POWER strategy when appropriate. Note that these activities can begin earlier in the instructional process.

Students keep a writing portfolio, which allows them to see the difference that the use of the strategy has made in the content of their writing. To create the portfolio:

1. Collect initial baseline probes to use in the initial conference and as part of the scaffolding process. These baseline probes also serve to illustrate the development of students' written compositions.
2. Take writing samples during strategy instruction to demonstrate student progress through the use of the POWER strategy.
3. Take a final sample, which will be included in the portfolio once it is determined that the student has reached mastery of strategy use.

Portfolios serve many purposes; the main purpose is to provide evidence of improved academic performance. These portfolios are evaluated by several people: students, teachers, parents, and administrators. After evaluating their own portfolio, students are questioned to find out whether or not they see an improvement in their writing skill and if they see the strategy as valuable to them or not. The teacher evaluates the portfolio to provide evidence of improved academic performance for grading purposes.

FINAL THOUGHTS

Writing is a complex task requiring attention to multiple processes. Negotiating and coordinating skills, knowledge, strategies, and conventions of written language can be difficult even for skilled writers. These processes are even more difficult for students with LD or ADHD. These students often lack the knowledge, skills, and strategies to be effective writers, and they do not understand that writing is purposeful. They have difficulty expressing their ideas; they focus on mechanical aspects of written communication, use unproductive strategies in their writing, and do not attend to critical writing elements. They also have problems monitoring the writing process (e.g., planning, composing, determining whether text makes sense). And, as we discussed in the previous chapter, students with LD or ADHD often lack the prerequisite skills necessary to effective writers, so it is also important to attend closely to these skills, particularly transcription skills and spelling.

Despite the difficulties inherent in the writing process, the evidence is clear that, through strategy instruction, students with LD or ADHD can be taught to attend to the critical elements of writing—planning, organizing, and revising—which can provide them with the knowledge, skills, and strategies they need to become effective writers.

CHAPTER 11

Strategies in Reading Comprehension

Reading comprehension is considered the "essence of reading" (Durkin, 1993). If readers can read the words but do not understand what they are reading, they are not really reading. Reading, at some level, is involved in all academic courses. Students are expected to read a variety of texts and comprehend them in order to gain knowledge. While reading comprehension in schools usually involves understanding textbook assignments, reading comprehension skills can also influence a student's ability to understand written directions, homework assignments, and other literature. The need to comprehend text is not exclusive to academic learning; it is also essential in everyday activities and to be successful in society (Mason et al., 2012). For example, students must acquire strong literacy skills to deal with the flood of information, especially from web-based resources, that they encounter daily. This flood of information requires students to be able to gather, comprehend, evaluate, and synthesize information from a variety of media forms and sources (National Governors Association Center for Best Practices [NGA] and Council of Chief State School Officers [CCSSO], 2010). In addition, it has been estimated that today's youth need more advanced literacy skills (i.e., comprehension of text) than previous generations to keep up with the increasing demands in the workplace (Biancarosa & Snow, 2006). Thus, improving students' reading comprehension can positively impact both educational outcomes and other important aspects of their lives.

Comprehension of text requires a wide variety of skills and cognitive processes. Students must be able to negotiate, manipulate, translate, and construct meaning from written language (King, 1994). Proficient readers not only read fluently, they also construct meaning through their interactions with text (Durkin, 1993). There is a reciprocal interaction between the reader and the ideas or message presented in a particular text. Good readers continuously construct and reconstruct meaning while reading. They are able to activate background knowledge prior to reading (prereading strategies), to monitor comprehension while reading (during-reading strategies), and to check for understanding after reading (postreading strategies; National Reading Panel, 2000). These strategies are automatic to good readers; however, many of these concepts seem to elude struggling readers, including students with LD. Thus, instruction for struggling readers must address these deficits.

Research on text comprehension demonstrates that students with LD or ADHD can be taught to use comprehension strategies (Bakken, Mastropieri, & Scruggs, 1997; Englert & Mariage, 1991a; Gardill & Jitendra, 1999; Idol, 1987; Johnson, Graham, & Harris, 1997; Johnson et al., 2012; Nelson, Smith, & Dodd, 1992). It is important to teach comprehension strategies in the primary grades; reading comprehension should be emphasized from the beginning rather than waiting until students have *mastered* the prerequisite skills of reading (National Reading Panel, 2000). Effective reading comprehension strategies should be taught explicitly, through direct explanation, modeling, and guided practice. Students should be made aware that the overall goal is improved reading comprehension, and they should understand the importance of the strategy to achieving that goal. The strategy should be demonstrated along with the metacognitive processes associated with it; students should be given ample opportunities to practice using the strategy and directed through the process until they have mastered it.

PROBLEMS FOR STUDENTS WITH LEARNING DISABILITIES

Students with LD have particular difficulty with many of the skills involved in comprehending text. By definition, students with LD experience an unexpected failure to learn. The overwhelming majority (at least 80%) of students with LD experience serious difficulty with learning to read (Gersten, Fuchs, Williams, & Baker, 2001). Clearly students with LD are not a homogeneous group; however, there are some commonalities that can be noted. Many students with LD show specific deficits in the area of phonological processing (decoding—sound–symbol correlation) and fluency (decoding with speed, accuracy, and expression). These deficits affect their ability to comprehend text. However, many other children with LD are able to read reasonably fluently but do not understand what they have read because of specific cognitive processing difficulties (Williams, 2003). Thus, some students with LD possess the cognitive abilities necessary to effectively comprehend text; however, for some reason they do so inefficiently or ineffectively (Gersten et al., 2001).

Reading comprehension involves strategic processing of language and concepts; students must be able to take in information from written language, organize that information in a logical manner, and construct meaning from that information. Students with LD often have greater difficulty with this process, and breakdowns occur because they are unable to regulate their cognitive processes in a purposeful, reflective manner (Gersten et al., 2001). Swanson and Alexander (1997) identified four particular cognitive processes that pose difficulties for students with LD: (1) phonological processing (noted earlier), (2) orthographic and semantic processing, (3) metacognition, and (4) working memory.

Orthographic and Semantic Processing

Orthographic (spelling) and semantic (word meaning) processing difficulties directly impact students' ability to comprehend text. If students are unable to negotiate spelling conventions or understand the meaning of words in text, it is not likely that they will be able to comprehend the material. Orthographic processing difficulties are common among students with LD. It is often difficult for these students to understand or manipulate the conventions of written language such as correct and incorrect spellings (Swanson & Alexander, 1997). Semantic processing (understanding the meaning of words) also presents difficulties for students with LD, who are often unable to create a meaningful representation of text. It is suggested that this is one reason for their reading difficulties (Swanson & Alexander, 1997): They have particular difficulty retrieving semantic information while reading. This inability to remember the meaning of words dramatically influences their ability to comprehend text.

Metacognition

Metacognition is essential to reading comprehension. The reader's awareness of and ability to regulate, monitor, and adjust cognitive actions are key components of comprehension (Swanson & Alexander, 1997). Good readers focus their attention (e.g., "What am I reading and why am I reading it?"), realize when there is a breakdown in comprehension, and apply fix-up strategies to gain comprehension of text (e.g., go back and reread, look at headings/figures in a text). Poor readers, including those with LD, often lack the awareness or ability necessary to regulate those various cognitive actions. Often, students with LD possess a degree of metacognition but lack strategies to properly utilize that knowledge. For example, they may be aware when a breakdown in comprehension occurs but lack the necessary fix-up strategies to achieve comprehension. Teaching students with LD procedures or strategies to enhance their metacognition can positively influence their text comprehension (Swanson & Alexander, 1997).

Working Memory

Working memory is the portion of memory used to process information (Swanson, 1996b). Working memory is essential to text comprehension; while reading, it is necessary to briefly store incoming information while other information is being added or manipulated. This is how text begins to evolve into meaningful information (Swanson & Alexander, 1997). However, working memory is a processing resource of limited capacity. It is able to hold only a limited number of "chunks" of information at a time, and then only for a matter of seconds. We are consciously aware of the information in our working memory; however, if we do not process the information, it will be lost. In other words, as soon as information is not being used, it disappears. To effectively comprehend text, one must be able to hold a small amount of information in working memory for a short time while simultaneously processing that information (Swanson & Alexander, 1997).

PREREQUISITE SKILLS

A variety of skills is necessary to successfully comprehend written material. The National Reading Panel, the Partnership for Reading, the National Institute for Literacy, the National Institute of Child Health and Human Development, and the U.S. Department of Education have identified five essential components to effective literacy instruction: (1) phonemic awareness, (2) phonological processing, (3) fluency, (4) vocabulary, and (5) text comprehension. These components are not independent of each other. A student's ability to manipulate sounds in spoken language (phonemic awareness) is a critical component, affecting the ability to understand that there is a predictable relationship between spoken and written sounds (phonics). Students must regulate those cognitive processes in order to read fluently and accurately (fluency). A student's ability to read fluently and to understand the meaning of novel words (vocabulary) directly affects his or her ability to comprehend text (text comprehension).

Effective instruction in each of these areas is crucial. Explicit, systematic instruction in early literacy skills has proven to be the most effective method for teaching these essential skills (National Reading Panel, 2000). Each skill builds on the next with the end goal of reading comprehension. Phonemic awareness is the ability to discern, reflect on, and manipulate the individual sounds in spoken words. Prior to learning to read print, children need to become aware of how the sounds in words work. Children who cannot discern and manipulate the phonemes of spoken words will have a difficult time learning how to relate these phonemes to graphemes (letters representing sounds) when they see them in written words (National Reading Panel, 2000). The ability to relate phonemes to written words is part of phonological processing. Phonological processing involves learning the alphabetic system; children must learn the letter–sound correspondences and spelling patterns, as well as be able to apply this knowledge to their reading. Phonological processing is consistently implicated in the ability of students with LD to successfully comprehend text. This is one of the most overt processes that presents difficulties for students' success with reading comprehension (Swanson & Alexander, 1997).

Reading fluency is also highly correlated with reading comprehension. Fluent readers are able to decode text with speed, accuracy, and expression. Reading fluently is dependent upon word recognition skill. Students who are not fluent readers often have difficulty gleaning the meaning of text (National Reading Panel, 2000). Meaning is often compromised by lack of fluency, resulting in unrewarding reading experiences, and reading is then avoided or done merely as a task to get finished, with little cognitive involvement (Cunningham & Stanovich, 1998).

Vocabulary is a prerequisite of reading comprehension because readers must know what *most* of the words mean before they can understand what is being read. Vocabulary and reading comprehension are both related to the meaning of print. Vocabulary is linked to the specific meaning of words, whereas reading comprehension covers larger units of meaning (i.e., themes or concepts). Vocabulary can be broken down into different categories: listening vocabulary, speaking vocabulary, reading vocabulary, and writing vocabulary (National Reading Panel, 2000). Each of these requires a different level of knowledge. Reading vocabulary requires that students recognize and understand various words or word parts in written text. A student's ability to recognize and understand words in text directly affects his or her ability to comprehend that text (National Reading Panel, 2000). Struggling readers and students with LD typically bring less vocabulary knowledge to a reading task, and consequently their comprehension suffers.

PREREADING STRATEGIES

Students with LD often possess a limited understanding of various text structures (the way ideas in text are organized) and often have limited knowledge of subject matter (Garner, 1987). They have difficulties specifically with the difference between narrative (story structure) and expository text structures (textbook or formal writing structure).

Narrative Text Structure

Narrative text structure is usually the first structure to which children are exposed and, not surprisingly, they are often more familiar with it than with other structures. Narratives generally involve a sequence of events that includes characters, actions, goals, and emotions. Skilled readers typically understand this series of events and expect the story to unfold in a certain way. This basic knowledge leads them to ask relevant questions about the story they are reading while they are reading it (Gersten et al., 2001). Less skilled readers often lack mastery of this schema and must be taught how text is structured and what relevant questions would be.

The Story Grammar Strategy

Short and Ryan (1984) taught students to use the Story Grammar strategy (see Figure 4.5, p. 64), which provides a strategic plan for selecting important aspects of the story information for further study. These students were taught to vocalize questions dealing with important story information, note questions in the margins, and underline story information that answered the Story Grammar questions. The Story Grammar strategy includes five questions:

1. Who is the main character?
2. Where and when did the story take place?
3. What did the main character do?
4. How did the story end?
5. How did the main character feel?

This strategy is unstructured; the procedural information is left out (i.e., exactly what steps the students will perform to use the strategy). Chapter 4 provides an example of how the Story Grammar strategy can be structured, as well as a sample implementation plan. When students were initially taught to use the Story Grammar strategy, they were given written text on which they could mark. This is not a luxury that is afforded to many classroom teachers; thus the sample implementation plan does not follow along exactly with Short and Ryan's (1984) study.

Expository Text Structure

As children progress through school, the demands change, with an increasing emphasis on comprehension of expository text. Typically, children are "learning to read" up through third grade. By fourth grade there tends to be a shift from "learning to read" to "reading to learn." Instruction for children in the primary grades relies heavily on reading stories for reading instruction. However, in fourth grade students are increasingly expected to work with expository text. Students with LD often have a difficult time gaining knowledge from expository text.

Often, difficulties are due to the fact that students with LD have limited knowledge of expository text structure. Unlike narrative text structures, children are not regularly exposed to expository text structures outside of the school environment. Several text structures provide useful information. Some are physical features such as headers, bold print, italics, tables, and figures. We discuss strategies that use text features in Chapter 13, which focuses on study skills. Anderson and Armbruster (1984) identified six major expository text structures (Table 11.1): (1) description, (2) temporal sequence of events, (3) explanation, (4) definition–example, (5) compare–contrast, and (6) problem–solution–effect. Good readers are aware of text structures and are able to make logical connections and create their own schema (representation) while reading text.

Research on expository text comprehension suggests that (1) awareness of text structure is acquired developmentally, (2) some text structures are more apparent and

TABLE 11.1. Examples of Expository Text Structures

Text structures	Explanation
Description	Text that illustrates a topic; a written account, representation, or explanation of something.
Temporal sequence of events	The time order in which things are arranged, actions are carried out, or events happen.
Explanation	A statement giving reasons for something or details of something.
Definition–example	Describing or stating something clearly and unambiguously, as well as providing an illustration that supports or provides more information.
Problem–solution–effect	A difficult situation, or matter, and how it is resolved, and how the change occurred as a direct result of the situation and resolution.

Note. See Anderson and Armbruster (1984) for more details.

easier for readers to grasp, and (3) skill at discriminating text structure and at using it appear to be central for comprehension of expository text (Gersten et al., 2001). If students are ill-equipped to negotiate and strategically process expository text, it will be difficult for them to gain knowledge from it. Teaching students strategies for negotiating and comprehending expository text can significantly improve their performance; knowledge of text structures leads students to ask themselves constructive questions about the text they are reading and to build the cognitive connections necessary for comprehension (Gersten et al., 2001).

The SCROL Strategy

The SCROL strategy was designed to improve student reading and learning from content-area texts (Grant, 1993). It is intended for students in middle and upper grades. The SCROL strategy (see Figure 4.2, p. 56) includes five steps: (1) *Survey* the headings; (2) write down any key words from the heading that might provide *Connections* between them; (3) *Read* the text looking for words and phrases that express important information about the headings; (4) *Outline* the text using indentations to reflect text structure; and (5) *Look back* at the text and check the accuracy of the major ideas and details. This strategy is intended to help students read and understand a variety of texts. The strategy encourages students to use text headings to aid their comprehension and help them find and remember important information. Chapter 4 provides additional information and an example of an implementation plan for the SCROL strategy.

DURING-READING STRATEGIES

While reading new, unfamiliar text, students with LD often lack strategies to assist them when their comprehension is disrupted. Monitoring comprehension is essential to the reading process and requires that students be actively involved at a metacognitive level. Unfortunately, as we mentioned earlier, students with LD are not actively involved at metacognitive level. However, through strategy instruction, students can be taught to be more actively involved with the reading material and to monitor their comprehension of the text.

Question Generation–Question Answering

The most common measure of a student's reading comprehension is answering questions at the end of a text (Graham & Wong, 1993). Answering questions after reading encourages students to focus on the important concepts in text; however, students with LD often have a difficult time with this task. One way to bolster student performance in question answering is to teach them to generate their own think-type questions (see next section). By generating think-type questions, students become more cognitively involved with the text. Question generation promotes active engagement with text and increases students' ability to monitor comprehension.

The Question-Generation Strategy

Davey and McBride (1986) taught upper elementary students how to generate two types of questions: those linking information across sentences and those related to the *most* important information (Table 11.2). First, students were taught the value of question generation while reading. Generating questions while reading promotes active involvement with text, cues the reader to focus on important concepts, and prompts the reader to think beyond what is provided in the text. Second, students were taught to differentiate between locate- and think-type questions. Locate-type questions merely pose a question that can be answered by directly restating information from the text (e.g., "What year was the first Nobel Peace Prize awarded?"). Think-type questions require additional cognitive and linguistic demands. Students are required to think beyond what is in the text and to state those thoughts in the form of a question. Good think-type questions help students remember key information, know if they need to reread, and anticipate test questions (e.g., "Why did the author use a graphic artist to describe ratios?"). Third, students were taught how to generate question stems for relating information from one part of the passage to information in another part (i.e., How did the author relate _____ to _____? Why did the author use _____ to describe _____?). Then students were taught important signal words to use in question stems (*what*, *why*, and *how*) and what an appropriate response would look like.

TABLE 11.2. Steps in Teaching Students a Question-Generation Strategy

Step 1. Provide rationale
- Explain why generation of think-type questions helps reading comprehension.

Step 2. Question type
- Explain the difference between locate- and think-type questions.
  - *Locate-type questions* can be answered directly from the text—for example, "What is the capital of Nebraska?"
  - *Think-type questions* require thinking beyond the text—for example, "Why did the author use a tunnel to describe her life?"

Step 3. Linking information
- Explain what a question stem is.
- Explain signal words for question stems: *What, Why, How.*
- Provide examples of question stems and what appropriate responses look like.
  Q: "What did the author say about _____ in the previous passage?"
  A: "The author said _____."
  Q: "Why did the author use _____ to explain _____ in the previous passage?"
  A: "The author used that as an example because _____."
  Q: "How does _____ relate to _____?"
  A: "_____ relates to _____ by _____."

Step 4. Self-monitoring
- Teach students how to self-monitor their performance of the question-generation strategy by using a checklist (Figure 11.1).

Note. Based on Davey and McBride (1986).

For example, "What did the author say about _____ in the previous passage? The author said _____." Finally, students were taught how to self-monitor their use of the question-generation strategy (Figure 11.1). Students also were presented with questions asking how well they felt they had done using the question-generation strategy.

Graphic/Semantic Organizers

Graphic organizers, originally called *structure overviews*, provide readers with new approaches to reading that are different from traditional, linear text presentation (Horton, Lovitt, & Bergerud, 1990). In this approach, a graphic aid is used to illustrate the structure of the text and the interrelations among concepts, providing readers with a clearer, more substantial understanding of what is being read (Chang, Sung, & Chen, 2002). Graphic organizers vary in structure and detail. Even though graphic representations of different texts will look different, the underlying principles and methods of application are very similar. They all convert linear information (text) into nonlinear graphic representations. Graphic organizers can be used with narrative or expository text.

How well did I identify important information?

5 = Excellent 4 = Good 3 = Satisfactory 2 = Somewhat 1 = Not at all

How well did I link information together?

5 = Excellent 4 = Good 3 = Satisfactory 2 = Somewhat 1 = Not at all

How well could I answer my question?

5 = Excellent 4 = Good 3 = Satisfactory 2 = Somewhat 1 = Not at all

Did my "think" question use different language from the text?

☐ Yes   ☐ No

Did I use good signal words?

☐ Yes   ☐ No

FIGURE 11.1. Question-generation strategy checklist.

The Story Map Strategy

Idol (1987) used a graphic organizer called the Story Map to improve students' reading comprehension. This technique was based on a schema–theory view of reading comprehension. This view emphasizes the development of an improved association between the reader's prior knowledge structures (schemas) and written text, and it helps students effectively apply story schemas to create a graphic representation. The Story Map (Figure 11.2) is a graphic representation of parts of a story and how they are interrelated. This framework draws the student's attention to elements common among narrative prose.

Students are taught to read the story and note, in some manner, the elements in the Story Map: (1) the setting, including characters, time, and place; (2) the problem; (3) the goal; (4) the action; and (5) the outcome. As mentioned earlier, this is an unstructured strategy; the exact procedure or structure to follow needs to be determined by the teacher. We provide an example of how this could be done in Chapter 4 (see pp. 50–69).

Paraphrasing/Note-Taking Strategies

One way to increase comprehension of text is to paraphrase while reading and/or to take notes. Strategies that explicitly teach students to monitor understanding while reading (e.g., check for understanding after a paragraph or section), identify important information, and paraphrase (e.g., orally or by taking notes) have been effective at increasing the comprehension of students who struggle to learn from text (e.g., students with LD or ADHD).

RAP

Several researchers have explored the effects of teaching students to paraphrase text using the paraphrasing strategy (Schumaker, Denton, & Deschler, 1984). The strategy, sometimes called the *RAP* strategy, has been successfully taught to students with and without disabilities across grade levels (see Graves, 1986; Graves & Levin, 1989; Hagaman & Reid, 2008; Hagaman et al., 2012). The three-step strategy helps students find and remember the main idea of the text they have read:

1. <u>R</u>ead a paragraph.
2. <u>A</u>sk myself, "What was the main idea of that paragraph? What are important details about that main idea?"
3. <u>P</u>araphrase or put the main idea and details into my own words.

By self-questioning and putting information into their own words, students are actively processing information in the text, which increases the likelihood that they will remember what they have read.

There are commercially available lesson plans for teaching the paraphrasing strategy (see Mason et al., 2012). However, it should be noted that these lessons have added

The setting

Who is in the story?

_____
_____
_____

When did the story happen?

_____
_____
_____

Where did the story happen?

_____
_____
_____

The problem, goal, or action

What did the main character do?

_____
_____
_____
_____

What happened next?

_____
_____
_____
_____

The outcome

How did the story end?

_____
_____
_____
_____
_____

FIGURE 11.2. Story Grammar sheet.

a step to the three-step RAP strategy. Specifically, prior to reading, students are asked to *think* before they beginning reading (e.g., "What is my purpose for reading this passage? What might I already know about this topic?"). When the "think step" is added to the RAP strategy, the acronym becomes *TRAP*. Adding the first step to create TRAP is important for increasing reading comprehension because it asks students to access prior knowledge and approach reading more strategically by determining the purpose for reading (e.g., as assignment, for fun). This change in the strategy also helps when introducing and selling the strategy because teachers can talk about the strategy helping to *TRAP* important information from a passage or chapter (Mason et al., 2012).

TWA

TWA is comprised of nine strategies in three phases of reading—before reading, while reading, and after reading (Mason, 2004). In the first phase, "Think before reading," students are asked to identify text structure and develop statements about what they already know and questions identifying what they want to learn. "While reading," students are taught to monitor their reading speed, check their understanding (e.g., reread if necessary), and make connections (e.g., relate new information to information they might already know). In the "After reading" phase, students are taught to identify the main ideas and summarize important information from the text. Several studies have found positive effects when teaching the TWA strategy to students with and without LD or ADHD (see Hedin, Mason, & Gaffney, 2011; Johnson et al., 2012; Mason, Hickey Snyder, Sukhram, & Kedem, 2006). In addition, prepared lesson plans for teaching TWA are available to teachers (see Mason et al., 2012).

POSTREADING STRATEGIES

Linking Comprehension Questions to Text

The ability to answer questions at the end of text *is* important; however, the ability to successfully search for appropriate information within a text to find the correct answer is of equal importance (Raphael & McKinney, 1983). As noted earlier, question answering is one of the primary means by which we assess a student's ability to comprehend text. This makes a student's ability to access appropriate information within a text a key factor in successfully comprehending text. Knowledge of the relationship between comprehension questions and the text used to answer them is a critical comprehension skill (Raphael & McKinney, 1983). Explicit instruction on this relationship can improve comprehension skills and dramatically affect reading comprehension.

The Question–Answer Relationship Strategy

Raphael and Wonnacott (1985) taught students to recognize the relationship between comprehension questions and the text answer sources; these question–answer relationships (QARs) were divided into three types (1) "right there" (text explicit), (2) "think and search" (text implicit), and (3) "on my own" (script implicit). A "right there" QAR is a question with an answer stated explicitly in the text within a single sentence. A "think and search" QAR is a question that requires the reader to integrate information across sentences or paragraphs. An "on my own" QAR is a question that requires the reader to draw from his or her own background knowledge to answer the question. Through a process of modeling and fading, students were taught to identify the type of QAR posed by particular questions. Students were led through examples and provided rationales for different QARs. Independent practice was increased once students had achieved mastery of the QAR strategy. Students were given passages and comprehension questions to assess their ability to identify the different QARs (Figure 11.3). For example, students would read a passage about early cowboys and then be given a question such as "For cowboys, what particular dangers were associated with a cattle drive?" The student would determine what type of QAR the question represented, locate the answer in the text, and answer the question on the appropriate line.

Summarizing

Text summarization requires the reader to generate a representation of the gist of a passage (Pressley & Harris, 1990). This strategy prompts students to identify the main

---

What made Albert Einstein a great scientist?

RIGHT THERE _____

THINK AND SEARCH _____

ON MY OWN _____

What is he best known for?

RIGHT THERE _____

THINK AND SEARCH _____

ON MY OWN _____

What type of disability did he have?

RIGHT THERE _____

THINK AND SEARCH _____

ON MY OWN _____

FIGURE 11.3. QAR task example.

idea of the passage, delete any unnecessary details, and run through the main points. In this way, students build their own schemas of the concepts and ideas presented in text, thereby increasing their understanding and memory of what was read (Nelson et al., 1992). Text summarization also prompts students to utilize metacognitive processes (awareness and control of the reading process) and cues them to attend to the structure of ideas within text and to how ideas relate to each other (Rinehart, Stahl, & Erickson, 1986). Improving students' metacognitive control enables them to better evaluate their reading and increases their awareness of the process necessary to comprehend text.

The Summary Skills Strategy

The summary skills strategy developed by Nelson and colleagues (1992) can be used to guide students' summarization of expository text. The strategy consists of three main steps: (1) identify and organize the main idea and important information, (2) identify important points the writer made about the main idea, and (3) clarify and revise the summary. These steps are broken down further into nine self-directional prompts (Table 11.3). Students are prompted through the series of steps to identify and organize the main idea and important information in the text and put them all into a summary form. Students are further prompted to clarify and revise their summaries.

TABLE 11.3. Summary Writing Guide

Step 1. Ask yourself—"What is the main idea?" Write it down.

Step 2. Ask yourself—"What important things did the writer say about the main idea?" Write down three important things the writer said.

Step 3. Check to make sure you understood what the main idea was and that you found three important things about it.

Step 4. Ask yourself—"What is the topic that I am going to write about?" Write a topic sentence for your summary.

Step 5. Ask yourself—"How should I order my ideas?" Put a "1" next to the idea you want to be first, put a "2" next to the idea you want to be second, and so on.

Step 6. Ask yourself—"Did I leave our any important information? Is there unimportant information that I can take out?"

Step 7. Write a summary about what you read.

Step 8. Read your summary. Ask yourself—"Is the summary clear?" If not, rewrite your summary.

Step 9. Ask a friend to read the summary and tell you if it is clear. Rewrite your summary (if necessary).

Note. Based on Nelson, Smith, and Dodd (1992).

Eight of the nine steps shown in Table 11.3 are aimed at generation of summary material, while the ninth is directed toward clarification of the text summary. The "generation" steps identify and organize the main idea and important information. In the first step students ask themselves, "What is the main idea?" and write it down. Texts vary in the explicitness of their main ideas. Students must be taught how to identify a main idea and its purpose. A main idea is the central theme; all the other ideas support this main one. Next, students are prompted to ask themselves "What important things did the writer say about the main idea?" and to write down the important points that the writer made. Students are thereby taught to identify supporting ideas, which help to further develop the main idea. The importance of information is determined by whether or not its exclusion would weaken the statement of the main idea.

Then, in Step 3, students are prompted to go back and check to make sure that they understood what the main idea was and the important points that the writer made. This step is to ensure that students check over what they identified as the main idea and the supporting details. Through checking, students may find that they did not have a clear notion of what the main idea was, or that the supporting ideas do not support what they thought was the main idea. At this point they may need to go back and restate the main idea. Step 4 prompts students to ask themselves "What is the topic that I am going to write about?" and to write a topic sentence for their summary. Students are instructed on how to create a topic sentence. Topic sentences are merely a restatement of the main idea in the form of a complete sentence. In Step 5 students are taught to rank their supporting ideas by asking themselves "How should I group my ideas?" and by putting a 1 next to the idea they want to be first, a 2 next to the idea they want to be second, and so on. In this way they are organizing their summary and possibly eliminating any unnecessary ideas.

In Step 6, students are prompted to ask themselves if they have left out any important information or left in any unimportant information they can take out. Students must look through the text again and determine whether or not they have unnecessarily included all relevant information, as well as whether or not they have included unimportant information. In Step 7 students are told to write a summary about what they read. By this point they should have a summary well planned and organized for composition. Step 8 starts the revision process; students are prompted to read their summary and ask themselves, "Is the summary clear?" and rewrite the summary (if necessary). Students need to determine whether or not their summary is an accurate representation of the text, and whether it highlights all the important points. In Step 9, the final step, students are prompted to have a classmate read their summary and to tell them if there is anything that is not clear. This peer review process is an additional step to ensure the clarity of the students' summaries.

IMPLEMENTATION PLANS

In this section we provide examples from various stages of implementation plans for the reading comprehension strategies previously mentioned.

Stage 1 for Question Generation: Developing and Activating Background Knowledge

Prior to teaching the strategy, it is necessary to evaluate students' background knowledge. Formal or informal assessments can be used to determine what skills students possess and what skills may be lacking; doing a task breakdown will provide the information for identifying the skills necessary to successfully complete the strategy (Table 11.4).

Stage 2 for Graphic/Semantic Organizers: Discussing the Strategy

This is the first stage in initiating strategy instruction when it is important to stress its relevance. During an initial conference the teacher discusses students' current performance. In order for students to be successful and able to self-regulate the strategy, they need to make a commitment to use the strategy; they need to "buy into" the value of the strategy. Thus it is important for the teacher to stress this value. Brainstorm situations

TABLE 11.4. Sample Task Breakdown for Question-Generation Strategy

Strategy	Skills	Assessment
Basic skills	Ability to read at the level of text presented	Students are given an assessment to determine appropriate independent reading levels.
	Ability to write	Given an informal assessment, students are asked to produce complete sentences.
Self-monitoring		
"How well did I identify important information?"	Ability to pick out important information	Provide students with a written text, require them to pick out the important information, and check to see how well they thought they did.
	Ability to critique own work	
"How well did I link information together?"	Knowledge of linking words and how to use them	Administer an informal assessment on linking words and usage.
"How well could I answer my question?"	Knowledge of how to answer a question completely	Administer an informal assessment on answering sentences completely.
"Did my 'think' question use different language from the text?"	Knowledge of "think" questions	Students are asked to define "think" questions and to provide an example.
"Did I use good signal words?"	Knowledge of signal words	Students are asked to list signal words and to explain their purpose.

wherein using this strategy or completing the given task accurately is important. For example, the following might be appropriate brainstorming ideas in response to the question "When would it be important for you to read and understand text?":

- For a test
- For an assignment
- To make an informed decision
- To learn more about something of interest
- To assemble something
- To operate equipment

As a last resort the teacher can use a behavioral contract, whereby the student tries the strategy and receives reinforcement for his or her effort.

A sample script for "selling" the strategy follows.

"This year we are doing a lot of reading! Sometimes it is a little difficult to keep everything straight. When we take our comprehension test, sometimes your memory of what was read is not too clear. Let's take a look at some of tests that we took this quarter. You really did a nice job [point out the positives]. However, if I look at the questions, there are some that aren't answered completely, and some that you just didn't seem to be too sure about. Earlier we mentioned that it is important to be able to read and comprehend text for assignments or for learning more about something. It appears that we could improve on this. Part of the reason you are having trouble is that no one ever taught you the tricks of how to read and comprehend text. The good news is that I have a trick to teach you that can really help you with your reading comprehension. You know how when you go on a trip, you use a map to guide you? Well, I have a 'map' to help guide you with your reading. It's called a 'semantic map' or 'graphic organizer.' *Semantic* means 'meaning'; this is a map to help you remember the important ideas in what you have read and to improve your reading comprehension."

Students need to "buy into" the value of using a strategy before you can move on. In this stage we also introduce the strategy steps and any prompts that will be given (see Table 11.2).

Stage 3 for Summarization: Modeling the Strategy

Here is an example of a think-aloud for a summarization strategy.

"OK, I just got done reading the section in my science book for class tomorrow. Ugh! I hope I can remember all of that information tomorrow when we have to answer questions. Sometimes it's hard for me to remember what I've read the night before. Hey, I know what I can do. My teacher just taught us how to use a summarization strategy to help us remember what we've read, and I can use my Summary Writing Guide to help me write a good summary; that will help me remember what I've read. OK, here goes! First, I need to think to myself, 'What is the main idea?' OK, I know that because the whole section was about invertebrates in the sea, and the different kinds. But what was the *main idea*? I think the main idea was that there are millions of different kinds of animals in the sea, and that they can be divided into three groups: (1) plankton, (2) benthos, and (3) nekton. OK, on to Step 2. I need to think to myself, 'What important things did the writer say about the main idea?' and write down the important things the writer said.

"OK, I already identified what I think is the main idea, and now I need to write down some of the important things that the writer said about invertebrates in the sea. I know that I need to find the important ideas in the reading so I can support my main idea, and that will help me remember better. Well, let's see . . . the author divided the invertebrates into three categories: plankton, benthos, and nekton. That's pretty important because everything else follows those three categories. If I didn't mention them, I wouldn't be able put the rest of the information into the right categories, and that's pretty important. OK, what else? Plankton live near the surface of the water, benthos live deep down on the seabed, and nektons swim between the top and bottom layers. Let's see, there are two kinds of plankton that live in the sea: (1) phytoplankton—plants, and (2) zooplankton—animals. Wow, some jellyfish are nearly 80 inches wide! That's cool, I'm going to write that down.

"Whew, this is going pretty well! I remember most everything that I read and *everything* that I wrote down! This should really help me answer questions tomorrow, and when it comes to the test I will be able to look at my summary to help me study! OK, what else? Let's see, I've talked about plankton, hmm . . . OK, now nekton. That's what's mentioned next in the text. I'm just going though the text and picking out the important details, and I don't want to miss any, so I will just start at the beginning and stop at the end. OK, nekton; what about nekton? Most of them are vertebrates, but not all—squid and octopus are nektons, but they are invertebrates. Last category, benthos; what about benthos? I already know that they live at the bottom of the sea. What else? OK, some benthos are animals that stay in one place (like coral), and some walk or crawl on the sea floor. Wow, I'm all done, that wasn't difficult at all!

"Let's see, that was Step 2, what is Step 3? Oh, yeah, I go back and check to make sure I understood what the main idea was and the important things the writer said about this topic. OK, I do understand the main idea and the important things. Good! What's next? Step 4: OK, I need to write a topic sentence. Let's see, we talked about topic sentences in class. I know that a topic sentence needs to express the main idea, and *all* the important ideas need to support that topic sentence. Hmm, how can I say that? Well, I could just say, 'Invertebrates that live in the sea can be classified in three different categories.' That's true! Well, do all my important details support that? Kind of, but not quite. I should add the three different categories of plankton, benthos, and nekton. That would make a great topic sentence. 'Invertebrates that live in the sea can be classified in three different categories: plankton, benthos, and nekton.' Great! Now Step 5, grouping my ideas. OK, I'm going to rank them *1, 2, 3* . . . that looks good.

"Step 6, I need to check my important information to see if I left anything out, or if I need to take out any unnecessary information. Hmm, I think I have all the important information, but do I have anything that is unnecessary? Yeah, I think that statement about the jellyfish is unnecessary; it's cool, but it doesn't really further develop the main idea. OK, good. Step 7—'Write a summary about what you read.' . . . That was easy; I just rewrote my topic sentence and put my important details into complete sentences. Step 8, I read my summary and it sounds pretty good, so I don't think I need to rewrite it. Step 9, ask a classmate to read it; I'll have Maci read it. She knows a lot about science. Wow, Maci thought it was good! That's great! I'm done, and I remember all the important parts of the reading. The summarization strategy really helped!"

Stage 4 for SCROL: Memorizing the Strategy

Memorizing the strategy is extremely important! As a student once said, "If you can't remember it, you can't use it" (Harris, personal communication, 2005). We want the students to focus on the task and not on the steps of the strategy. Memorization also frees up working memory. The specific memorization activities themselves are not critical. There are many appropriate activities. The important aspects of the activities is whether or not they facilitate memorization. You will need to plan and prepare the memorization activities and monitor their effectiveness. Many strategies use acronyms that can help students memorize the strategy (e.g., SCROL); however, students must be able to do more than simply name the steps. They must know and understand what must be done at each step of the strategy. For example, to memorize SCROL, students might pair up. Then one student can give the letter (e.g., S) and the other state the step and what must be done.

Stage 5 for Question–Answer Relationship: Supporting the Strategy

Scaffolding is important in this stage. With scaffolding it is possible to gradually transfer strategy performance from teacher to student. Students need to be given adequate time and support to master the strategy.

Content Scaffolding

Students are given a simple passage to read. The teacher and students then go over the passage and the comprehension questions at the end of the passage. Together they determine what type of QAR each comprehension question represents and answer those questions on the appropriate line. The teacher directs the process, and the students provide answers to teacher-directed questions (i.e., "What type of QAR does this question represent? Is the information found directly in one sentence of the text? Do you need to look in more than one sentence or paragraph to find the answer? Is this a question that requires you to think on your own?").

Task Scaffolding

Students are taught one question–answer relationship at a time. First, they are taught to locate information in text to answer "right there" questions, then how to locate information in text to answer "think and search" questions. Finally, students are taught how to utilize the information in text to answer "on my own" questions.

During collaborative practice, the teacher prompts students to use their QAR categories to answer comprehension questions. The teacher demonstrates the use of the QAR categories though modeling. In subsequent lessons the teacher asks the students to fill in the QAR categories and describe how they knew which category the question represented. Finally, students are given comprehension questions and the QAR categories and expected to determine the category and to answer the questions correctly.

Material Scaffolding

Students are given a QAR prompt card (Figure 11.4) to use with the comprehension questions at the end of each reading passage given. Initially, this prompt serves as a guide to remind students of the question–answer relationships and how those relationships can help them answer comprehension questions. Students are given multiple opportunities to practice using their QAR strategy until they are able to do so independently and to successfully answer comprehension questions.

QAR Helper

What type of question is this?

RIGHT THERE
Can the information be found in one sentence of the text?

THINK AND SEARCH
Can the information be found in two or more of the sentences or paragraphs in the text? Does it require me to put the information together?

ON MY OWN
Does this question require me to use my background knowledge of the subject?

FIGURE 11.4. QAR scaffolding example.

Stage 6 for Summarization: Independent Performance

At this stage the student is ready to use the strategy independently. The teacher's main task is to monitor the student's performance and check on proper and consistent use of the strategy. However, it is important to keep in mind that our main goal is improved academic performance. Teachers must evaluate whether or not the strategy is being used and whether or not academic performance has improved. Generalization may also be a concern. Students will not always generalize strategies to appropriate situations; they will need to be prompted and encouraged to do so. Note that activities to promote generalization should occur very early in the process. For example, in the discussion stage (Stage 2) teachers and students typically list situations where a strategy could or should be used.

To promote generalization, students should be encouraged to use the strategy in other content areas when they are required to read. All team teachers should be informed about the use of the strategy, the language, the prompts, and what is required at each step. All team teachers should be given a wall chart to hang up in their room as a reminder for students to use the Summary Writing Guide strategy when appropriate.

Students should be assessed regularly using the comprehension questions at the ends of their texts. These scores should be recorded and tracked for trends in progress. The goal is improved academic performance, and if performance isn't improving, a reteaching of the strategy may be necessary. Once students are successful in using the strategy and answering comprehension questions, their performance should be monitored periodically. Even when students have reached the independent performance stage, they should be monitored to ensure proper use of the strategy. If students deviate from the given summarization strategy, performance should be evaluated, but action should be taken only if performance is no longer improving.

FINAL THOUGHTS

Reading is one of the most important skills students gain in school. No student can succeed without well-developed comprehension skills. Improving a student's comprehension of text can have a positive and lifelong impact on learning outcomes. In closing, we should stress that instruction in comprehension strategies should begin early and continue throughout a student's academic career.

CHAPTER 12

Strategies in Mathematics

$\mathbf{M}$athematics is a core academic competency. Mastering basic mathematic skills (e.g., knowledge of basic facts, problem solving) is critical for successful functioning in society. We are constantly confronted with problems that involve mathematics skills. These might range from "Do I have enough money to pay for these three items I want to purchase?" to "I have to go 30 miles to a meeting that takes place in 30 minutes—how fast do I have to drive to get there on time?" Mastering the skills and strategies necessary to solve these problems is critical for functioning effectively in society and in the workplace (Chesloff & Maier, 2012; Patton, Cronin, Bassett, & Koppel, 1997). Over the last 10 years, math achievement has steadily increased (National Center for Education Statistics, 2011); however, our level of mathematics achievement is still a matter of national concern, as research suggests that American children have serious deficits in many areas (Jitendra & Xin, 1997; Xin & Jitendra, 1999).

For the purposes of this chapter, we limit our discussion to three major areas of mathematics: basic facts, computation procedures, and word-problem solving. Knowledge of basic math facts is a foundational for more advanced operations. Fluency with mathematics requires students to learn and store basic facts (e.g., $3 + 5 = 8$; $9 \times 7 = 63$) in long-term memory, and then to rapidly and accurately recall and apply them. Computational procedures are also fundamental. Students must master procedures involved in computations such as long division, place value, and regrouping. They must also remember and apply these procedures correctly while simultaneously recalling and utilizing basic facts. Finally, students are required to develop and utilize word-problem-solving skills. Here students are confronted with word problems that require them to identify important information, conceptualize how to solve the problem, define appropriate equations, and solve equations. Again, knowledge of basic facts and computational procedures must also be accessed and utilized.

PROBLEMS FOR STUDENTS WITH LEARNING DISABILITIES

Math disabilities (MD; also termed *dyscalculia* or *developmental dyscalculia*) are a serious educational problem. Studies suggest that 5–10% of all school-age children have some type of serious deficit in mathematics (Murphy, Mazzocco, Hanich, & Early, 2007). MD are independent of intelligence in that students with very high IQs may also have math disabilities (Butterworth & Relgosa, 2007). MD may occur in isolation (i.e., the only difficulties are in math) or in combination with reading disabilities. It is thought that the problems of students with both MD and reading disabilities are due to underlying language deficits that may or may not be accompanied by numerical deficits (Jordan, 2007).

Difficulties experienced by children with MD span all three areas (basic facts, computation procedures, and problem solving). Children with MD are extremely heterogeneous; however, some problems commonly occur (Geary, 2003). These include:

- Poor understanding of concepts underlying mathematical procedures
- Problems with counting and using counting to solve problems
- Use of immature or inappropriate strategies
- Difficulty with fact retrieval
- Difficulty coordinating and monitoring steps in computation
- Difficulty in word-problem solving
- Working memory deficits

On the whole, children with LD are only slightly behind typically achieving peers in terms of development of number concepts (Geary, Hamson, & Hoard, 2000). But some commonly occurring problems, such as difficulty with counting concepts, have been demonstrated (Geary, Bow-Thomas, & Yao, 1992; Geary, Hoard, & Hamson, 1999). For example, children may believe that nonsequential counting (i.e., skipping some items and counting them later) will result in an incorrect count (Geary, 2003). Another example would be failure to grasp the commutative principle. Students who did not understand this principle would not understand that 8×5 is the same problem as 5×8. Poor understanding of number concepts can inhibit the use of advanced strategies and may affect ability to detect procedural errors (Geary, 2003). Counting problems are a serious concern because counting serves as an important preskill in the mastery of basic addition facts. Difficulty counting can inhibit the development of basic addition facts. Children with LD may be developmentally delayed in the use of counting to solve arithmetic problems. They may also fail to perceive the link between counting and problem solving. Many see counting as simply a rote activity (Geary, 2003).

Use of appropriate strategies is also a concern. Many children either fail to develop or fail to utilize more advanced strategies. For example, many children with LD don't gradually switch from counting to direct retrieval of math facts (Geary, Widaman, Little, & Corimer, 1987). Thus, these children use an inefficient means of retrieval. Memory problems are a major factor in poor mathematic performance. Children with LD commonly produce more errors in math fact retrieval than their peers. Research suggests that children with LD may have problems in storing basic facts in long-term memory and accessing them readily. Errors in retrieval may be due to problems inhibiting irrelevant information and/or associations (Geary et al., 2000). For example, with a problem such as 6 + 2, many will answer 7, the next number after 6. For complex problems (i.e., those that involve a number of operations), children with LD frequently make procedural errors. They may omit steps (e.g., fail to regroup) or have difficulty performing steps in the correct sequence. Procedural errors in computation appear to be due to problems in monitoring and coordinating the sequence of problem-solving steps (Russell & Ginsberg, 1984). Problems with working memory are common and are thought to be related to procedural difficulties (Geary, Hoard, Nugent, & Byrd-Craven, 2007).

Solving word problems is often extremely difficult for children with LD. The difficulties with word-problem solving go well beyond problems with decoding. Parmar, Cawley, and Frazita (1996) found that students with LD had difficulties representing problems, identifying salient information, and choosing the appropriate arithmetic operations. Word problems may contain irrelevant information, and solving them may require multiple operations or steps that can also cause serious problems (Fuchs & Fuchs, 2003). Thus, word problems place a number of demands on children's cognitive processing. These problems are exacerbated by the fact that mathematics instruction for children with LD often is focused on memorization of facts and computation skills at the expense of instruction on application of mathematics in problem-solving situations (Bottge, 1999; Parmar et al., 1994).

PREREQUISITE SKILLS

A list of all the possible prerequisite skills for mathematics would be beyond the scope of this chapter. There are, however, three major areas of preskills that are extremely important for successful development of mathematical skills: number sense, basic mathematics principles, and basic facts rules in mathematics. These prerequisites are critical to the development of skill with basic facts, computation procedures, and problem solving. In this section we discuss each preskill.

Number Sense

Number sense is a concept that refers to "a child's fluidity and flexibility with numbers, the sense of what numbers mean, and an ability to perform mental mathematics and look at the world and make comparisons" (Gersten & Chard, 1999, p. 20). Children with a good number sense have a "feel" for math. They can see patterns in numbers and have mastered concepts such as *greater than, less than,* and *equal to.* Van de Walle (1998) lists five components of number sense:

1. Well-understood number meanings (e.g., 3 corresponds to a certain quantity)
2. Awareness of multiple relationships among numbers (e.g., a set of 6 objects can be made with 2 sets of 3 or a set of 4 plus a set of 2)
3. Recognition of the relative magnitude of numbers (e.g., 5 is larger than 2)
4. Knowledge of the effects of operations on numbers (e.g., adding makes the number bigger)
5. Knowledge that numbers measure things in the real world

One of the key components of a good number sense is a well-developed counting ability. Counting involves the ability to produce number words and the knowledge that the number words have a one-to-one relationship with the set being counted. Counting is also a critical preskill for the development of knowledge of basic addition facts. Mastery of basic addition facts initially depends on counting-based strategies (Garnett, 1992). Children go through four stages in the mastery of basic addition facts:

1. *Count all*: Given 3 + 2, the student counts 1, 2, 3, 4, 5 to get the answer (i.e., counts all the numbers).
2. *Count on*: Given 2 + 5, the student begins at one addend and counts 2, 3, 4, 5, 6, 7.
3. *Count on from larger addend or shortcut sum*: Given 2 + 5, the student begins at the larger addend and counts 5, 6, 7.
4. *Memory*: Given 2 + 5, the student just "knows" the answer.

Obviously children with impaired counting skills will have difficulty progressing to the memory level where knowledge is automatic. Counting skills are also used in strategies for teaching basic facts, as we discuss later. Garnett (1992) recommended frequent practice in counting. This includes counting by 1's, 2's, and 5's. After students can count forward fluently, teachers should also attend to counting backward to provide the groundwork for subtraction skills.

Basic Mathematics Principles

A number of critical principles are considered foundational for mathematical understanding and apply to many different levels of mathematics. Harniss, Carnine, Silbert, and Dixon (2002) noted the following set of critical principles:

- *Place value*: The position of a number provides information about the value of the number.
- *Expanded notation*: Numbers can be reduced to their underlying units (e.g., the number 437 is equal to four 100's plus three 10's, plus seven 1's).
- *Commutative property*: The order of numbers in an equation does not affect the result (e.g., 8 + 7 = 7 + 8). This is true for addition and multiplication, but not subtraction and division.
- *Associative property*: The grouping of numbers in an equation can be changed without changing the result; for example, (8 + 7) + 4 = 8 + (7 + 4). Again, only addition and multiplication are associative.
- *Distributive property*: Numbers in an equation can be redistributed; for example, $7 \times (8 + 4) = (7 \times 8) + (7 \times 4)$.
- *Equivalence*: The quantity on one side of the = sign is equal to the quantity on the other.

These principles, which Harniss and his colleagues (2002) term "big ideas," cut across all of basic mathematics and are critical for understanding mathematics and solving equations. For example, the commutative principle means that 5×4 is the same as 4×5. This, in turn, means that rather than having to memorize 100 basic addition facts, it's only necessary to learn 50, which decreases the memory burden significantly. Many children with LD do not understand the commutative principle and would think that the two problems were actually different.

Basic Facts Rules

For each of the four operations (addition, subtraction, multiplication, and division) there is an underlying set of rules. These rules are helpful in mastering the basic facts because they help to "chunk" facts into groups that are related. This chunking, in turn, can help reduce the demands on working memory and enable long-term storage in memory. These chunks can also be utilized as the basis for strategies, as we show later. Figure 12.1 shows the basic facts rules for addition, subtraction, multiplication, and division.

INSTRUCTION IN MATHEMATICS

In the sections that follow, we present examples of strategies for basic facts, computation procedures, and word-problem solving. We selected basic facts because they are the foundation for all mathematics skills; students must master basic facts if they are to progress in mathematics. Computation involves application of basic facts to solve more advanced problems, which requires students to learn and follow an effective procedure. Many children with LD have difficulty following a procedure. Word-problem solving was selected because it is a problem area for many children, and it is a critical area because it can help children develop problem-solving skills for real-world problems.

BASIC MATH FACTS STRATEGIES

Addition

Addition facts are the first in a series of fact families that must be learned. Basic facts are often taught by rote repetition—an extremely inefficient method for several reasons. First, it requires learning 100 facts by rote and thus ignores the commutative principle. Second, and more importantly, it does not provide any framework to help students organize information to be learned. As we noted earlier, facts that are organized and related are much easier to learn than unrelated facts. Thornton and Toohey (1985) developed a chunking strategy to simplify instruction in basic addition facts. This is an unstructured strategy that takes advantage of basic facts rules and simple mnemonics to group math facts by the strategy needed for recall. Chunking the addition facts into groups based on the strategy used to recall the addition fact makes is easier for students to recall the facts. These are the groups:

- *Count-ons*. These are the facts that involve adding 1 or 2 (e.g., 5 + 1 or 6 + 2). Students are prompted to start big, count on, and to "feel the count."
- *Zeros*. These are the facts that involve adding 0 (e.g., 3 + 0 or 8 + 0). For this set, students are taught that plus 0 stays the same.

Addition	Subtraction	Multiplication	Division
The Order Rule (or commutative principle) *The 0 Rule*: any number plus 0 is the number. *The 1's Rule*: any number plus 1 is 1 more than the number. *The 9's Rule*: any single-digit number greater than 0 added to 9 results in the addend number minus 1 plus 10. *The 10's Rule*: any single-digit number added to 10 results in the 0 being changed to the number being added.	*The 0 Rule*: any number minus 0 is the number. *The 1's Rule*: any number minus 1 is 1 less than the number (count backwards by 1). *The Same Number Rule*: any number minus itself is 0. *The Addition/ Subtraction Relationship Rule*: in a subtraction problem, the answer added to the number being subtracted equals the top number. Thus to solve 12 – 9, teach the student "What number plus 9 equals 12?"	*The 0 Rule*: any number times 0 equals 0. *The 1's Rule*: any number times 1 equals the number. *The 2's Rule*: any number times 2 is double the number. Thus 8 × 2 is equal to 8 + 8. *The 5's Rule*: any number times 5 is equivalent to counting by 5's the number of times indicated by the multiplier. Thus 5 × 4 is counting by 5's four times. *The 9's Rule*: when multiplying by 9, the answers can be found by taking 1 from the multiplier to get the number in the 10's position, and then adding enough to that number to make 9. For example, 9 × 5—take 1 from 5 to get the number of 10's (i.e., 4) then add enough to 4 to make 9 (i.e., 5), thus the answer is 45.	*The 0 Rule*: 0 divided by any number is 0. *The 1's Rule*: any number divided by 1 is the number. *The 2's Rule*: any number divided by 2 is half the number. *The 9's Rule*: when dividing by 9 the answer is 1 more than the number in the 10's column. For example, 54 ÷ 9 = 6 (6 is 1 more than the number in the 10's column). *The Multiplication/ Division Relationship Rule*: to solve for 32 ÷ 4, think what number times 4 equals 32? The quotient times the divisor equals the dividend.

FIGURE 12.1. Basic facts rules.

- *Doubles.* These are the facts with identical addends (e.g., 4 + 4 or 6 + 6). Students are taught to associate the facts with a picture. For example, 4 + 4 could be the "spider fact" because a spider has 8 legs; 6 + 6 could be the "dozen eggs" fact.
- *Near doubles.* These are facts, such as 5 + 4 or 8 + 7, which are close to being doubles. Students are taught to relate these facts to their doubles. For example, if 4 + 4 = 8, then 5 + 4 must be 1 more. So 5 + 4 must equal 9.
- *9's.* The 9's facts (e.g., 9 + 4) follow a pattern. Count backward 1 from the small number and put the 1 in front. For example, for 9 + 4 the student would count backward 1 from 4 to get 3 and put the 1 in front (13). Students are taught to use this pattern.
- *10's.* The 10's facts are all the facts that sum to 10 (e.g., 7 + 3, 6 + 4). A 10 frame (see Figure 12.2) is used to teach these facts. Student are taught to remember the 10 frame.
- *Near 10's.* The near 10's (e.g., 9 + 2 or 8 + 4) are similar to the near doubles. Students are reminded to relate these facts to the appropriate 10's fact. For example, if 8 + 2 = 10, then 8 + 4 must be 12.

The key to this strategy is that all fact groups use a similar strategy for retrieval. Note that some facts are in more than one family. For example, 5 + 5 would be a double and a 10's fact. The strategy does not cover all addition facts (i.e., 7 + 5, 8 + 4, 8 + 5, 8 + 6). This small group of facts must be taught separately. They can be approached as "10's plus extras," or simply as extra facts and taught through memorization.

Multiplication

Multiplication facts are another important fact family. Once again, these facts are amenable to an approach that utilizes a chunking strategy. Wood and her colleagues (Wood & Frank, 2000; Wood, Frank, & Wacker, 1998) have developed and validated an effective strategy for teaching multiplication facts. The strategy divides the multiplication facts into six families: 0's, 1's, 2's, 5's, 9's, and pegwords (see Chapter 14 for more on

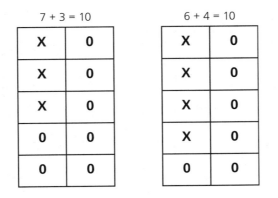

FIGURE 12.2. Ten-frame examples. A 10 frame is a container that has 10 separate receptacles. Manipulatives are used to illustrate the various combinations that add to 10.

pegwords). Facts are taught in this order. Note that the pegword facts are used for the 15 facts that do not fall into any of the first five families. Figure 12.3 shows the multiplication facts charts. Each fact family has its own strategy. In the case of the 2, 5, and 9 families, the strategy is combined with a graphic designed to serve as a mnemonic. Pegword facts use key words (i.e., the pegword) in sentences. Students are taught to associate the words with numbers (e.g., door = 4; gate = 8; dirty = 30; shoe = 2). Pegwords are put into sentences that combine illustrations to help the child learn and remember facts. For example, the problem $4 \times 8 = 32$ is represented by the sentence "Door on gate by dirty shoe" combined with a representation of these images.

Students are taught each fact family in turn. After all fact families have been mastered, students are taught to (1) scan a problem; (2) determine if one of the numbers is *0, 1, 2, 5,* or *9*; (3) if so, use the appropriate strategy; (4) if not, remember the pegword. When teaching, the strategy self-instructions are modeled and stressed (e.g., "This problem has a *9*, so I can use my 9's strategy"). As always, instruction should stress that successful use of the strategy will help the student to get the right answer. Note that this strategy would follow naturally from the addition facts strategy previously discussed. The procedures are quite similar, and one fact family from the addition strategy, the

FIGURE 12.3. Multiplication strategy charts. From Wood and Frank (2000). Copyright 2000 by the Council for Exceptional Children. Reprinted by permission.

doubles, could be used for the 2's in the multiplication strategy. Commercial materials are available that use this approach to chunk strategies for multiplication facts (Liautaud & Rodreguez, 1999).

COMPUTATION STRATEGIES

Many students with LD struggle with computational procedures. Solving problems such as 34 × 7 or 456 + 895 requires students to remember necessary basic facts, the necessary steps, and how to order the steps. This can strain working memory for students with LD. As a result, they may forget the order of operation, regroup improperly, fail to regroup, or even develop improper algorithms. A number of strategies are useful for helping students remember and follow computational procedures. Figure 12.4 shows examples of computation strategies. These strategies typically consist of a mnemonic that serves to cue the student to remember and perform steps to correctly solve

---

DIVISION STRATEGY

Division. Remember *Does Mama Sell Biscuits Really?*:
  Does (Divide)
  Mama (Multiply)
  Sell (Subtract)
  Biscuits (Bring Down)
  Really (Remainder)

_____ Divide	_____ Divide	_____ Divide
_____ Multiply	_____ Multiply	_____ Multiply
_____ Subtract	_____ Subtract	_____ Subtract
_____ Bring Down	_____ Bring Down	_____ Bring Down
_____ Remainder	_____ Remainder	_____ Remainder
124 ÷ 7	66 ÷ 4	861 ÷ 9

MULTIPLICATION STRATEGY

Multiply. Remember MAMA:
  Multiply the 1's column.
  Across Do I need to go across to the 10's?
  Multiply the bottom 1's digit with the top 10's digit.
  Add any number that was carried in Step 2.

_____ Multiply	_____ Multiply	_____ Multiply
_____ Across	_____ Across	_____ Across
_____ Multiply	_____ Multiply	_____ Multiply
_____ Add	_____ Add	_____ Add
17	3 5	6 4
× 8	× 3	× 7

FIGURE 12.4. Examples of computation strategies.

problems. It is often useful to combine these types of strategies with self-monitoring. The self-monitoring serves to cue the student to perform all steps of the strategy in the correct order. As the student gains fluency with the strategy, the self-monitoring can be faded. Note that it is also possible to develop customized strategies for students. The process for creating customized computational strategies, developed by Dunlap and Dunlap (1989), was discussed in Chapter 7 (p. 114).

WORD-PROBLEM-SOLVING STRATEGIES

Many children with LD struggle with word problems. Word-problem solving requires students to apply basic facts and computational skills to novel situations. There are two components to word-problem solving (Jitendra, Hoff, & Beck, 1999). The first is *problem representation*, which entails translation of a problem from words into a meaningful combination of (typically) written symbols on paper (e.g., diagrams), actual objects (e.g., manipulatives), or mental imagery (Janvier, 1987). Constructing an effective representation is a prerequisite to understanding the quantitative relationships in a problem. The second is *problem solution*, which entails selection and application of appropriate mathematical operations based on the representation. Problem solution includes both solution planning and execution of appropriate mathematical operations. Research strongly suggests that two critical components for successful word-problem solving are explicit instruction in problem solving and the use of graphic representation of word problems such as diagrams (van Garderen, 2007).

Diagrams

Diagrams can be extremely helpful for students with MD and offer several benefits (van Garderen, 2006): (1) They reduce demands on working memory; (2) as visible reminders, diagrams allow for both teacher and student to monitor progress; (3) they are flexible and can be used for many different types of problems; and (4) they can be used as a part of a strategy. Note that using and creating effective diagrams is a skill that must be explicitly taught to students, especially those with LD (van Garderen, 2006). Simply telling students to "make a diagram" will not be effective. There are two basic types of diagrams: pictorial and schematic (Hegarty & Kozhenikov 1999). Pictorial diagrams depict the appearance of what is described in the problem; schematic diagrams depict the relations described in the problem (see Figure 12.5 for examples). The use of schematic diagrams is associated with successful problem solving, whereas the use of pictorial diagrams is associated with *unsuccessful* problem solving (van Garderen, 2007). Diagrams are an important part part of schema strategies (see below) that are effective for students with LD.

Four types of diagrams are commonly used (van Garderen, 2007; see Figure 12.6):

- Line diagrams—link points together with lines. They are useful to show how quantities may be combined in a problem.
- Matrices or tables—show relationships between two or more sets of information.

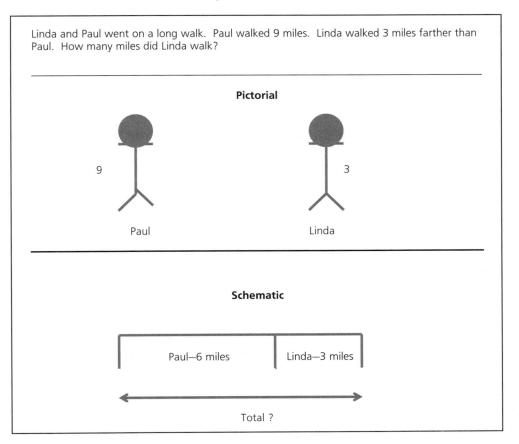

Linda and Paul went on a long walk. Paul walked 9 miles. Linda walked 3 miles farther than Paul. How many miles did Linda walk?

Pictorial

9   Paul   3   Linda

Schematic

Paul—6 miles   Linda—3 miles

Total ?

FIGURE 12.5. Examples of pictorial and schematic diagrams.

- Tree diagrams—show diverging or converging paths. They are useful in showing possible numbers of alternatives.
- Part–whole—show relationships between parts and the whole. They are useful for grouping components of a problem together.

Visualize

The visualize strategy (van Garderen, 2007) is designed to help students learn to create diagrams and use them to solve word problems. It uses the mnemonic RV-PCC along with self-instructions to guide students through the steps of the strategy. The steps in the visualize strategy follow:

1. *Read.* The students read the problem and check to see if they understand it.
2. *Visualize the problem.* Students draw a diagram of the problem and then assess it to determine whether it accurately shows how the parts of the problem are related. They rearrange the elements in the diagram if needed.

Line. Jordan wanted to get to the beach. The beach was 35 miles away. Jordan rode his bike for 16 miles. Then he walked another 8 miles. How far did Jordan need to go to reach the beach?

| 16 miles | 8 miles | ? |

35 mile to beach

Matrix/Table. While Heidi was walking home, she saw many people walking their dogs. Each person walked only one dog. She counted 48 legs. How many people and how many dogs were there?

5 people =10	5 dogs = 20	30 legs
6 people = 12	6 dogs = 24	36 legs
7 people = 14	7 dogs = 28	42 legs
8 people = 16	8 dogs = 32	48 legs

Tree. Michah went to the museum. He wanted to try each activity at each booth. There were 4 booths. Each of the booths had a drawing activity, a physical activity, and guessing activity. How many activities would Michah do in total?

Part–Whole. Cynthia bought a red rose and a white rose for $26. She paid $11 for the red rose. How much did the white rose cost?

Total = 26

| Red = 11 | White = ? |

FIGURE 12.6. Examples of schematic diagrams.

3. *Plan how to solve the problem.* Here students determine what operations and how many steps are needed to solve the problem. After making the plan, students use their diagram to determine if the plan makes sense.

4. *Compute the answer.* Students solve the problem using the plan from the previous stage. They also check to see that their operations were done in the correct order.

5. *Check the answer.* Students check their answer to see if it makes sense. If not, they go back to their plan and ask for help if they need it.

During instruction, students also are taught important background information: (1) why they should use diagrams and how diagrams can be helpful; (2) rules to use when creating a diagram (i.e., there is no need to draw everything, drawings don't have to look realistic, and don't take to long making a diagram); (3) how to use symbols or graphic codes in diagrams (e.g., using the letter *b* for the number of beans); (4) how to use question marks to indicate unknowns; and (5) the major types of diagrams and how to use them.

SOLVE IT!

To solve a word problem, students must read the problem, decide what to do, solve the problem, and check that the answer is reasonable. The SOLVE IT! strategy (Montague, 2006) is designed to help students "understand the mathematical problems, analyze the information presented, develop logical plans to solve problems, and evaluate their solutions" (Montague, Warger, & Morgan, 2000, p. 111). SOLVE IT! is a structured strategy that uses explicit instruction to teach problem-solving steps. SOLVE IT! features a series of steps, each of which incorporates self-instructions and self-monitoring (i.e., *say, ask, check*). Students are taught to carefully read problems, paraphrase them, analyze the information, form a plan, solve the problems, and assess their solutions. SOLVE IT! involves the following steps:

1. *Read for understanding.* Students are taught to read a problem and ask themselves if they understood the problem. They also remind themselves to check for understanding as they work the problem.
2. *Put the problem in their own words.* Students are taught to put the problem in their own words and to find and underline important information. Students are taught to ask themselves what the question is and what the problem is asking for.
3. *Draw a picture or diagram.* Students are taught to represent the problem in a picture or diagram, and to check to see if their representation includes the important information in the problem.
4. *Make a plan to solve the problem.* Students identify the steps that will be involved in solving the problem and the operations (e.g., addition, subtraction, mulitiplication) that they will need. They write the symbols for the needed operations and check to see if the plan makes sense.
5. *Estimate the answer.* Students estimate what the final answer should look like by rounding numbers. They will check their final answer against this estimate.
6. *Do the problem.* Students compute the answer to the problem. They are taught to ask themselves to check their answer against their estimate, whether all operations were done in the correct order, and to ask whether the answer makes sense.
7. *Check the answer.* Finally, students check their computation and determine if it is correct and ask for help if needed.

Schema-Based Strategies

The wide variety of possible word problems is one factor that makes them more difficult for students. The ability to organize word problems into a small number of groups with common characteristics that can then be represented and solved simplifies the difficulty of word problems greatly. Schema-based strategies approach word problems from this perspective. Schemas are representations of word-problem structures. Schemas "capture both the patterns of relationships as well as their linkages to operations" (Marshall, 1995, p. 67). Thus, schema-based approaches allow students to both understand how to represent problems and to identify the correct operations for solving them (Jitendra, DiPipi, & Perron-Jones, 2002). An advantage of schema-based approaches is that when one piece of information is retrieved, other information that is linked to it will also be activated (Jitendra et al., 2002; Marshall, 1995). The most typical types of word-problem schemas in elementary and middle schools are *change, equalize, combine, compare, vary,* and *restate* (Riley, Greeno, & Heller, 1983; Van de Walle, 1998). Figures 12.7 and 12.8 show examples of problem types for each schema.

Jitendra and her colleagues (Jitendra, 2007; Jitendra & Hoff, 1996; Jitendra et al., 1998, 1999, 2000) have developed and validated a schema-based approach to word-problem solving. The strategy requires students to learn the types of schemas to mastery and to match each schema with the appropriate diagram (developed by Marshall, 1995). The diagram serves to remind students to record the important information and to cue the appropriate arithmetic operation. The steps in the strategy follow:

1. *Identify problem schemas*: Students are taught the types of schemas to mastery and how to differentiate between them through the use of several examples.
2. *Create an appropriate diagram*: Students are then taught how to appropriately diagram the different types of schemas (Figure 12.9). The diagrams serve as graphic organizers that help students organize and remember important information.
3. *Flag the missing element with a question mark*: The missing element, or the answer that the problem is requesting, is then flagged with a question mark. The question mark lets students know that they must use a mathematical operation to figure out the number to go in that box or circle (Figure 12.9).
4. *Apply the appropriate operation to solve the problem*: The type of schema and diagram will dictate the operation to be used. Students will need to be taught which operation goes with which type of schema and diagram (Figure 12.9).
5. *Ask if the answer made sense*: Once students have solved the problems, they are to check to see if the answers make sense (e.g., if the operation is addition, then the answer should be greater than both the addends). Students could use estimating to determine if their answers are reasonable.
6. *Check the work*: Students should be taught to "work the problem backward." Working a problem backward requires students to do the opposite operation to determine whether or not the answer is correct (e.g., subtraction → addition, multiplication → division).

Note that all of these steps must be taught to a high degree of mastery. Figure 12.9 shows examples of how a graphic organizer could be used with the different types of story problems. Commercial lesson plans to teach the schema approach to work-problem solving are now available (Jitendra, 2007).

Change
 Results unknown
 Dr. Gerber has 6 golf balls. Dr. Lloyd gave him 8 more. How many golf balls does Dr. Gerber have?

 Sue has 21 cats. She gave 11 to John. How many cats does Sue have left?

 Change unknown
 Reese had 7 baseballs. Chris gave him some of her baseballs. Now Reese has 23 baseballs. How many baseballs did Chris give Reese?

 John has 12 slices of pizza. He gave some pizza to Stan. Now John has 3 slices of pizza. How many slices did John give to Stan?

 Start unknown
 Torri had some hamburgers. Then Wendy gave her 7 hamburgers. Now Torri has 18 hamburgers. How many hamburgers did Torri have at the beginning?

 Trevor had some cows. He gave 6 cows to Maci. Now Trevor has 22 cows. How many cows did Trevor have before he gave some to Maci?

Equalize
 Mike has 7 dollars. Ron has 14 dollars. How many dollars does Mike need to have as many as Ron?

 Javon has 25 trading cards. Fred has 11 trading cards. How many cards would Javon have to give away to have as many as Fred?

Combine
 Total set unknown
 Melody has 5 flowers. Emma has 9 flowers. How many flowers do they have in total?

 Subset unknown
 Emma and Leigh have 28 rabbits altogether. Leigh has 13 rabbits. How many rabbits does Emma have?

Compare
 Difference unknown
 Alex has 11 books. Joe has 5 books. Alex has how many more books than Joe?
 Laura has 17 pens. Ross has 11 pens. Ross has how many fewer pens than Laura?

 Compared quantity unknown
 Andy has 4 computers. Matt has 8 more computers than Andy. How many computers does Matt have?

 Laura has 23 books. Ross has 6 fewer books than Laura. How many books does Ross have?

 Referent unknown
 Jorge has 10 DVDs. He has 3 more DVDs than Cindy. How many DVDs does Cindy have?
 Nirbhay has $17. He has $9 less than Alan. How many dollars does Alan have?

FIGURE 12.7. Addition and subtraction word-problem types.

Vary
Size of groups unknown
In Steve's basketball camp there are 5 balls for 25 players. How many players must share each ball?

Whole unknown
George worked picking up bottles for 6 days. He earned $54 for each day he picked up bottles. How much did George earn?

Compare
Referent unknown (compared is part of referent)
Mike and Ron bought some cherries. Mike bought 4 pounds of cherries. Ron bought one-third as many cherries as Mike. How many cherries did Ron buy?

Compared unknown (compared is part of referent)
Stan and Michalla both got speeding tickets. The amount that Stan had to pay was one-half the amount that Michalla had to pay. Stan had to pay $40. How much did Michalla have to pay?

Compared unknown (compared is multiple of referent)
John has 20 doughnuts. Evie has 4 times as many doughnuts as John. How many doughnuts does Evie have?

Restate
Susan and Lynette took a walk. Lynette walked half as far as Susan. If Susan walked 18 miles, how far did Lynette walk?

FIGURE 12.8. Multiplication and division word-problem types.

IMPLEMENTATION PLANS

In this section, we provide partial examples of implementation plans for the math strategies previously discussed.

Stage 2 for Computation Strategies: Discussing the Strategy

This is the first stage in initiating the strategy when it is important to stress its relevance. During an initial conference the teacher discusses the students' current performance. It is also important for the teacher to stress the value of the strategy. Brainstorm with the students on situations wherein using this strategy or completing the given task accurately is important. For example, the following might be appropriate brainstorming

Change Problem

Frank has 8 seashells. Edward gave him 8 more. How many sea shells does Frank have now?

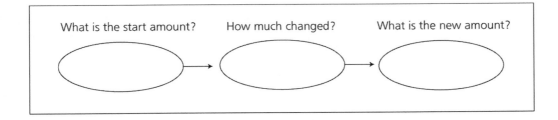

Vary Problem

In Steve's basketball camp there are 5 balls for 25 players. How many players must share each ball?

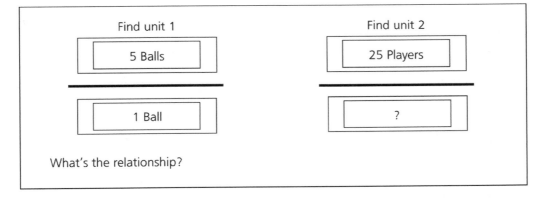

FIGURE 12.9. Examples of graphic organizers for word problems.

ideas in response to the question "When would it be important for you to make accurate math calculations?"

- Balancing your checkbook
- Trying to figure out if you have enough money to buy what you want
- Following a recipe
- Measuring anything
- Building a house
- Fixing your car

- Planning next year's crops
- For a test
- For an assignment

As we noted earlier some students may be unsure about, or reluctant to try, a strategy. If this occurs, we recommend the use of a behavioral contract. The student agrees to try using the strategy for a set period of time. In return, the student receives an agreed-upon reinforcer (e.g., extra computer time).

A sample script for "selling" the strategy follows:

"Math is everywhere! We came up with a lot of instances where it would be important to make accurate math calculations. We decided that it is really important when we are balancing our checkbook, and seeing if we have enough money to buy that new CD we want. Math is a very important part of our lives, whether we like it or not. Sometimes it's difficult to remember all of the different steps in various math calculations, or our 'computational procedures.' One procedure we have been using a lot, and one that is giving many of us difficulties, is multiplication of multidigit numbers (i.e., 10's, 100's, 1,000's). We have been working on this for a while now in math, and I've noticed that many of you are having difficulty remembering the procedures. It's important to remember the procedures; if you don't follow the correct procedure, you won't get the correct answer. This problem has been affecting your grades. Let's take a look at some of your recent quiz scores. You really did a nice job _____ [point out the positives]. However, there seems to be a breakdown in your procedural methods because you are getting quite a few incorrect. Earlier we mentioned that it is important to be able to make correct math calculations for assignments, quizzes, or tests; it appears that we could improve on this. The good news is that I have a way that can really help you with your multiplication procedures. It's a 'trick' to help you remember the multiplication computation procedures. This trick is a strategy called *MAMA*. Just like your mom's help, this strategy will help you! It should make multiplication easier for you, and your grades will improve."

In this stage we also introduce the strategy steps and any prompts that will be given (Figure 12.10).

Stage 3 for SOLVE IT!: Modeling the Strategy

The teacher will need to use a think-aloud to demonstrate the use of the strategy. Here is an example of a think-aloud for SOLVE IT!

"OK, I am doing my math homework. Things are going just fine; I know how to do these subtraction problems with regrouping when they are written out in standard form. OK, but now I am up to the last section and they are *story problems*! Story problems always give me trouble! Ugh, what can I do? Oh, yeah, the other day we talked about a trick that could help us with our story problems; it was called the

---

MAMA

Step 1: Multiply the 1's column.

Step 2: Across—do I need to go across to the 10's?

Step 3: Multiply the bottom 1's digit with the top 10's digit.

Step 4: Add any number that was carried in Step 2.

FIGURE 12.10. Prompt sheet for the MAMA strategy.

'SOLVE IT!' strategy. I'll try it now. OK, first I need to *Read* for understanding. Being able to read the problem is important, but it's even more important that I understand what I've read. If I don't understand it, I'll never be able to pull out all of the necessary information to solve it.

"At each step in the SOLVE IT! strategy I am supposed to follow three steps: (1) Say, (2) Ask, and (3) Check. So, at this step I need to *say*: 'Read the problem. If I don't understand, read it again.' OK, so I'll read the problem. The problem says: 'Taylon has 427 head of cattle on his ranch. Sydni has 605 head of cattle on her ranch. How many more cattle does Sydni have than Taylon?' All right, I read the problem, now what? I need to *ask* myself, 'Have I read and understood the problem?' Well, I read the problem; did I understand it? I think so. Now I can just go to the next step and check for understanding as I solve the problem. I double-check to make sure I understand the problem while I'm attempting to solve it. Now what do I need to do? The next step is to *Paraphrase* the problem in my own words, so I *say*: 'Underline the important information. Put the problem in my own words.' Well, I know that the number of cattle is important. I know that because the question asks me 'How many more?' Numbers in story problems are usually important.

"OK, now I need to put the problem in my own words. Sydni has more cows than Taylon. She has 605, and he has 427. How many more does she have? This is going pretty smooth; now I need to *ask*: 'Have I underlined the important information?' Yes, I underlined the number of cattle each rancher had. Those are the numbers I need to work with. Good. Now, 'What is the question? What am I looking for?' The question is, 'How many more head of cattle does Sydni have than Taylon?' So, I'm looking for how many MORE. OK, now I need to *check* that the information goes with the question. So, the question asks how many head of cattle? That's the information that I underlined; that's right then. It's helpful to do these checks to make sure I'm not messing up or leaving out important steps along the way.

"What's next? *Visualize* a picture of a diagram. I know what a diagram is. That's like a graph or a web. OK, I need to *say*: 'Make a drawing or diagram.' All right, I've drawn my graphic representation. Now I need to *ask*: 'Does the picture fit the problem?' Well, it shows Sydni's ranch with her cattle, and Taylon's ranch with his cattle; yes, it does fit the problem! Let's keep going! Next, I need to *Hypothesize* a plan to solve the problem. What does *hypothesize* mean? I know in science it means to make an educated guess, so I think this step means I need to make an educated guess at a plan to solve this problem. I'm now supposed to *say*: 'Decide how many steps and operations are needed. Write the operation symbols (+, −, ×, ÷). This problem has only one step.' I need to find the difference between Taylon's herd and Sydni's herd. I already know how many cattle each of them has; all I need to do is find the difference. I know that *difference* almost always means subtraction, so I will write down a −. Now, I need to *ask*: If I do subtraction, what will I get? Well, I will get a number smaller than my largest number, but I don't know what that will be until I actually solve the problem.

"OK, so I know that I only need to perform one operation, and that operation is subtraction. This sounds like a reasonable plan. Now, I need to *check* that the plan makes sense. Well, I already said that it sounds reasonable. That means I think my plan makes sense. How will I know? Let's see, what's my next step? My next step is to *Estimate* and predict my answer. That will help me to make sure my plan makes sense. All right, on to the next step; I need to *say*: 'Round the numbers, do the problem in my head, and write the estimate.' OK, so if I round the larger number, 605, I get 600. I round the larger number first because I know with subtraction the larger number is always on top. All right, now the other number, 427, and I get 400. Now I need to do the problem in my head (600 − 400 = 200) and write the estimate, so I'll write down *200*. Now, I need to *ask*: 'Did I round up and down?' Well, I only rounded down, but that's because I know when I round, if a number is less than 5 I round down, but if a number is 5 or greater I round up. In both of the numbers that I was rounding, the second digit was less than 5, so I rounded down. I still need to *ask*: 'Did I write the estimate?' Yes, I wrote it on the board.

"Now, I need to *check* that I used important information. Yes, I did! I used the information that I underlined. I didn't even realize it at first, but having the numbers underlined really helped me find the correct information. Wow, this is going very well; this strategy is really helping me with my story problem. What's next? *Compute*, or do the arithmetic. I'm finally ready to solve the problem. I feel very confident that I'm going to be able to SOLVE IT! Let's see, 605 − 427 = ? OK, I got it, 178. Now, I need to *ask*: 'How does my answer compare with my estimate? Does my answer make sense? Are the decimals or money signs in the right place?' Well, my answer is very close to my estimate; if I rounded my answer, I would get my estimate! I think I did it—my answer definitely makes sense. There are no decimals or money symbols, so I don't need to worry about that. Almost done, only one more step! I need to *Check* to make sure everything is right. So, I *say*: 'Check the computation.' OK, I used the correct operation, and my estimate is close to my answer, but I'm not sure if it's completely accurate. How can I make sure my answer is correct? Well, we usually check our work by performing the opposite operation; even though this is a story problem this should still work—all I'm doing is subtraction! OK, so I can do addition to check. I will add my answer to the number I subtracted, and I should get the larger number. I already know how to do this! All right, so 178 + 427 = 605; yes, I got it right!

"Next, 'Have I checked every step? Have I checked the computation? Is my answer right?' Yes, I checked every step (I only had one), I checked my computation by doing the opposite operation, and I determined that I had the correct answer! Finally, I need to *check* that everything is right. If not, go back. Then ask for help if I need it. Well, I already asked myself these questions, and I determined that I got the right answer, so I don't need to go back or ask for help. I did it! I did it, and I know I got it all right. Wow, when I try and make sure I use the appropriate strategy, story problems aren't so bad! That was actually kind of fun!"

Stage 5 for Schema-Based Strategies: Supporting the Strategy

Students need to automatically recognize the various types of schemas used. They also need to be able to identify the features of the semantic relations in the problem and check the salient element of the chosen problem schema. Based on Jitendra's (Jitendra et al., 1998) procedures, scaffolding should include the following:

1. The teacher models collaboratively with students. Students help identify critical elements or constraints of the word problems.

- Students practice identifying the different problem types in the story situations (e.g., Change, Group, and Compare).
- Students translate the information (i.e., read and understand the word problem).
- Students map the features of the situation onto the schema diagrams (Figure 12.9).

2. The teacher reviews the problem schemas through collaborative modeling. Any student misconceptions should be addressed immediately, and explicit feedback provided along with additional modeling.

- Equations, instead of word problems, are presented; however, the teacher still *reads* a word problem to the students.
- The teacher should use a facilitative questioning procedure for students to identify the semantic features of the problem.
- The teacher then demonstrates how critical elements of the specific problem are translated and mapped on the schema diagrams (Figure 12.9).
- The missing element is flagged with a question mark.

3. Instruction is given on the second strategy step. During this stage, students should be given explicit feedback on their ability to synthesize the steps of the strategy. The teacher should use guided practice and modeling, and provide immediate corrective feedback at each step in the instructional process.

- The teacher explains how to find the total amount in the word problem by focusing on the specific information in the problem. For example:
  - *Change problem*: Students will need to determine if the problem ends with more or less than the beginning amount.
    - ending state = total when the change results in an increase
    - beginning state = total when the change results in a decrease
  - *Compare problem*: Students compare the value of the referent and compare objects to determine the greater quantity, or the total.
  - Students must read the comparison or difference statement in the word problem.
  - Students are taught a generalizable rule based on the part–whole concept for determining the operation to be used. They must examine the part of the situation that is unknown and whether it represents the whole or the part to be solved.
    - If the whole is *not* known, then add to find total.
    - If the whole *is* known, then subtract to the other (part) amount.

Initially, students should be given only one type of problem; after they are able to successfully use the strategy with that type of problem, others should be introduced one at a time.

Stage 5 for Basic Multiplication Strategies: Supporting the Strategy

Scaffolding is important in this stage. With scaffolding it is possible to gradually transfer strategy performance from teacher to student. Students need to be given adequate time and support to master the strategy.

Content Scaffolding

Students are given simple multiplication problems. The teacher and students then go over the problems and the use of the different strategies. Together they determine which type of multiplication strategy is appropriate, and they solve the problem together. The teacher directs the process and the students provide answers to teacher-directed questions (i.e., "What type of multiplication strategy does this problem represent? What do we need to remember to solve this problem?").

Task Scaffolding

Students are taught one multiplication strategy at a time, first the "0 strategy" for multiplication to mastery, then each additional strategy, as listed in Figure 12.3.

During collaborative practice the teacher prompts students to use their various multiplication strategies to solve problems. The teacher demonstrates the use of the various multiplication strategies though modeling. In subsequent lessons the teacher asks students to identify the strategy necessary to solve the problem and asks how they knew which strategy to use (the teacher directs the process). Finally, students are given a set of multiplication problems and expected to choose the appropriate multiplication strategy and answer the questions correctly.

Material Scaffolding

Students are given prompt cards with multiplication strategies (Figure 12.3) to use with their independent math work. Initially, the prompts serve as a guide to remind them of various multiplication strategies, and the cues that go with each. Students are provided with multiple opportunities to practice using their multiplication strategies, until they are able to do so independently and to successfully solve basic multiplication problems.

Stage 6 for Computational Strategies: Independent Performance

At this stage the student is ready to use the strategy independently. The teacher's main task is to monitor the student's performance and check on proper and consistent use of the strategy. It is important to keep in mind that our main goal is improved academic performance. Teachers must evaluate whether or not the strategy is being used, if it is being generalized to other appropriate situations, and whether or not academic performance has improved. Students will not always generalize strategies to appropriate situations; they will need to be prompted and encouraged to do so.

To promote generalization, students are encouraged to use the strategy in other content areas where they are required to compute mathematical calculations. All team teachers should be informed about the use of the strategy, the language, the prompts, and what is required at each step. All team teachers are given a wall chart to hang up in their room as a reminder for students to use the computational strategies when appropriate.

Students should be assessed regularly, using independent work, quizzes, and tests, specifically in math class. These scores are recorded and tracked for trends in progress. The goal is improved academic performance, and if performance isn't improving, a reteaching of the strategies may be necessary. Once students are successful in using the strategies, their performance should be monitored periodically. Even though they have reached the independent performance stage, they should be monitored to ensure proper use of the strategy. If students deviate from the given computation strategies, performance should be evaluated and action taken only if performance is no longer improving.

FINAL THOUGHTS

There is good evidence that strategies can be effective for all the levels of mathematics included in this chapter. In fact, because it is often highly procedural and rule based, mathematics is a natural area for strategy instruction. Still, there are some areas (e.g., algebra, geometry) that have not been well studied or have not been studied with students with LD. In these cases, teachers would need to construct their own strategies using a task analysis as a guide. An accurate task breakdown, combined with the SRSD model, should be helpful when there are no existing strategies.

CHAPTER 13

Study Skills Strategies

The term *study skills* refers to a wide variety of skills necessary to be successful in any academic setting. These skills include note taking, test taking, homework completion, and general school "survival skills" (e.g., coming to class prepared, being organized, and paying attention in class) (Smith & Smith, 1989). These skills become more important as students progress through school and are particularly critical at the secondary level, where teachers expect students to display these "responsible behaviors" (Snyder & Bambara, 1997). Effective study skills can make the difference between academic success versus failure, and can often lead to positive outcomes across multiple academic settings (Gettinger & Seibert, 2002). In contrast, lack of survival skills can increase the risk of academic problems (e.g., failing a course or failing to learn course content) (Krishnan, Feller, & Orkin, 2010).

As they mature, successful learners display appropriate, self-directed behavior in order to gain information (Schumaker & Deshler, 1988). This information comes from a wide variety of source books, as well as material presented in class. Successful learners are strategic in gaining information; they devise plans and gather information in a systematic fashion (Olson & Platt, 2000). For example, they listen while the teacher is delivering instruction, take notes, ask questions, answer questions, and contribute to the discussion. When given an assignment, successful students use class time efficiently, consult textbooks and other appropriate sources of information to answer questions, and complete assignments in a timely manner. These skills are essential to academic success. Unfortunately, many students with LD or ADHD lack efficient and effective study skills strategies. As a result, by the time students with LD or ADHD reach secondary school, they are typically well below their peers in terms of content-area knowledge (e.g., social studies, science, math) (Scruggs, Mastropieri, Berkeley, & Graetz, 2010).

When compared to normally achieving peers, students with LD or ADHD have trouble with note-taking skills, error monitoring, test-taking strategies, and ability to scan a textbook for information (Carlson & Alley, 1981). These deficits should not be too surprising given the problems with self-monitoring and with adopting a strategic approach to tasks that we have discussed previously. Teaching study skills strategies for note taking, test-taking, and organization to help with time management and assignment completion can help students with LD or ADHD become more successful and independent (Olson & Platt, 2000; Reid & Johnson, 2012; Scruggs et al., 2010). Effective study strategies can represent the key to independent learning for students with LD or ADHD, and can make the difference between academic success and academic failure (Bos, Coleman, & Vaughn, 2002).

PROBLEMS FOR STUDENTS WITH LEARNING DISABILITIES OR ATTENTION-DEFICIT/HYPERACTIVITY DISORDER

Because of current inclusive practices, students with LD or ADHD generally spend all or most of their day in the general education classroom (e.g., Schnoes et al., 2006) . However, the general education classroom is often not set up for students with LD or ADHD to succeed. From around fourth grade and up, most instruction is delivered in a lecture format. This delivery style demands effective note taking, adequate writing skills, and rapid and efficient information processing. Students must be able to focus on salient information, accurately remember important details, and retrieve this information for assessments or examinations. This type of instructional delivery puts students with LD or ADHD at a definite disadvantage (Scruggs et al., 2010). Without the necessary cognitive skills, background knowledge, and appropriate strategies, they may flounder. Thus it is important that students be taught strategies to focus and enhance their efforts. Students with LD or ADHD have several characteristics that negatively affect their study skills.

Lack of Coordinated Strategies

Learning is an active process. Study skills, such as taking notes, completing homework, or taking a test, require a student's active engagement both cognitively and metacognitively. Successful students are actively involved in academic tasks and understand that their success is due to their effort and their use of effective strategies. In contrast, as we discussed in Chapter 1, students with LD or ADHD are likely to lack appropriate strategies and background knowledge and to possess a negative belief about their academic abilities. Note that problems with strategies are not due to an inability to learn or profit from appropriate strategies; instead, it is that these students have difficulties developing and deploying strategies (Johnson & Reid, 2011). In order to be successful in the general education classroom, students must be actively engaged in learning activities and utilize effective strategies.

Focus on Irrelevant Information

Gaining information in the general education classroom is based largely on a student's ability to focus on important information. Study skills require students to differentiate between relevant and irrelevant information. For example, when taking notes from a lecture or text, students must be able identify and to write down key information. This prerequisite puts students with LD or ADHD at a disadvantage; they do not often *devote* attention to learning. They may not be able to identify what information is important, or they may focus on irrelevant information, distractions in the classroom, or other elements that are not related to a learning task. They also may need to focus attention on receiving information (i.e., decoding text, understanding lecture language), rather than on processing the information relevant to the task (Kops & Belmont, 1985).

Working Memory Deficits

Research indicates students with LD or ADHD have smaller working memories for verbal information than their normally achieving peers (Martinussen & Major, 2011; Swanson & Trahan, 1992). This deficit affects their ability to encode, organize, and process information. It also puts students with LD or ADHD at a distinct disadvantage in terms of study skills, because study skills can place extreme demands on working memory. For example, while accessing basic skills such as transcription, spelling, and outlining, note taking requires a student to (1) attend to information presented verbally and/or visually in a lesson, (2) focus on important information, (3) remember the information, (4) organize the information, and (5) condense or synthesize information.

Inability to Make Appropriate Generalizations

Students are often expected to use information or skills previously learned and generalize them to appropriate situations. This is often necessary in order to gain new information. For example, a common strategy for reading a chapter in a textbook is to skim the headings; note charts, graphs, or figures that may be important; ask yourself questions about the material; and activate prior knowledge before reading. Successful students know that this strategy will be useful for a wide variety of tasks, and they can appropriately generalize this strategy. Students with LD or ADHD, however, are not likely to make these appropriate generalizations; if they do know strategies, they often do not generalize these strategies to other appropriate situations. Students must be taught generalization of skills and strategies to other appropriate situations.

Poor Writing Skills

Many academic activities require students to turn information known, heard, or read into intelligible written language (e.g., taking tests, taking notes, and completing assignments). Englert and Raphael (1988) noted that students with LD experience greater difficulties than their nondisabled peers with the demands of writing. They experience difficulties with planning, organizing, and revising their writing, as well as with basic transcription skills. Transcription skills, which include handwriting and spelling, are often overlooked but can be critical (Graham & Harris, 2000). Because of poor transcription skills, many students with LD exhibit writing that is practically indecipherable—even to them!

Lack of Organization

Students with LD often approach complex tasks in a disorganized fashion. The lack of a planful, step-by-step approach to academic tasks means that these students may waste time or use ineffective or inefficient approaches to task completion. Organizational skills are especially important in the case of tasks that involve multiple steps (e.g., doing a book report). Organizational problems are common among students with ADHD or LD (Johnson & Reid, 2011) and can result in their failing to complete tasks that are otherwise well within their capabilities.

PREREQUISITE SKILLS

When teaching students study skills strategies, it is critical to consider the prerequisite skills necessary for them to be successful. Study skill prerequisites include (1) recording, (2) organizing, (3) remembering, and (4) using information appropriately (Gettinger & Seibert, 2002).

Recording

Recording includes writing/transcription skills. It is necessary for students to be able to successfully record information; if information is written incorrectly, it will be difficult for them to successfully complete the academic task. For example, students are required to record their assignments (i.e., assignments given verbally or posted in the classroom, generally on the board); an incorrect recording of the assignment would most likely result in an incomplete assignment. If the student is lucky, the teacher will allow him or her to redo the assignment; however, this will often result in a loss of points and a very frustrated student. Students are also required to write/record while gaining and demonstrating knowledge. Writing is commonly used for test taking, assignment completion, and note taking.

Organizing

Organization of information is crucial to a student's success in the general education classroom. Organized information is easier to store in long-term memory and easier to retrieve when needed. The ability to organize incoming information, from text or lecture, is a make-it or break-it skill in the inclusive classroom. If students are unable to organize incoming information in a meaningful fashion, they will not be able to understand that information. If they are not able to relate what they have learned in an organized fashion, they will not be able to demonstrate their knowledge on assignments or examinations.

Remembering

The ability to recall information is essential to a student's academic success. Assessments and examinations are designed to test a student's ability to recall previously learned material. If a student is unable to remember or recall information, then it is difficult to say that he or she has "learned" that information. Many mnemonic strategies are extremely effective at improving memory for academic material. Because this area is so important, we deal with strategies designed to help with information storage and retrieval in the next chapter.

Appropriate Use

Gaining information, understanding it, and remembering it are all necessary skills in the classroom, but the ability to appropriately use the information is arguably the most important. Students must be able to use information to demonstrate their knowledge as well as to develop additional skills. Being able to use information appropriately is the reason for learning it in the first place.

INSTRUCTION IN STUDY SKILLS

Olson and Platt (2000) made the following recommendations for planning study skills instruction for students with LD:

1. The study skills should be functional, meaningful, and determined by the needs of the students.
2. Students need to be convinced that the study skills are useful, necessary, and effective in solving problems.
3. The instruction should be direct, organized, and sequential, with instructor modeling, many examples presented, difficult points explained, and student progress monitored.
4. Instruction should show which study skills can be used, how they can be used, and when and why they are beneficial.
5. The instructional materials used with the students should be motivating, meaningful, relevant, and easy to understand.

In the sections that follow, we focus on four major areas of study skills: (1) note-taking skills, (2) homework (task) completion, (3) test-taking strategies, and (4) classroom survival strategies.

NOTE-TAKING STRATEGIES

Taking notes is an important means of organizing information, and accurate note taking is essential in most content-area classrooms (Deshler, Ellis, & Lenz, 1996). Students who record and review their personal lecture notes perform better on tests than do students who just listen to lectures (Kiewra, 1987). Taking notes requires students to receive information and process it simultaneously. This requirement places demands on working memory and decreases the cognitive processing abilities available for organizing and storing information (Kiewra, 1987). The effective note taker uses working memory capacity to simultaneously attend to, store, and manipulate information selected from the lecture, while also transcribing ideas just previously presented and processed (Kiewra & Benton, 1988).

In order to manipulate information for note taking, students must be able to hold information and process it at the same time. The more information they are required to process in working memory, the less space they have left to hold information to transcribe. Awareness of demands on working memory is important in note taking. Humans are probably able to deal with only two or three items of information at a time, when required to process rather than merely hold information (Sweller, van Merrienboer, & Paas, 1998). Thus, it becomes important to reduce demands on working memory for students with LD or ADHD, who already may have difficulties in this area.

Note taking involves more than just writing. It also involves comprehension of the lecture or text, and the organization and production of intelligible text. Students must be able to select relevant information from a lecture or text, maintain that knowledge while integrating it with new and old ideas, and then select the information to be transcribed (Kiewra, 1987). Typically, students with learning disabilities try to take notes verbatim (Suritsky, 1992). These students' inability to process information in a timely manner makes the task of note taking laborious and extremely frustrating. Students with lower information-processing ability record fewer notes and tend to have lower achievement; one possible reason for their lower achievement is their somewhat terse note taking (Kiewra, 1987).

Teachers will often allow students to tape-record lectures or use copies of peers' notes, but neither strategy helps students compensate for comprehension deficits or distinguish subtle differences among similar concepts (Deshler & Graham, 1980). Using another student's notes is usually not as effective as using those generated by the student him- or herself, but it can be done to compensate for note-taking deficiencies. However, providing students with notes during a lecture can be beneficial. When students are provided with complete and organized notes (rather than being required to review their own notes), they perform better (Kiewra, 1984). Notes should be available for the students during the lecture to act as an effective retrieval cue later (Benton, Kiewra, Whitfill, & Dennison, 1993). Although it is effective to have students listen to lectures and review a set of provided notes, this is not best practice. Students are able to recall more information from well-done personally recorded notes than from notes provided to them (Kiewra, 1984). Thus, it is highly beneficial to assist students in improving the notes they generate themselves.

Lazarus (1988, 1991) taught students to used guided notes to improve the content of their notes. Guided notes are a skeleton outline containing the main ideas and related concepts of a lecture, with designated spaces for students to complete as the lecture proceeds. The type and amount of information can vary depending on the subject matter and the student's skill level. One of the key aspects of guided notes is providing for maximum student response, meaning that students have numerous opportunities to fill in blanks and to receive feedback. Figure 13.1 is an example of a skeleton outline containing only the most fundamental information (main ideas and key concepts) that provides students with several opportunities to fill in the rest (Lazarus, 1996). Notes will vary depending on students' needs.

Note the review tally in the upper right-hand corner of the sample notes. Students can put checkmarks in the Reviewer Tally to keep track of how many times they use or review the notes. This will allow them to monitor their efforts in learning the material. Reviewing notes is important, because it promotes mastery of the content. However, be realistic and don't provide too many spaces, as students may see them as one more requirement and get frustrated (Lazarus, 1996). Lazarus (1996) provided some practical tips for developing skeleton outlines: (1) Use existing lecture notes, (2) use a consistent format, and (3) provide for maximum student response.

Review Tally __ __ __ __ __ __

Volcanoes

I. Volcanoes are _____

   Types of volcanoes are:

   A. _____

   B. _____

   C. _____

II. How volcanoes are formed:

   A. _____

   _____

   B. _____

   _____

   C. _____

   _____

III. Hazards posed by volcanoes include:

   A. _____

   B. _____

   C. _____

FIGURE 13.1. Guided notes example.

Use Existing Lecture Notes

Guided notes are most effective if created from existing lecture notes (Lazarus, 1996). Creating guided notes from existing lecture notes helps students follow both the lecture and the notes; each provides a cue for the other. If students get lost in the lecture, they should be able to find their place by using the guided notes, and vice versa. Using existing lecture notes is easier for the teacher and provides students with a comprehensive outline of the lecture. The amount of information provided will vary depending on a particular student's level of need. Guided notes should, at the least, contain the main ideas covered in the lecture. It may also be beneficial to include key phrases, definitions, related issues, and contrasting viewpoints to avoid confusion (Lazarus, 1996).

Use a Consistent Format

Using a consistent format that corresponds with the structure of the lecture helps students use guided notes efficiently (Lazarus, 1996). If the notes follow the lecture format, students are able to focus on the information being provided instead of figuring out where they are in their notes. In fact, the format should parallel the sequence of the lecture; it should correspond with the structure and content of the course. This method will provide organized information to facilitate note taking and aid in comprehension and retention of the material. Providing a consistent format will also help in review. The consistency of the notes will assist students in recalling information presented in the lecture; if the notes mirror the lecture, then students will have a much easier time remembering the information presented in the lecture.

Provide for Maximum Student Response

Students should be given numerous opportunities to respond and receive feedback while using the guided notes (Lazarus, 1996). The more opportunity students have to use the guided notes, the more effective and efficient they will become. Lazarus (1996) noted several ways in which students and teachers can use guided notes.

1. During lectures, show examples of completed copies of the guided notes on an overhead (see Figure 13.2). By covering the slide and revealing each related phrase as it is discussed, teachers give students access to accurate information in a way that helps them keep their place.
2. Visual cues such as blanks, alphabet letters, and labels (see Figure 13.1) on the students' copies of the notes convey the amount and type of information to record. For example, the letters *A* through *C* under Roman numeral *I* ("Types of volcanoes") alert students that three examples will be presented.
3. Although a chapter in a textbook may take a week or more to cover in class, give the students copies of the guided notes for the entire chapter before you give them their reading assignment. Students may then use the guided notes as a reading guide while reading the assignment.

Volcanoes

 I. Volcanoes are <u>holes in the earth which allow lava, ash, and hot gasses to escape.</u>

   Types of volcanoes are:

   A. <u>Shield</u>

   B. <u>Cinder cone</u>

   C. <u>Composite</u>

 II. How volcanoes are formed:

   A. <u>Shield volcanoes are formed by runny lava that flows for miles leaving wide shallow</u>
      <u>slopes.</u>

   B. <u>Cinder cone volcanoes are formed by lava shot into the air that fall to earth.</u>

   C. <u>Composite volcanoes are formed by lava, volcanic ash, and rock.</u>

 III. Hazards posed by volcanoes include:

   A. <u>Red hot lava flows</u>

   B. <u>Volcanic ash</u>

   C. <u>Pyroclastic flows</u>

FIGURE 13.2. Completed guided notes example.

4. Holding a 5- or 10-minute supervised review period at the end of each class gives you an opportunity to evaluate students' guided notes and provide corrective feedback and reinforcement. This not only gives students review time, but also provides them with the opportunity to clarify any confusing information in their notes before the notes are reviewed.

5. Provide guided notes for all students in the class. This way, *all* students benefit, and the student(s) with LD is not singled out.

Guidelines for Making Guided Notes

Lazarus (1996) provided some tips for making guided notes. To create guided notes, first highlight information from existing lecture notes to create the skeleton for students to use. Then copy the highlighted information. Highlight the additional information, using a marker in a second, transparent shade, so that you can simply add the information to the original guided notes. Use this template to make transparencies. These tips work nicely when you are working from existing lecture notes; however, if you are just creating lecture notes, it may be easier to start with a skeleton outline and let that guide your lecture. Initially, preparing guided notes takes about 1–2 hours per chapter; however, they can be used repeatedly.

HOMEWORK/TASK COMPLETION

Homework provides students with opportunities to practice skills learned in the class-room (Polloway, Epstein, & Foley, 1992), and it can be one of the most efficient ways to improve their academic performance (Cancio, West, & Young, 2004). However, for students with LD or ADHD, homework may produce mixed outcomes (Hughes, Ruhl, Schumaker, & Deshler, 2002). In order for students to benefit from homework, teachers must assign appropriate tasks, and students must complete those tasks. Teachers must be mindful of students' varying levels of independent functioning or provide them with the support necessary to complete their homework successfully; students must actually complete the homework. Students with LD or ADHD encounter a number of problems with homework. They frequently misunderstand what has been assigned. Because of organizational deficits, they often fail to gather the necessary materials to complete the assignment (Gureasko-Moore, DuPaul, & White, 2007; Polloway et al., 1992). They also have difficulty recording assignments, managing their time, focusing on homework, monitoring progress, and maintaining effort if the task becomes difficult (Hughes et al., 2002).

Glomb and West (1990) taught high school students to use a homework comple-tion strategy. This strategy was designed to teach students how to plan assignments and monitor their academic work for (1) completeness of assignment, (2) accuracy with which they followed all of the directions or performance standards for the assignment, and (3) neatness. Students were first taught to identify what to do before starting home-work and after completing homework, particularly in regard to completing indepen-dent seatwork or homework assignments. Important steps before homework comple-tion included understanding the requirements of the given assignment, preparing to complete the assignment (i.e., gathering all necessary materials), and determining how the assignment would be completed (i.e., time frame, any additional resources). Steps after completing homework included reviewing for accuracy and completeness, mak-ing any necessary changes, and handing it in on time.

The WATCH strategy (Figure 13.3) consists of four steps: (1) *W*rite down an assign-ment when it is given and write the due date; (2) *A*sk for clarification or help on the assignment if needed; (3) *T*ask-analyze the assignment and schedule the tasks over the days available to complete the assignment; and (4) *C*heck all work for completeness, accuracy, and neatness. Students can use an assignment planner, which can help them to carry out each step; planners are an excellent way to monitor students' use of the strategy. The planner can also prompt students with questions such as "Do I under-stand the assignment?" and "Do I need help?" These cues are part of the self-instruction component of the strategy.

Expectations vary for different classes and for different teachers. Because the moni-toring component of this strategy includes checking for completeness, accuracy, and neatness (CAN) of assignments, teachers will need to teach students performance stan-dards for these three and how to evaluate their work according to each standard. Per-formance standards will vary depending on the content area and the teacher's expecta-tions, and they should reflect expectations the teacher has established for the class. The assignment planner can have the acronym *CAN* on it to cue students to check tasks for completeness, accuracy, and neatness (Figure 13.3). Lesson plans for the WATCH strategy are commercially available (Mason et al., 2012).

TEST-TAKING STRATEGIES

For middle and high school students, tests generally make up the majority of a student's grade in a content-area class. Students with LD have particular difficulty with the skills required to take a test. Preparing for tests is often problematic because of these students' difficulties with organization, comprehension, memory, task completion within time limits, self-doubt, and "test-wiseness" (Olson & Platt, 2000).

Ritter and Idol-Maestas (1986) noted that test anxiety, carelessness, poor use of time, and confusion are serious problems for test takers. The additional pressures of time limits, different forms of response, recalling previously learned information, and writing it into an understandable form pose problems; students are expected to work independently and read the directions, read the questions, remember the correct response, and write the correct response. Each of these tasks requires a unique set of skills that is essential to performing well on a test (Ritter & Idol-Maestas, 1986).

☐ **W**rite down an assignment, and **W**rite the due date
☐ **A**sk for clarification or help on the assignment if needed
☐ **T**ask-analyze the assignment and schedule the tasks over the days available
☐ **Ch**eck all work for **C**ompleteness, **A**ccuracy, and **N**eatness

"Do I understand the assignment?"
"Do I need help?"

Class: Social Studies   **Date:** 8/13

Assignment: Read Chapter 12 and answer the comprehension questions
                         at the end.

Task Analysis:

➢ **Date:** 8/13—Survey the chapter/questions; read pages 38–43 and take notes
➢ **Date:** 8/14—Read pages 44–49 and take notes
➢ **Date:** 8/15—Answer questions
➢ **Date:**
➢ **Date:**

Due Date: 8/16 _____   Before turning in Check for:

☐ **C**ompleteness

☐ **A**ccuracy

☐ **N**eatness

FIGURE 13.3. Example of a completed WATCH sheet.

Teaching students test-taking strategies can dramatically improve their test-taking abilities, as well as their scores on tests. One approach to improving students' test scores is to help them become "test-wise." Test-wiseness is described as a student's capacity to use the characteristics and formats of a test and/or the test-taking situation to earn a high score (Scruggs & Mastropieri, 1988). Skills involved in test-wiseness include time-use strategies, error-avoidance strategies, guessing strategies, and deductive reasoning strategies (Scruggs, Bennion, & Lifson, 1985). Test-wiseness is independent of subject-matter knowledge; the focus is on adapting oneself to the test structure (e.g., if the test is a multiple-choice test, one needs to be prepared to discriminate between correct and incorrect information) (Ritter & Idol-Maestas, 1986).

Simmonds, Luchow, Kaminsky, and Cottone (1989) designed the SPLASH (Table 13.1) test-taking strategy for taking multiple-choice tests. This is a preparation strategy as well as an actual test-taking strategy that helps student become more test-wise. The SPLASH acronym stands for the following skills:

1. *Skim the entire test*. Students skim the test to get a general idea of what will be required of them (i.e., how many questions, what types of questions, areas of proficiency and deficiency). This will help them make a plan for attacking the test.

2. *Plan your strategy*. Once students have a general idea of the test, they must plan their strategy. This strategy generally includes time constraints, knowledge, and where to begin. Students should first answer all questions to which they know the answers.

3. *Leave out difficult questions in a planned manner*. Omitting difficult questions in a planned manner means that students have an idea of which questions they will come back to first.

4. *Attack the questions you know immediately*. This focuses students' attention on information that they understand. Once they have answered all the questions for which they immediately know the answers, they should move on to any questions of which they were unsure.

TABLE 13.1. The SPLASH Strategy

S—Skim the test.

P—Plan your strategy.

L—Leave out tough questions.

A—Attack questions you know.

S—Systematically guess.

H—Housecleaning; leave a few minutes to fill in all answers, check computer forms, clean up erasures.

Note. Based on Simmonds, Luchow, Kaminsky, and Cottone (1989).

5. *Systematically guess*. After exhausting other strategies (i.e., skimming for areas of proficiency, answering all questions that they are sure of, and planning how to attack the skipped questions), students should take their best guess at an answer.

6. *Housecleaning*. Finally, students should leave 5–10% of their time to ensure that they have filled in all answers, checked computer forms, and cleaned up erasures.

Subjective or essay/short-answer tests require different skills than objective tests. Often students with LD approach essay questions in a haphazard manner (Simmonds et al., 1989); they tend to jump right into writing without doing any sort of planning—Scardamalia and Bereiter (1987) termed this "knowledge telling." Little attention is directed toward the goal of answering the question; students will simply write down whatever it is they may know about the topic, and not take into consideration the goal of answering the question. Mapping can provide a more strategic approach and can be introduced as an effective strategy to facilitate appropriate responses to essay questions (Marshak, 1984). The organization of a map provides a graphic representation of the essay's flow. Figure 13.4 shows a graphic organizer (map) for answering essay questions. Students using this map must be taught what an acceptable essay answer looks like. This strategy can be used to demonstrate that structure and organization influence the content and cohesiveness of essays (Simmonds et al., 1989). The first sentence in any essay is the topic sentence, which states what the essay is about; all subsequent sentences should reflect the topic sentence. Subsequent sentences, called *supporting sentences*, elaborate, explain, and defend the position of the topic sentence. The final sentence in any essay answer is a concluding sentence that wraps up all the points made and brings the focus back to the topic sentence.

CLASSROOM SURVIVAL STRATEGIES

Up till now all of our strategies have dealt with academics. However, in the general education classroom it is sometimes necessary to provide students with a "survival strategy" that addresses organization and motivation. We have already discussed several monitoring strategies (i.e., strategies students can use to monitor their progress toward a goal). This final study skills strategy is a combination of a monitoring strategy and a *motivational* strategy; motivational strategies are designed to maintain motivation and minimize negative thoughts or feelings (Ellis & Lenz, 1987). Students with LD do not generally use monitoring or motivational strategies, which can lead to much frustration as well as failure.

The PREPARE strategy (Ellis & Lenz, 1987) was designed as a classroom survival strategy to help students mentally prepare for class. Students can use the PREPARE strategy to monitor their class preparation behaviors; the PREPARE strategy also includes a motivational substrategy, PSYC. The PREPARE strategy contains six main steps: (1) *P*lan locker visits; (2) *R*eflect on what you need and get it; (3) *E*rase personal needs (personal issues that do not have to do with class); (4) *PSYC* yourself up (*P*—Pause

Topic Sentence

_____

_____

_____

_____

Supporting Details

_____	_____	_____
_____	_____	_____
_____	_____	_____
_____	_____	_____
_____	_____	_____

Concluding Sentence

_____

_____

_____

FIGURE 13.4. Example of a graphic organizer for answering essay questions.

for an attitude check, *S*—Say a personal goal related to the class, *Y*—Yoke in negative thoughts, *C*—Challenge yourself to good performance); (5) *Ask yourself where class has been and where class is going* (a brief review of what you have learned and what you will be learning); (6) *Review notes and study guide*; and (7) *Explore the meaning of teacher's introduction*.

IMPLEMENTATION PLANS

As with previous chapters, we provide partial examples of implementation plans for each of the strategies previously presented.

Stage 1 for Guided Notes: Developing and Activating Background Knowledge

Prior to teaching the strategy, it is necessary to evaluate the students' background knowledge. Formal or informal assessments can be used to determine which skills the students possess and which skills they lack; doing a task analysis will provide the information for identifying the skills necessary to successfully complete the strategy (Table 13.2).

Stage 2 for WATCH: Discussing the Strategy

This is the first stage in initiating the strategy when it is important to stress its relevance. During an initial conference the teacher discusses the students' current performance. In order for students to be successful and able to self-regulate the strategy, they need to make a commitment to use the strategy; they need to "buy into" the value of the strategy. Thus it is important for the teacher to stress this value. Brainstorm with the students on situations wherein using this strategy or completing the given task accurately is important. For example, the following might be appropriate brainstorming ideas in response to the question "When would it be important for you to complete an assignment?":

- To pass a class—and get to use the car
- At work when you're given something to do
- So your parents will be proud of you
- So you can play sports

A sample script for "selling" the strategy follows:

"The other day, we came up with a list of instances when it would be important to complete an assignment. Since we are here in school, the obvious one was to pass a class. Passing a class provides other motivations: getting to use the car, being able to play in the big game on Friday night, not having to take the class over, or maybe

TABLE 13.2. Example of Task Breakdown for Guided Notes

Strategy	Skill	Assessment
Basic skills	Writing/copying	Given a spelling test using terms from the given content area, the student will be able to spell the words correctly with 80% accuracy.
	Reading from the board (transparency projection)	Given the task of copying a passage from the board, the student will be able to copy everything with 100% accuracy.
Guided notes (format)	Knowledge of main ideas, key phrases, definitions, related issues, and contrasting viewpoints	Given a familiar passage from the student's textbook, the student will highlight main ideas, key phrases, definitions, related issues, and contrasting viewpoints, using specific colors to identify each, with 100% accuracy.
	Understanding standard outline format (i.e., I for major headings, A for main ideas under major headings, and so on)	Given a standard outline format, the student will be able to fill in each blank with the correct title (i.e., major heading, main ideas, and so on).
	Knowledge of lecture format	Given a simple lecture on familiar material, the student will be able to follow along and note major concepts with 90% accuracy.
Using the guided notes	Distinguishing relevant information	Given a familiar passage with a task that the student can perform, the student will be able to highlight all information relevant to completing the task with 90% accuracy.
	Writing and listening at the same time	Given a list orally, the student will be able to listen and write the correct list at the same time with 100% accuracy.
	Ability to put information into an organized format (guided notes)	Given a skeleton outline and a simple passage, the student will be able organize the information in the passage.

even getting on the honor roll. There are lots of reasons to complete your assignments, but sometimes it's hard to get it all done! I used to have a difficult time with this too, but now I have secret weapon. It's a strategy called *WATCH*. This strategy helps me organize myself so I can get my work turned in on time. Yes, as teachers we still have work! This strategy has really helped me, and I would like to teach it to you to help you too. I would hate it if any of you had to miss something important just because you didn't get an assignment done."

Stage 3 for SPLASH: Modeling the Strategy

The teacher will need to use a think-aloud to demonstrate the use of the strategy. Note how self-statements are used to focus attention and to redirect maladaptive thoughts.

"OK, here goes another science test. I always have such a hard time taking these tests! I just don't even know where to begin. Wait a minute, in class we've been working on this test-taking strategy called *SPLASH*; I think I'll use that strategy to help me. Let's see, what do I need to do first? SPLASH . . . oh, yeah, the *S* in SPLASH stands for 'Skim the entire test.' OK, I'll skim the test . . . it looks like there are 50 questions, 40 multiple choice, and 10 true–false. I like true–false questions; I usually seem to know those answers right away. I also saw some key words that I know; I'm sure I'll know those answers, but I also saw some words whose meaning I can't remember right now. *Great,* now what am I going to do? I know there are some of those questions that I *can't* answer!!! Well, no need to focus on that; that won't help me! What's next in my strategy? That *may* help me!

"OK, *S . . . P*—the next step in the SPLASH strategy is to 'Plan my strategy once I have a general idea of the test.' Well, I know I have the whole hour to take the test, but some questions may take me longer than others (like those ones I'm not sure about), so I should start with the ones that I know for sure! I think I'll start with the true–false questions, since I like those. Then, I'll answer the multiple-choice ones. The next step in my SPLASH strategy is *L*—'Leave out any difficult questions.' That will be easy—I already saw a few that I don't know; I'll leave those out. I like that step! OK, on to the next step. What's next? I've done *S* for *skimmed*, *P* for *planned*, and *L* for *left out* the hard ones; now I need to *A*—'Attack the questions I know immediately.' OK, I will start with the true–false ones . . . . Done—I knew most of those, but there was that one that I left out, because I'm just not sure about it. That's OK, according to my SPLASH strategy I'm supposed to leave out the difficult ones! I sure did that! OK, I've answered all the questions that I'm sure about, but I still have about 10 left! Now what? OK, back to SPLASH, *S . . . P . . . L . . . A . . . S*—stands for 'Systematically guess.' Well, I have a pretty good idea about most of these; answering all the questions that I was sure about helped me to remember some of the other things that I had forgotten, but there is still that true–false one that I have no idea about. I will just have to guess; I have a 50/50 chance at getting the right answer; I like those odds! OK, now what? SPLAS . . . *H*—stands for 'Housecleaning'; I need to make sure that my paper is clean, and that I have all of my answers marked clearly. Wow, I'm done! That was so much easier using my SPLASH strategy. I don't feel like I wasted any time, and I feel pretty good about how I did!"

Stage 4 for PREPARE: Memorizing the Strategy

Memorizing the strategy is extremely important! We want the students to focus on the task and not on the steps of the strategy. The specific activities themselves are not nearly as important. There are many appropriate activities. The important aspects of the activities are whether or not they facilitate memorization. The teacher will need to plan and prepare the activities and monitor their effectiveness. Previous chapters have provided examples of how to instruct effectively at this stage. Memorization of the PREPARE strategy could be promoted in a similar fashion.

Stage 5 for Guided Notes: Supporting the Strategy

Scaffolding is important in this stage. With scaffolding it is possible to gradually transfer strategy performance from teacher to student. Students need to be given adequate time and support to master the strategy.

Content Scaffolding

Students are given completed guided notes and a skeleton outline. The teacher and students go over the notes and discuss the components of the skeleton outline. The teacher directs the process and the students provide answers to teacher-directed questions (e.g., "What is the first major heading?" "Where would this definition go?" "What is the key concept here?").

Students are given a skeleton outline, some familiar text, and they are asked to fill in the skeleton outline. The teacher posts the completed guided notes on the overhead so that students can check their outlines against the completed outline. The teacher provides any support necessary in order for the students to be successful.

Task Scaffolding

During collaborative practice while lecturing, the teacher questions the students as to what part of their skeleton outline they should fill in. The teacher then fills in the outline and explains why the information should be placed in that particular location. In subsequent lessons the teacher will ask the students where information from lectures should go, have them fill in the appropriate space, and then the teacher will explain why that information needs to be in that particular location. Finally, the students will say where the information should go, fill in the skeleton outline, and explain why that information should be in that particular location.

Material Scaffolding

Students are given several skeleton outlines. Initially, outlines containing most of the information are provided (Figure 13.2). Over time outlines will provide less information but still provide the structure and key information (Figure 13.1). Eventually, the skeleton outlines will be faded completely; at this point students should have reached the mastery level of taking notes and being able to work independently.

Stage 6 for SPLASH: Independent Performance

At this stage the student is ready to use the strategy independently. The teacher's main task is to monitor the student's performance and check on proper and consistent use of the strategy. With our main goal being improved academic performance, it is necessary to monitor student progress with the strategy. Teachers must evaluate whether or not the strategy is being used, if it is being generalized to other appropriate situations, and whether or not academic performance has improved. Records of student achievement on tests should be kept and monitored.

Teachers need to keep in mind the fact that students will not always generalize strategies to appropriate situations; they will need to be prompted and encouraged to do so. To promote generalization, students should be encouraged to use the strategy in other content areas where they are required to take tests (i.e., most all of them). All team teachers should be informed about the use of the strategy, the language, the prompts, and what is required at each step. All team teachers are given a wall chart to hang up in their room as a reminder for students to use the SPLASH strategy when appropriate.

Even though students have reached the independent performance stage, they should be monitored to ensure proper use of the strategy. If students deviate from the given SPLASH strategy, performance should be evaluated, but action taken only if performance is no longer improving.

FINAL THOUGHTS

Study skills are an important part of any student's repertoire. The need for well-developed study skills becomes progressively greater as the student moves from elementary, to middle, to high school settings. Although these skills are critical for academic success, in our opinion they are too often overlooked because of the focus on basic academic skills at the elementary level, and the focus on content areas at the middle and high school levels. We would urge teachers to consider teaching organizational, study skills, and test-taking strategies as early as possible. These strategies will be useful then and will only become more important over time. Unfortunately, there was not space here to present many excellent study skill strategies. For more information on study skills strategies, we refer the reader to Gettinger and Siebert (2002).

CHAPTER 14

Mnemonics

$\mathbf{W}$hat's the capital of Bolivia? What are the parts of the nucleus of an atom? What's the fourth planet from the sun? What are three reasons for the start of the Civil War? Students are commonly called upon to answer questions such as these in classes, assignments, and examinations. This means that students must be able to efficiently and effectively store information in long-term memory and retrieve it on demand. As with other academic tasks, using strategies can help with storing and retrieving information. However, as we've previously discussed, students with LD do not spontaneously use appropriate and effective strategies that could help them remember. Thus, teachers should be aware of the need not only to teach content, but to also provide students with strategies to help them store and retrieve important information. One very effective type of memory strategy is a mnemonic.

A *mnemonic* is a strategy designed to help students store and retrieve information. Most students, at one point, have learned a mnemonic strategy, although they may not have heard the word *mnemonic* (Scruggs & Mastropieri, 2000). For example, many students have learned the acronym ROY G. BIV to help them remember the colors of the rainbow. Each letter in the acronym represents one of the colors of the rainbow (i.e., red, orange, yellow, green, blue, indigo, violet). Another example that would be familiar to music students is the phrase "Every good boy does fine," used to help students remember the notes on the lines of the treble clef: *e, g, b, d,* and *f*. These are examples of how mnemonics can be used to remember factual or detailed information. Mnemonics can also be used to help us remember the order of steps in a process. For example, Please excuse my dear Aunt Sally is a first-letter mnemonic used to remember the order of operations in algebraic problems (parenthesis, exponents, multiply, divide, add, and subtract) (Mastropieri & Scruggs, 1991).

Mnemonic strategies have been used for thousands of years. The ancient Greeks used a form of mnemonics, the method of loci, to help orators remember their speeches.

This strategy involves remembering a series of very familiar places or locations, such as the route taken from school to home, and pairing images of one piece of information with each place. For example, to remember a shopping list of hot dogs, ice cream, and cat food, you might pair up images of (1) hot dogs rolling down your driveway, (2) ice cream melting on the stoplight at the first intersection, and (3) a hungry cat in a shopping cart in the grocery store parking lot. The shopping list information can then be easily retrieved by mentally retracing one's route and recalling each of the items placed on the "mental map" (Schoen, 1996). Though this may sound strange, the method of loci is actually highly effective. This unconventional method illustrates an important point: The method is not what is important; what is important is how well it facilitates the different memory processes (i.e., encoding, storage, and retrieval) (Schoen, 1996).

There's a good reason why mnemonic strategies have been used for so long. Research clearly demonstrates that mnemonic techniques are superior to traditional methods of instruction when teaching the acquisition and recall of highly factual information (e.g., science and social studies information). For example, Mastropieri, Sweda, and Scruggs (2000) reported that using mnemonic strategies for social studies in an inclusive classroom raised the average test scores of students with LD from 36 to 75%, and that students responded very positively to the use of mnemonics. Similarly, Mastropieri, Scruggs, Bakken, and Brigham (1992) found that mnemonics were effective in teaching U.S. states and capitals. Finally, Scruggs, Mastropieri, Levin, and Gaffney (1985) found that mnemonics could be used to teach multiple attributes of minerals (e.g., hardness scale, color, and their uses), and that mnemonic instruction was more effective than direct instruction or free study. On the whole, mnemonics have proven to be highly effective in improving retention of information in specific content areas—most notably, science—for students with LD (Mastropieri & Scruggs, 1998; Scruggs & Mastropieri, 1990, 1992; Therrien, Taylor, Hosp, Kaldenberg, & Gorsh, 2011). Reviews of research (Scruggs & Mastropieri, 2000; Scruggs et al., 2010) have found that instruction that utilized mnemonics led to significant improvement in learning over traditional approaches. Moreover, the majority of the studies reviewed were done with students with LD.

There are many different types of mnemonic strategies, each of which can be used for multiple purposes. In this chapter we present examples of the five main types of mnemonic strategies based on the classification developed by Mastropieri and Scruggs: (1) acronyms and acrostics, (2) mimetics, (3) symbolics, (4) key words, and (5) pegwords.

PROBLEMS FOR STUDENTS WITH LEARNING DISORDERS OR ATTENTION-DEFICIT/HYPERACTIVITY DISORDER

As you will recall from Chapter 1, one of the most salient characteristics of students with LD is a problem with memory. Many students with LD do not efficiently encode and retrieve information from long-term memory, and there is good reason to suspect that students with ADHD also have problems in this area (Perugini, Harvey, Lovejoy, Sandstrom, & Webb, 2000; Reck, Hund, & Landau, 2010). Memory is critical to intellectual functioning and learning (Swanson & Saez, 2003). The ability to recall information is directly linked to a student's ability to learn, and therefore obviously a key component to academic success. Swanson and Saez (2003) identified two reasons why memory is a critical area of focus for students with LD or ADHD.

1. *Memory reflects applied cognition; that is, memory functioning reflects all aspects of learning* (p. 182). In schools, measures of learning are generally measures of memory (i.e., basic math facts, vocabulary, and reading comprehension). The way we measure whether or not students have learned content is to assess their memory of the information. If a student is unable to apply or recall new information, it is difficult to determine whether or not learning has occurred.

2. *Several studies suggest that the memory skills used by students with LD do not appear to exhaust, or even tap, their abilities; therefore, we need to discover instructional procedures that can capitalize on this underdeveloped potential* (p. 182). The problems with recall of factual information for students with LD or ADHD are probably not due to a deficient memory. Rather they are due to the failure to use strategies or to the use of ineffective or inefficient strategies. Students with LD have the potential to learn; however, unless they are taught how to recall information and use their cognitive abilities effectively, they will never reach their full academic potential.

According to Mastropieri and Scruggs (1991), learning occurs most efficiently when new information can be linked to previously acquired information. That is, learning is a knowledge-based process that requires the active involvement of the learner to make connections between known information and to-be-learned information. Students with LD or ADHD often fail to make these important mental "connections" between known and unknown information. This inability often results in school failure in the form of poor performance on tests and a general loss of information in content areas (Scruggs & Mastropieri, 2000). Because gaining knowledge requires learners to possess some knowledge, students must not only understand the new information presented to them, but must continually test, modify, and build upon or replace existing knowledge (Gaskins & Elliot, 1991). This presents problems for students with LD or ADHD; many times they do not possess the prerequisite knowledge required to make learning meaningful and lasting. Research indicates that students who have a firmly established knowledge base will be able to easily assimilate and apply new information. Students with impoverished background knowledge bases are clearly at a distinct disadvantage. Mastropieri and Scruggs called this phenomenon the "Matthew effect," whereby the "informationally rich" become richer, and the "informationally poor" (students with LD or ADHD) become poorer. This is a vicious cycle; the best way to break it is to provide students with a solid knowledge base, as well as with strategies to promote the acquisition of future information.

ACRONYMS AND ACROSTICS: THE "FIRST-LETTER" STRATEGIES

Acronyms

Most of us are familiar with acronyms. Acronyms are formed by taking the first letters of the words in a title or list of facts and combining them into a word. Each letter in an acronym represents the first letter of a word on a list of information to be learned or remembered. Acronyms serve as convenient shorthand representations of information. For example, it's much easier to say *NASA* than *National Aeronautics and Space Administration*, or to say *KFC* as opposed to *Kentucky Fried Chicken*. Generally, this type of mnemonic is most helpful when the items to be remembered are familiar and concrete. With only the first letter as a prompt, students must be familiar enough with the responses for that to serve as an adequate cue (Mastropieri & Scruggs, 1991). For example, a highly effective acronym for people studying U.S. geography is HOMES, an acronym for the five Great Lakes. Each letter in the acronym HOMES represents a different lake: *H*uron, *O*ntario, *M*ichigan, *E*rie, and *S*uperior.

This strategy is highly effective, but *only* for people who are familiar with the names of the Great Lakes. Here, the first letter is typically enough to evoke the correct response. If students were not familiar with the names, they would need to be taught them first, so that the first letter could serve as an adequate cue. Students would also need to be taught a way to associate the acronym HOMES with the names of the Great Lakes so that they could retrieve it for later use (Mastropieri & Scruggs, 1998). This process is similar to the *key word* process of recoding, relating, and retrieving (discussed in detail later in the chapter). For this example, students could be taught to relate the acronym HOMES to the Great Lakes by visualizing "homes" built around the edges of the Great Lakes (providing a picture of this scene would be even better). For retrieving the names, the students would need to remember the visual image of homes built on the edge of the lakes, come up with the acronym HOMES, and use the first-letter cues to come up with *H*uron, *O*ntario, *M*ichigan, *E*rie, and *S*uperior (Mastropieri & Scruggs, 1998).

Acronyms are an excellent way to organize information; you've probably noticed that many of the strategies we have presented use acronyms in the name. For example:

- SCROL—textbook reading strategy
- WWW, What = 2, How = 2—narrative writing strategy
- FAST DRAW—solving word problems
- POW + TREE—expository writing strategy
- COPS—mechanical revision strategy
- SCAN—content revision strategy
- WATCH—homework completion strategy
- SPLASH—test-taking strategy
- PREPARE—general classroom survival strategy

There's a good reason for this. The acronym serves to help organize the steps in the strategy, stimulate memory of the strategy steps, and cue the order of steps.

Acrostics

An acrostic is a sentence in which the first letter of each word doubles as part of a mnemonic that represents the information to be learned and remembered. An example was provided at the beginning of this chapter for the notes on the lines of the treble clef, *every good boy does fine.* Another example would be "*Queen Hannah gave Mr. Potter every CD collected.*" This assists in remembering the step in the scientific method of experimental research: *question, hypothesis, gather materials, perform experiment, collect data,* and *conclusion.* Acrostics can also be used to remember the spelling of difficult words (e.g., "*A rat in the house may eat the ice cream!*" for the word *arithmetic*). Acrostics are sometimes used to help cue the steps in a strategy. For example, "*Does McDonald's sell cheeseburgers?*" can be used to help remember the steps in long division:

- Does _____ go into _____?
- Multiply to find out.
- Subtract.
- Check to make sure the result is smaller.
- Bring down.

When an acronym or an acrostic alone is not effective or practical, the two can be combined. For example, when remembering the order of the planets from the sun, a combination can be used: "*My very exciting man, JSUN, plays!*" for Mercury, Venus, Earth, Mars, Jupiter, Saturn, Uranus, Neptune, and Pluto. Students would need to be able to remember which part of the sentence was an acronym, and which part was an acrostic; however, this would not be difficult if the students were familiar enough with the information to be remembered (i.e., the planets).

MIMETICS

The term *mimetic* literally means imitating or mimicking something. In the case of mnemonic strategies, a mimetic is simply a pictorial representation of the information that is to be learned. Many content areas require students to learn content that is concrete and that can easily be depicted in an illustration (Mastropieri & Scruggs, 1991). If the content is already familiar and meaningful to the student, then a mimetic is likely to be effective. For example, in social studies content introduced is often familiar and meaningful to students. Students studying the Industrial Revolution would be familiar with the technology in 1800s that changed life in the United States (e.g., textile mills, mass production, the Erie Canal, the national road, and steamboats and railroads) (Figure 14.1). To teach this content, the teacher would present the picture and note how the mill was by the national road and the steamboats and steam engines were bringing goods for mass production. The teacher would remind the students that when they needed to remember something about technology in the 1800s, they should remember the picture of how the steamboat and steam engines brought material along the national road to the textile mills. By reconstructing this information mimetically, students would achieve greater recall of the information. We should stress that it is critical for the students to already be familiar with the content. For example, Mastropieri and Scruggs (1991) described the use of a mimetic showing convoys protecting U.S. oil tankers in the Persian Gulf. However, because the students were unfamiliar with the word *convoy*, the mimetic was not effective.

FIGURE 14.1. A mimetic representation of the Industrial Revolution. This picture depicts the major innovations of the 1800s leading to the Industrial Revolution: (1) textile mills, (2) assembly lines, (3) interchangeable parts, (4) steam engines, (5) the Erie Canal, and (6) the national roadway.

SYMBOLICS

Symbolics are similar to mimetics. Both use illustrations to represent information. Symbolics differ in that they are used to depict abstract information. Political cartoons are an excellent example of symbolics. Symbolics are used in the same manner as mimetics. As with mimetics, students must be familiar with the content. This is a serious concern because of the abstract nature of the content of symbolics. For example, most of us are familiar with the symbols used for Republicans (an elephant) and Democrats (a donkey). However, students with LD do not always know this association (Mastropieri & Scruggs, 1991). Symbolics are used in much the same manner as mimetics. Figure 14.2 provides an example of a symbolic mnemonic for the three branches of government and what each branch represents. Again, it is important to remember that students *must* be familiar with the symbols used to represent each branch in order for this particular mnemonic to be effective. If these symbols are unfamiliar, it would be necessary to teach these associations first.

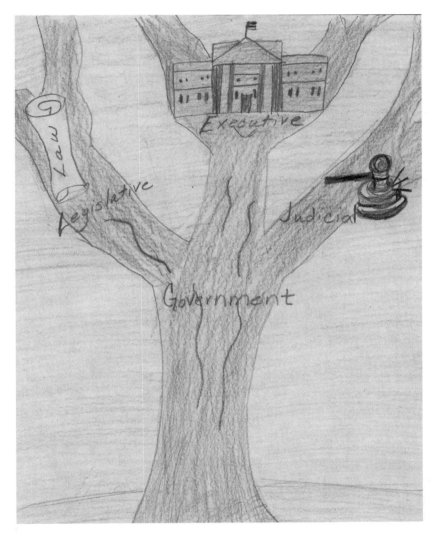

FIGURE 14.2. A symbolic representation of the three branches of government.

KEY WORDS

The key word method was initially developed as a technique for foreign vocabulary learning. It is rooted in the elaboration of unfamiliar vocabulary words or concepts (Atkinson, 1975). This is accomplished by making information to be recalled more concrete through association with visual images (mental pictures or actual illustrations) in which the key word and target word or concept are interacting in a meaningful way (Foil & Alber, 2002; Scruggs & Mastropieri, 2000). Key words are first chosen by examining terms for any salient or prominent acoustic characteristic they may hold in common, and then linking or integrating the key word with the to-be-learned word or concept via an interactive mental image (Pressley, Levin, & Delaney, 1982; Smith, 1985). The key word method can be described as a chain with two links connecting a new word to its definition (Atkinson, 1975). This is facilitated through a three-step process involving (1) recoding, (2) relating, and (3) retrieving new information (Levin, 1988).

1. *Recoding:* Teachers must choose a key word that sounds like the vocabulary word to be learned. The word should be acoustically similar, familiar to the students, and concrete enough to be easily pictured.
2. *Relating*: Once a key word has been chosen, it must be related, or linked, to the response or to-be-learned information. This can be done via a sentence, a visual mental image, or, better yet, in a picture in which the student can see the key word interacting with the to-be-learned information.
3. *Retrieving*: After "recoding" the vocabulary word into a key word and relating it to the information to be learned through a sentence, visual image, or picture, students will need to be taught how to retrieve the definition.
   a. Have students think of the key word when they are asked for the definition of the vocabulary word.
   b. Students then need to think back to the interactive picture with the key word and definition.
   c. Finally, students retrieve the definition from the information in the picture (Mastropieri & Scruggs, 1991).

For example, suppose that the student needed to remember that *caballo* means horse in Spanish. One might select *cab* for a key word because it is acoustically similar to *caballo*. Then the teacher would create a picture relating the key word (*cab*) to the target word (*caballo*). For example, here the obvious choice might be a picture of a horse driving a cab (Figure 14.3). Finally, the teacher would help the child construct a retrieval path to remember the meaning of *caballo*. The teacher would tell the child, "When you hear the word *caballo*, remember the key word *cab*. Then remember the picture of the cab with the horse driving. This will help you remember that *caballo* means horse." The student would practice this sequence a few times to ensure that he or she was able to follow the three steps (i.e., recode, relate, retrieve). Remember that mnemonic strategies involve more than just pictures. Teachers need to teach students a retrieval path for information. Figure 14.4 shows additional examples of key words.

The key word method can also serve as the basis for a strategy. The LINCS strategy (Ellis, 1992) is a key word vocabulary strategy designed to assist students to independently generate key words for target vocabulary. LINCS is an acronym for the following steps:

1. List the parts. Write the word on a study card and list the most important parts of the definition on the back (Figure 14.5).

   Example: If the vocabulary word is *chrysalis*, the student would write this word on the front of the card and write the definition, "pupa of a moth or butterfly enclosed in a cocoon," on the back.
2. Imagine a picture. Create a mental picture and describe it.

Caballo (cab) = horse

<u>Recoding</u>: *Caballo* sounds like the familiar, concrete word *cab*.
    (1) *Cab* sounds like *caballo*.
    (2) A *cab* is familiar to most students.
    (3) A *cab* is concrete enough to be easily pictured.

<u>Relating</u>: Depict the information to be remembered (*horse*) interacting with the key word (*cab*).

<u>Retrieving</u>:
    1. Have students think of the key word *cab* when they are asked for the definition of *caballo*.
    2. Students then need to think back to the interactive picture of the horse driving the cab.
    3. Finally, students retrieve the definition from the information in the picture.

FIGURE 14.3. A key word mnemonic example.

    Example: For the word *chrysalis* the student might think of a crystal ball with a cocoon and a butterfly in it.

3. <u>*Note a reminding word*</u>. Think of a familiar word that sounds like the vocabulary word.

    Example: For the word *chrysalis* the student might think of the familiar words *crystal ball* and write them on the bottom half of the front side of the card.

4. <u>*Construct a LINCing story*</u>. Make up a short story about the meaning of the word that includes the reminding word.

    Example: The fortuneteller looked into her crystal ball and saw a pupa in a chrysalis turning into a butterfly.

5. <u>*Self-test*</u>. Test your memory forward and backward.

Example: Look at the words *chrysalis* and *crystal ball* on the front of the card and say what is on the back of the card ("pupa of a moth or butterfly enclosed in a cocoon"): "The fortuneteller looked into her crystal ball and saw a pupa in a chrysalis turning into a butterfly." The student should also look at the back of the card to self-test the vocabulary word and the key word.

A slight variation on this strategy would be to have students not only create a LINCing story, but to also create a LINCing picture. Students can create their own LINCing

Ocho = eight

The key word to remember is *ouch!*
When you hear *ocho*, think of the figure 8 hurting its foot and yelling out the word "Ouch!"

Zapatos = shoes

The key word to remember is *pot*.

When you hear the word *zapatos*, think of a bunch of shoes being used as flowerpots.

Beringia = land bridge that connects Asia and North America

The key word to remember is *bear*.

When you hear *beringia*, think of a bear stretching over the water to make a bridge connecting Asia and North America.

FIGURE 14.4. Additional examples of key word mnemonics.

Chrysalis

Fold here

Crystal ball

---

pupa of a moth or butterfly enclosed in a cocoon

The fortuneteller looked into her crystal ball and saw a pupa in a cocoon turning into a butterfly.

---

pupa of a moth or butterfly enclosed in a cocoon

The fortuneteller looked into her crystal ball and saw a pupa in a cocoon turning into a butterfly.

FIGURE 14.5. An example of the LINCS strategy.

picture and put it next to their LINCing story on their word cards (see bottom of Figure 14.5). The picture can then serve as an additional cue to the meaning of the word. Note that the Association for Supervision and Curriculum Development (2002) has a video that shows examples of how the LINCS strategy should be taught.

PEGWORDS

The pegword method uses "peg" words, or rhyming proxies, for numbers (e.g., one—bun, two—shoe, three—tree). Here are some commonly used pegwords for the numbers 1–10.

- One = *bun,* or *gun,* or *sun*
- Two = *shoe*
- Three = *tree*

- Four = *door* or *floor*
- Five = *hive*
- Six = *sticks*
- Seven = *heaven*
- Eight = *gate*
- Nine = *vine, line,* or *lion*
- Ten = *hen*

Figure 14.6 shows an example of pegword–key word combinations.

Pegwords can be helpful in remembering virtually any numbered or ordered sequences of information (e.g., the order of U.S. presidents; the kingdom, phylum, and class of living organisms; causes or factors leading up to world conflicts). The pegword method is particularly useful in remembering the specific location of an item within a sequence (see Mastropieri & Scruggs, 1991). This method is often used with the key word method to facilitate the recall of information that is ordered or numbered (Mastropieri & Scruggs, 1991). For example, when learning the periodic table of elements, remembering that the atomic number for carbon is 6 is much easier when one visualizes a car (key word of carbon) made of sticks (the pegword for 6) (Figure 14.7). This key word–pegword combination helps make the association between carbon and its place in the periodic table. The pegword method is particularly useful in the social and physical/life sciences, which typically require classification, organization, and hierarchical categorizations of oftentimes seemingly unrelated information and events.

Research has shown that the combination of key words and pegwords can be extremely effective. For example, Mastropieri and Scruggs (1991) showed that the combination of key words and pegwords could be used to help students remember a mineral's place on the hardness scale along with major uses. An example would be the mineral wolframite, which is number 4 on the hardness scale. The researchers used a picture of a wolf (the key word for wolframite) on a floor (the pegword for 4), turning on a light bulb (a major use for wolframite). Key words and pegwords have also been used successfully with basic math facts. Greene (1999) showed that hard-to-remember multiplication facts could be taught using pegwords for the math fact (e.g., for 6 × 7 the key words would be *sticks* and *heaven*) and a key word (*warty shoes*) for the product (42).

A key word–pegword combination can be used if numbered or sequential information is associated with unfamiliar names of things (Mastropieri & Scruggs, 1991). For example, students learning about five early Western philosophers (Epicurus, Socrates, Plato, Xeno, and Aristotle) could use a combination of key words and pegwords (see Figure 14.8 for examples) to remember their names. After they have been taught the key words (recoded names to be learned) and the sentences for relating the information in order, students would need to be taught how to retrieve the information. It is important to practice all the steps in the retrieval process so that students can tell you the correct answer as well as how they arrived at it (Mastropieri & Scruggs, 1991). This is an important link; if there is an interruption in the retrieval process, the information is likely to be forgotten (i.e., students will not know how to retrieve the information).

Key Word–Pegword Combination

	Recode–Key Word		
Cornea	Corn	The sun makes the corn grow.	
Iris	Iris (flower)	There is an iris in the shoe.	
Pupil	Pupil (student)	The pupil is under the tree.	
Lens	Lens (glasses)	There are lenses on the door.	

FIGURE 14.6. Combining pegwords and key words.

Carbon (car) = atomic number 6 (sticks) – a "car" made of "sticks."

FIGURE 14.7. A pegword mnemonic example.

FINAL THOUGHTS

Mnemonic strategies can be a valuable tool for teachers. However, it is important to realize their limitations. They are intended to assist with factual learning. Thus, the range of application may be somewhat limited. Still, as we noted earlier, recall of factual information is extremely important in its own right. Factual information is more than rote learning. Without a sound factual informational base it is incredibly difficult to progress academically.

In closing, we present some frequently noted comments/questions about mnemonics and their application in the schools taken from Mastropieri and Scruggs (1991).

- *"Making all those mnemonics is so much work; teachers don't have the time."* The key here is to remember to start small. One teacher we know had a problem with a health class that required memorizing a great deal of vocabulary. She decided to develop one set of mnemonics a year. She started with the 20 terms that caused the most problems. After 3 years she had addressed most of the problem terms, and her students with LD were doing much better in the course. Remember also that in the long run mnemonics will actually save you time because they will reduce the time spent in teaching that content. Think of the time spent developing mnemonics as an investment!

- *"I can't draw well enough to make the pictures."* Luckily the quality of the picture doesn't matter much. So long as the picture is recognizable, mnemonics will be effective. It's also possible to use clip art or cut out pictures from magazines to help make the pictures. Drawing on the skills of students in art classes is another possibility.

- *"Won't all those pictures confuse students?"* Not really. The brain's capacity for storing information is virtually unlimited. The problem is in retrieving it and this is what makes mnemonics so effective. They provide a retrieval path that makes recalling information much easier. It is possible to put too much content in a lesson. So teachers do need to be sensitive to how much information to present in a lesson.

Philosopher	Recode–Key Word	Relate	Pictorial recoding	Retrieve
Socrates	Socks	I wear **socks** with my **shoes**.		To remember the second major philosopher, my pegword for *two* is shoe. I remember the shoe with a sock in it. *Sock* is my key word for *Socrates*. That helps me remember that Socrates is the second major philosopher.
Plato	Plate	Why is that **plate** up in the **tree**?		To remember the third major philosopher, my pegword for *three* is tree. I remember the tree with a plate stuck in it. *Plate* is my key word for *Plato*. That helps me remember that Plato is the third major philosopher.
Aristotle	Airplane	The **airplane** was flying so low, it hit a bee**hive**.		To remember the fifth major philosopher, my pegword for *five* is hive. I remember the airplane that flew so low, it hit a beehive. *Airplane* is my key word for *Aristotle*. That helps me remember that Aristotle is the fifth major philosopher.

FIGURE 14.8. Combining key words and pegwords.

- *"Mnemonics stress pictures. What about 'auditory learners'?"* The notion that there are different types of learners is quite common. However, there is little if any research to support the notion that some students learn best via visual or auditory teaching. What research has shown is that mnemonics are universally beneficial for students who lack strategies to help with recall of information.

- *"Shouldn't students learn to make their own mnemonics?"* Students can learn to make their own mnemonics. We discussed one strategy—LINCS—in which students do exactly that. The question is not whether students can make their own mnemonics, but whether there is any *advantage* to having them do so. When students make their own mnemonics, it takes much more time than when teachers create the mnemonics. This should be considered. However, it is also possible that creating their own mnemonic could be more effective for some students.

References

Alderman, M. K. (1999). *Motivation for achievement: Possibilities for teaching and learning.* Mahwah, NJ: Erlbaum.

Alderman, M. K., Klein, R., Seeley, S., & Sanders, M. (1993). Preservice teachers as learners in formation: Metacognitive self-portraits. *Reading Research and Instruction, 32,* 38–54.

Alexander, P. A., Graham, S., & Harris, K. R. (1998). A perspective on strategy research: Progress and prospects. *Educational Psychology Review, 10,* 129–154.

Alloway, T. P., Gathercole, S. E., Kirkwood, H. J., & Elliott, J. E. (2009). The cognitive and behavioral characteristics of children with low working memory. *Child Development, 80,* 606–621.

Anderson, T. H., & Armbruster, B. B. (1984). Content area textbooks. In R. C. Anderson, J. Osborn, & R. J. Tierney (Eds.), *Learning to read in American schools* (pp. 193–226). Hillsdale, NJ: Erlbaum.

Andrews, G. R., & Debus, R. (1978). Persistence and the causal perception of failure: Modifying cognitive attributions. *Journal of Educational Psychology, 70,* 154–166.

Armbruster, B. B., Lehr, F., & Osborn, J. (2001). *Put reading first: The research building blocks for teaching children to read: Kindergarten through grade 3.* Washington, DC: National Institute for Literacy.

Association for Supervision and Curriculum Development. (2002). Teaching students with learning disabilities in the regular classroom: Tape 2 (using learning strategies). Retrieved from *http://shop.ascd.org.*

Atkinson, R. C. (1975). Mnemonic techniques in second-language learning. *American Psychologist, 30,* 821–828.

Bakken, J., Mastropieri, M., & Scruggs, T. (1997). Reading comprehension of expository science material and students with learning disabilities: A comparison of strategies. *Journal of Special Education 31*(3), 300–324.

Bandura, A. (1986). *Social foundations of thought and action.* Englewood Cliffs, NJ: Prentice Hall.

Bandura, A. (1988). Self-regulation of motivation and action through goal systems. In V.

Hamilton, G. H. Browder, & N. H. Frijda (Eds.), *Cognitive perspectives on emotion and motivation* (pp. 37–61). Dordrecht, The Netherlands: Kluwer Academic.

Bandura, A. (1993). Perceived self-efficacy in cognitive development and functioning. *Educational Psychologist, 28,* 117–148.

Bandura, A. (1997). *Self-efficacy: The exercise of control.* New York: Freeman.

Barkley, R. A. (2006). *Attention-deficit/hyperactivity disorder: A handbook for diagnosis and treatment* (3rd ed.). New York: Guilford Press.

Barkley, R. A., Copeland, A. P., & Sivage, C. (1980). A self-control classroom for hyperactive children. *Journal of Autism and Developmental Disorders, 10,* 75–89.

Bauer, R. H. (1987). Control processes as a way of understanding, diagnosing, and remediating learning disabilities. In H. L. Swanson (Ed.), *Advances in learning and behavioral disabilities: Memory and learning disabilities* (pp. 41–81). Greenwich, CT: JAI Press.

Benbow, M., Hanft, B., & Marsh, D. (1992). Handwriting in the classroom: Improving written communication. In C. Royeen (Ed.), *AOTA self-study series: Classroom applications for school-based practice* (pp. 6–60). Rockville, MD: American Occupational Therapy Association.

Benton, S. L., Kiewra, K. A., Whitfill, J. M., & Dennison, R. (1993). Encoding and external-storage effects on writing processes. *Journal of Educational Psychology, 85,* 267–280.

Berninger, V., Mizokawa, D., & Bragg, R. (1991). Theory-based diagnosis and remediation of writing disabilities. *Journal of School Psychology, 29,* 57–79.

Berninger, V., Vaughan, K., Abbott, R., Abbott, S., Rogan, L., Brooks, A., et al. (1998). Early intervention for spelling problems: Teaching functional spelling units of varying size with a multiple-connection framework. *Journal of Educational Psychology, 90,* 587–605.

Berninger, V. W., Vaughan, K. B., Abbott, R. D., Rogan, L., Brooks, A., Reed, E., et al. (1997). Treatment of handwriting problems in beginning writers: Transfer from handwriting to composition. *Journal of Educational Psychology, 89*(4), 652–666.

Biancarosa, C., & Snow, C. E. (2006). *Reading next: A vision for action and research in middle and high school literacy—a report to Carnegie Corporation of New York* (2nd ed.). Washington, DC: Alliance for Excellent Education.

Boom, S. E., & Fine, E. (1995). STAR: A number-writing strategy. *Teaching Exceptional Children, 27*(2), 42–45.

Borkowski, J. G., Estrada, M. T., Milstead, M., & Hale, C. A. (1989). General problem solving skills: Relations between metacognition and strategic processing. *Learning Disability Quarterly, 12,* 57–70.

Borkowski, J. G., Weyhing, R. S., & Carr, M. (1988). Effects of attributional retraining on strategy-based reading comprehension in learning-disabled students. *Journal of Educational Psychology, 80,* 46–53.

Bos, C. S., Coleman, M., & Vaughn, S. (2002). Reading and students with E/BD: What do we know and recommend? In K. L. Lane, F. M. Gresham, & T. E. O'Shaughnessy (Eds.), *Interventions for children with or at risk for emotional and behavioral disorders* (pp. 87–103). Boston: Allyn & Bacon.

Bottge, B. A. (1999). Effects of contextualized math instruction on problem solving of average and below-average achieving students. *Journal of Special Education, 33,* 81–92.

Broden, M., Hall, R. V., & Mitts, B. (1971). The effects of self-recording on the classroom behavior of two eighth-grade students. *Journal of Applied Behavior Analysis, 4,* 191–199.

Browder, D. M., & Minarovic, T. J. (2000). Utilizing sight words in self-instruction training for employees with moderate mental retardation in competitive jobs. *Education and Training in Mental Retardation and Developmental Disabilities, 35,* 78–89.

Brown, R. T., & Wynne, M. E. (1984). An analysis of attentional components in hyperactive and normal boys. *Journal of Learning Disabilities, 17,* 162–167.

Bryan, T., & Wheeler, R. (1972). Perception of learning disabled children: The eye of the observer. *Journal of Learning Disabilities, 5,* 484–488.

Butler, D. L., & Winne, P. H. (1995). Feedback and self-regulated learning: A theoretical synthesis. *Review of Educational Research, 65,* 245–281.

Butterworth, B., & Relgosa, V. (2007). Information processing deficits in dyscalculia. In D. B. Berch & M. M. Mazzocco (Eds.), *Why is math so hard for some children?: The nature and origins of mathematical learning difficulties* (pp. 65–81). Baltimore, MD: Brookes.

Cancio, E. J., West, R. P., & Young, K. R. (2004). Improving mathematics homework completion and accuracy of students with EBD through self-management and parent participation. *Journal of Emotional and Behavioral Disorders, 12*(1), 9–22.

Carlson, S. S., & Alley, G. R. (1981). *Performance and competence of learning disabled and high-achieving high school students in essential cognitive skills* (Research Report No. 53). Lawrence: University of Kansas, Institute for Research in Learning Disabilities.

Carnine, D., Silbert, J., Kame'enui, E. J., & Tarver, S. (2004). *Direct instruction reading* (4th ed.). Upper Saddle River, NJ: Prentice Hall.

Case, L. P., Harris, K. R., & Graham, S. (1992). Improving the mathematical problem-solving skills of students with learning disabilities: Self-regulated strategy development. *Journal of Special Education, 26,* 1–19.

Cassel, A. J., & Reid, R. (1996). Use of a self-regulated strategy intervention to improve word problem solving skills of students with mild disabilities. *Journal of Behavioral Education, 6,* 153–172.

Ceci, S., Ringstorm, M., & Lea, S. (1981). Do language learning disabled children have impaired memories?: In search of underlying processes. *Journal of Learning Disabilities, 14,* 159–163.

Chang, K. E., Sung, Y. T., & Chen, I. D. (2002). The effect of concept mapping to enhance text comprehension and summarization. *Journal of Experimental Education, 71*(1), 5–23.

Chapman, J. (1988). Cognitive–motivational characteristics and academic achievement of learning-disabled children. *Journal of Educational Psychology, 80,* 357–365.

Chase, C. (1986). Essay test scoring: Interaction of relevant variables. *Journal of Educational Measurement, 23,* 33–41.

Cheek, E. H., Jr., & Cheek, M. C. (1983). *Reading instruction through content teaching.* Columbus, OH: Merrill.

Chesloff, J. D., & Maier, L. (2012, July 8). Viewpoint: Math skills needed for the future workforce. Available from *www.masslive.com/opinion/index.ssf/2012/07/viewpoint_math_skills_needed_f. html.*

Cunningham, A. E., & Stanovich, K. E. (1998). What reading does for the mind. *American Educator, 22*(1–2), 8–15.

Daniels, H., & Bizar, M. (2005). *Teaching the best practice way: Methods that matter, K–12.* York, ME: Stenhouse.

Davey, B., & McBride, S. (1986). Effects of question-generation training on reading comprehension. *Journal of Educational Psychology, 78,* 256–262.

De La Paz, S., & Graham, S. (1995). Dictation: Application to writing for students with learning disabilities. In T. Scruggs & M. Mastropieri (Eds.), *Advances in learning and behavioral disorders* (Vol. 9, pp. 227–247). Greenwich, CT: JAI Press.

De La Paz, S., & Graham, S. (1997). Strategy instruction in planning: Effects on the writing performance and behavior of students with learning difficulties. *Exceptional Children, 63,* 167–181.

Deshler, D. D., Ellis, E. S., & Lenz, B. K. (1996). *Teaching adolescents with learning disabilities: Strategies and methods* (2nd ed.). Denver, CO: Love.

Deshler, D. D., & Graham, S. (1980). Tape recording educational materials for secondary handicapped students. *Teaching Exceptional Children, 12,* 52–54.

Dickson, S. V., Collins, V. L., Simmons, D. C., & Kame'enui, E. J. (1998). Metacognitive strategies: Instruction and curricular basics and implications. In D. Simmons & E. Kame'enui (Eds.), *What reading research tells us about children with diverse learning needs* (pp. 361–380). Mahwah, NJ: Erlbaum.

Diener, C. I., & Dweck, C. S. (1978). An analysis of learned helplessness: Continuous changes in performance, strategy, and achievement cognitions following failure. *Journal of Personality and Social Psychology, 36*, 451–462.

Dunlap, L. K., & Dunlap, G. (1989). A self-monitoring package for teaching subtraction with regrouping to students with learning disabilities. *Journal of Applied Behavior Analysis, 22*, 309–314.

DuPaul, G. J., & Stoner, G. (2003). *ADHD in the schools: Assessment and intervention strategies* (2nd ed.). New York: Guilford Press.

Durkin, D. (1993). *Teaching them to read* (6th ed.). Boston: Allyn & Bacon.

Dweck, C. S. (1975). The role of expectations and attributions in the alleviation of learned helplessness. *Journal of Personality and Social Psychology, 31*, 674–685.

Dweck, C. S., & Leggett, E. L. (1988). A social-cognitive approach to motivation and personality. *Psychological Review, 95*, 256–273.

Ellis, E. S. (1992). *LINCS: A starter strategy for vocabulary learning.* Lawrence, KS: Edge.

Ellis, E. S., & Lenz, K. (1987). A component analysis of effective learning strategies for LD students. *Learning Disabilities Focus, 2*, 94–107.

Engelman, S., & Bruner, E. (1974). *DISTAR Reading I.* Chicago: Science Research Associates.

Englert, C. S., Hiebert, E. H., & Stewart, S. R. (1985). Spelling unfamiliar words by an analogy strategy. *Journal of Special Education, 19*, 291–306.

Englert, C. S., & Mariage, T. V. (1991a). Making students partners in the comprehension process: Organizing the reading "POSSE." *Learning Disability Quarterly, 14*, 123–138.

Englert, C. S., & Mariage, T. V. (1991b). Shared understandings: Structuring the writing experience through dialogue. *Journal of Learning Disabilities, 24*(6), 330–342.

Englert, C. S., & Raphael, T. E. (1988). Constructing well-informed prose: Process, structure and metacognitive knowledge. *Exceptional Children, 54*, 513–520.

Englert, C. S., Raphael, T. E., & Anderson, L. (1985). *Teaching cognitive strategies to the mildly handicapped: A classroom intervention study* (The Cognitive Strategy Instruction in Writing Project). Project funded by the U.S. Department of Education Office of Special Education Programs. East Lansing: Michigan State University.

Fisher, D., & Frey, N. (2008). *Improving adolescent literacy: Content area strategies at work* (2nd ed.). Upper Saddle River, NJ: Merrill Prentice Hall.

Flavel, J. H. (1979). Metacognition and cognitive monitoring: A new area of cognitive developmental inquiry. *American Psychologist, 34*, 906–911.

Fletcher, J. M., Lyon, G. R., Barnes, M. A., Stuebing, K. K., Francis, D. J., Olson, R., et al. (2002). Classification of learning disabilities: An evidence-based evaluation. In R. Bradley, L. Danielson, & D. P. Hallahan (Eds.), *Identification of learning disabilities: Research to practice* (pp. 185–250). Mahwah, NJ: Erlbaum.

Fletcher, J. M., Morris, R. D., & Lyon, G. R. (2003). Classification and definition of learning disabilities: An integrative perspective. In H. L. Swanson, K. R. Harris, & S. Graham (Eds.), *Handbook of learning disabilities* (pp. 30–56). New York: Guilford Press.

Foil, C. R., & Alber, S. R. (2002). Fun and effective ways to build your students' vocabulary. *Intervention in School and Clinic, 37*, 131–139.

Frank, A. R., & Brown, D. (1992). Self-monitoring strategies in arithmetic. *Teaching Exceptional Children, 24*(2), 52–53.

Fuchs, L. S., & Fuchs, D. (2003). Enhancing the mathematical problem solving of students with mathematical disabilities. In H. Swanson, K. R. Harris, & S. Graham (Eds.), *Handbook of learning disabilities* (pp. 306–322). New York: Guilford Press.

Fuchs, D., Fuchs, L. S., & Compton, D. L. (2004). Identifying reading disabilities by responsiveness-to-instruction: Specifying measures and criteria. *Learning Disability Quarterly, 27,* 216–227.

Gardill, M. C., & Jitendra, A. K. (1999). Advanced Story Map instruction: Effects on the reading comprehension of students with learning disabilities. *Journal of Special Education, 33*(1), 2–17.

Garner, R. (1987). Strategies for reading and studying expository text [Special issue: Current issues in reading comprehension]. *Educational Psychologist, 22*(3–4), 299–312.

Garnett, K. (1992). Developing fluency with basic number facts: Intervention for students with learning disabilities. *Learning Disabilities Research and Practice, 7,* 210–216.

Gaskins, I., & Elliot, T. (1991). *Implementing cognitive strategy instruction across the school: The benchmark manual for teachers.* Cambridge, MA: Brookline Books.

Geary, D. C. (2003). Learning disabilities in arithmetic: Problem-solving differences and cognitive deficits. In H. Swanson, K. R. Harris, & S. Graham (Eds.), *Handbook of learning disabilities* (pp. 199–212). New York: Guilford Press.

Geary, D. C., Bow-Thomas, C. C., & Yao, Y. (1992). Counting knowledge and skill in cognitive addition: A comparison of normal and mathematically disabled children. *Journal of Experimental Child Psychology, 54,* 372–391.

Geary, D. C., Hamson, C. O., & Hoard, M. K. (2000). Numerical and arithmetical cognition: A longitudinal study of process and concept deficits in children with learning disability. *Journal of Experimental Child Psychology, 77,* 236–263.

Geary, D. C., Hoard, M. K., & Hamson, C. O. (1999). Numerical and arithmetical deficits in learning disabled children: Relation to dyscalculia and dyslexia. *Aphasiology, 15,* 635–647.

Geary, D., Hoard, M., Nugent, L., & Byrd-Craven, J. (2007). Strategy use, long-term memory, and working memory capacity. In D. B. Berch & M. M. Mazzocco (Eds.), *Why is math so hard for some children?: The nature and origins of mathematical learning difficulties* (pp. 83–105). Baltimore, MD: Brookes.

Geary, D. C., Widaman, K. F., Little, T. D., & Cormier, P. (1987). Cognitive addition: Comparison of learning disabled and academically normal elementary school children. *Cognitive Development, 2,* 249–269.

Gersten, R., & Chard, D. (1999). Number sense: Rethinking arithmetic instruction for students with mathematical disabilities. *Journal of Special Education, 33,* 18–28.

Gersten, R., Fuchs, L., Williams, J., & Baker, S. (2001). Teaching reading comprehension strategies to students with learning disabilities: A review of research. *Review of Educational Research, 71*(2), 279–320.

Gettinger, M. (1991). Learning time and retention differences between nondisabled students and students with learning disabilities. *Learning Disability Quarterly, 14,* 179–189.

Gettinger, M., & Seibert, J. K. (2002). Contributions of study skills to academic competence. *School Psychology Review, 31,* 350–365.

Glomb, N., & West, R. P. (1990). Teaching behaviorally disordered adolescents to use self-management skills for improving the completeness, accuracy, and neatness of creative writing homework assignments. *Behavioral Disorders, 15*(4), 233–242.

Goldstein, K. (1936). The modifications of behavior consequent to cerebral lesions. *Psychiatric Quarterly, 10,* 586–610.

Graham, L., & Wong, B. Y. L. (1993). Comparing two models of teaching a question–answering strategy for enhancing reading comprehension: Didactic and self-instructional training. *Journal of Learning Disabilities, 26*(4), 270–279.

Graham, S. (1983a). The effect of self-instructional procedures on LD students' handwriting performance. *Learning Disability Quarterly, 6,* 231–244.

Graham, S. (1983b). Effective spelling instruction. *Elementary School Journal, 83,* 560–567.

Graham, S. (1990). The role of production factors in learning disabled students' compositions. *Journal of Educational Psychology, 82,* 781–791.

Graham, S. (1999). Handwriting and spelling instruction for students with learning disabilities: A review. *Learning Disability Quarterly, 22,* 78–98.

Graham, S. (2000). Should the natural learning approach replace the traditional spelling instruction? *Journal of Educational Psychology, 92,* 235–247.

Graham, S. (2006). Writing. In P. Alexander & P. Winne (Eds.), *Handbook of educational psychology* (pp. 457–477). Mahwah, NJ: Erlbaum.

Graham, S. (2010). Want to improve children's writing?: Don't neglect their handwriting. *American Educator, 33,* 23.

Graham, S., Berninger, V. W., & Abbott, R. D. (1997). Role of mechanics in composing of elementary school students: A new methodological approach. *Journal of Educational Psychology, 89,* 170–182.

Graham, S., & Freeman, S. (1986). Strategy training and teacher- vs. student-controlled student conditions: Effects on LD students' spelling performance. *Learning Disability Quarterly, 9,* 15–22.

Graham, S., & Harris, K. R. (1989). Components analysis of cognitive strategy instruction: Effects on learning disabled students; compositions and self-efficacy. *Journal of Educational Psychology, 6,* 221–236.

Graham, S., & Harris, K. R. (1992). *Helping young writers master the craft: Strategy instruction and self-regulation in the writing process.* Cambridge, MA: Brookline Books.

Graham, S., & Harris, K. R. (1996). Self-regulation and strategy instruction for students who find writing and learning challenging. In C. M. Levy & S. Randall (Eds.), *The science of writing: Theories, methods, individual differences, and applications* (pp. 347–360). Mahwah, NJ: Erlbaum.

Graham, S., & Harris, K. R. (1997). Self-regulation and writing: Where do we go from here? [Commentary]. *Contemporary Educational Psychology, 22,* 102–114.

Graham, S., & Harris, K. R. (2000). The role of self-regulation and transcription skills in writing and writing development. *Educational Psychologist, 35,* 3–12.

Graham, S., & Harris, K. R. (2003). Students with learning disabilities and the process of writing: A meta-analysis of SRSD studies. In H. L. Swanson, K. R. Harris, & S. Graham (Eds.), *Handbook of learning disabilities* (pp. 323–344). New York: Guilford Press.

Graham, S., & Harris, K. R. (2011). Writing and students with disabilities. In J. Kauffman & D. Hallahan (Eds.), *Handbook of special education* (pp. 422–433). London: Routledge.

Graham, S., Harris, K. R., & Hebert, M. (2011). It is more than just the message: Presentation effects in scoring writing. *Focus on Exceptional Children, 44,* 1–12.

Graham, S., Harris, K. R., & MacArthur, C. (2004). Writing instruction. In B. Wong (Ed.), *Learning about learning disabilities* (3rd ed., pp. 281–313). Orlando, FL: Academic Press.

Graham, S., Harris, K. R., & Mason, L. (2005). Improving the writing performance, knowledge, and self-efficacy of struggling young writers: The effects of Self-Regulated Strategy Development. *Contemporary Educational Psychology, 30,* 207–241.

Graham, S., Harris, K. R., & McKeown, D. (2013). The writing of students with learning disabilities, meta-analysis of Self-Regulated Strategy Development writing intervention studies, and future directions: Redux. In H. L. Swanson, K. R. Harris, & S. Graham (Eds.), *Handbook of learning disabilities* (2nd ed., pp. 405–438). New York: Guilford Press.

Graham, S., Harris, K. R., & Reid, R. (1992). Developing self-regulated learners. *Focus on Exceptional Children, 24,* 1–16.

Graham, S., Harris, K. R., & Sawyer, R. (1987). Composition instruction with learning disabled students: Self-instructional strategy training. *Focus on Exceptional Children, 20*(4), 4–11.

Graham, S., & Hebert, M. (2010). *Writing to reading*. Washington, DC: Alliance for Excellence in Education.

Graham, S., & MacArthur, C. (1988). Improving learning disabled students' skills at revising essays produced on a word processor: Self-instructional strategy training. *Journal of Special Education, 22*(2), 133–152.

Graham, S., MacArthur, C., Schwartz, S., & Page-Voth, T. (1992). Improving the compositions of students with learning disabilities using a strategy involving product and process goal setting. *Exceptional Children, 58*, 322–344.

Graham, S., McKeown, D., Kiuhara, S., & Harris, K. R. (2012). A meta-analysis of writing instruction for students in the early grades. *Journal of Educational Psychology, 104*(4), 879–896.

Graham, S., & Miller, L. (1979). Spelling research and practice: A unified approach. *Focus on Exceptional Children, 12*, 1–16.

Graham, S., & Miller, L. (1980). Handwriting research and practice: A unified approach. *Focus on Exceptional Children, 13*, 1–16.

Graham, S., Morphy, P., Harris, K. R., Fink-Chorzempa, B., Saddler, B., Moran, S., et al. (2008). Teaching spelling in the primary grades: A national survey of instructional practices and adaptations. *American Educational Research Journal, 45*, 796–825.

Graham, S., & Perin, D. (2007a). A meta-analysis of writing instruction for adolescent studies. *Journal of Educational Psychology, 99*, 445–476.

Graham, S., & Perin, D. (2007b). *Writing next: Effective strategies to improve writing of adolescents in middle and high schools—a report to Carnegie Corporation of New York*. Washington, DC: Alliance for Excellence in Education.

Graham, S., & Weintraub, N. (1996). A review of handwriting research: Progress and prospects from 1980 to 1994. *Educational Psychology Review, 8*, 7–87.

Graham, S., Weintraub, N., & Berninger, V. W. (1998). The relationship between handwriting style and speed and legibility. *Journal of Educational Research, 91*(5), 290–297.

Grant, R. (1993). Strategic training for using text headings to improve students' processing of content. *Journal of Reading, 36*, 482–488.

Graves, A. W. (1986). Effects of direct instruction and metacomprehension training on finding main ideas. *Learning Disabilities Research, 1*, 90–100.

Graves, A. W., & Levin, J. R. (1989). Comparison of monitoring and mnemonic text-processing strategies in learning disabled students. *Learning Disabilities Quarterly, 12*, 232–236.

Greene, G. (1999). Mnemonic multiplication fact instruction for students with learning disabilities. *Learning Disabilities Research and Practice, 14*, 141–148.

Gureasko-Moore, S., DuPaul, G., & White, G. (2007). Self-management of classroom preparedness and homework: Effects on school function of adolescents with attention deficit hyperactivity disorder. *School Psychology Review, 36*, 647–664.

Hacker, D. J. (1998). Definitions and empirical foundations. In D. Hacker, J. Dunlosky, & A. Graesser (Eds.), *Metacognition in educational theory and practice* (pp. 1–23). Mahwah, NJ: Erlbaum.

Hackney, C. S., & Lucas, V. H. (1993). *Zaner-Bloser Handwriting: A way to self-expression, grade 2M*. Columbus, OH: Zaner-Bloser.

Hagaman, J., Casey, K., & Reid, R. (2012). The effects of a paraphrasing strategy on the reading comprehension of young students. *Remedial and Special Education, 33*, 110–123.

Hagaman, J., & Reid, R. (2008). The effects of the paraphrasing strategy on the reading comprehension of middle-school students at-risk for failure in reading. *Remedial and Special Education, 29*, 222–234.

Hallahan, D. P., Kauffman, J. M., & Lloyd, J. W. (1996). *Introduction to learning disabilities*. Boston, MA: Allyn & Bacon.

Hallahan, D. P., Lloyd, J. W., Kosiewicz, M. M., Kauffman, J. M., & Graves, A. W. (1979). Self-monitoring of attention as a treatment for a learning disabled boy's off-task behavior. *Learning Disability Quarterly, 2,* 24–32.

Hallahan, D. P., Marshall, K. J., & Lloyd, J. W. (1981). Self-recording during group instruction: Effects on attention to task. *Learning Disability Quarterly, 4,* 407–413.

Hallahan, D. P., & Sapona, R. (1983). Self-monitoring of attention with learning disabled children: Past research and current issues. *Journal of Learning Disabilities, 15,* 616–620.

Hammill, D., & Larsen S. (1974). The effectiveness of psycholinguistic training. *Exceptional Children, 41,* 5–14.

Hanna, P. R., Hanna, J. S., Hodges, R. E., & Rudorf, E. H., Jr. (1966). *Phoneme–grapheme correspondence as cues to spelling improvement* (USDOE Publication No. 32008). Washington, DC: U.S. Government Printing Office.

Harniss, M. K., Carnine, D. W., Silbert, J., & Dixon, R. C. (2002). Effective strategies for teaching mathematics. In E. Kame'enui, D. Carnine, R. Dixon, D. Simmons, & M. Coyne (Eds.), *Effective teaching strategies that accommodate diverse learners* (pp. 121–148). Columbus, OH: Merrill.

Harris, K. R. (1982). Cognitive behavior modification: Application with exceptional students. *Focus on Exceptional Children, 15*(2), 1–16.

Harris, K. R. (1986a). The effects of cognitive-behavior modification on private speech and task performance during problem solving among learning-disabled and normally achieving children. *Journal of Abnormal Child Psychology, 14,* 63–76.

Harris, K. R. (1986b). Self-monitoring of attentional behavior versus self-monitoring of productivity: Effects on on-task behavior and academic response rate among learning disabled children. *Journal of Applied Behavior Analysis, 19,* 417–423.

Harris, K. R. (1990). Developing self-regulated learners: The role of private speech and self-instructions. *Educational Psychologist, 25,* 35–49.

Harris, K. R., & Graham, S. (1992). Self-regulated strategy development: A part of the writing process. In M. Pressley, K. R. Harris, & J. Guthrie (Eds.), *Promoting academic competence and literacy in schools* (pp. 277–309). San Diego, CA: Academic Press.

Harris, K. R., & Graham, S. (1996). *Making the writing process work: Strategies for composition and self-regulation.* Cambridge, MA: Brookline Books.

Harris, K. R., & Graham, S. (1999). Programmatic intervention research: Illustrations from the evolution of Self-Regulated Strategy Development. *Learning Disability Quarterly, 22,* 251–262.

Harris, K. R., Graham, S., & Freeman, S. (1988). Effects of strategy training on metamemory among learning disabled students. *Exceptional Children, 54,* 332–338.

Harris, K. R., Graham, S., Mason, L. H., & Friedlander, B. (2008). *Powerful writing strategies for all students.* Baltimore, MD: Brookes.

Harris, K. R., Graham, S., & Pressley, M. (1992). Cognitive behavioral approaches in reading and written language: Developing self-regulated learners. In N. N. Singh & I. L. Beale (Eds.), *Current perspectives in learning disabilities: Nature, theory, and treatment* (pp. 415–451). New York: Springer-Verlag.

Harris, K. R., Graham, S., & Mason, L. H. (2003). Self-regulated strategy development in the classroom: Part of a balanced approach to writing instruction for students with disabilities. *Focus on Exceptional Children, 35,* 1–16.

Harris, K. R., Lane, K. L., Graham, S., Driscoll, S., Sandmel, K., Brindle, M., et al. (2012). Practice-based professional development for self-regulated strategies development in writing: A randomized controlled study. *Journal of Teacher Education, 63*(2), 103–119.

Harris, K. R., & Pressley, M. (1991). The nature of cognitive strategy instruction: Interactive strategy instruction. *Exceptional Children, 57,* 392–403.

Harris, K. R., Santangelo, T., & Graham, S. (2010). Metacognition and strategies instruction in writing. In H. S. Waters & W. Schneider (Eds.), *Metacognition, strategy use, and instruction* (pp. 226–256). New York: Guilford Press.

Hedin, L., Mason, L. H., & Gaffney, J. (2011). TWA plus prompted discourse: Reading comprehension effects for three students with learning disabilities. *Preventing School Failure, 55,* 148–157.

Hegarty, M., & Kozhenikov, M. (1999). Types of visual-spatial representations and mathematical problem solving. *Journal of Educational Psychology, 91,* 684–689.

Heward, W. L. (2002). Ten faulty notions about teaching and learning that hinder the effectiveness of special education. *Journal of Special Education, 36,* 186–205.

Hinshelwood, J. (1917). *Congenital word blindness.* London: Lewis.

Horton, S. B., Lovitt, T. C., & Bergerud, D. (1990). The effectiveness of graphic organizers for three classifications of secondary students in content area classes. *Journal of Learning Disabilities, 23*(1), 12–22.

Hughes, C. A., Ruhl, K. L., Schumaker, J. B., & Deshler, D. (2002). Effects of instruction in an assignment completion strategy in the homework performance of students with learning disabilities in general education classes. *Learning Disabilities Research and Practice, 17,* 1–18.

Hux, K., Reid, R., & Luggert, M. (1994). Self-instruction training following neurological injury. *Applied Cognitive Psychology, 8,* 259–271.

Idol, L. (1987). Group story mapping: A comprehension strategy for both skilled and unskilled readers. *Journal of Learning Disabilities, 20*(4), 196–205.

Idol, L., & Croll, B. J. (1987). Story-mapping training as a means of improving reading comprehension. *Learning Disability Quarterly, 10,* 214–230.

Individuals with Disabilities Education Improvement Act. 20 U.S.C. § 1400 (2004).

International Dyslexia Association. (2008). *Spelling and dyslexia.* Retrieved from *www.ldonline.org/article/24882/*

Isaacson, S., & Gleason, M. M. (1997). *Mechanical obstacles to writing: What can teachers do to help students with learning problems?* Hillsdale, NJ: Erlbaum.

Jacobson, L. T., & Reid, R. (2010). Self-Regulated Strategy Development: Improving the persuasive essay writing of high school students with ADHD. *Exceptional Children, 76,* 157–174.

Janvier, C. (1987). Representation and understanding: The notion of function as an example. In C. Janvier (Ed.), *Problems of representation in the teaching and learning of mathematics* (pp. 67–71). Hillsdale, NJ: Erlbaum.

Jitendra, A. K. (2007). *Solving math word problems.* Austin, TX: PRO-ED.

Jitendra, A. K., DiPipi, C. M., & Perron-Jones, N. (2002). An exploratory study of schema-based word-problem-solving instruction for middle school students with learning disabilities. *Journal of Special Education, 36,* 23–38.

Jitendra, A. K., Griffin, C. C., McGoey, K., Gardhill, M. K., Bhat, P., & Riley, T. (1998). Effects of mathematical word-problem solving by students at risk or with mild disabilities. *Journal of Educational Research, 91,* 345–355.

Jitendra, A. K., & Hoff, K. (1996). The effects of schema-based instruction on the mathematical word-problem solving performance of students with learning disabilities. *Journal of Learning Disabilities, 29*(4), 422–431.

Jitendra, A. K., Hoff, K., & Beck, M. M. (1999). Teaching middle school students with learning disabilities to solve word problems using a schema-based approach. *Remedial and Special Education, 20,* 50–64.

Jitendra, A. K., Hoppes, M. K., & Xin, Y. P. (2000). Enhancing main idea comprehension for students with learning problems: The role of summarization strategy and self-monitoring instruction. *Journal of Special Education, 34,* 127–139.

Jitendra, A. K., & Xin, Y. P. (1997). Mathematical word-problem-solving instruction for students with mild disabilities and students at-risk for math failure: A research synthesis. *Journal of Special Education, 30*, 412–438.

Johnson, J., & Reid, R. (2011). Overcoming executive function deficits with students with ADHD. *Theory into Practice, 50*, 61–67.

Johnson, J., Reid, R., & Mason, L. (2012). Improving the reading recall of high school students with ADHD. *Remedial and Special Education, 33*, 258–268.

Johnson, L., & Graham, S. (1990). Goal setting and its application with exceptional learners. *Preventing School Failure, 34*, 4–8.

Johnson, L., & Graham, S. G. (1997). The effects of goal setting and self-instruction on learning a reading comprehension strategy: A study of students with learning disabilities. *Journal of Learning Disabilities, 30*, 80–91.

Johnson, L., Graham, S., & Harris, K. R. (1997). The effects of goal setting and self-instruction on learning a reading comprehension strategy: A study of students with learning disabilities. *Journal of Learning Disabilities, 30*(1), 80–91.

Jordan, N. C. (2007). Do words count?: Connections between mathematics and reading difficulties. In D. B. Berch & M. M. Mazzocco (Eds.), *Why is math so hard for some children?: The nature and origins of mathematical learning difficulties* (pp. 107–120). Baltimore, MD: Brookes.

Kamann, M. P., & Wong, B. Y. L. (1993). Inducing adaptive coping self-statements in children with learning disabilities through self-instruction training. *Journal of Learning Disabilities, 26*, 630–639.

Kanfer, F. H. (1977). The many faces of self-control, or behavior modification changes its focus. In R. B. Stuart (Ed.), *Behavioral self-management* (pp. 1–48). New York: Brunner/Mazel.

Kauffman, J. M. (1996). Research to practice issues. *Behavioral Disorders, 22*, 55–60.

Kavale, K. A., & Forness, S. R. (1996). Social skills deficits and learning disabilities: A meta-analysis. *Journal of Learning Disabilities, 29*, 226–237.

Kiewra, K. A. (1984). Acquiring effective notetaking skills: An alternative to professional notetaking. *Journal of Reading, 27*, 299–302.

Kiewra, K. A. (1987). Notetaking and review: The research and its implications. *Instructional Science, 16*, 233–249.

Kiewra, K. A., & Benton, S. L. (1988). The relationship between information-processing ability and notetaking. *Contemporary Educational Psychology, 13*, 33–44.

King, A. (1994). Guiding knowledge construction in the classroom: Effects of teaching children how to question and how to explain. *American Educational Research Journal, 31*(2), 338–368.

Kistner, J., Osborn, M., & LeVerrier, L. (1988). Causal attributions of learning-disabled children: Developmental patterns and relation to academic progress. *Journal of Educational Psychology, 80*, 82–89.

Kops, C., & Belmont, I. (1985). Planning and organizing skills of poor school achievers. *Journal of Learning Disabilities, 18*, 8–14.

Krishnan, K., Feller, M., & Orkin, M. (2010). Goal setting, planning, and prioritizing: The foundations of effective learning. In L. Meltzer (Ed.), *Promoting executive function in the classroom* (pp. 57–85). New York: Guilford Press.

Lazarus, B. D. (1988). Using guided notes to aid learning disabled students in secondary mainstream settings. *The Pointer, 33*, 32–36.

Lazarus, B. D. (1991). Guided notes, review, and achievement of secondary students with learning disabilities in mainstream content courses. *Education and Treatment of Children, 14*, 112–127.

Lazarus, B. D. (1996). Flexible skeletons. *Teaching Exceptional Children, 23*, 34–40.

Lerner, J. (2000). *Learning disabilities: Theories, diagnosis, and teaching strategies* (8th ed.). New York: Houghton Mifflin.

Levin, J. R. (1988). Elaboration-based learning strategies: Powerful theory = powerful application. *Contemporary Educational Psychology, 13*, 191–205.

Liautaud, J., & Rodreguez, D. (1999). *Times tables the fun way* (3rd ed.). Sandy, UT: Key.

Licht, B. G. (1983). Cognitive–motivational factors that contribute to the achievement of learning-disabled children. *Journal of Learning Disabilities, 16*, 483–490.

Licht, B. G. (1993). Achievement-related beliefs in children with learning disabilities: Impact on motivation and strategic learning. In L. Meltzer (Ed.), *Strategy assessment and instruction for students with learning disabilities* (pp. 195–220). Austin, TX: PRO-ED.

Lienemann, T. O., & Reid, R. (2008). Using self-regulated strategy development to improve expository writing with students with attention-deficit/hyperactivity disorder. *Exceptional Children, 74*, 471–486.

Lindsley, O. R. (1964). Direct measurement and prosthesis of retarded behavior. *Journal of Education, 147*, 62–81.

Lloyd, J. W., Bateman, D. F., Landrum, T. J., & Hallahan, D. P. (1989). Self-recording of attention versus productivity. *Journal of Applied Behavior Analysis, 22*, 315–323.

Locke, E. A., & Latham, G. P. (1990). *A theory of goal setting and task performance.* Englewood Cliffs, NJ: Prentice Hall.

Lovitt, T. C., & Curtis, K. A. (1969). Academic response rate as a function of teacher- and self-imposed contingencies. *Journal of Applied Behavior Analysis, 2*, 49–53.

Lyon, G. R., Fletcher, J. M., & Barnes, M. C. (2003). Learning disabilities. In E. J. Mash & R. A. Barkley (Eds.), *Child psychopathology* (2nd ed., pp. 520–586). New York: Guilford Press.

Maag, J. W. (2004). *Behavior management: From theoretical implications to practical applications.* Belmont, CA: Wadsworth.

Maag, J. W., Reid, R., & DiGangi, S. A. (1993). Differential effects of self-monitoring attention, accuracy, and productivity. *Journal of Applied Behavior Analysis, 26*, 329–344.

MacArthur, C., & Graham, S. (1987). Learning disabled students' composing under three methods of text production: Handwriting, word processing, and dictation. *Journal of Special Education, 21*(3), 22–42.

MacArthur, C., Schwartz, S., & Graham, S. (1991). A model for writing instruction: Integrating word processing and strategy instruction into a process-based approach to writing. *Learning Disabilities Research and Practice, 6*, 230–236.

Mace, F. C., Belfiore, P. J., & Hutchinson, J. M. (2001). Operant theory and research on self-regulation. In B. Zimmerman & D. Schunk (Eds.), *Self-regulated learning and academic achievement* (pp. 39–65). Mahwah, NJ: Erlbaum.

Mace, F. C., & Kratochwill, T. R. (1988). Self-monitoring. In J. C. Witt, S. N. Eliott, & F. M. Gresham (Eds.), *Handbook of behavior therapy in education* (pp. 489–522). New York: Plenum Press.

Marr, D., Windsor, M., & Cermak, S. (2001). Handwriting readiness: Locatives and visuomotor skills in the kindergarten years. *Early Childhood Research and Practice, 3*. Retrieved from *http://ecrp.uiuc.edu/v3n1/marr.html*.

Marshak, D. (1984). Study skills: Their values and why they should be taught. *NASSP Bulletin, 68*, 103–107.

Marshall, S. P. (1995). *Schemas in problem solving.* New York: Cambridge University Press.

Martin, G., & Pear, J. (2003). *Behavior modification: What it is and how to do it* (7th ed.). Upper Saddle River, NJ: Prentice Hall.

Martinussen, R., & Major, A. (2011). Working memory weaknesses in students with ADHD: Implications for instruction. *Theory into Practice, 50*, 68–75.

Martinussen, R., & Tannock, R. (2006). Working memory impairments in children with attention deficit hyperactivity disorder with and without comorbid language learning disorders. *Journal of Clinical and Experimental Neuropsychology, 28*, 1073–1094.

Mason, L. H. (2004). Explicit self-regulated strategy development versus reciprocal questioning: Effects on expository reading comprehension among struggling readers. *Journal of Educational Psychology, 96,* 283–296.

Mason, L. H., Benedek-Wood, E., & Valasa, L. (2009). Quick writing for students who struggle with writing. *Journal of Adolescent and Adult Literacy, 53,* 313–322.

Mason, L. H., Hickey Snyder, K., Sukhram, D. P., & Kedem, Y. (2006). Self-regulated strategy development for expository reading comprehension and informative writing: Effects for nine 4th grade students who struggle with learning. *Exceptional Children, 73,* 69–89.

Mason, L. H., Kubina, R., & Taft, R. (2009). Developing quick writing skills of middle school students with disabilities. *Journal of Special Education, 44,* 205–220.

Mason, L. H., Reid, R., & Hagaman, J. L. (2012). *Building comprehension in adolescents. Powerful strategies for improving reading and writing in content areas.* Baltimore, MD: Brookes.

Mastropieri, M. A., & Scruggs, T. E. (1991). *Teaching students ways to remember: Strategies for learning mnemonically.* Cambridge, MA: Brookline Books.

Mastropieri, M. A., & Scruggs, T. E. (1998). Enhancing school success with mnemonic strategies. *Intervention in School and Clinic, 33,* 201–208.

Mastropieri, M. A., Scruggs, T. E., Bakken, J., & Brigham, F. J. (1992). A complex mnemonic strategy for teaching states and capitals: Comparing forward and backward associations. *Learning Disabilities Research and Practice, 7,* 96–103.

Mastropieri, M. A., Sweda, J., & Scruggs, T. (2000). Teacher use of mnemonic strategy instruction. *Learning Disabilities Research and Practice, 15,* 69–74.

McKinney, J. D., & Feagans, L. (1983). Adaptive classroom behavior of learning disabled students. *Journal of Learning Disabilities, 16,* 360–367.

Meichanbaum, D. (1977). *Cognitive-behavior modification: An integrative approach.* New York: Plenum Press.

Mercer, C. (1997). *Students with learning disabilities* (5th ed.). Upper Saddle River, NJ: Prentice Hall.

Moats, L. C. (2005). How spelling supports reading. *American Educator, 29,* 12–22, 42–43.

Montague, M. (2006). Self-regulation strategies for better math performance in middle school. In M. Montague & A. K. Jitendra (Eds.), *Teaching mathematics to middle school students with learning difficulties* (pp. 89–107). New York: Guilford Press.

Montague, M., Graves, A., & Leavell, A. (1991). Planning, procedural facilitation, and narrative composition of junior high students with learning disabilities. *Learning Disabilities Research and Practice, 6,* 219–224.

Montague, M., Warger, C., & Morgan, T. (2000). SOLVE IT!: Strategy instruction to improve mathematical problem solving. *Learning Disabilities Research and Practice, 15,* 110–116.

Moser, L., Fishley, K., Konrad, M., & Hessler, T. (2012). Effects of the copy–cover–compare strategy on acquisition, maintenance, and generalization of spelling sight words for elementary students with attention-deficit/hyperactivity disorder. *Child and Family Behavior Therapy, 34,* 93–110.

Murphy, J., Hern, C., McLaughlin, T. F., & Williams, R. L. (1990). The effects of the copy, cover, and compare approach to increasing spelling accuracy with learning disabled students. *Contemporary Educational Psychology, 15,* 378–386.

Murphy, M., Mazzocco, M., Hanich, L., & Early, M. (2007). Characteristics of children with mathematics learning disability (MLD) varies as a function of the cutoff criterion used to define MLD. *Journal of Learning Disabilities, 40,* 458–478.

Murray, C., Goldstein, D. E., & Edgar, E. (1997). The employment and engagement status of high school graduates with learning disabilities through the first decade after graduation. *Learning Disabilities Research and Practice, 12,* 151–160.

National Center for Education Statistics. (2011). The nation's report card: Mathematics 2011: National assessment of educational progress at grades 4 and 8 (NCES-2012-458). Washington, DC: U.S. Department of Education, Institute of Education Sciences. Retrieved from *http://nationsreportcard.gov/math_2011/math_2011_report*.

National Center for Learning Disabilities (NCLD). (2010). *What is dysgraphia?* Retrieved from *www.ncld.org/types-learning-disabilities/dysgraphia/what-is-dysgraphia*.

National Governors Association Center for Best Practices (NGA) and Council of Chief State School Officers (CCSSO). (2010). *Common Core State Standards Initiative, Common Core State Standards for English language arts and literacy in history/social studies, science, and technical subjects*. Washington, DC: Author. Retrieved from *www.corestandards.org/assets/Appendix_A.pdf*.

National Reading Panel. (2000). *Teaching children to read: An evidence-based assessment of the scientific research literature on reading and its implications for reading instruction* (NIH Publication No. 00-4769). Washington, DC: National Institute of Child Health and Human Development.

Nelson, J. R., Smith, D. J., & Dodd, J. M. (1992). The effects of teaching a summary skills strategy to students identified as learning disabled on their comprehension of science text. *Education and Treatment of Children, 15*(3), 228–243.

Nelson, R. O., & Hayes, S. C. (1981). Theoretical explanations for reactivity in self-monitoring. *Behavior Modification, 5*, 3–14.

Newcomer, P. L., & Barenbaum, E. M. (1991). The written composing ability of children with learning disabilities: A review of literature from 1980 to 1990. *Journal of Learning Disabilities, 24*, 578–593.

Olson, J. L., & Platt, J. M. (2000). *Teaching children and adolescents with special needs* (3rd ed.). Upper Saddle River, NJ: Prentice Hall.

Ormrod, J. E. (1985). Proofreading The Cat in the Hat: Evidence for different reading styles of good and poor spellers. *Psychological Reports, 57*, 863–867.

Orton, S. J. (1937). *Reading, writing, and speech problems in children*. New York: Norton.

Parmar, R. S., Cawley, J. F., & Frazita, R. R. (1996). Word problem solving by students with and without mild disabilities. *Exceptional Children, 62*, 415–429.

Parmar, R. S., Cawley, J., & Miller, J. (1994). Differences in mathematics performance between students with learning disabilities and students with mild retardation. *Exceptional Children, 60*, 549–563.

Patton, J. R., Cronin, M. E., Bassett, D. S., & Koppel, A. E. (1997). A life skills approach to mathematics instruction: Preparing students with learning disabilities for the real-life math demands of adulthood. *Journal of Learning Disabilities, 30*, 178–187.

Perugini, E., Harvey, E., Lovejoy, D., Sandstrom, K., & Webb, A. H. (2000). The predictive power of combined neuropsychological measures of attention-deficit/hyperactivity disorder in children. *Child Neuropsychology, 6*, 101–114.

Polloway, E. A., Epstein, M. H., & Foley, R. (1992). A comparison of homework problems of students with learning disabilities and nonhandicapped students. *Learning Disabilities Research and Practice, 7*, 203–209.

Polloway, E. A., Miller, L., & Smith, T. E. C. (2003). *Language instruction for students with disabilities* (3rd ed.). Denver, CO: Love.

Porath, L. (2012). *LAMPS lesson plans*. Unpublished manuscript, University of Nebraska–Lincoln.

Pressley, M., Borkowski, J. G., & Schnieder, W. (1987). Cognitive strategies: Good strategy users coordinate metacognition and knowledge. In R. Vasta & G. Whitehurst (Eds.), *Annals of child development* (Vol. 5, pp. 89–129). Greenwich, CT: JAI Press.

Pressley, M., & Harris, K. R. (1990). What we really know about strategy instruction. *Educational Leadership, 48*, 31–34.

Pressley, M., Levin, J. R., & Delaney, H. D. (1982). The mnemonic keyword method. *Review of Educational Research, 52,* 61–91.

Pressley, M., & Woloshyn, V. (1995). *Cognitive strategy instruction that really improves children's academic performance.* Cambridge, MA: Brookline Books.

Rafferty, L. (2011). Step-by-step: Teaching students to self-monitor. *Teaching Exceptional Children, 43,* 50–58.

Raphael, T. E., & McKinney, J. (1983). An examination of fifth- and eighth-grade children's question–answering behavior: An instructional study in metacognition. *Journal of Reading Behavior, 15*(3), 67–86.

Raphael, T. E., & Wonnacott, C. A. (1985). Metacognitive training in question-answering strategies: Implementation in a fourth-grade developmental reading program. *Reading Research Quarterly, 20,* 286–296.

Reck, S., Hund, A., & Landau, S. (2010). Memory for object locations in boys with and without ADHD. *Journal of Attention Disorders, 13,* 505–515.

Reetz, L., & Rasmussen, T. (1988). Arithmetic mind joggers. *Academic Therapy, 24,* 79–82.

Reid, R. (1992). *A brief multiplication strategy.* Unpublished manuscript, University of Nebraska–Lincoln.

Reid, R. (1993). Implementing self-monitoring interventions in the classroom: Lessons from research. *Monograph in Behavior Disorders: Severe Behavior Disorders in Youth, 16,* 43–54.

Reid, R. (1996). Self-monitoring for students with learning disabilities: The present, the prospects, the pitfalls. *Journal of Learning Disabilities, 29,* 317–331.

Reid, R. (1999). Attention-deficit/hyperactivity disorder: Effective methods for the classroom. *Focus on Exceptional Children, 32*(4), 1–20.

Reid, R., & Harris, K. R. (1989). Self-monitoring of performance. *LD Forum, 15,* 39–42.

Reid, R., & Harris, K. R. (1993). Self-monitoring of attention versus self-monitoring of performance: Effects on attention and academic performance. *Exceptional Children, 60,* 29–40.

Reid, R., Harris, K. R., Graham, S., & Rock, M. (2012). Self-regulation among students with LD and ADHD. In B. Wong & D. Butler (Eds.), *Learning about learning disabilities* (pp. 141–173). New York: Elsevier.

Reid, R., & Johnson, J. (2012). *Teacher's guide to ADHD.* New York: Guilford Press.

Reid, R., & Lienemann, T. O. (2006). Self-regulated strategy development for written expression with students with attention-deficit/hyperactivity disorder. *Exceptional Children, 73,* 53–68.

Reid, R., Trout, A., & Schartz, M. (2005). Self-regulation interventions for children with attention-deficit/hyperactivity disorder. *Exceptional Children, 71,* 361–377.

Reynolds, C. J., Hill, D. S., Swassing, R. H., & Ward, M. E. (1988). The effects of revision strategy instruction on the writing performance of students with learning disabilities. *Journal of Learning Disabilities, 21*(9), 540–545.

Richards, R. (2008). *Writing made easier: Helping students develop automatic sound/symbol correspondence.* Retrieved from *www.ldonline.org/article/5893.*

Riley, M., Greeno, J., & Heller, J. (1983). Development of children's problem solving ability in arithmetic. In H. Ginsburg (Ed.), *The development of mathematical thinking* (pp. 153–196). New York: Academic Press.

Rinehart, S. D., Stahl, S. A., & Erickson, L. G. (1986). Some effects of summarization training on reading and studying. *Reading Research Quarterly, 21*(4), 422–438.

Ritter, S., & Idol-Maestas, L. (1986). Teaching middle school students to use a test-taking strategy. *Journal of Educational Research, 79,* 350–357.

Rivera, D. P. (1997). Mathematics education and students with learning disabilities: Introduction to the special series. *Journal of Learning Disabilities, 30,* 2–19.

Rock, M. L. (2005). Use of strategic self-monitoring to enhance academic engagement, productivity, and accuracy of students with and without exceptionalities. *Journal of Positive Behavioral Interventions, 7*(1), 3–17.

Rock, M. L., & Thead, B. K. (2007). The effects of fading a strategic self-monitoring intervention on students' academic engagement, productivity, and accuracy. *Journal of Behavioral Education, 16,* 389–412.

Rogers, L., & Graham, S. (2008). A meta-analysis of single subject design writing intervention research. *Journal of Educational Psychology, 100,* 879–906.

Rooney, K. J., Hallahan, D. P., & Lloyd, J. W. (1984). Self-recording of attention by learning disabled students in the regular classroom. *Journal of Learning Disabilities, 17,* 360–364.

Russell, R. L., & Ginsburg, H. P. (1984). Cognitive analysis of children's mathematical difficulties. *Cognition and Instruction, 1,* 217–244.

Salahu-Din, D., Persky, H., & Miller, J. (2008). *The nation's report card: Writing 2007* (NCES 2008-468). National Center for Education Statistics, Institute of Education Sciences, U.S. Department of Education, Washington, DC.

Scardamalia, M., & Bereiter, C. (1987). Knowledge telling and knowledge transforming in written composition. In S. Rosenberg (Ed.), *Advances in applied psycho-linguistics: Vol. 2. Reading, writing, and language learning* (pp. 142–175). Cambridge, UK: Cambridge University Press.

Schnoes, C., Reid, R., Wagner, M., & Marder, C. (2006). ADHD among students receiving special education services: A national survey. *Exceptional Children, 72,* 483–496.

Schoen, L. M. (1996). Mnemopoly: Board games and mnemonics. *Teaching of Psychology, 23,* 30–32.

Schumaker, J. B., Denton, P. H., & Deshler, D. D. (1984). *The paraphrasing strategy.* Lawrence: University of Kansas.

Schumaker, J. B., & Deshler, D. D. (1988). Implementing the Regular Education Initiative in secondary schools: A different ball game. *Journal of Learning Disabilities, 21,* 26–31.

Schumaker, J. B., Deshler, D. D., Nolan, S., Clark, F. L., Alley, G. R., & Warner, M. M. (1981). *Error monitoring: A learning strategy for improving academic performance of LD adolescents* (Research Report No. 34). Lawrence: Institute for Research in Learning Disabilities, University of Kansas.

Schunk, D. H. (1987). Peer models and children's behavioral change. *Review of Educational Research, 57,* 149–174.

Schunk, D. H. (1990). Goal setting and self-efficacy during self-regulated learning. *Educational Psychologist, 25,* 71–86.

Schunk, D. H. (2001). Social cognitive theory and self-regulated learning. In B. Zimmerman & D. H. Schunk (Eds.), *Self-regulated learning and academic achievement* (pp. 125–151). Mahwah, NJ: Erlbaum.

Scruggs, T. E., Bennion, K., & Lifson, S. (1985). Analysis of children's strategy use of reading achievement tests. *Elementary School Journal, 85,* 479–484.

Scruggs, T. E., & Mastropieri, M. (1988). Are learning disabled students "test-wise"?: A review of recent research. *Learning Disabilities Focus, 3,* 87–97.

Scruggs, T. E., & Mastropieri, M. A. (1990). Mnemonic instruction for students with learning disabilities: What it is and what it does. *Learning Disability Quarterly, 13,* 271–280.

Scruggs, T. E., & Mastropieri, M. A. (1992). Classroom applications of mnemonic instruction: Acquisition, maintenance, and generalization. *Exceptional Children, 58,* 219–229.

Scruggs, T. E., & Mastropieri, M. A. (2000). The effectiveness of mnemonic instruction for students with learning and behavior problems: An update and research synthesis. *Journal of Behavioral Education, 10,* 163–173.

Scruggs, T. E., Mastropieri, M., Berkeley, S., & Graetz, J. (2010). Do special education interventions improve learning of secondary content?: A meta-analysis. *Remedial and Special Education, 31*, 437–449.

Scruggs, T. E., Mastropieri, M. A., Levin, J. R., & Gaffney, J. S. (1985). Facilitating the acquisition of science facts in learning disabled students. *American Educational Research Journal, 22*, 575–586.

Shankweiler, D., & Lundquist, E. (1993). On the relations between learning to spell and learning to read. *Haskins Laboratories Status Report on Speech Research, 113*, 135–144.

Shapiro, E. S., & Cole, C. L. (1994). *Behavior change in the classroom: Self-management interventions.* New York: Guilford Press.

Shapiro, E. S., DuPaul, G. J., & Bradley-Klug, K. L. (1998). Self-management as a strategy to improve the classroom behavior of adolescents with ADHD. *Journal of Learning Disabilities, 31*, 545–555.

Shaywitz, S. E. (2003). Neurobiological indices of dyslexia. In H. L. Swanson, K. R. Harris, & S. Graham (Eds.), *Handbook of learning disabilities* (pp. 514–531). New York: Guilford Press.

Short, E. J., & Ryan, E. B. (1984). Metacognitive differences between skilled and less skilled readers: Remediating deficits through story grammar and attribution training. *Journal of Educational Psychology, 76*, 225–235.

Simmonds, E. P. M., Luchow, J. P., Kaminsky, S., & Cottone, V. (1989). Applying cognitive learning strategies in the classroom: A collaborative training institute. *Learning Disabilities Focus, 4*, 96–105.

Skinner, C. H., McLaughlin, T. F., & Logan, P. (1997). Cover, copy, and compare: A self-managed academic intervention effective across skills, students, and settings. *Journal of Behavioral Education, 7*, 295–306.

Smith, B. W., & Sugai, G. (2000). A self-management functional assessment-based behavior support plan for a middle school student with EBD. *Journal of Positive Behavior Interventions, 2*, 208–217.

Smith, G., & Smith, D. (1989). Schoolwide study skills program: The key to mainstreaming. *Teaching Exceptional Children, 21*, 20–23.

Smith, S. M. (1985). A method for teaching name mnemonics. *Teaching of Psychology, 12*, 156–158.

Smolen, L., Newman, C., Walthen, T., & Lee, D. (1995). Developing student self-assessment strategies. *TESOL Journal, 5*, 22–26.

Snyder, M., & Bambara, L. (1997). Teaching secondary students with learning disabilities to self-manage classroom survival skills. *Journal of Learning Disabilities, 30*, 534–544.

Spear-Swerling, L. (2006). The importance of teaching handwriting. *LDOnline.* Retrieved from *www.ldonline.org/spearswerling/The_Importance_of_Teaching_Handwriting.*

Stanovich, K. (1986). Matthew effects in reading: Some consequences of individual differences in the acquisition of literacy. *Reading Research Quarterly, 21*, 360–406.

Stipek, D. (1993). *Motivation to learn: From theory to practice.* Boston: Allyn & Bacon.

Stone, C. A., & Conca, L. (1993). The origin of strategy deficits in children with learning disabilities: A social constructivist perspective. In L. J. Meltzer (Ed.), *Strategy assessment and instruction for students with learning disabilities* (pp. 23–59). Austin, TX: PRO-ED.

Strauss, A. A., & Lehtinen, L. E. (1947). *Psychopathology and education of the brain-injured child.* New York: Grune & Stratton.

Swanson, H. L. (1993). Principles and procedures in strategy use. In L. Meltzer (Ed.), *Strategy assessment and instruction for students with learning disabilities* (pp. 61–92). Austin, TX: PRO-ED.

Swanson, H. L. (1996a). Information processing: An introduction. In D. K. Reid, W. Hresko, & H. L. Swanson (Eds.), *Cognitive approaches to learning disabilities* (pp. 251–285). Austin, TX: PRO-ED.

Swanson, H. L. (1996b). Learning disabilities and memory. In D. K. Reid, W. Hresko, & H. L. Swanson (Eds.), *Cognitive approaches to learning disabilities* (pp. 187–314). Austin, TX: PRO-ED.

Swanson, H. L. (1999a). Cognition and learning disabilities. In W. Bender (Ed.), *Professional issues in learning disabilities* (pp. 415–460). Austin, TX: PRO-ED.

Swanson, H. L. (1999b). *Interventions for students with learning disabilities: A meta-analysis of treatment outcomes.* New York: Guilford Press.

Swanson, H. L., & Alexander, J. (1997). Cognitive processes and predictors of word recognition and reading comprehension in learning-disabled and skilled readers: Revisiting the specificity hypothesis. *Journal of Educational Psychology, 89*(1), 128–158.

Swanson, H. L., Cochran, K. F., & Ewers, C. A. (1990). Can learning disabilities be determined from working memory performance? *Journal of Learning Disabilities, 23,* 59–67.

Swanson, H. L., Harris, K. R., & Graham, S. (Eds.). (2003). *Handbook of learning disabilities.* New York: Guilford Press.

Swanson, H. L., & Sachs-Lee, C. (2000). A meta-analysis of single-subject-design intervention research for students with LD. *Journal of Learning Disabilities, 33,* 114–136.

Swanson, H. L., & Saez, L. (2003). Memory difficulties in children and adults with learning disabilities. In H. L. Swanson, K. R. Harris, & S. Graham (Eds.), *Handbook of learning disabilities* (pp. 182–198). New York: Guilford Press.

Swanson, H. L., & Trahan, M. R. (1992). Learning disabled readers: Comprehension of computer mediated text—the influence of working memory, metacognition, and attribution. *Learning Disabilities Research and Practice, 7,* 74–86.

Sweller, J., van Merrienboer, J. J. G., & Paas, F. G. W. C. (1998). Cognitive architecture and instructional design. *Educational Psychology Review, 10,* 251–296.

Therrien, W., Taylor, J., Hosp, J., Kaldenberg, E., & Gorsh, J. (2011). Science instruction for students with learning disabilities: A meta-analysis. *Learning Disabilities Research and Practice, 26,* 188–203.

Thornton, C. A., & Toohey, M. A. (1985). Basic math facts: Guidelines for teaching and learning. *Learning Disabilities Focus, 1*(1), 44–57.

Thurber, D. N. (1993). *D'Nealian handwriting ABC book: Cursive.* Reading, MA: Addison Wesley.

Tompkins, G. (2002). *Language arts: Content and teaching strategies* (5th ed.). Upper Saddle River, NJ: Pearson Merrill Prentice Hall.

Torgesen, J. K. (1984). Memory processes in reading disabled students. *Journal of Learning Disabilities, 18,* 350–357.

Troia, G. A., & Graham, S. (2002). The effectiveness of a highly explicit, teacher-directed strategy instruction routine: Changing the writing performance of students with learning disabilities. *Journal of Learning Disabilities, 35*(4), 290–305.

Troia, G. A., & Graham, S. (2003). Effective writing instruction across the grades: What every educational consultant should know. *Journal of Educational and Psychological Consultation, 14,* 75–89.

U.S. Department of Education. (2008). *Thirtieth annual report to Congress on the implementation of the education of the handicapped act.* Washington, DC: U.S. Government Printing Office.

U.S. Department of Education. (2010). Individuals with Disabilities Education Act (IDEA) data. Retrieved from *www.ideadata.org/StateLevelFiles.asp.*

Van de Walle, J. A. (1998). *Elementary and middle school mathematics: Teaching developmentally* (3rd ed.). New York: Longman.

van Garderen, D. (2006). Teaching visual representation for mathematics problem solving. In M. Montague & A. K. Jitendra (Eds.), *Teaching mathematics to middle school students with learning difficulties* (pp. 72–88). New York: Guilford Press.

van Garderen, D. (2007). Teaching students with LD to use diagrams to solve mathematical word problems. *Journal of Learning Disabilities, 40,* 540–553.

Vaughn, S., & Bos, C. S. (2012). *Strategies for teaching students with learning and behavior problems* (8th ed.). Upper Saddle River, NJ: Pearson.

Weiner, B. (1979). A theory of motivation for some classroom experiences. *Journal of Educational Psychology, 71,* 3–25.

Weiner, B. (1992). *Human motivation: Metaphors, theories, and research.* Newbury Park, CA: Sage.

Williams, J. P. (1988). Identifying main ideas: A basic aspect of reading comprehension. *Topics in Language Disorders, 8,* 1–13.

Williams, J. P. (2003). Teaching text structure to improve reading comprehension. In H. L. Swanson, K. R. Harris, & S. Graham (Eds.), *Handbook of learning disabilities* (pp. 293–305). New York: Guilford Press.

Winne, P. H. (1997). Experimenting to bootstrap self-regulated learning. *Journal of Educational Psychology, 89,* 397–410.

Witt, J. C. (1986) Teachers' resistance to the use of school-based interventions. *Journal of School Psychology, 24,* 37–44.

Wood, D. K., & Frank, A. R. (2000). Using memory-enhancing strategies to learn multiplication facts. *Teaching Exceptional Children, 32*(5), 78–82.

Wood, D. K., Frank, A. R., & Wacker, D. P. (1998). Teaching multiplication facts to students with learning disabilities. *Journal of Applied Behavior Analysis, 32,* 323–338.

Wood, R. W., Webster, L., Gullickson, A., & Walker, J. (1987). Comparing handwriting legibility with three teaching methods for sex and grade level. *Reaching Improvement, 24,* 24–30.

Wong, B. Y. L. (1986). A cognitive approach to teaching spelling. *Exceptional Children, 53,* 169–173.

Wong, B. Y. L. (2000). Writing strategies instruction for expository essays for adolescents with and without learning disabilities. *Topics in Language Disorders, 20*(4), 29–44.

Wong, B. Y. L., Harris, K. R., & Graham, S. (1991). Academic applications of cognitive-behavioral programs with learning disabled students. In P. C. Kendall (Ed.), *Child and adolescent therapy: Cognitive-behavioral procedures* (pp. 245–275). New York: Guilford Press.

Wong, B. Y. L., & Wilson, M. (1984). Investigating awareness of and teaching passage organization in learning disabled children. *Journal of Learning Disabilities, 17,* 477–482.

Wong, B. Y. L., Wong, R., & Blenkinsop, J. (1989). Cognitive and metacognitive aspects of learning disabled adolescents' composing problems. *Learning Disability Quarterly, 12,* 300–322.

Xin, Y. P., & Jitendra, A. K. (1999). The effects of instruction in solving mathematical word problems for students with learning problems: A meta-analysis. *Journal of Special Education, 32,* 207–225.

Zabala, D., Minnici, A., McMurrer, J., Hill, D., Bartley, A. P., & Jennings, J. (2007). *State high school exit exams: Working to raise test scores.* Washington, DC: Center on Education Policy.

Index

Page numbers in *italic* indicate figures

"Ability," "incremental" definition of, 11
Academic outcomes, maladaptive attributions, 9
Academic performance
    assessment, 43–44, 60
    monitoring, 42
Acronyms, 267–268
Acrostics, 268–269
Addition
    addition word-problem types, *237*
    basic facts rules, 227, *228*
    See also Basic addition facts
Addition/Subtraction Relationship Rule, *228*
Analogies, 20–21
Anxiety, coping with, 98–103
Assessment
    in the SCROL strategy, 51–52, *53*, 60
    self-evaluation, 79–81
    of self-monitoring, 76
        of attention, 93
        of performance, 95
    in SRSD
        of actual strategy use, 44
        of changes in performance, attitudes, and
            cognition, 43–44
        considering the level of evaluation needed, 43
        importance of, 42–43
        including students as coevaluators, 43
        portfolio procedures, 45

of strategy use over time and in new
    situations, 44–45
while instruction is in progress, 44
in the Story Grammar strategy, 60–61, *62*, 69
of student knowledge, 34, 36
Association for Children with Learning
    Disabilities, 3
Associative property, 226
Attention-deficit/hyperactivity disorder (ADHD)
    deficiencies in working memory, 23
    strategy instruction approach and, 14
    students with learning disabilities and, 2
Attention deficits, 8
Attitudes, assessment, 43–44
Attributions
    dimensions of, 23–24
    maladaptive, 9
    retraining when discussing strategies, 36
    strategy instruction and, 24–26
    suggestions for changing, 25, *26*

Background knowledge, development and
    activation
    for the COPS strategy, 174–175
    for guided notes, 260
    for the question-generation strategy, 217
    for the SCROL strategy, 50–52, *53*
    in SRSD, 33–36

299